July 6, 1999

Dear Professor,

As the newest "first author" of *Principles and Types of Speech Communication*, I am pleased to welcome you to the 14th Edition.

The overarching goal of this revision is to expand on twin commitments that make this text a leading one in the discipline: a commitment to cultural sensitivity with concrete advice to students on how they can talk effectively in a culturally diverse society, and a commitment to the best research base of any basic book in the field. As such, the text retains core concepts which have been its trademark (e.g., Monroe's Motivated Sequence) and leads the field with respect to bringing the best research in both humanistic and social science traditions to bear on the principles and practices of public communication.

In this new edition, we have focused renewed attention throughout the textbook on the issue of how one uses cultural information in making sound rhetorical choices, and have devoted a new specific chapter, Chapter 4, to strategies that one might use in creating community while being sensitive to the diversity that marks contemporary audiences.

We have also focused attention not only on what resources the World Wide Web brings to bear on the search for information, but also on its potential for being biased or inaccurate. Students are presented with guidelines for evaluating the information obtained. In addition, we discuss the use of PowerPoint in organizing and presenting information.

We continue the tradition of making this a solid scholarly treatment of public communication by drawing on contemporary research. While remaining accessible through the use of clear explanations, we challenge students to stretch their minds as they contemplate speaking in public settings. The relationship between theory and practice has been strengthened with respect to a continued commitment to critical thinking and to the application of ethical principles in making appropriate rhetorical choices.

Finally, in addition to the customary focus on ceremonial speaking, we also focus attention on speaking at meetings and conferences, with renewed emphasis on the speech to entertain, the keynote speech, and panel participation.

If you have any questions, or suggestions for more making this an even more useful textbook, don't hesitate to contact me via email(McKerrow@ohio.edu).

Sincerely,

Raymie E. McKerrow
Professor, Rhetorical Studies
Ohio University

ISBN 032105578 ①

Principles & Types of Speech Communication, 14th Edition,

offers a COMPLETE learning and teaching package...

For Instructors:

INSTRUCTOR'S MANUAL
0-321-06324-4

TESTBANK
0-321-06325-2

TRANSPARENCIES
0-321-07526-9

POWERPOINT PRESENTATION ON CD-ROM
0-321-07524-2

TESTGEN CD-ROM
(COMPUTERIZED TEST BANK)
0-321-06326-0

ESL GUIDE FOR PUBLIC SPEAKING
0-321-02079-0

TEACHING PUBLIC SPEAKING
0-321-00386-1

ASSESSMENT GUIDE FOR PUBLIC SPEAKING
0-321-02078-2

GREAT IDEAS FOR TEACHING SPEECH (GIFTS)
0-321-02081-2

STUDENT SPEECHES VIDEO-2000 EDITION
0-321-07536-6

SELECTION OF STUDENT SPEECHES VIDEO
0-321-02253-X

ADDRESSING YOUR AUDIENCE VIDEO
0-321-40598-6

SPEAKER APPREHENSION VIDEO
0-321-02256-4

CRITIQUING STUDENT SPEECHES VIDEO
0-321-02255-6

VIDEO GUIDE TO PUBLIC SPEAKING
0-321-02080-4

For Students:

New!

Online Study Guide at www.awlonline.com/mckerrow

Discount subscription to Newsweek magazine (ask your local sales representative for more information)

Available for FREE when ordered bundled with the text:

SPEECH WRITER'S WORKSHOP CD-ROM
0-321-07535-8

STUDENT GUIDE TO POWERPOINT
0-321-04926-8

PUBLIC SPEAKING GUIDE FOR STUDENTS
0-06-501292-5

STUDYING COMMUNICATION BOOKLET
0-673-97005-1

BRAINSTORMS BOOKLET: A GUIDE TO CREATIVE THINKING
0-673-98136-3

SPEECH WRITER'S WORKSHOP (MAC) 0-321-02801-5

SPEECH WRITER'S WORKSHOP (WIN) 0-321-02453-2

Principles and Types of Speech Communication

Principles and Types of Speech Communication

Fourteenth Edition

Raymie E. McKerrow
Ohio University

Bruce E. Gronbeck
The University of Iowa

Douglas Ehninger

Alan H. Monroe

 **LONGMAN**

An imprint of Addison Wesley Longman, Inc.

New York • Reading, Massachusetts • Menlo Park, California • Harlow, England
Don Mills, Ontario • Sydney • Mexico City • Madrid • Amsterdam

Editor-in-Chief: Priscilla McGeehon
Acquisitions Editor: Michael Greer
Development Manager: Lisa Pinto
Marketing Manager: Megan Galvin
Supplements Editor: Mark Gerber
Full Service Production Manager: Joseph Vella
Project Coordination, Text Design,
   and Electronic Page Makeup: York Production Services
Cover Designer/Manager: Nancy Danahy
Cover Illustration/Photo: © Diana Ong/SuperStock
Photo Researcher: Mira Schachne
Senior Print Buyer: Hugh Crawford
Printer and Binder: Quebecor-Fairfield
Cover Printer: Coral Graphic Services, Inc.

For permission to use copyrighted material, grateful acknowledgment is made to the copyright holders on pp. 419–420, which are hereby made part of this copyright page.

Library of Congress Cataloging-in-Publication Data
Principles and types of speech communication / Raymie E. McKerrow . . .
   [et al.] . — 14th ed.
      p.   cm.
   Includes bibliographical references and index.
   ISBN 0-321-04425-8 (hardcover)
   1. Public speaking.   2. Oral communication.   I. McKerrow, Ray E.
PN4121.P72   2000
808.5'1—dc21   99-27668
                                                         CIP

Please visit our Website at http://www.awlonline.com.

ISBN 0-321-04425-8

12345678910—ARF—02010099

Brief Table of Contents

Contents

Part Four TYPES   295

CHAPTER 13   *Speeches to Inform*   297

A Note to Students and Teachers

Principles and Types of Speech Communication has been a mainstay in the basic speech course, a celebrated leader in communication studies, for over half a century because it not only follows but also sets educational standards in this field. Longevity comes from adaptability to varied conditions. This book always has looked both backward and forward: backward to the timeless principles of speech that are central to the Euro-American cultural experience since the ancient Greeks, and forward to the latest research and the leading challenges of today and tomorrow. The fourteenth edition of this book follows in that tradition.

The overarching goal of this revision is to strengthen those features that have made *Principles and Types of Speech Communication* a pre-eminent book within the field: a commitment to cultural sensitivity with concrete advice to students on how they can talk effectively in a culturally diverse society, and a commitment to the best research base of any basic book in the field. As such, the text retains core concepts which have been its trademark (e.g., Monroe's Motivated Sequence) and leads the field with respect to bringing the best research in both humanistic and social science traditions to bear on the principles and practices of public communication. At the same time, the language of the text continues to be accessible to the entering college undergraduate. Conceptually complex ideas are introduced in a way that makes them both understandable and applicable to the act of speaking in public settings. Furthermore, it is written for students who are computer-literate and who often rely more on Internet sources than paper library sources for their speech materials. Developing competent communicators with a sophisticated understanding of public communication is the ultimate goal. Presenting a text that instructors will be proud to use as an exemplar of the best the field has to offer is the means to achieve that goal.

HIGHLIGHTS OF THIS REVISION

Some have criticized current public speaking textbooks for "dumbing down" content" to such an extent as to lose credibility. This text moves in the opposite direction. With a commitment to clarity in the presentation of concepts as the underlying principle, we introduce materials that are at the cutting edge of scholarship within the discipline, and illustrate their connection to the practice of communicating in public settings. As will be noted below, a new chapter focusing on the importance of communicating in a culturally diverse society, with specific advice on how to accommodate difference, is a key feature of this revision. Beyond a commitment to illustrating how one communicates in a culturally diverse society, this revision introduces research on such topics as performance theory and its role in oral presentations and devotes specific attention to assessing the credibility of information obtained via the World Wide Web. The issue of assessment leads directly into another pervasive feature of this revision—a commitment to illustrating critical thinking skills, and their use in preparing for and critiquing public discourse. Thus, this revision highlights four specific achievements in differentiating this text from its predecessor and from others in the field:

1. A pervasive connection to culture studies as it assists in approaching and analyzing public discourse in a culturally diverse society.

There is a specific *new* chapter devoted to the issue of how one uses cultural information in making specific choices in language, arguments, etc. While other texts have focused, as does this text, on illustrations throughout the chapters, we have developed the connection between culture and public speaking as a means of introducing students to the importance of attending to cultural differences. We offer specific strategies for unifying diverse audiences without losing a sense of who you are as the speaker. Beyond that, we have expanded the use of diverse examples from people of color—to further illustrate the issues of concern, as well as to indicate the style of reasoning/speaking. For example, to our knowledge, we are the first text to make extensive use of contemporary Native American speakers as exemplars. The audience analysis chapter and the informative and persuasive speaking chapters draw on the strategies noted in the new cultural life chapter. Recognizing that ideas and their acceptance are culture-bound is a major thrust of this revision.

2. A pervasive attention to the role of new technologies in communicating (from critically assessing web-based resources to using Powerpoint in presentations).

While the World Wide Web is a fantastic resource for students with easy access, it also is a highly problematic information source with respect to information accuracy. Sites are established to promote specific points of view, and students need to be aware of the potential for bias and inaccuracy in assessing web-based information. We focus on this issue in the information gathering chapter, and raise it again in the context of gaining an understanding of audiences through the use of the World Wide Web.

The use of PowerPoint is discussed in the chapter on visual communication—strategies for making powerpoint more than a convenient outline of content are reviewed; the goal is to enhance the presentation's ability to convey ideas, not simply to impress the audience with one's technical skill. In addition, there is a separate booklet on the use of PowerPoint that provides further instruction on how to use it as an outlining tool and as an aid in presentations.

3. **A thoroughgoing introduction of scholarship bearing on public communication, including but not limited to performance theory as it affects orality, culture studies, and persuasion theory.**

This text has a long and well established reputation for the currency of its research base. In this edition, as already noted, we introduce a special chapter that takes advantage of recent research in culture studies. We also add new information drawn from performance theory in relation to physical presence in speaking (the rhetoric of the body). Other additions include:

- Recent advances in motivational psychology (we are the only text to introduce more recent research on motivation, such as that drawn from McClelland);
- The concept of "collective memory" or "collective desire" as a resource in audience analysis and its role in ceremonial speaking;
- The role of fantasy theme analysis as it contributes to research on audiences;
- A renewed and updated emphasis on how public language (in the guise of political correctness debates, etc.) functions.

4. **A focus on meetings and conferences as typical settings for public presentations.**

While a business and professional communication course may offer more extended discussion of these issues, not all students will have the opportunity to avail themselves of this experience. Hence, we have reworked materials in earlier editions so as to focus attention on the kinds of experiences that will occur as you enter the workplace. Guidelines for speaking at meetings and conferences also continues the practical, applied focus of this text. Highlighting keynote addresses and after-dinner speaking also provides students with an understanding of the role of these kinds of "special occasion" addresses.

KEY STRENGTHS OF THE TEXT

In addition to the focus on what is new, *Principles and Types of Speech Communication* has earned its reputation because of traditional strengths, and we have been sure to retain those characteristics here. The following are key ingredients of a continuing commitment to a textbook that offers a clear and useable blend of theory and performance skills:

1. Connecting theory to practice.

Although known for its solid grounding in rhetorical and communication research, this book maintains its focus on the actual experience itself: creating and presenting an effective public speech. For example, in keeping with the increased emphasis on oral communication skills—skills needed to both prepare and deliver effective speeches, we have continued the **"How To"** **boxes.** Each of these boxes contains specific advice on how the concepts discussed can be used in a specific illustration, thereby putting theory into practice. The continued use of **"Communication Research Dateline" boxes** also underscores the dual focus on grounded knowledge and practical advice to speakers.

2. Focus on both speechmaking in society and student presentations in classrooms.

This book has an obligation to compel communication studies' students to reflect seriously upon the electronic revolution and its implication for responsible dialogue between and among citizens. Throughout the text we utilize examples and illustrations that focus attention on contemporary political, economic, religious, and social issues. We ask students to analyze these issues in a manner that will help them construct arguments and appeals that reflect their own beliefs and resonate with their audience's beliefs, desires, and needs. Simultaneously, we recognize that as a reader, you are seeking to survive and grow in your own environment—the college communication classroom. Thus, you'll find many of our examples, illustrations, and sample speeches drawn from campus life as well as from student speakers. This book not only asks you to assess your skills where you are, but also to look ahead to the experience of building community through communication after your college years.

3. A continued commitment to critical thinking.

The chapter on argumentation focuses attention on the use of fallacies, both in terms of their "illogicality," and in terms of their potential as rhetorically effective arguments (e.g., the controversy over Clinton's "lie" reduces to an attack on personal character that may well be persuasive and appropriate, even though it is an ad hominem—to the person instead of the issue—attack).

Critical thinking is not only about assessing arguments for logicality or validity. It also implies a close attention to language choices in front of a diverse audience, and to choices about how one organizes a presentation. Throughout the text, we highlight the importance of thinking about rhetorical choices that one may make in addressing specific audiences—the engagement of ideas and audiences is a matter of choice: it does matter what one says, and how one says it in most circumstances. The "how to" boxes noted above are one means of focusing attention on choices. The illustrations drawn from current political and social discourse—how public discourse choices (such as the "failed apology" from Clinton) affect future rhetorical choices also presents public speaking as it influences public affairs.

4. A continued commitment to the importance of ethics.

Our **"Ethical Moments" boxes** were among the most positively received features of previous editions. In this edition we have included discussions of plagiarism, sexism, the ethics of credibility and hyperemotionalism, ghost writing, and statistical sleight-of-hand. Public speaking involves moral decisions, both in terms of the choices one makes to "tell the truth" about what one knows, as well as to say what one believes in ethically responsible ways. Audiences tire quickly of speakers whose veracity is founded on technical understandings, as the controversy over whether and in what sense Clinton engaged in a "lie" or perjured himself would suggest.

5. Streamlined coverage for today's public speaking classroom.

Without losing sight of what has made this text a valuable part of the communication field since its introduction in 1935, we have made several structural changes in this new edition:

- The chapter on "Getting Started" now follows the introductory chapter so that students can more quickly move to the practical matter of "what do I do next?" Instructors will find it easier to provide an overview of the basics as a precursor to the first speaking assignment.
- The strategies for gaining and maintaining attention have been integrated with the specific advice on building introductions and conclusions.
- We have integrated "motivational appeals" into those chapters where their use is a priority—in the informative and persuasive speaking chapters. This will allow instructors to highlight those appeals most likely to be effective as they focus attention on strategies for informing and persuading audiences.
- We also have tightened the "ceremonial" chapter and moved the "speech to entertain" to a new chapter focusing on speaking at meetings and conferences. This allows us to highlight the use of the "keynote" and "after-dinner" speech in a more appropriate context.

6. Continued pedagogical support.

Both teachers and students need to be well supported in the educational process. *Principles and Types of Speech Communication,* fourteenth edition, continues to be a leader in pedagogical support. Each chapter closes with a clear **summary** and a list of the **key terms** used in the chapter. These will be helpful in recalling concepts and building a vocabulary with which to discuss public communication events. Among those ancillaries offered for instructors are multiple videos on topics such as speaker apprehension and audience analysis and a guide on how to use them; an Instructor's Manual that includes elements covered in the previous edition's Speaker's Resource Book as well as tips for teaching; bibliographies; chapter reviews for lecturing; and additional tested exercises.

Overall, we know that this edition of the most popular public-speaking textbook of the twentieth century has merged traditional and innovative features to keep it at the forefront of communication studies. It is based on a speech skills tradition, which assures educators that course outcomes can be tested in concrete ways, and yet it lives and breathes the liberal arts tradition, which makes the basic speech course but an introduction to the world of communication studies—to the scientific, theoretical, historical, and critical study of public communication and social life. What we seek through this revision is nothing less than the most refined, sophisticated research-driven, application-oriented textbook available on the market. We are convinced that you will find *Principles and Types of Speech Communication* to be a solid yet malleable teaching and learning instrument.

SUPPLEMENTARY MATERIALS

The ancillary package for the fourteenth edition of *Principles and Types of Speech Communication* includes the following instructional resources:

Resources for Instructors

Instructor's Manual

The Instructor's Manual includes chapter overviews, discussion and critical thinking questions, a wealth of valuable classroom activities, and suggestions for further reading.

Test Bank

The Test Bank contains hundreds of challenging and thoroughly revised multiple choice, true-false, short answer, and essay questions along with an answer key. The questions closely follow the text chapters and are cross-referenced with corresponding page numbers.

TestGen-EQ 2.0 CD-ROM

The printed Test Bank is also available electronically through our computerized testing system, TestGen-EQ 2.0. This fully networkable test-generating software is now available in a cross-platform CD-ROM. TestGen-EQ's friendly graphical interface enables instructors to view, edit, and add questions, transfer questions to tests, and print tests in a variety of fonts and forms. Search and sort features allow instructors to locate questions quickly and arrange them in a preferred order. Six question formats are available, including short-answer, true-false, multiple-choice, essay, matching, and bimodal.

PowerPoint CD-ROM

New to this edition, the transparency masters will now be available as PowerPoint presentation slides on CD-ROM.

Overhead Transparency Package

A set of 75 four-color acetate transparencies is available to adopters. The set includes graphs, charts, and tables from the text.

Teaching Public Speaking

This introduction to teaching the public speaking course offers suggestions for everything from lecturing to designing classroom assignments to incorporating cultural diversity into lesson plans. Essential for graduate teaching assistants and first-time instructors, it may also provide new insight to the more experienced professor. An extensive bibliography and a listing of media resources is also included.

Assessment Guide for Public Speaking

This useful booklet contains suggestions to help instructors assess student progress. It establishes realistic goals for students as they acquire essential public speaking skills such as how to research topics, how to plan and deliver speeches, and how to use language more effectively. Based on NCA guidelines for "Assessing College Student Competency in Speech Communication," this guide is invaluable for instructors who want to develop criteria for proficiency assessment.

Great Ideas for Teaching Speech (GIFTS)

This unique supplement offers instructors a myriad of creative ideas for enlivening their public speaking course. All of the assignments found in GIFTS have been successfully employed by experienced public speaking instructors in their classrooms.

ESL Guide for Public Speaking

The ESL Guide for Public Speaking provides strategies and resources for instructors teaching in a bilingual or multilingual classroom. It also includes suggestions for further reading and a listing of related websites.

Longman's Public Speaking Video Library

Longman's video collection includes a wide variety of films on topics such as preparation for public speaking, critiquing student speeches, speaker apprehension, and audience assessment. We also offer a variety of accompanying printed video guides. Please contact your local sales representative for more information on titles and availability.

Resources for Students

The Speech Writer's Workshop and Brainstorms CD-ROM

A virtual handbook for public speaking, this exciting public speaking software is now available on CD-ROM. The software includes five separate features: (1) a *speech handbook* with tips for researching and preparing speeches, plus information about grammar, usage, and syntax; (2) a *speech workshop,* which guides students through the speech writing process while displaying a series of questions at each stage; (3) a *topics dictionary,* which gives students hundreds of ideas for speeches—all divided into subcategories to help students with outlining and organization; and (4) a *citation database* that formats bibliographic entries in MLA or APA style; and (5) *Brainstorms: How to Think More Creatively About Communication . . . or About Anything Else.*

Student Guide to PowerPoint

Designed to introduce students to PowerPoint, this student guide explains how to use the program as a tool for planning, organizing, and delivering oral presentations. The supplement covers all of the requisite skills for mastering

PowerPoint, including outlining, designing, and modifying slides; using graphics and animations; and presenting a slide show.

Studying Communication

This booklet introduces students to the field of communication and to the way in which research in the discipline is conducted. The booklet also offers students a variety of practical suggestions for how to get the most out of their study of communication, including how to read a textbook, how to take a test, and how to write a paper for a communication course.

Online Course Companion (http://www.awlonline.com/mckerrow)

This Online Course Companion (OCC) provides valuable resources for both students and instructors using *Principles and Types of Speech Communication,* fourteenth edition. Students will find information about the book and the authors, interactive practice tests, and links to related sites. There's also a link to *The Podium,* Longman's public speaking web page, which contains information about all of our public speaking texts and a variety of public speaking activities. Instructors will have access to complete text and supplement information, a syllabus builder, and an array of other material to help manage their classes.

Brainstorms

This unique booklet integrates creative thinking into the communication course. *Brainstorms* explores the creative thinking process (its nature, values, characteristics, and stages) and its relationship to communication. It also provides 19 specific tools for thinking more creatively about communication (or anything else). The discussion of each tool includes its purposes, techniques, and an exercise to get started. Creative thinking sidebars and relevant questions add to the interactive pedagogy.

Acknowledgments

We owe a great debt to those instructors who took time to review the previous edition:

Mike Allen, University of Wisconsin, Milwaukee
Carold M. Barnum, Southern Polytechnic State University
L.R. Chudomelka, Arkansas State University, Beebe
Dayle C. Hardy-Short, Northern Arizona University
Thomas B. Harte, Southeast Missouri State University
Sally O. Hastings, Western Kentucky University
Susan A. Jasko, Montclair State University
Julie R. Mactaggart, University of Minnesota-Twin Cities
Angela M. Mason, Beaufort County Community College
David B. McLennan, Peace College
Jean E. Perry, Glendale Community College
Richard Quianthy, Broward Community College
James W. Reed, Glendale Community College
Roy Schwartzman, University of South Carolina
Gary J. Semonella, Riverside Community College
James Monroe Stewart, Tennessee Technological University
Jennifer Tighe, Xavier University

Gratitude is due to the University of Iowa's Obermann Center for Advanced Studies, especially its director Jay Semel and operating magician Lorna Olson; the facilities provided by the Center helped the revision proceed smoothly. Thanks as well to Jakob and Ingrid Gronbeck, who continue to contribute their talents for library research and attempt to keep their father current. Gratitude is owed as well to Gayle and Matthew McKerrow for their constant encouragement and continued support.

We also thank Addison Wesley Longman for the resources and talents it invested in this project. This edition was executed under the careful watch of our Acquisitions Editor, Donna Erickson, and the word-by-word manuscript preparation was overseen by Production Coordinator Elsa van Bergen. We also appreciate the assistance of the Permissions Department in keeping us legal. We were pleased with the efforts of Marketing Manager Megan Galvin. And finally, we thank the group of talented sales representatives who carried this book onto the campuses and ultimately to you.

You, of course, are the bottom line. We thank you for examining and using this book. Your own personal commitment to excellence as a public communicator will be enhanced here and you will find new ways both to improve your own fortunes and to build a better community in a culturally diverse world. Your commitments are ours as well and we remain ever mindful of our obligation to enable you to succeed as ethical communicators.

Raymie E. McKerrow
Bruce E. Gronbeck

Part One
THE PROCESS OF SPEAKING PUBLICLY

What other power [than eloquence] could have been strong enough either to gather scattered humanity into one place, or to lead it out of its brutish existence in the wilderness up to our present condition of civilization as [people] and as citizens, or, after the establishment of social communities, to give shape to laws, tribunals, and civic rights?

Cicero
De oratore I.33

Chapter 1

The Academic Study of Public Speaking

"Why take a speech class? I've been speaking all of my life!"

"How in the world can you justify using expensive college and university resources on something as technique-oriented as public speaking?"

"Sure, the business school needs to require speaking—accountants need all of the help they can get!—but why require it of the rest of us?"

"Ok, maybe our international students profit from taking this class, but not somebody from Detroit, Michigan!"

"If you want to take the easiest class at this school, sign up for public speaking!"

Teachers of public speaking have listened to these sorts of comments for all their years in the classroom. The course is too easy, or it's too hard. It's too technique- or too theory-oriented. It should be required, or it should be thrown out. Then, the first speech must be delivered, and the comments change:

What should I talk about?

How should I start my speech?

Why am I doing this? What do I want to achieve?

How should I stand? What do I do with my hands?

What if they can't understand my awkward English pronunciation?

What if someone asks a question I can't answer?

What if I forget what I want to say?

As a student in a public speaking class, you're likely to feel a range of emotions: fear of what might happen to you in the middle of a speech, excitement at the prospect of learning how to better control yourself and your words in front of an audience, boredom when reading some of the chapters in this book, smugness when you find yourself saying, "I already know [or do] that!" or even anger at being asked to do something you'd rather not do publicly.

While the prospect of speaking in public seems scary, exciting, boring, or whatever other emotion you experience when you're about to talk, learning to channel your perfectly natural feelings in positive directions to come across as being poised, prepared, and even persuasive is why you are here. In addition, you're in this class because many people in higher education believe public speaking is something that well-educated, community-oriented people must be able to do well. Further, as the quotation from Cicero at the beginning of this unit indicates, the power of speech in building community is worthy of study. Preserving your own identity while creating a community is a special challenge as the next century looms before us.

We can't deal with all of your feelings and all of the reasons that you should (or should not) be in this classroom. But, as you start into a process that Cicero said will make you *vir bonus, dicendi peritus*—"the good person, speaking well"—we will ask you to think about some important questions:

1. Why should you study public speaking at the collegiate level of education?
2. Why is public speaking itself important to you in your public roles in society?
3. What are the primary skills you need to work on in a college-level class in public speaking?
4. What if you're deathly afraid of speaking publicly?
5. What ethical obligations do you assume every time you rise to say a few words publicly?

STUDYING PUBLIC SPEAKING IN HIGHER EDUCATION

Your first questions about a class in public speaking probably should focus on *why:* Why in the world should you be in this room with these people? And the second might be, ok, if it's a good idea for me to be here, how should a collegian go about studying public talk? Let's examine those questions seriously.

The Need for Speech Training

Actually, if you ask even speech teachers why students need such training, you'll find no unanimity in their answers. Some will stress the *social imperative:* speech skills are necessary for all social beings, and speech training was mandated by the federal government as long ago as 1978, in the Primary and Secondary Education Act. Speech skills are necessary for any individual to participate in public events, or, as pioneer rhetorical critics Lester Thonssen and A. Craig Baird noted some fifty years ago, "the fundamental purpose of oral discourse is social coordination or control."[1] The ability to control—to make function smoothly—various social events and confrontations also has been important to students of speech, as Kenneth Burke noted, because the public arena is "the Scramble, the Wrangle of the Market Place, the flurries and flare-ups of the Human Barnyard, the Give and Take, the wavering line of pressure and counterpressure, the Logomachy, the onus of leadership, the Wars of Nerves, the War. . . . Rhetoric is concerned with the state of Babel after the Fall . . . [in] the lugubrious regions of malice and the lie."[2] Speech skills must be sharpened through study and practice, because otherwise, you could not participate with maximum effect in public events and, worse, could be victimized by unscrupulous others.

That last point suggests another: You learn about the technicalities of public speaking not only to be a better maker of messages but also to be a more sophisticated receiver of public talk. There is a *consumer imperative* to speech education. Roderick Hart has written that a student of speech must engage in both "reflective complaining" and "reflective compliments," that a student must become someone "who knows when and how to render an evaluation."[3] To understand how public communication works, you must have an understanding of basic processes and varied techniques, a vocabulary for talking about both, and some sense as to what kinds of standards can be used to make value judgments about speeches. A good course in public speaking teaches you as much about listening to as about making speeches.

Finally, behind any solid courses in public speaking is an *intellectual imperative:* in fact, speech training is an important part of a liberal arts education. This has been so since Isocrates made it central to his training of the orator-statesmen of fourth-century B.C.E. Greece:

> For [the power to speak publicly] it is which has laid down laws concerning things just and unjust, and things honourable and base; and if it were not for these ordinances [i.e., of public speech] we should not be able to live with one another. It is by this also that we confuse the bad and extol the good. Through this we educate the ignorant and appraise the wise; for the power to speak well is taken as the surest index of a sound understanding, and discourse which is true and lawful and just is the outward image of a good and faithful soul.[4]

In this grand conception, the study of human speech is the study of the ethics, practical philosophy, and most eloquent expressions of the human spirit: the essence of the liberal arts. In exceptional instances—Abraham Lincoln at Gettysburg in 1863; Martin Luther King, Jr., at the Washington Monument a century later—public speaking can rise to the pinnacle upon which Isocrates mounted it. Even when it doesn't, studying speech still becomes part of most other liberal arts disciplines. Political policy is made through speeches, as in presidential inaugural addresses. People construct their sense of common identity, as when Sojourner Truth urged us to understand that black women face the same problems as their white sisters in "Ain't I A Woman?" Some speeches read like good literature, as, for example, does William Faulkner's speech accepting the Nobel Prize in 1950 (see Chapter 10 on language). Speeches become vehicles for studying the classical era, other languages, and different cultures. While public speaking per se is a practical art

Sojourner Truth was an eloquent spokesperson for emancipation and women's rights.

that people use to make decisions in the here-and-now, the act of speaking can be examined politically, psychologically, socially, aesthetically, philosophically, and culturally to great educational effect.

You take courses in public speaking for social, protective, and intellectual reasons—and, of course, to improve your own self-confidence and sense of empowerment. That's why you need speech training.

Ways to Learn More About Public Speaking

There are, of course, many different ways to learn about public speaking. Your instructor probably won't have you pursue all of them, but some certainly will be part of his or her pedagogy. Consider:

1. *A speech classroom is a laboratory and, hence, an ideal place for experimentation.* You should try to develop new skills in the assigned speeches. Tell a story in the conclusion, use PowerPoint or some other computer project for making visual aids, or deliver a speech from in front of rather than behind a lectern. The speech classroom is a comparatively safe environment for experimentation.
2. *Practice new speech techniques on friends, in a variety of settings, and in the speech classroom.* Practicing public speaking is every bit as important as practicing music instruments, football plays, or job-related behaviors. You can't just read about speaking and then do it well. Speaking skills develop through the hit-and-miss process of practice: in the privacy of your own room, in front of friends willing to humor you, in other classes, and, of course, in your speech classroom. Get feedback wherever you can.
3. *Work on your speech consumer skills as well.* In your lifetime, you'll be exposed to thousands upon thousands of public messages in the form of speeches, classroom pitches, TV ads, and Internet dialogues. Practicing listening—trying to accurately comprehend and fairly evaluate what others say formally—develops skills that are equally as important as speaking skills.
4. *Learn to criticize expertly the speeches of others.* You can use this book as a tool for analyzing speeches you find in print (e.g., with the *Speech Index*),[5] hear in person, or access electronically. Especially when working with historical or contemporary political material, you can find helpful explanatory and interpretative materials via tables of contents and searchable electronic materials assembled by professional organizations.[6] Studying speeches closely will give you useful tips on how to improve your own speaking styles.

Through activities both inside and outside your speech classroom, speaking and analyzing the speeches of others, you will develop and hone the skills that will make you a more productive and successful member of society.

THE FUNCTIONS OF ORAL COMMUNICATION IN SOCIETY

What, then, are the central goals of public speakers considered from the viewpoint not of themselves but of the organizations, agencies, and other publics of which they are parts? In what ways do we build community through public speaking as the millennium dawns?

Public Speaking in the Age of Diversity

First and foremost, to speak in public is to declare yourself to be a member of a community. By "going public" with your ideas, you demand that others accept you and your suggestions as being worthy of consideration. Asserting this right to be heard and taken seriously, especially when that right has been denied, is a vital part of our history. Without Frederick Douglass, a former slave who urged the abolition of slavery, we would be less than we are today. In the language of his times, Douglass said, "Men may combine to prevent cruelty to animals, for they are dumb [mute] and cannot speak for themselves; but we are men and must speak for ourselves, or we shall not be spoken for at all."[7] Martin Luther King, Jr.'s "Dream" may not yet be fully realized, but the legacy of Douglass lives on as African Americans continue to speak on behalf of their cultural heritage. Similarly, the women attending the Seneca Falls, New York, convention for women's rights in 1848 argued they should be allowed to talk publicly. Originally, they had been assigned to watch the proceedings from the gallery, but they were determined to define their own rights. The words of Elizabeth Cady Stanton give eloquent testimony to the need to speak:

> I should feel exceedingly diffident to appear before you at this time . . . did I not feel that woman herself must do this work. . . . Man cannot speak for her, because he has been educated to believe that she differs from him so materially, that he cannot judge of her thoughts, feelings, and opinions by his own.[8]

Speaking in public, then, is a personal declaration of your beliefs and values, or of your right to be a representative of your community. Not to speak is to engage in silence. Silence can make you disappear, become invisible, a nonperson in the eyes of others: the Jews of Hitler's Germany were talked about as "silent animals" in *Mein Kampf*. American slaves were thought of as the personal property of slave owners. Native Americans were viewed as children, and treated as such. Whole segments of populations have been—and continue to be—treated as outcasts in their own land (and even "cleansed" in ethnic genocide, as in the Kosovo tragedy). When whole peoples are silenced, whether through force or other forms of intimidation, they are in danger of elimination.

The connection between the right to be heard publicly and being accepted as a human being with a distinct cultural heritage is trivialized at the expense of human freedom. If one can speak, what of the community from which, or to which, one speaks? The words *community* and *communication* both derive from the common Latin root words *cum* (meaning "with") and *munis* (meaning "public work"). Communities are defined by public talk; human conversation creates, sustains, and alters the sense of community one has with another. Such groups are created and maintained symbolically: as Boy Scouts or Girl Scouts who take their oaths together, as members of a church congregation who together recite the Lord's Prayer, as people stand and cease talking as the national anthem plays at the start of a hockey game.

Public speech, whether as part of a ritual performance or as a specific address to right social wrongs, has as a side benefit the maintenance or alteration of communities to which we belong. In our culturally diverse land, maintaining community is a special right of those whose culture differs from others. With maintenance comes the obligation of respecting differences between cultures, even in the same physical community.

In 1989, Henri Mann Morton, a member of the Cheyenne nation, addressed a multicultural conference and gave voice to the long-standing concern for preserving **cultural diversity** in these words:

> I am the granddaughter of those who welcomed many of our grandmothers and grandfathers—your grandparents—to this country. It is now our country.
>
> We were multi-tribal; heterogeneous as the indigenous people of America, and following Anglo contact exchanged the term "multi-tribal" for "multicultural," so we could embrace those who came to live with us. Prior to non-Indian contact, we as American Indians were culturally diverse. We were familiar with the concept of "cultural diversity," and recognized that those cultural differences made us strong. Cultural diversity made for strength—there was/is strength in cultural diversity. Cultural diversity makes our country strong. It has made us a great nation and we all have an opportunity to achieve the American dream.[9]

On the opening night of the 1992 Democratic National Convention in New York City, the third keynote speech was given by the late Barbara Jordan, the former congresswoman from Texas who in 1976 became the first female African American to keynote a national political party convention. Dealing forthrightly with the issue of race relations in this country, she implored her listeners to recognize and value difference in the midst of unity:

> We are one, we Americans, and we reject any intruder who seeks to divide us on the bases of race and color. We honor cultural identity. We always have, we always will. But separateness is not allowed. Separateness is not the American way. We must not allow ideas like political correctness to divide us and cause us to reverse hard-won achievements in human rights and civil rights. Xenophobia has no place in the Democratic party. We seek to unite people, not divide them.
>
> As we seek to unite people, we reject both white racism and black racism. This party, this party, this party will not tolerate bigotry under any guise. Our strength, our strength in this country is rooted in our diversity. Our history bears witness to that fact. E pluribus unum. "From many, one." It was a good idea when our country was founded, and it's a good idea today.[10]

That two speeches by female members of minority groups would deal with matters of cultural diversity, racial divisions, and social unity was no accident. We were then—and we continue to be—rocked by a series of incidents that suggest the country has not escaped the danger of splitting apart along racial lines. From the "Rodney King incident" to the incendiary (to many) lyrics of rapper Ice-T's song "Cop Killer" to Spike Lee's film *Malcolm X* to the allegations surrounding the Fuhrman tapes at the O. J. Simpson trial, to the slaughter of classmates because of difference in Littleton, Colorado, in 1999 maintaining a sense of community while preserving diversity has been sorely tried.

Social division along racial lines is but one of the cleavages that appear nightly on television. Men battle women for elected office, for managerial and entry-level jobs, for custody of children during divorce proceedings, and over charges

For Nelson Mandela, speech is a powerful means of maintaining cultural identity and fostering community.

of sexual discrimination and harassment. College and university campuses are alive with debate over "political correctness": concern about giving members of the political left or right access to student audiences, about racial and gender quotas in faculty hiring, about what constitutes sexual or racial harassment, and about what authors should be read in basic literature and history classes.[11]

The remarks of Morton and Jordan illustrate that even mainstream public spokespersons have become frustrated by the divisions threatening to crack open this country. The difficulty was articulated clearly by Jordan: We believe in and regularly affirm **cultural diversity,** even while we know it is essential that we maintain social unity to achieve common goals, both locally and globally. Many have rejected the old notion of this country as the "melting pot"—a metaphor indicating that people's separate cultures somehow are assimilated into one homogeneous "American" culture. Jesse Jackson's "rainbow coalition" of many colors is one way of expressing the kind of tension articulated by Jordan: Seen in the sky, the rainbow is at the same time "one" and "many." Achieving community while preserving diversity remains a challenge, but that challenge can be met, in part, through common activity. People who work together, play together, fight a common enemy, or seek a common goal usually find out that people are people. When men and women teach together, they better appreciate each other's strengths; when Latinos and whites serve on community boards together, they generally discover shared hopes for their neighborhoods.

Sharing work and play can lead to shared views, but mere association is not enough. Most people need more than proximity to know and understand each other, and this fact gives rise to the second means—and the focus of this book: People need to talk. They need to chat about their teenage years, children, disgust with local government, favorite basketball teams, and commitments. They need to argue over abortion or statehood for the District of Columbia or tax credits for kids in college. They need to verbally construct bridges between female and male, brown and white, immigrant and Native American. In their diversity, they must speak to become one.

Public speaking is a primary vehicle for recognizing individual identity even as a group of people seeks to share common ideas, values, action plans, and identities. If we had no need to share information and ideas, attitudes and values, plans and projects, or images of what we hold in common, we wouldn't need to talk. But we have those needs, we do talk publicly, and we must become better at such talk.

Achieving Personal and Collective Goals Through Public Talk

Even as you pursue the public expression of your individual identity in front of others, you also forward important shared or collective goals via speech. Both speaking and listening skills are important, because for centuries, *public communication* has been the glue that holds societies together. A sense of sharing— the *"withness"* part of the Latin root of the English word *communication*—bonds people together. More specifically, public speeches perform four important functions for a community:

For Senator Ben Nighthorse Campbell of Colorado, the "Indian Way" places greater value on contributions to society than on acquisition of material possessions.

1. *Speeches are used for self-definition.* Especially on occasions such as Memorial Day, the Fourth of July, dedications of community centers, and political conventions, communities define themselves, indicating what they stand for and what it means to be a member of that community, in speeches. That's why we all look to each other as we speak to sense who we are. ("As one speaks so she or he is" is an aphorism from the time of the Roman orator Seneca.)

2. *Speeches are used to spread information through a community.* The president announces the latest plans for a European economic summit through public talk. The surgeon general holds a press conference to update AIDS research findings. The mayor uses a radio interview to spread the word about next week's downtown jazz festival. Most information, of course, is distributed via print or electronic display, but spoken information is so much more personalized that important ideas often are spoken directly to you. Even when offering ideas across national boundaries, world leaders still speak through translators because of the personal nature of talk.

3. *Speeches are used to debate questions of fact, value, and policy in communities.* Human beings always have fought through their differences with each other. As civilizations advanced, however, verbal controversy began to replace physical combat, and the art of public debate was born. From the government to the workplace, arguing one's way to a decision is an important function of talk.

4. *Speeches are used to bring about individual and group change.* For centuries, persuasion has been the heart of public talk. The earliest books about public speaking dealt exclusively with persuasion as the most important kind of talk. Societies must adapt to changes in their environments, values, and practices; if change is to occur, most people must be persuaded to accept it.

Speechmaking, therefore, performs four broad social functions in communities. Whether one is talking about community broadly (as in a community of nations) or narrowly (as in a community of friends), collectivities simply could not exist and work without multiple forms of public communication. So, even as you grow, develop, and learn how to better achieve your own social, political, economic, and religious goals through improving your speaking knowledge and skills, you also become a better public servant, a more useful instrument for helping your organizations and the public itself find their collective goals.

SKILLS AND COMPETENCIES NEEDED FOR SUCCESSFUL SPEECHMAKING

Because public speaking is an interactive process through which people transact various kinds of business, you must acquire certain skills (psychomotor abilities) and competencies (mental abilities to identify, assess, and plan responses to communication problems). From the beginning of your coursework, four basic qualities merit your attention:

- *Integrity*
- *Knowledge*

- *Sensitivity to both listener needs and speaking situations*
- *Oral skills*

Integrity

Your reputation for reliability, truthfulness, and concern for others is your single most powerful means of exerting rhetorical influence. Integrity is important, especially in an age of diversity, when various groups in a fragmented culture are wary of each other and of each other's purposes. Listeners who haven't had personal experience with a particular subject or with representatives of particular social groups must be convinced of your concern for them. You must earn their trust while speaking if you are to succeed.

Knowledge

No one wants to listen to an empty-headed windbag; speakers must know what they're talking about. So, for example, even though you may have personal experience with criterium bike-racing, do some extra reading, talk with other bikers and shop owners, and find out what aspects of the topic interest potential listeners before giving a speech about it.

Rhetorical Sensitivity

Sometimes we talk publicly for purely *expressive* reasons—simply to give voice to ourselves. Usually, however, we speak for *instrumental* reasons—to pass on ideas or influence how others think or act. The most successful speakers are "other directed," concerned with meeting their listeners' needs and solving their problems through public talk. These speakers are rhetorically sensitive to others.

Rhetorical sensitivity refers to speakers' attitudes toward the process of speech composition.[12] More particularly, rhetorical sensitivity is the degree to which speakers recognize that all people are different and complex and, hence, must be considered individually; adapt their messages and themselves to particular audiences; consciously seek and react to audience feedback; understand that, in some cases, silence is better than speaking; and work at finding the right set of arguments and linguistic expressions to make particular ideas clear and attractive to particular audiences. Being rhetorically sensitive doesn't mean saying only what you think an audience wants to hear. Rather, it's a matter of careful self-assessment, audience analysis, and decision making. What are your purposes? To what degree will they be understandable and acceptable to others? To what degree can you adapt your purposes to audience preferences while maintaining your own integrity and self-respect? These questions demand that you be sensitive to the needs of listeners, of speaking situations, and of your own need for self-respect. Being a rhetorically sensitive speaker attests to your competence as a communicator.

Oral Skills

Fluency, poise, voice control, and coordinated body movements mark you as a skilled speaker. These skills don't come naturally; they develop through attention to the advice offered in this textbook and putting that advice into practice. As you practice inside and outside the classroom, your aim is to refine your skill as an animated, natural, and conversational speaker. Many competent public speakers—discounting those speaking in the highly ceremonial situations of politics and re-

HOW TO

ENHANCE YOUR CREDIBILITY AS A SPEAKER

Research has verified the following generalizations, among others:

1. References to yourself and your experience—provided you're not boasting or excessive—tend to increase your perceived trustworthiness and competence. References to those acknowledged as authorities tend to increase your perceived trustworthiness and dynamism.
2. Using highly credible authorities to substantiate your claims increases your perceived fairness.
3. If you can demonstrate that you and your audience share common beliefs, attitudes, and values, your overall credibility will increase.
4. Well-organized speeches are more credible than poorly organized speeches.
5. The more sincere you are, the better your chance of changing your listeners' attitudes.[13]

ligion—seem to be merely *conversing* with their audiences. That should be your goal: to practice being yourself while engaging others in public conversation.[14]

OVERCOMING SPEECH ANXIETY

As you think about speaking publicly, you're likely to feel some anxiety, because you don't want to fail. This fear of failure or embarrassment may be even stronger than your desire to speak, leading to speech anxiety.

Research distinguishes between two kinds of speech anxiety: state apprehension and trait apprehension.[15] **State apprehension** refers to the anxiety you feel in particular settings or situations. For example, perhaps you can talk easily with friends but are uncomfortable when being interviewed for a job. This sort of apprehension is also known as *stage fright,* because it's the fear of performing that leads to your worries about embarrassing yourself. Extreme stage fright has physiological manifestations: clammy hands, weak knees, dry mouth, and a trembling or even cracking voice. Its psychological manifestations include mental blocks (forgetting what you're going to say), vocal hesitation and nonfluency, and an internal voice that keeps saying you're messing up your speech. The knowledge that you're being evaluated by others intensifies these anxious moments.

Although some aspects of nervousness are characteristic of the situation, others are a part of your own personality. This kind of apprehension, called **trait apprehension,** refers to your level of anxiety as you face any communication situation. A high level of such anxiety may lead people to withdraw from any situation that requires interpersonal or public communication with others.

HOW TO

MANAGE YOUR FEAR OF PUBLIC SPEAKING

There are positive ways of reducing such apprehension in the classroom setting:

1. *Realize that tension and nervousness are normal and, in part, even beneficial to speakers.* Learning how to control fear and make it work for you is the key to relieving tension. Tension can provide you with energy and alertness. As adrenaline pours into your bloodstream, you experience a physical charge that increases bodily movement and psychological acuity. A speaker who isn't pumped up may come across as dull and lifeless.

2. *Take comfort that tension is physiologically reduced by the act of speaking.* As you talk and discover that your audience accepts and understands what you're saying, your nervousness will dissipate. Physiologically, your body is using up the excess adrenaline it generated; psychologically, your ego is getting positive reinforcement. The very act of talking aloud reduces fear.

3. *Talk about topics that interest you.* Speech anxiety arises in part because of self-centeredness; sometimes you're more concerned with your personal appearance and performance than with your topic. One means of reducing this anxiety is to select topics that thoroughly interest you—topics that take your mind off yourself.

4. *Talk about subjects with which you're familiar.* Confidence born of knowledge increases your perceived credibility and helps you control your nervousness. Knowing something about the subject may be part of the answer: subject mastery is related closely to self-mastery.

5. *Analyze both the situation and the audience.* The more you know about the audience and what is expected of you, the less there is to fear. In the speech classroom, students usually are less nervous during their third speech than during their first, because they're more comfortable with the audience and more aware of the demands of the situation. Careful analysis of an audience and its expectations goes a long way toward reducing a natural fear of the unknown.

6. *Speak in public as often as you can.* Sheer repetition of the public-speaking experience will not eliminate anxiety, but it will give you greater confidence in managing your apprehension. Speaking several times in front of the same group can help reduce your fright. Speaking up in class discussions, engaging in conversations with friends and others, and contributing ideas or thoughts in meetings of organizations to which you belong also will gain you more knowledge about the strategies that work for you in reducing nervousness.

There are no shortcuts to developing self-confidence about speaking in public. For most of us, gaining self-confidence is partly a matter of psyching ourselves up and partly a matter of experience. The sick feelings in your stomach may well always be there, at least momentarily, but they needn't paralyze you. As you gain experience with each of the essential steps—from selecting a subject to practicing the speech—your self-confidence as a speaker will grow.[16]

SPEAKING THE CULTURE IN ETHICAL WAYS

Being perceived by listeners as a person with socially grounded, ethical principles is vital to your success as a speaker. In helping people define who they are, assembling and packaging information for others, and seeking to persuade them to think or act in a certain way, you run into many ethical questions. Is it ethical to make explicitly racial references when defining a people? Should you tell both sides of the story when giving people information on a new wonder drug? Can you in good conscience suppress certain kinds of information when you're trying to change people's minds? These—and hundreds of other—ethical questions arise as you prepare and deliver speeches. Whether you want to or not, you make decisions with moral implications many, many times—even when you're building a comparatively simple speech. The principles offered here are not exhaustive, but they give a sense of what is at stake.

BEING A PRINCIPLED SPEAKER

1. *Honesty is the best policy.* This old aphorism, tainted by the practices of speakers seeking to bend the truth or not provide it at all, still holds true as a starting point for deciding what to say—or not to say—in a public setting.
2. *Maximize audience responsibility for decision making.* Public speaking in a democratic society demands openness with respect to information. Whether you are informing or persuading, respect your audience enough to allow them to make a decision based on all the information and support you have to offer.
3. *Maximize help while minimizing harm to others.* Your reasons for speaking out should result in actions that would help rather than harm other individuals. Inciting listeners to believe or act in a manner that produces physical or emotional harm to others is a misuse of communication's power.
4. *Place your ego at the service of others, not simply of yourself.* While self-interest and a sense of self-esteem go a long way toward making you a successful speaker, the purpose is not simply to display your ability but rather to put it at the service of the community.
5. *Follow both the letter and the spirit of the law.* Your language should be within legal bounds; the question of libelous or harassing language should never arise in the speaking situation.
6. *When in doubt, think of how this audience would expect and want you to talk.* This standard is more complex than it sounds, perhaps because audience expectations are complicated. So, for example, a congregation expects a

minister or rabbi to point out their shortcomings, even to disapprove of parts of their lifestyles. Therefore, thinking of an audience's behavioral standards doesn't mean that you always must act as they would. Rather, what's important is to think of your society's range of acceptable and unacceptable beliefs, attitudes, values, and behaviors as you prepare to talk. Sometimes, you'll decide to conform to them; other times, you'll decide to challenge them. What's important is that you make ethical decisions after having thought about listener reactions and be ready for the consequences, whether or not you reflect their moral standards when you talk. That's what we mean by "speaking the culture in ethical ways."[17]

No one can presume to tell you precisely what ethical codes you should adhere to when giving a speech. Given this textbook's educational mission, however, we'll regularly raise ethical questions and urge you to deal with them by considering simultaneously your own moral code and those of your listeners. Throughout this book, you'll encounter "Ethical Moments." These features are designed to confront you with a problem; working through ethical dilemmas will make you a more thoughtful speaker.

CHAPTER SUMMARY

While some might prefer not to be taking a collegiate-level public speaking class, there are sound reasons for doing so. Social, consumer, and intellectual imperatives justify this sort of educational activity. By treating the classroom as a lab, practicing speaking skills in multiple settings, learning better listening as well as speaking skills, and studying speeches and speech research, you encounter many routes to improving your skills and knowledge.

There are special challenges to studying public speaking in our time. We live in an Age of Diversity, characterized by a fragmented population and subgroups within society that are separated from each other even while needing a sense of the whole to live together. Speaking skills are important to society, because we collectively use speeches for self-definition; information giving; debate about questions of fact, value, and policy; and debate about individual and social change.

Because public speaking is a complex transaction, you need certain skills and competencies to be successful: integrity, knowledge, rhetorical sensitivity, and oral skills. Whenever you talk publicly, you also must consider the ethical dimensions of your act of communication.

KEY TERMS

cultural diversity (pp. 9, 10)

rhetorical sensitivity (p. 13)

state apprehension (p. 14)

trait apprehension (p. 14)

ASSESSMENT ACTIVITIES

1. To learn to assess both your own and other's speeches, watch a speech on videotape; pause each time something strikes your attention—jot down notes as you watch and listen. After viewing the speech several times, answer the following questions:

   a. Does the speech seek to define community, share information, take a position in a debate, or call for social change? Does it have more than one of these general purposes? If so, which predominates? Why do you think this is so?

   b. Does the speaker appear to be rhetorically sensitive to the situation and the audience? Given the content, structure, and style of the speech, what is the image the speaker appears to have of the audience? Does the speaker view listeners as passive consumers or as active, intelligent critics of the message?

   c. What attitudes might the audience bring to this speech? Why would they be listening to the speaker?

   d. How would you rate the speaker's skills and competencies? Does the speaker seem knowledgeable, self-assured, and trustworthy? Does the speaker's use of verbal and nonverbal communication result in a message that is clear, forceful, and compelling? Why, or why not?

   e. List at least three ways the speaker could improve on this particular speech.

2. Explore a recent public event in which the ethics or credibility of a person was called into question. Prepare a three to four-minute presentation in which you briefly summarize the ethical issue. Then, add your own views as to whether the person was fairly accused and, if so, what you think of the choice the person apparently made.

REFERENCES

1. Lester Thonssen and A. Craig Baird, *Speech Criticism: The Development of Standards for Rhetorical Appraisal* (New York: The Ronald Press, 1948), 5.

2. Kenneth Burke, *The Grammar of Motives and the Rhetoric of Motives* (orig. pub. 1945, 1950; Cleveland: Meridian Books, 1962), 547.

3. Roderick P. Hart, *Modern Rhetorical Criticism*, 2nd ed. (Boston: Allyn and Bacon, 1997), 34.

4. Isocrates, *Isocrates II* (including *Antidosis*), translated by George Norlin (Cambridge, MA: Harvard University Press), 327.

5. Roberta Briggs Sutton, ed., *Speech Index: An Index to 259 Collections of World Famous Orations and Speeches for Various Occasions*, 4th ed. rev. & enl. (Metuchen, NJ: Scarecrow Press, 1966); and Charity Mitchell, *Speech Index: An Index to Collections of World Famous Orations and Speeches for Various Occasions*, 4th ed. suppl., 1966–1980 (Metuchen, NJ: Scarecrow Press, 1982).

6. For example, 19 professional journals are indexed in Ronald J. Matlon and Sylvia P. Ortiz, eds., *Index to Journals in Communication Studies Through 1990* (Annandale, VA: National Communication Association, 1992), while you can find indexes to 24 journals, abstracts to articles from the six published by NCA, 1978–1995, and full searchable texts to those six, 1991–1995, on a CD-ROM, *Comm Search*, 2nd ed. (Annandale, VA: National Communication Association, 1998). Check the NCA's Web site for more information: http://www.natcom.org.

7. Frederick Douglass, "Speech at the National Convention of Colored Men

(1883)," reprinted in *The American Reader: Words That Moved a Nation,* ed. Diane Ravitch (New York: HarperCollins, 1990), 172.

8. Elizabeth Cady Stanton, "Speech at the Seneca Falls Convention, 1948," reprinted in *Man Cannot Speak For Her,* vol. 2, *Key Texts of the Early Feminists,* ed. Karlyn Kohrs Campbell (New York: Praeger, 1989), 42.

9. Henri Mann Morton, "Strength through Cultural Diversity," in *Native American Reader,* ed. J. Blanche (Juneau, AL: Denali Press, 1990), 196–197.

10. Barbara Jordan, keynote address to the 1992 National Democratic Party Convention, July 13, 1992, New York City, telecast on the C-SPAN television network; personal transcription.

11. For a readable study of the so-called "culture wars" understood from a communication perspective, see Todd Gitlin, *The Twilight of Common Dreams: Why America Is Wracked by Culture Wars* (New York: Henry Holt, 1995).

12. See Roderick P. Hart and Don M. Burks, "Rhetorical Sensitivity and Social Interaction," *Speech [Communication] Monographs* 47 (1980): 1–22.

13. Still the most complete bibliography on credibility research is Stephen W. Littlejohn, "A Bibliography of Studies Related to Variables of Source Credibility," *Bibliographic Annual of Speech Communication, 1971,* ed. Ned A. Shearer (Annandale, VA: National Communication Association, 1971), 1–40. For a more recent overview, see James B. Stiff, *Persuasive Communication* (New York: Guilford Press, 1994), ch. 5, "Source Characteristics in Persuasive Communication," 89–106.

14. The goal of achieving an up-close-and-personal relationship with others through public talk was one of the mainstays of communication in oral societies. See Walter J. Ong, *Orality and Literacy: The Technologizing of the Word* (New York: Methuen, 1982), 45–46, for his discussion of oral culture talk as "empathetic and participatory rather than objectively distanced" (45).

15. James McCroskey, "Oral Communication Apprehension: A Summary of Current Theory and Research," *Human Communication Research* 4 (1977): 78–96.

16. Also relevant is the research on shyness, made popular by Philip Zimbardo, a psychologist at Stanford University. For summaries of this research, see John A Daly and James C. McCroskey, eds., *Avoiding Communication: Shyness, Reticence, and Communication Apprehension* (Thousand Oaks, CA: Sage, 1984); and Philip Zimbardo, *Shyness: What It Is, What to Do About It,* rev. ed. (Reading, MA: Addison-Wesley, 1990).

17. For a more complete discussion of these and other principles, see James Benjamin and Raymie E. McKerrow, *Business and Professional Communication: Concepts and Practices* (New York: Longman Educational Publishers, 1994).

Chapter 2

Getting Started: Basic Tips for Speech Preparation and Delivery

The first chapter provided an introduction to the study of public speaking, with an overview of the basic skills needed for success as a speaker. Because you will be asked to present speeches before you've actually read all—or even most—of the chapters, this early chapter provides a "safety valve" of sorts by presenting an overview of speaking as practice: planning what to say and how to say it. All speech teachers have heard students say, "Well, yeah, I knew what I wanted to do. I just lost it!" When their teachers probe a little—Did you find and carefully arrange supporting arguments? Did you phrase your key ideas ahead of time?—the answer is usually "No, I just thought it would all happen as I planned it in my head."

If you've had a similar experience, you know that public speaking takes preparation. Although this chapter won't cover all that you can learn about the intricacies and shortcuts of speech preparation and speechmaking, it will provide you with sufficient information so that you can think and act in a more rhetorically sound way and can get through the initial speech assignments with confidence you are on the right track. Having a **rhetorical frame of mind** means thinking your way strategically through the decisions you need to make as you prepare for any speech: (**1**) *selecting the subject;* (**2**) *narrowing the subject;* (**3**) *determining your purposes, including central ideas and claims;* (**4**) *considering the audience and occasion;* (**5**) *gathering the speech material;* (**6**) *making an outline;* and (**7**) *practicing aloud in preparation for standing in front of an audience and presenting your ideas.* Working through these steps in a systematic manner will keep you from wandering aimlessly through the library or waiting endlessly at your desk for inspiration. This chapter reviews each step to provide a basic foundation for planning your presentation.

There's no magical formula for getting ready to speak. However, if you pay close attention to these seven steps—either in the order presented here or in another that works for you—you'll be ahead of the game and ready for an audience. In this chapter, we also supplement these seven steps with additional subjects that will help you develop your first speech: how to decide on an ap-

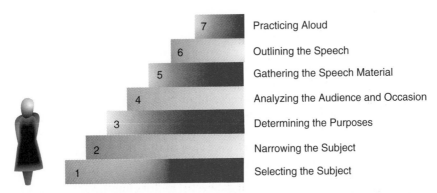

FIGURE 2.1   The Essential Steps in Planning, Preparing, and Presenting a Speech

propriate method of presentation, how to project self-confidence, and how to evaluate presentations. Becoming a critical listener, as we will note in Chapter 3, is as important as learning to speak well.

SELECTING THE SUBJECT

Oddly, one of the most difficult jobs many speakers in classrooms face is choosing a subject. When you are confronted with a speech assignment, the following guidelines will help you select a subject that's appropriate to the rhetorical situation.

Select a subject about which you already know something and can find out more. Begin with an inventory of what you already know. This will help you focus your ideas and distinguish between strong and weak choices (i.e., less familiar topics are weaker choices). If you need to update statistical data or locate additional examples to flesh out your basic knowledge, consider whether the needed information is readily accessible. Research is easier if you know something about the subject, because you have a better idea regarding potential sources of information. Selecting a familiar topic also increases your self-confidence as you rise to speak.

Select a subject that interests you and your audience. First, resist the temptation to speak on an issue that is more interesting to the audience than it is to you. This can be a disastrous choice, because gathering information will be unexciting and your presentation will reflect your lack of enthusiasm. If you have a personal interest in an issue, however, your commitment will come across to the audience. You'll find that researching the issue is more interesting and that preparing the speech becomes easier. Conversely, talking without regard to your audience may leave you with a subject that only interests an audience of one—you. You need to balance your needs and interests with those of the audience. A topic may interest listeners for one or more of the following reasons:

- *It concerns their health, happiness, or security.* For instance, you might talk to senior citizens about changes in Medicare or to college students about recent employment trends.

- *It offers a solution to a recognized problem.* You may suggest ways your group could raise funds to participate in a national competition or ways college students might volunteer within the community.
- *It is surrounded by controversy or conflict of opinion.* You might speak on the proposed relocation of a town dump to a site near your campus or on proposed strategies to implement recycling in the community.
- *It provides information on a misunderstood or little understood issue.* You might speak to a local business group about the community service contributions of college students or to the class about services provided by the campus writing and math centers.

Select a topic appropriate to the occasion. Several factors may limit your degree of freedom in selecting an appropriate subject. Often, however, the freedom to choose an appropriate subject will be virtually unlimited. An in-class speech assignment may ask that you seek to inform or persuade but give you the freedom to select a subject. Consider whether the occasion is the right setting for what you want to accomplish: a demonstration speech on body-building might go over very well in your speech classroom, but bringing a dog to class to demonstrate training commands may not work equally well. Likewise, the speech on body-building may not be appropriate at the dedication of a new senior citizens' center, but a speech describing the need for exercise at all ages and how to get the most out of the new center's exercise room would be fitting. In each instance, your choice would be affected as much by your personal interests as by the needs of the audience. At other times, your speech topic will be determined—at least in part—by the group to whom you will speak. Usually, you are invited to speak because you have specific expertise or knowledge to share with the group. As part of the invitation, you'll be asked to address a particular issue, policy, or question that relates to your work, community involvement, or special skills. In a classroom, the instructor may limit choices by requiring you to consider only certain issues or subject areas or even by placing certain topics (e.g., "how to put a clarinet together," "how to kill a chicken"—these have been real topics in the past!) "off-limits."

In sum, whether the topic is a free choice or is assigned, it's advantageous to approach it in ways that play off your strengths. Any speech must reflect interests that you and your audience share, and it must be appropriate to the speaking occasion. Playing off your strengths means talking about a subject you can handle. Playing off your audience's interests means finding an approach to that subject that engages them.

NARROWING THE SUBJECT

A general subject is of little value until it's narrowed down to a manageable size. Narrowing a subject to a more precise topic for a speech involves three primary considerations.

Narrow your subject so that you can discuss it adequately in the time allotted for the speech. If you are responding to an in-class speech assignment that will last 5 to 7 or 8 to 10 minutes, you can't begin to do justice to "The History of the

Olympics Since Early Times." Instead, you might give an overview of the newest sports recognized for winter or summer Olympic competition, or you might discuss "Olympics and Terrorism," with specific attention to the bombing in Atlanta. Fit the topic's breadth to the time you have to speak.

Narrow your subject to meet the specific expectations of your audience. Listeners expecting an informative presentation on clear-cutting rain forests may be upset if you request their financial support for an environmental group formed to counter the devastation. The announced purpose of the meeting, the demands of the particular context, and the traditions of the group can influence an audience's expectations of what it is to hear. Violate audience expectations only when you feel it's absolutely essential, and be prepared for—and willing to accept—the consequences if you break with those expectations.

Gauge your subject to the comprehension level of the audience. If, for example, you want to talk about laser technology or the existence of "black holes" to stu-

HOW TO

NARROW A TOPIC: AN ILLUSTRATION

1. Identify a broad subject you know and care about—for example, science fiction.
2. Identify subtopics of the broad subject area that also interest you. For example, subtopics of science fiction might include the following:
   - The differences between science fiction and fantasy
   - The nature of "hard science" in science fiction novels
   - Major writers of science fiction: Heinlein, LeGuin, Asimov, McCaffrey
3. Ask five questions about each subtopic:
   - Which of these possible subtopics is of most interest to me?
   - Is the audience likely to be interested in the topic?
   - Is it appropriate to the occasion?
   - Can I cover it in the time available?
   - Will the audience comprehend it?
4. Narrow each subtopic until you can answer "yes" to all the questions above.

Time constraints might limit the first general topic to "*two or three* major differences between science fiction and fantasy" and the third to "*a single* major writer or a writer's *major series.*" Because you really aren't that excited about the differences between fantasy and science fiction, it would be difficult to seem enthusiastic when speaking; hence, that topic would be dropped. The audience's lack of background knowledge might cause you to discard the hard science topic if you have only 8 to 10 minutes to present your speech.

dents in your speech class, you should focus your attention on basic principles. If the audience is a group of senior physics majors, however, the nature and complexity of the material you present would necessarily change.

The process of narrowing may lead to a subject that is "best" for a particular occasion, or as the "How to" illustration indicates, it may leave you with several possibilities. If this is the case, you need to decide which subject, given your time limit, will best fit your interests as well as those of the audience. Which topic can you make the most interesting—which will be the most engaging for you and your audience?

DETERMINING THE PURPOSES

Once you know what you want to talk about, the next task is to consider a series of "why's" already implicit in much that's been discussed: Why do *you* wish to discuss this subject? Why might an *audience* want to listen to *you*? Why is this topic appropriate to *this occasion*? These questions can be answered by considering the following four points in sequence:

1. Think about the *general purposes* that people have in mind when they speak in public.
2. Consider your own *specific purposes*.
3. Focus on the *central idea* or *claim* that expresses the principal message you wish to communicate.
4. Create a *title* for the presentation that captures your goals and tells the audience the focus of your central idea or claim.

Finally, we examine strategic considerations relevant to selecting purposes.

General Purpose

What is the mental state you wish your listeners to be in when you complete the speech? For example, are you trying to tell them something they do not—but should—know? Are you seeking to alter how they feel about a social, economic, or political issue? Are you interested in having them do something as a result of your speech? Do you want them to laugh and learn at the same time?

FIGURE 2.2 The General Purposes of Speech

To Inform	Clear Understanding
To Persuade	Acceptance of Ideas
To Actuate	Action
To Entertain	Enjoyment and Comprehension

Answering "yes" to one of these questions will help focus your general purpose on the "end state" you wish to create in your audience. Asking "What is the general purpose of your speech?" sets up the following **general purposes:**

- *inform*
- *persuade*
- *actuate*
- *entertain*

Although these "end states" are not mutually exclusive (you may make a moral point through humor), they are sufficiently discrete for us to treat them as individual purposes. We'll consider the types of speeches that accompany each of these general purposes later in the book, with a major emphasis on the processes of informing and persuading. In this section, we consider the major goals of informative, persuasive, actuative, and entertaining speeches.

To Inform.   The general purpose of a **speech to inform** is to help listeners understand an idea, concept, or process or to widen their range of knowledge. This is a primary goal of elected officials when they seek to explain their actions to constituents; of college professors when they teach chemistry, speech, philosophy, art, or any other subject; and of supervisors when they explain how to use new equipment. Conveying new information changes the level or quality of knowledge your listeners possess. By providing examples, statistics, illustrations, and other materials containing data and ideas, you seek to expand or alter their concrete knowledge about an idea, policy, process, concept, or event. The message must be *comprehensive, accurate,* and *timely* to accomplish your informative goal. For example, an informative speech on the dangers of credit card debt must give an overview of the national scope of the problem, especially if the focus is on college students. It also must provide factual information about how such debt builds, what interest rates are being charged (and how they compare with other credit card interest rates), and how students can avoid being caught in the debt cycle. Because this speech may well relate to audience experience, you need to be sure you have accurate and complete information.

To Persuade or to Actuate.   The purpose of a **speech to persuade** or a **speech to actuate** is to influence listeners' minds or actions. Because both have similar goals, we consider them together. It may be argued that all speeches are persuasive to some degree, but in many situations, speakers have outright persuasion or action as their primary purpose.[1] For example, promoters and publicists try to make you believe in the superiority of certain products, persons, or institutions. Social action group leaders exhort tenants to believe in the need for city codes to protect their rights. Politicians debate campaign issues and strive to convince voters that they will best represent their interests in state legislatures, Congress, or the White House. For our purposes, speeches designed to influence belief and attitudes will be referred to as *persuasive speeches.* Speeches that go a step further to move the audience to adopt specific actions (e.g., "buy my product," "join the protest," "vote for the preferred candidate") will be referenced as *actuative speeches*. The distinguishing feature of an actuative speech is that instead of stopping with an appeal to beliefs or attitudes, you ask your listeners to alter their behavior in a specified way.

To influence or alter your listeners' beliefs and actions, you need to present well-ordered arguments that are supported by facts, figures, examples, and the opinions of experts. You also need to do more than simply state facts. To change minds and move people to action, you must be sensitive to both the rational and the motivational aspects of audience psychology, topics that will be discussed at length in later chapters. For the present, keep in mind the principle that facts alone, even if "airtight" as far as the case for change is concerned, often are insufficient to change behavior. Consider all of the information connecting cigarette, cigar, and pipe smoking to various forms of cancer—as well as to the issue of secondary smoke effects. If facts alone were sufficient, wouldn't more people decide to stop smoking? If you or a friend smokes, what about the current information is insufficient to warrant a change in behavior? What motivational appeal will lead a listener to take action in such an instance? Thus, persuasion and actuation involve far more complex tasks than simply telling people what you think.

To Entertain.   To entertain, amuse, or provide other enjoyment for listeners frequently is the general purpose of an after-dinner speech, but talks of other kinds also may have enjoyment as their principal aim. A travel lecture, for example, contains information, but it also may entertain an audience through exciting, amusing tales of adventure—or misadventure. Club meetings, class reunions, and similar gatherings of friends may provide the opportunity to "roast" one or more of the people present. In these situations, the effective use of humor is a key ingredient in being judged funny as opposed to tasteless by the audience.

A **speech to entertain** is *not* just a comic monologue. The humor in speeches to entertain is purposeful. Even the humor at a roast is intended to convey affection and genuine appreciation for the talents of the person being "honored" by friends and colleagues. Humor also can have a social role: humorist Will Rogers used his radio talks and commentaries on political realities during the Depression to help create a sense of American unity and common effort. More recently, Whoopi Goldberg, Sinbad, Paula Poundstone, and others have used humor to call attention to social issues. In short, a speech to entertain is humorous yet serious.

As you have learned, to inform, persuade, actuate, and entertain are the general purposes that guide your reason for speaking. Just as subjects are narrowed to subtopics, and often further, your general purpose must be narrowed to more specific ones to focus your audience's attention on the content of your presentation.

Specific Purposes

Given your topic, what specifically do you want the audience to know, value, or do? Within the context of a general purpose, a **specific purpose** focuses your attention on the particular, *substantive* goal of the presentation. Once you determine your specific purpose, you can describe the exact response you want from your listeners: "I want my audience to understand the classification scheme for levels of professional baseball." In this instance, you want to inform your audience (general purpose), but more specifically, you want to teach them about the different levels of expertise they're likely to encounter at the various levels of professional baseball.

You may have more than one specific purpose for a speech. Some may be clearly expressed and others held privately. For example, you tell your listeners precisely what you want them to understand or do as a consequence of listening to your presentation. You also hope to make a good impression on the audience or receive a high grade for the presentation, but you are not likely to make these purposes explicit.

Specific purposes can be short-term or long-term. If you are speaking to class members on the value of eating fat-free foods, your short-term purpose may be to get a decent grade, but your long-term objective might be to change their eating habits.

Theoretically, you may have any number of public and private, short-term and long-term specific purposes when you speak. Practically, however, you should reduce your list of goals to a *dominant* one: *the response you wish to elicit from the audience.* Formulated into a clear, concise statement, this specific purpose delineates exactly what you want the audience to understand, enjoy, feel, believe, or do.

STATING SPECIFIC PURPOSES: AN ILLUSTRATION

You've just decided on your topic for a speech that you'll give in one of your classes: the impact of MTV on recent presidential election campaigns. While your classmates may have seen some of the events, they probably do not have the "whole picture" with respect to MTV's participation. Hence, your overall objective may be to expand the audience's knowledge of MTV's role. More precisely, your specific purposes would include:

1. In terms of the subject, you want to provide background on MTV's actions in the 1988 campaign, contrast this with the 1992 and 1996 "Rock the Vote" campaigns, and finally, discuss MTV's involvement in the 2000 campaign. You also want to highlight the specific events that took place, including interviews with the candidates. Finally, you want to cover the actual impact MTV's role had in terms of voter participation.

2. In terms of yourself, a private goal may be the hope that if they understand the role MTV plays, they also will see the value of greater participation in political campaigns and in voting. Undoubtedly, you want to convey to the class—and to the instructor—a sense that you understand what it means to plan and prepare an informative speech. You want to show the students and instructor that you are knowledgeable and competent to speak on the issue. The first specific purpose addresses a long-term goal of creating understanding and expanding

knowledge. The personal goals are private rather than public. All of these specific goals can be summarized, however, in a statement of *the* dominant specific purpose: "to expand the audience's knowledge of MTV's role."

Central Idea or Claim

For most speakers, this step flows directly from the preceding one. Can you state your message in a single sentence? If you are seeking to explain an idea or inform an audience about a process or event, that sentence is the **central idea.** It is a declarative statement that summarizes your speech: "Why Pete Rose was banned from selection into the Baseball Hall of Fame." On the other hand, a **claim** expresses the intent of your argument: "Why Pete Rose should be eligible for election to the Baseball Hall of Fame." Thus, *central ideas are characteristic of informative speeches, whereas claims form the core of persuasive and actuative speeches.* Speeches to entertain also have a controlling thought—either as *a central idea aiming to convey information* or as *a claim aiming to make a moral point or exhort the audience to action.*

Both central ideas and claims share the same function: They identify the primary thrust of your message. Precise phrasing of your central idea or claim is crucial, because it focuses the audience's attention on *your* reasons for speaking rather than on *their* reasons for listening.

Precise phrasing of your central idea or claim is important, because your wording captures the essence of your subject matter and purpose and focuses audience attention on your reasons for speaking.

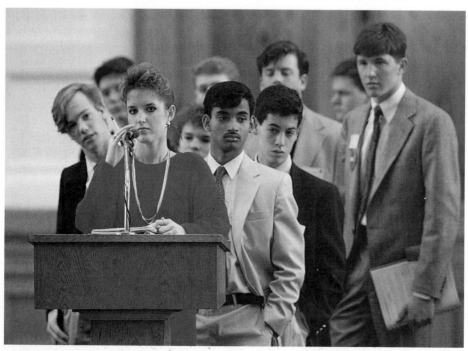

General Purpose	Inform	Persuade/Actuate	Entertain
Specific Purpose	Central Idea (preview main points)	Claim (preview main points)	Central Idea or Claim (preview main points)

FIGURE 2.3   Central Ideas and Claims

Phrasing Central Ideas.   Assume that you're giving an informative speech on the relationship between business and social causes. Each of the following central ideas suggests a different emphasis for the speech:

1. The Jerry Lewis Telethon for the Muscular Dystrophy Association (MDA) illustrates how corporations can assist social causes.
2. Ben Cohen of Ben and Jerry's fame illustrates how one can make money and donate to worthy causes.
3. American corporate largesse is not limited to the United States.

A speech on central idea one would be developed differently than a speech on idea two or three; each would use different kinds of material for support or illustration. The first version would stress the history of the Telethon and the amount of research funded over the years. The second version would use the same theme but develop it through a close analysis of one specific company known for its commitment to social action. The third version would change the focus to how various American corporations have assisted people in Third World countries.

Phrasing a Claim.   Phrasing your claim can be an even more crucial preparatory step than casting the central idea, because the wording colors the emotional tone of the message and its line of development. It also suggests the relationship between you and your audience. Note how you can vary the audience's perception of your intensity:

1. Clear-cutting in the world's rain forests is *unwise.*
2. Clear-cutting in the world's rain forests is *a despicable act.*
3. Clear-cutting in the world's rain forests is *a moral outrage.*

As you move from version one to three, feelings are phrased with greater intensity; each successive version expresses your attitude in harsher, more graphic language. In the next examples, note how you can vary the reasons for taking some course of action:

1. Make use of the Writing Lab, because it will help you in your English courses.

2. Make use of the Writing Lab, because you will get higher grades in all courses in which writing is expected.

3. Make use of the Writing Lab, because better writing will lead to better jobs on graduation.

As these examples illustrate, your listeners may choose to act for a variety of reasons, so phrase your claim in a way that captures what you think will be the most compelling ones for *this particular audience.*

You also can vary the evaluative criteria for judging something:

1. The city's landfill is an *eyesore.* (aesthetic judgment)

2. The city's landfill is a *health hazard.* (personal safety judgment)

3. While the city's landfill is *cheaper* than other solid-waste removal options, we should explore other means of handling garbage. (political value judgment)

Each claim condemns a community facility: The first version judges the landfill's lack of beauty, the second considers its safety and health costs, and the third acknowledges it is a cheaper alternative but implies the community should value safety more than economic cost. In each case, selecting particular criteria will control the main features of the speech's ultimate development: to focus on the values of judging aesthetics in relation to community development, to emphasize the facts related to health and safety, and to seek an accommodation based on economic considerations.

When you've decided on the general and specific purposes of your speech and considered how to phrase the central ideas and claims, you can start developing your speech outline. These points will focus your research efforts, because they will indicate the type and quantity of information needed to accomplish your goals. More important, succinctly phrased central ideas and claims will enable you to *preview the main points* of your speech. As you flesh out the central idea or claim, it may become apparent that two or three main points will be necessary to cover the subject. For example, if you are talking about MTV, you could indicate to the audience how the speech would develop by leading into the main points in this manner: "In explaining the role played by MTV in the recent election, I will focus on three key points: prior activities by MTV, the specific events it was involved with in the recent election, and the impact its role had on voter participation among young viewers of voting age."

INTEGRATING GENERAL AND SPECIFIC PURPOSES WITH CENTRAL IDEAS AND CLAIMS

The following examples illustrate the outline process:

Informative Speech

Subject: Business and social action

General Purpose: To inform

Specific Purposes: Indicates dominant purpose, recast as central idea

The Jerry Lewis Telethon for MDA illustrates how corporations can assist social causes

Ben Cohen of Ben and Jerry's fame illustrates how one can make money and donate to worthy causes

American corporate largesse is not limited to the United States

Central Idea: Ben and Jerry's provides a prototype for businesses seeking to become socially responsible.

Actuative Speech

Subject: Housing conditions of migrant farm workers

General Purpose: To actuate

Specific Purposes: Indicates dominant purpose, recast as claim

To illustrate with specific cases the substandard housing provided for migrant laborers

To force farmers hiring migrant laborers to provide adequate housing

To be perceived favorably by the audience

To overcome opposition from farmers to this proposal

Claim: Farmers/owners hiring migrant laborers must provide adequate housing.

Central ideas and claims make different demands on the audience. Whereas central ideas explain and clarify information, claims give audiences reasons to believe or act in a certain way. A speech to entertain encompasses both possibilities, because its goal may include either informing or persuading an audience.

Wording the Title

To complete your initial thinking about purposes, you often will want to decide on **wording the title.** It may seem odd or even unnecessary to consider a title during the preliminary stages of speech preparation, but there are several concrete advantages to doing so. First, a title highlights the key concept or idea that the speech content will reflect. Second, speakers often are required to announce titles ahead of time to allow for publicizing the event. Just as a title helps the speaker focus on content, it also assists those who might attend in deciding whether the speaker's subject is of interest. The following guidelines will assist you in selecting and phrasing a title.

A title should be relevant to you, the audience, and the occasion. If you were to give a speech on business and political ethics, you might consider a title such as "The Eleventh Commandment," as did the speaker who claimed that the commandment "Thou shalt not steal" had been supplanted in some business and political circles by another: "Thou shalt not get caught."

A title should be provocative. Linda G. Stuntz, the acting deputy secretary of energy for the Bush administration, delivered a speech entitled "The Environmentally Ugly American" at MIT's Center for Energy and Environmental Policy Research. The title reflected the image of the inconsiderate American and focused attention on her primary claim "that while the United States, of course, has challenges . . . we are hardly the evil empire of environmental deregulation that some would have you believe."[2] The title was worded in such a way that audience members would not know for certain which side of the issue she would defend.

A title should be productive. Titles should convey to the audience the central idea or claim or, at the very least, give them a reason to attend to the message. Provocative titles become unproductive when they turn off significant portions of the audience, hence lessening a speaker's chance of a fair hearing.

The title should be brief. Imagine the effect of announcing your title as "The Effects upon High-Track, Mean-Track, and Low-Track High School Juniors of Pretesting for Senior Year Competency Testings." In addition to not being terribly clear, the title is far too long and doesn't stimulate curiosity in your audience. A better choice might be "Tracking Juniors: A Means to Successful Testing as Seniors?" or "A Pretest in Time Saves Nine—or More." These latter two titles may lack some precision, but they are decidedly more provocative than the first choice.

When committing to a title for advance publicity, select a general phrase. If you must commit to a title well in advance, you want to preserve flexibility in how you develop the speech itself. The title "Ben and Jerry's: A Socially Responsible Company" is sufficiently precise to give the audience an idea of your general topic while allowing you to alter the development of the subject as you plan the speech.

Strategic Considerations

The preceding discussion focused on general and specific purposes in terms of the *desired response* you wish to obtain from your audience. What remains is to examine some of the reasons you may elect to (or have been asked to) inform, persuade, or entertain your audience. Some of the factors that determine your actual decisions include an assessment of risks taken, the listeners' authority to act, their preexisting attitudes, the nature of the speech occasion, and the time available to speak.

Taking Risks.   There are times we must ask ourselves how much we are willing to risk personally in front of others. For example, suppose you work for a firm that you're convinced is patently sexist in its promotion policies; the past record clearly suggests that it seldom promotes women to upper-level managerial positions. You find that you are given a chance to talk about promotions at an open meeting of the firm. How far do you go? What do you say? Your **private aim** may be to get your frustrations heard, regardless of the consequences. Your **ultimate aim** may be to get some women—including, perhaps, yourself—into higher managerial positions. How you balance these purposes and the degree to which you put your own job at risk become real rather than theoretical issues.

Listeners' Authority or Capacity to Act.   For a speaker to demand of students that they should "abolish all required courses" is futile; any decision concerning course requirements is in the hands of the faculty. In this case, the listeners' **authority to act** is nonexistent. As a speaker, limit your specific purposes and claims to behaviors that are clearly within the domain of the audience's authority or power.

Listeners' Preexisting Attitudes.   If your listeners' **preexisting attitudes** are hostile to your message, you might be able to convince them in a single speech that there's merit in your side of the issue. You'll be hoping for too much, however, if you expect the audience to disavow their current beliefs and embrace yours or take positive action based on your request.

The Nature of the Speech Occasion.   Under most conditions, you automatically will seek to speak in a way that is in tune with what audiences expect on the occasion. Violating audience expectations can have negative consequences; hence, you should willingly go "against the grain" only when your principles dictate a need to "say what needs saying" regardless of the audience's attitude. Be willing to accept the audience's anger should you disappoint them. On most occasions, you will find it easy and natural to adapt your specific purpose to the mood and spirit of the occasion.

Time Limits.   The person assigning the speech, those inviting you to speak, or the occasion itself may dictate **time limits**—the amount of time you will have available. You need to adjust what you hope to accomplish to fit the time constraints of the rhetorical situation. For example, you may be able to induce a hostile audience to postpone a decision without talking very long. If your goal is to change their feelings and convictions so they endorse your proposal, however, you'll need more than a few minutes. Similarly, if your subject is complex, a 15-minute speech may achieve listener comprehension but not convince the audience to act. Don't try to secure a response that an audience cannot give in the time available. Knowing more about the audience and the occasion will assist you in making sound strategic choices.

ANALYZING THE AUDIENCE AND OCCASION

A good speech is one that reflects your interests while being seen as responsive to the interests, preferences, and values of the audience. You must regularly ask yourself: "How would I feel about this topic if I were in their place?" "How can I adapt this material to their interests and habits, especially at points where their experiences and understanding differ from mine?" To answer such questions, you need to analyze the people that compose your audience— their age range, gender, social-political-economic status, culture, backgrounds, prejudices, and fears. In a public speaking class, you can estimate these factors by listening to comments made during class discussions and by asking some class members what they think. In other circumstances, gathering this information is more difficult, and it requires you to become more creative in assessing the audience. Among the kinds of information you may wish to gather, consider the following:

The audience's knowledge of and attitude toward you. What does the audience already know about you, and what information would be useful to convey your own expertise? Have they had a chance to form an opinion about you as a speaker?

The audience's knowledge of and attitude toward the topic. What they know and how they feel about the topic is critical. You may bore them if you simply duplicate their existing knowledge, and you may anger them if you ignore their own attitudes. Regardless of how it's done, **audience analysis** is a primary determinant of success. You also need to consider the setting and circumstances in which you're speaking.

Are there specific rules or customs that you need to know and follow? You need to be aware of anything that will affect the audience's reception of you or your message. When Ross Perot spoke to an African-American audience during his 1992 presidential campaign, his continued use of "you people" was an affront to those present, because it widened the gulf between the races. What is the cultural mix of the audience likely to be, and how will that affect what you want to say and how you express your ideas?

How long will you have to speak? Will you precede or follow other speakers who could influence your reception? If you overtalk your time limit, it may be the same as "overstaying your welcome." When others also will speak, knowing your "place" in the line-up will help you adapt to an audience who has heard too many speeches already.

What impact will events before or after your speech have on topic selection, phrasing of your central idea or claim, or supporting materials? As we will note later, timing is a critical variable. The fact that President Clinton waited seven months before admitting that his relationship with Monica Lewinsky was inappropriate made his criticism of Independent Counsel Ken Starr vulnerable to Republican criticism. The "fitting moment" for his admission had come and gone.

Will the physical circumstances support your speaking style? If not, can you alter them? Speaking to an audience when some people are positioned behind pillars, as in a residence hall dining room, can make for anxious moments. You may have to move further from a lectern than normal so that parts of the audience can see you more easily, at least part of the time. Examining such issues in advance is the key. You want to be as forewarned and as comfortable as possible with the circumstances you face when it's your time to speak.

GATHERING THE SPEECH MATERIALS

Once you've analyzed the audience and context of the speech, you're ready to assemble some ideas and information to support your central idea or claim. You need to:

- Assess what information you think is needed to accomplish your objectives.
- Reflect on what you already know.
- Figure out how much of it is relevant to your central idea or claim.
- Investigate where additional information can be found, if needed.
- Obtain the needed additional information, if any.

ETHICAL MOMENTS

ETHICS AND PUBLIC SPEAKING

Occasionally in this book, we'll include a boxed area devoted to "ethical moments"—ethical decisions public speakers must make in preparing and delivering their talks. Some of these moments will fit you and your circumstances, and some will not. In either case, we hope that you'll take a moment to think about the problems presented and their solutions. Some of these problems might be discussed in class. Here are some typical ethical questions that you might face in the speeches you'll give this term:

1. When is it fair to borrow other people's ideas and words, and when is it not?
2. You recognize that a major portion of a speaker's informative speech came from an article that you read last week. The speaker does not cite the source.

During the critique session, should you blow the whistle on the speaker?
3. An article says exactly what you intended to say about the use of pesticides on garden vegetables. Then, you find a more recent article claiming that new research contradicts the first article. Should you ignore the new evidence?

You will face ethical moments such as these regularly, both in your speech classroom and throughout your life. Taking a few moments to consider such situations, and even to articulate your position in discussion, can save you many embarrassing times later. Know what your moral stands are—and know why you take them—*before* you face ethical dilemmas on the platform.

In almost every speech situation, you will need to gather additional information to develop, expand, or reinforce what you already know and believe. You may wish to talk to others, such as friends or local experts, to check out your perceptions. Critical listening is important here. You undoubtedly will want to gather other materials from newspapers, magazines, books, government documents, or radio and television programs. You'll soon learn of some traditionally solid sources: the "News of the Week in Review" section of the *New York Times;* articles in *Time, Newsweek,* and *U.S. News and World Report;* journal articles surveyed in *Readers' Guide to Periodical Literature* and more specialized indexes; and all of the annuals, yearbooks, almanacs, and so on that fill the reference area of your library. Surfing the World Wide Web is another great means of obtaining information, but as we will note, the accuracy and comprehensiveness of this information must be carefully scrutinized. Computerized index searches also will be helpful as you seek new information or supporting material for your ideas. (We will review these and other resources in Chapter 6.)

OUTLINING THE SPEECH

Once you've compiled your materials, you have to sort them. Developing a preliminary outline of your main ideas will help. An outline lets you see how your various materials relate to your central idea or claim, shows where you have plenty of (or too little) material, and makes the structure of your speech clear. You'll probably jockey back and forth between your materials and your outline, looking for just the right fit between what you *know* and what you can *justify* publicly to a critical audience.

We will examine outlining in more detail later. For now, follow these rules:

- Arrange your main ideas in a clear and systematic order.
- Arrange the subpoints under each main idea in a manner that clearly illustrates their connection to the main point.
- Preserve the unity of your speech by making sure that each point, whether a main point or a subpoint, directly relates to your specific purpose and central idea or claim.

PRACTICING ALOUD

With your outline completed, you're ready for the most terrifying task of preparation: practicing your speech. This is not easy! You can feel like a fool talking aloud in your room. The sound of your voice rings hollow, and you find that some of the materials you wrote out come off as simplistic, clichéd, stiff, or silly. Nevertheless, practicing aloud is essential if you're to improve some of the decisions you've already made and work on your delivery skills.

Give practice a chance. It can, quite literally, save your communicative life. Talk through your outline in a confident, conversational (not a mumbling) tone that will help you get used to the sound. Repeatedly read through the outline until you've made all changes that seem useful and until you can express each idea clearly and smoothly. Practice until the ideas flow easily, all the time talking in a conversational voice. Finally, if you dare, get a friend to listen to your speech, give you direct feedback, and help you practice making eye contact with a real person.

These steps—from selecting and narrowing a subject through practicing aloud—take you to the brink of public speaking with real audiences. Good work on preparation pays off in effective performance.

DELIVERING YOUR SPEECH CONFIDENTLY

For most beginners, delivering their first speeches is very difficult. Many feel anxious and nervous: "I'm too nervous to stand up there." "What do I do with my hands?" "Will people think I'm a jerk?" Self-doubts, whether from actual

Appearing confident helps put your audience at ease as they listen to your ideas.

fright or a more general lack of self-confidence, creep into every speaker's mind; the trick is to learn to control them. In the remaining part of this chapter, we examine three strategies for self-control: selecting the right method of presentation, focusing not on yourself but on capturing and holding the attention of your listeners, and communicating self-confidence.

Selecting the Method of Presentation

Which method should you use to present your speech? Your choice should be based on several criteria, including any restrictions imposed by your instructor: type of speaking occasion, the seriousness and purpose of your speech, audience analysis, and your own strengths and weaknesses as a speaker. Attention to these considerations will help you decide whether your method of presentation should be impromptu, memorized, read from a manuscript, or extemporaneous.

The Impromptu Speech.   As the name suggests, the **impromptu speech** is delivered on the spur of the moment, with little preparation. The speaker relies entirely on previous knowledge and skill. When an instructor in a meteorology class calls on you for an explanation of the jet stream's course through the atmosphere, for example, you don't have time to prepare more than a quick list of three or four words to remind you of points you want to make. Impromptu speeches are given in rhetorical emergencies—at public meetings, in classes, in conventions. When using this method, try to focus on a single idea, carefully relating all significant details to it. This way, you'll avoid the rambling, incoherent remarks this method too often produces.

The Memorized Speech.   The **memorized speech** is written out word for word and is committed to memory. Few speakers can do this well; it presents problems for most of us. Instead of sounding conversational, a memorized speech often results in a stilted presentation. Speakers tend to pause too often while trying to remember the words, or they rush past ideas so as not to forget the words. In either case, meaning is at the expense of memory. This form is well-suited to drama, as in the speeches of a Shakespearean play, or to intercollegiate competition in original oratory. For general purposes, it is not a recommended method of presentation.

The Read Speech.   Like the memorized speech, the **read speech** is written out, but in this method, the speaker reads from the manuscript. If extremely careful wording is required—as in the president's annual message to Congress, in which a slip could undermine domestic or foreign policies—the read speech is appropriate. It also is used in presentations of scholarly papers, where exact, concise, often technical exposition is required. Reading a speech while retaining a conversational style is more difficult than it sounds. No matter how experienced you are, when you read your message, you'll inevitably sacrifice some of the freshness and spontaneity necessary for effective speechmaking. You'll also have trouble reacting to feedback and may be tempted to use more formal, written language. If you do use this method, talk through the speech over and over to ensure an effective oral style.

The Extemporaneous Speech.   Representing a middle course between the memorized or read speech and the impromptu speech, the **extemporaneous speech** requires careful planning and a good outline. This chapter has been preparing you to present an extemporaneous speech. Working from your outline, practice the speech aloud, and express the ideas somewhat differently each time through it. Use the outline to fix the order of ideas in your mind, and try out various wordings to develop accuracy, conciseness, and flexibility of expression. Through such preparation, you'll be able to deliver the actual speech from a few notes.

If the extemporaneous method is used carelessly, the result will resemble a bad impromptu speech, which sometimes leads to confusion about these two terms. When used well, however, this method produces a speech that is nearly as polished as a memorized one but is more relaxed, flexible, and spontaneous—hence, more like natural conversation than the other methods. The best lecturers at your college or university undoubtedly are extemporaneous speakers. Most of the advice in this textbook assumes the use of the extemporaneous method.

Communicating Self-Confidence

The second matter you need to think about when speaking in front of a real audience is yourself. In Chapter 1, we discussed speech anxiety and some ways to overcome it. Now you need to consider how to convey an air of dynamism and self-assuredness to your listeners. Many students ready to give their first speech ask, "How should I deliver my speech? How can I communicate a sense of self-confidence to an audience?" The following guidelines are a start to answering those questions:

1. *Be yourself.* Act as if you were having an animated conversation with a friend. Avoid an excessively rigid posture, but don't become so comfortable in front of the group that you sprawl all over the lectern. If there is a table, avoid the temptation to simply perch on the table while talking. When you speak, you want your listeners to focus on your ideas rather than on their form of presentation.

2. *Look at your listeners.* Watch the listeners' faces for reactions. Without this feedback, you can't gauge your effectiveness or make adjustments as you speak. In addition, people tend to mistrust anyone who doesn't look directly at them. They also may get the impression you don't care about them and aren't interested in their reactions. *In speaking, the eyes have it!*

3. *Communicate with your body as well as your voice.* Realize that as a speaker, you're being seen as well as heard. Bodily movements and changes in facial expression can help clarify and reinforce your ideas. Keep your hands at your sides so that when you feel an impulse to gesture, you can do so easily. If there is no lectern and you're working from an outline, use a hard backing to hold the papers firm. (This also makes your nervousness less visible!) If you're using notecards, hold them up so you can see them clearly rather than hiding them. Your speech will flow more smoothly if your outline or notecard is easy to read from as well. As you speak, don't become so relaxed you curl your papers or fold your cards. Let your body move as it responds to your feelings and message. If you hear a tremor in

your voice or see one in your hand, remember that neither is as notice-
able to listeners as it is to you. Overall, if you're being yourself, appropriate bodily responses will flow from the act of communicating.

LEARNING TO EVALUATE SPEECHES

The classroom serves as a laboratory for studying and evaluating speech materials and delivery. The evaluation form on the opposite page is designed to help
sharpen your critical listening skills as well as your sensitivity to the fundamentals
of the speechmaking process. A recent study of this and other evaluation forms
indicated that one can discriminate between good and not-as-good speeches
through the use of such rating instruments.[3] You can use it to evaluate speeches
in classrooms, settings around your campus or community, and televised presentations on C-SPAN and other networks. Depending on the assignment, the audience, and the demands of the occasion, some checkpoints on this form will be
more significant and applicable than others. For now, use the form as a general
guide; later, concentrate on those parts that are relevant to specific assignments.

What makes a "good" speech? While the answer to this question will vary
among listeners, a positive "yes" to the following questions highlights some of
the key issues involved:

- Does the speaker appear sincerely interested in the consequences of his
  or her speechmaking? That is, is the speaker willing to assume responsibility for what happens as a result of presenting ideas?
- Does the speaker take time at the beginning to indicate interest in—and
  appreciation for—divergent points of view? Does the speaker appear
  willing to consider opinions or perspectives other than those he or she is
  advancing?
- Is the information comprehensive and accurate insofar as it is possible to
  obtain credible information on the topic being addressed?
- If central ideas or claims are advanced, are they supported with up-to-
  date and credible testimony, statistics, examples, and other supporting
  materials?
- Is the presentation understandable? That is, can you fathom what the
  speaker is talking about? Is the organization clear? Is the language appropriate? Is the delivery easy to listen to?

As you participate regularly in speech evaluations, even of early classroom assignments, use these broad questions and others that seem appropriate to raise in
providing direct feedback to your classmates. Constructive criticism is both positive and negative—but it always is personally supportive. Telling someone what
worked, as well as what you think should be changed, provides beginning speakers with much-needed feedback, and it forces you—the listener—to formulate
your own thoughts and come to grips with your own standards and expectations.
In this way, both you and the speaker gain. As another strategy in this class, read

Name:
Topic:
Occasion: **Speech length**

Introduction (15 points)
Gained audience's attention
Established speaker's credibility and good will
Revealed nature of topic as central idea or claim
Prepared audience for rest of speech (forecasting)

Body (40 points)
Main points clearly identified
Each main point developed with appropriate materials
Topic development appropriate for this occasion, audience
Logical arrangement of ideas
Transitions used effectively
Appropriate support (examples, testimony, statistics) used
Clear source citation
Relation to and inclusion of audience
Appropriate use of visual aids (if needed/used)

Conclusion (15 points)
Prepared audience for end
Reinforced central idea or claim in an appropriate manner

Presentation and Delivery (30 points)
Extemporaneous delivery
Enthusiasm for subject
Gestures/movements appropriate
Facial expressions appropriate
Eye contact appropriate
Pronunciation clear, accurate
Appropriate word choice for occasion, audience
Vocal variety
Fluent expression

FIGURE 2.4   Evaluation Form

Source: Adapted from Carlson and Smith-Howell, "Classroom Public Speaking Assessment: Reliability and Validity of Selected Evaluation Instruments," Communication Education *44 (April 1995): 87–97.*

the sample speeches in this book, analyzing them systematically to isolate the communication cues that facilitate listener comprehension and acceptance.

ASSESSING A SAMPLE SPEECH

The following speech by Dena Craig of Sante Fe Community College (New Mexico) is well adapted to a student audience and a persuasive speech assignment.[4] The initial paragraph introduces the issue, and the second paragraph indicates the major problem to be addressed, and provides a clear preview of the main ideas and the order in which they will be discussed. Paragraphs 3 through 6 indicate the hazards associated with cigar smoking. Paragraphs 7 through 12 suggest why cigar smoking, though hazardous, has become popular. Paragraph 13 marks a transition from reviewing the problem to considering the solution in the next paragraphs (14–17). The final paragraphs (18–19) provide a fitting ending to the speech with a specific plea for action.

CLEARING THE AIR ABOUT CIGARS

Dena Craig
Santa Fe Community College
Coached by Ann Scroggie

Introduction

Denzel Washington, after finishing a hard day's work on an action film, unwinds with a premium Churchill cigar. Linda Evangelista walks down the runway modeling the latest fashions and holding a Cheroot cigar between her fingers. Jack Nicholson, after winning the Academy Award for best actor, celebrates with an expensive Macanudo cigar. Are they cool? Cigars may be smelly and expensive, but they are the hottest societal trend. Each year, according to the *Wall Street Journal*, February 8, 1998, Americans consume over 5.2 billion cigars annually. This represents a 53 percent increase in the last five years. /1

Central Idea

Alarmingly, despite potential carcinogenic effects, cigars carry no Surgeon General warning and users mistakenly believe that since they don't inhale, there is little danger. This is simply not true. Until recently, modern tobacco research has failed to illustrate the composition, use and effects of cigars, focusing its attention instead on cigarettes. But the fact remains, cigars are also toxic and addicting. Unlike cigarettes, cigars are completely unregulated. Today, we will look at first the dangers of cigar smoking; second, examine the reasons for the lack of control; and finally, suggest workable solutions to reduce the risk. /2

Problems:
Technical

Since cigar smokers don't usually inhale, the dangers have always appeared negligible and, consequently, cigars have long had a benign quality. Many of us can remember a favorite uncle who always kept a stogie close at hand. And of course, many famous people smoke cigars: Winston Churchill, Groucho Marx, Bill Cosby, Bill Clinton and Demi Moore. But recent research is clearing the air about cigars, and what it reveals shouldn't surprise us: where there's smoke, there's fire! /3

Cigar smoking is dangerous to the smoker because the toxicity level determined during the slow curing process produces tars and nicotine which are readily absorbed into the mucous when placed in the mouth or absorbed into the skin when the moistened tip is held between the fingers. The problem is further complicated by the fact that the nicotine content varies from .77 to 21.2 percent, depending on how the cigar was made. Given the nature of cigars and their production, it is clear that there cannot be a one-size-fits-all method of researching its effects. /4

The American Health Foundation, July 1997, equates one large cigar to the toxicity of an entire pack of cigarettes. Cigar smokers might spend one full hour smoking a cigar, but will spend several hours holding the unlit cigar, thus allowing more absorption of the toxic ingredients. /5

It cannot be denied that cigars produce poisons and that these poisons, in turn, lead to an array of health problems. *Newsweek,* July 21, 1997, indicates that cancers of the mouth, lung, larynx, pancreas, and esophagus are all associated with cigar smoking, and those risks are amplified if you drink alcohol while you puff. Furthermore, and perhaps more important to nonsmokers, the 23 poisons and 43 carcinogens released in cigar smoke make second-hand inhalation much more hazardous than second-hand cigarette smoke. James Repace, an advisor to the National Cancer Institute, states, "If you have to breathe second hand smoke, cigar smoke is a lot worse than cigarette smoke." And we all are familiar with that lingering, musty odor that is cigar smoke; that's because we all have inhaled it, and at it's current pace, cigars will soon replace cigarettes as the preferred weapon of smokers. Clearly, we are all affected. Cigars are poison to those who smoke and everyone else who breathes air polluted with cigar smoke. /6

Problems:
Social

Despite these risks, cigars have become the fashionable trend of the 90s. Upscale cigar stores, lounges, and magazines have become a booming business. The magazine *Cigar Aficionado,* now six years old, is highly successful. It commands advertising rates comparable to *People* and *Time,* and many famous people such as Denzel Washington in February of 1998 have graced its cover. But somehow all the cigar smoking has escaped the restrictions visited upon cigarette smoking. The *New York Times,* which wouldn't touch anything advocating cigarette smoking, happily runs full-page ads for *Cigar Aficionado.* /7

Cigar smoking has been made to look good, fun and even sexy. Celebrity endorsers are having a drastic effect on the popularity of cigars. Basketball star Michael Jordan has been on the cover of *Sports Illustrated* with a cigar in his mouth. What kind of message is this sending to children? Arnold Schwarzenagger, whom we once saw standing on the White House lawn telling us to lead a healthy life, graced one of *Cigar Aficionado's* early covers. /8

Further, cigars are attracting a variety of people, including a growing number of women. According to *Fortune Magazine,* April 15, 1996, men often describe women cigar smokers as sexy. Tomina Edmark, author of *Cigar Chic—A Women's Perspective,* insists that every woman should smoke a cigar. She goes on to say that cigar smoking is good for relationships. /9

Too many teenagers are listening to this kind of advice. Because according to *Cancer Weekly Plus* June 9, 1997, "more than a quarter of American teenagers have smoked a stogie in the past year." What makes this even worse is that two-thirds of the students who bought cigars said they were rarely or never asked their age. /10

Not only are sales unregulated, but the federal government has closed its eyes to the cigar industry in that it does not have regulations concerning content, additives, or processing. According to *Medical Update,* September 1997, the law does not require the package health warning on cigars that is found on cigarettes and other tobacco products, so users may not be aware of health risks. In addition, despite the fact that most cigars are imported, there are no regulations to monitor the quality of the product, for example, whether pesticides were used in growing tobacco, thus posing another risk to the smoker. /11

According to *Post Graduate Medicine,* September 1997, many cigar smokers believe that if they just chew on cigars instead of smoking them that it reduces the cancer risk—but that just raises the risk of mouth cancer. Many cigar smokers believe that if they don't inhale the smoke they are free from the dangers. This is simply not true. Because of the alkaline quality of cigars, the smoke does not need to be inhaled to get the nasty array of effects. It is these myths which cause society to misunderstand the dangers of cigars. /12

It is apparent that the cigar smoking fad is growing and is here to stay despite the risks involved. So what can be done to address this. /13

Solutions

In April 1998, the Centers for Disease Control released a report confirming that the most recent research clearly demonstrates that cigars can be more harmful than cigarettes. It further indicates that the full extent of the risks is unknown due to the variables of importation, packaging, size, additives and smoking patterns. /14

Therefore, on the national level, the first step must be additional research. Extensive research on the variation of product types and smoking patterns is needed to fully understand the dangers of cigars. According to the *Journal of the American Medical Association,* July 2, 1997, there are few long term studies to indicate the extent of the harmful effects. Thus, it is necessary for the Centers for Disease Control to conduct an extensive study to quantify the exact harms. Secondly, money must be allocated to launch a national education program, similar to the anti-smoking campaign of cigarettes, to make the public fully aware of the harmful effects of cigars. Thirdly, the federal government must enact regulations that require warning labels on all brands–domestic and imported–and exact standards regarding the composition of cigars as well as any pesticides used in growing tobacco. /15

On the state level: stiff penalties, including both fines and imprisonment must be implemented. Next, states must enforce laws which prohibit the sale of cigars to minors. And third, following the precedent of the Florida lawsuit against cigarette producers, advertising must be curtailed to prohibit cigar manufacturers from promoting their deadly products along interstates, in airports and in newspapers. /16

Finally on a personal level, first and most obvious, don't smoke cigars because they can kill you. If you're addicted to the high nicotine content, get help. Second, don't passively allow others to pollute your air with cigar smoke. Whether you're shy or just think you're being polite, stand up for yourself because their smoke can destroy your health. Finally, we must all act to bring to cigars the same stigma that hangs over cigarettes. /17

By implementing these responsible measures, we can extinguish its popularity and ensure that we begin tomorrow's day with a breath of fresh air. /18

Conclusion

Denzel Washington smoking a Churchill, Linda Evangelista, now pregnant, smoking a Cheroot, Jack Nicholson smoking a Macanudo, Arnold Schwarzenagger, Bill Cosby, Bill Clinton, Demi Moore and Michael Jordon all smoking cigars, and all well respected by children and adults . . . well they are not cool. Hollywood may glamorize cigars, and cigar lounges may sell them, but the fact remains, cigars may be a trend, but addiction never goes out of style. /19

CHAPTER SUMMARY

In preparing a speech, the competent speaker must follow seven essential steps: selecting the subject, narrowing the subject, determining the central idea or claim, analyzing the audience and occasion, gathering the speech material, making an outline, and practicing aloud. Going through these steps prepares you to deliver speeches to audiences. In preparing an initial speech, the competent speaker will be able to:

- Select an appropriate method of presentation (impromptu, memorized, read, extemporaneous).
- Communicate confidence.
- Use the evaluative questions and form as a check on the adequacy of your presentation.

KEY TERMS

actuative speeches (p. 26)

audience analysis (p. 34)

authority to act (p. 33)

central idea (p. 28)

claim (p. 28)

extemporaneous speech (p. 38)

general purposes (p. 25)

impromptu speech (p. 38)

memorized speech (p. 38)

persuasive speeches (p. 25)

preexisting attitude (p. 33)

private aim (p. 32)

read speech (p. 38)

rhetorical frame of mind (p. 20)

specific purpose (p. 26)

speech to actuate (p. 25)

speech to entertain (p. 26)

speech to inform (p. 25)

speech to persuade (p. 25)

time limits (p. 33)

ultimate aim (p. 32)

wording the title (p. 31)

ASSESSMENT ACTIVITIES

1. Listed below are two groups of three statements about a single topic. Read all three statements in each group, and write what you believe to be the claim of the group's message. Compare your phrasing of the claims with those of members of your class.

   I. a. Many prison facilities are inadequate.

   b. Low rates of pay result in frequent job turnovers in prisons.

   c. Prison employees need on-the-job training.

   II. a. There is a serious maldistribution of medical personnel and service.

   b. The present system of delivering medical service is excellent.

   c. Rural areas have a shortage of doctors.

2. Rewrite the following statements, making each one into a clear and concise central idea for a speech.

   a. Today, I would like to try to get you to see the way in which the body can communicate a whole lot of information.

   b. The topic for my speech has to do with the high amount of taxes people have to pay.

   c. A college education might be a really important thing for some people, so my talk is on a college education.

Now rewrite statements (b) and (c) as claims. Be ready to present your versions in a class discussion.

3. Following the principles and guidelines presented in this chapter, prepare a 3- to 4-minute speech to inform. Narrow the subject carefully so that you can do it justice in the allotted time. Concentrate on developing ways to gain and hold the audience's attention. Hand in an outline along with a brief analysis of the audience and the occasion when you present the speech. In your analysis, indicate why you think your approach to attention will work in this situation.

4. Working in small groups, prepare an "Issues Survey." Each group member will come to class prepared with five suitably narrowed subjects for an informative speech and five for a persuasive speech (there may be some overlap). Discuss your lists with your group, and sort out overlapping ideas to develop one list (there may be more than five topics listed for informative and for persuasive speeches). Have one person collate the list in readable form and bring copies for everyone in the next class. Using a simple three-point scale (1—very interesting; 2—interesting; 3—very uninteresting), have class members respond to the subject lists of the various groups. The instructor and one or two students will collate responses and prepare a master copy for everyone in class. Select one informative or persuasive topic that scores among the lowest (i.e., most uninteresting) on this final list, and develop a speech that has arousing audience interest as a specific purpose.

REFERENCES

1. It can be argued that all speeches are persuasive. *Any* change in a person's stock of knowledge, beliefs, attitudes, or ways of acting represents the kind of adjustment in mental and emotional state that can be attributed to persuasion as long as symbols were employed to induce the change. From a psychological perspective, it may be argued that it's impossible to separate "informative" and "persuasive" messages. We're taking a *rhetorical* perspective, in which the symbols used to evoke a certain kind of response as well as the strategies employed in that process provide an *orientation* that's overtly one of informing, persuading, actuating, or entertaining an audience. Hence, you'll find separate discussions of these later in this book. For a cogent discussion of persuasion, see Deirdre D. Johnston, *The Art and Science of Persuasion* (Dubuque, IA: Brown and Benchmark, 1994), ch. 1; and Gary C. Woodward and Robert E. Denton, Jr., *Persuasion and Influence in American Life* (Prospect Heights, IL: Waveland, 1988), ch. 1.

2. Linda G. Stuntz, "The Environmentally Ugly American," *Vital Speeches,* 58 (June 15, 1992): 527.

3. Robert E. Carlson and Deborah Smith-Howell, "Classroom Public Speaking Assessment: Reliability and Validity of Selected Evaluation Instruments." *Communication Education* 44 (April 1995): 87–97.

4. Dena Craig, "Clearing the Air About Cigars," *Winning Orations 1998.* Reprinted by permission of Larry Schnoor, Executive Secretary, Interstate Oratorical Association, Mankato, MN.

Chapter 3

Setting the Scene for Community in a Diverse Culture: Public Speaking and Critical Listening

I arrived in Hong Kong ready to teach to a predominantly Chinese audience. Over the next four weeks, this veteran classroom lecturer was undone and remade. What I had been doing in the classroom on a university campus for several years bore little resemblance to the approach I learned, through trial and several errors, to take by the time I finished teaching. While several students spoke excellent English, and wrote well in response to questions on exams, they were not familiar with most of the early examples I attempted to use in explaining concepts, nor were they familiar with my "style" of asking questions. Adapting my lectures to the audience and situation became easier as I began to draw on illustrations familiar to them. I also learned to speak slower and to avoid common idiomatic expressions that only one raised in the United States might understand. In short, all of the elements of the process of public speaking were revamped or adapted to enable learning to take place in a less frustrating environment.

The experience just outlined is a real one. Speaking to a diverse audience in a U.S. college classroom is one thing; speaking to a predominantly non-native English-speaking audience is quite another. The experience brings home in clear terms what is at stake in the process of getting one's ideas heard. In the example, class members were polite and cordial at all times—even the student who responded with "I haven't a clue what you just said" smiled as he spoke. Not all audiences may be as forgiving, as the expectation that you will adapt to their level of knowledge and skill in listening may govern their responses. In either case, the information offered in this chapter, as the example suggests, cannot be "taken for granted."

In the initial chapters, we set forth the rationale for the academic study of public speaking and outlined the basic tasks ahead of you. Before going into greater detail, this chapter provides a model of the speechmaking process, and it introduces a critical component that must be considered in all encounters, whether interpersonal or public: the process of critical listening.

BASIC ELEMENTS OF THE SPEECHMAKING PROCESS: A MODEL

Overview: A Model of the Process

Speechmaking is comprised of a number of elements: A *speaker,* the primary communicator, gives a speech, which is a continuous, purposive oral *message,* to the *listeners,* who provide *feedback* to the speaker. Their exchange occurs through various *channels* in a particular communication *situation* and *cultural context.* Before considering each of these elements individually, one way to conceptualize this process is to think in terms of your daily interactions with friends, significant others, instructors, and strangers. You bring to these interactions a specific "self-image"—how you want others to see you in a particular interaction, such as poised, self-confident, scared, responsible, or contrite. You also have an "image of the other" who is listening to you. You may see the person(s) as responsible, cooperative, or maybe as highly critical of you and your ideas. Your listener likewise has a specific self-image to project in that particular setting and a particular image of you as the communicator. He or she may see you as petulant, responsible, and appropriately contrite (or may expect, as the American people did with President Clinton, more "contriteness" than was displayed in his now-famous "apology" that wasn't). In any case, the message that is communicated and heard by your listener(s) must touch, in some way, on all of these competing images—it must accommodate them so as to bring closure to the communication event. If you are seen by your listener as irresponsible and petulant while you see yourself as responsible and justified in your complaint, and if your listener sees himself as open-minded and flexible while you see him as judgmental and rigid, what chance is there for your message—however it is phrased—to be communicated effectively? In this particular scenario, communication success will be difficult to achieve. As our opening example suggests, communicating effectively is far more difficult in many situations than it may appear at first. Meeting the obligations imposed by the setting or the audience while holding true to your sense of yourself as a person may not always be easy. Reflect on the model presented in Figure 3.1 as you consider the more specific illustrations of the speechmaking process.

The Speaker

A speaker must consider four key elements in every speech exchange or transaction[1]: his or her *purpose; knowledge of subject and communication skills; attitudes toward self, listeners, and subject;* and *degree of credibility.*

The Speaker's Purpose.   Every speaker talks to achieve a goal. That goal can be as simple as a desire for social exchange or as complex as the desire to alter someone's ideas and actions. Your purpose or goal may be to entertain, call attention to a problem, refute an assertion, ward off a threat, or establish or maintain your status or power.

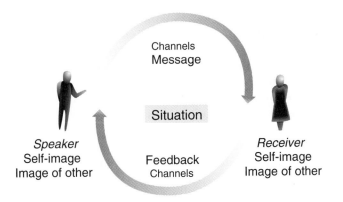

FIGURE 3.1   A Model of the Communication Process

The Speaker's Knowledge.   Your knowledge of the subject affects the character of your message and your effectiveness. If you have only surface knowledge of a topic, listeners feel cheated; they want you to say something important, new, relevant, and interesting. You also need to say it in a way that is understandable and enjoyable. In the chapters that follow, we address both areas, with an emphasis on communication goals, finding and assembling relevant information, organizing messages in coherent and powerful ways, illustrating them visually, and delivering them in a manner that convinces the audience you care about them.

The Speaker's Attitudes.   Your attitudes toward yourself, your listeners, and your subject significantly affect what you say and how you say it. As suggested earlier, we all have mental pictures of ourselves—self-concepts or **self-images** of the kinds of individuals we are and of how others perceive us.[2]

Your self-image—along with the self you wish to project in a specific situation—influences how you speak. Drawing on the opening example, suppose you're giving a speech in class about your experience communicating with international students. If you have little confidence in your abilities and haven't done any research beyond your own limited experience, you'll tend to speak hesitantly. Your voice will become weak, your body stiff, and you'll watch the walls rather than your audience. If you're convinced you know more than anyone else in class, however, you might move to the other extreme, becoming overbearing, disregarding listeners' needs, or riding roughshod over their feelings. Doing research will improve your confidence in speaking in the first instance, and recognizing that your knowledge, while extensive, may not be complete will temper your expression in the second. Balancing research with sensitivity to your audience's own self-image will go a long way toward presenting ideas in keeping with a self-image you would like to project in that setting.

Part of your treatment of audiences comes from your power relations with them and the ways in which you perceive them—as instructors or fellow students, as supervisors or employees, as subordinates or equals. Giving a speech about cross-cultural communication in front of a teacher who is grading you involves an unequal power relationship; giving the same speech to a student research committee of which you're a member involves a relatively equal power relationship. As power relationships change, you adjust your speaking style accordingly.

Your comfort level in a specific setting also affects how you approach the speech. For example, a speech classroom will make you feel awkward at first, and that feeling will affect your speeches. As you grow more at home in this setting, however, your attitudes will improve—and so will your skills. Most people take a while to get used to speaking in church or synagogue, club, or civic group.

The Speaker's Credibility.   Your listeners' estimation of your credibility will affect their reception of your message. Speaker **credibility** is the degree to which an audience judges a communicator as trustworthy, competent, sincere, attractive, and dynamic. The idea of credibility is rooted in the classical Greek concept of **ethos,** which means character. Research has demonstrated repeatedly that a speaker who can raise an audience's estimation of his or her trustworthiness, competency, sincerity, attractiveness, and dynamism will heighten the impact of any speech. As *Time* reported in the aftermath of President Clinton's "apology" speech to the nation, 51 percent did not believe him when he indicated that he did not ask anyone to lie. After all, he had lied 7 months earlier about his relationship with Monica Lewinsky. As Peggy Noonan observed, "after seven long months, what we got was four minutes of petulance and prevarication."[3] Sometimes speeches don't improve one's credibility.

As these generalizations suggest, you and your message are inseparable in people's minds. Your audience's perception of you is the key—Aristotle called it the most important aspect of persuasion—to your effectiveness.

The Message

Your messages often are referred to as your ideas or information. In public speaking, three aspects of the message—*content, structure,* and *style*—are especially important.

The Content of the Message.   A speech's **content** is the substantive and valuative materials that form your view of the issues that need to be covered. You make choices in forming any presentation, because you will have more material than you can use. Those choices affect the meaning of the message being conveyed. For example, the content of a speech on notebook computers is more than a recitation of brands, model numbers, and features; it is the way that information is shaped for an audience's use. You could shape it as an informational presentation ("The following criteria—price, performance, and use—provide a useful way to organize the variables involved in purchasing a notebook computer") or as a persuasive speech ("Three factors—price, preference in disk operating systems, and uses—should guide your decision on which notebook computer to purchase"). In both cases, the central idea changes the nature of the content and how it is perceived and understood by the audience.

The Structure of the Message.   Any message you transmit is, of necessity, structured in some way, simply because you say some words first, others second, and so on. The clarity with which you phrase your central idea will in large part, determine how you structure your message. As the previous examples suggest, the pattern imposes coherence on a subject that seems bewildering in its complexity. To keep the structure clear to the audience, numbering your points, ("First I'll discuss, . . . next I will . . . and finally, I'll . . .") or providing other internal summaries ("Having reviewed price, let's next consider performance.") will help the audience keep track of where you are in during the presentation.

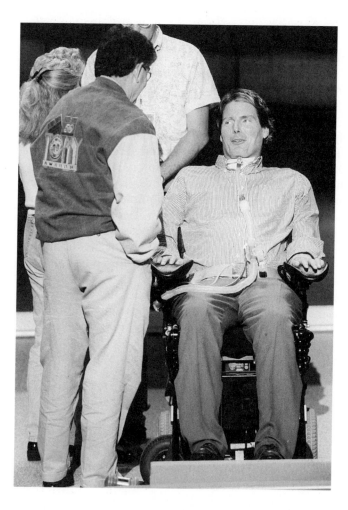

Christopher Reeve has spoken eloquently on behalf of the handicapped.

The Style of the Message.   Just as you must select and arrange the ideas you wish to convey to listeners, so too must you select words, arranging them in sentences and using them to reveal your self-image to others. Selecting and arranging words and revealing yourself to be a certain kind of person are matters of style. Styles can be personal or impersonal, literal or ironic, plain or elevated, and even philosophical or poetic. Such labels refer to particular combinations of vocabulary, syntax (sentence structure), and images of the speaker. What we call *style,* therefore, really has little to do with the elegance (stylishness) of language. Rather, it refers to those aspects of language that convey impressions of you, details of the world, and emotional overtones.

The Listener

Like speakers, listeners have purposes in mind; they are partners in speech transactions. The way they think about what is said is affected by their *purposes, knowledge of and interest in the subject, level of **listening** skills,* and *attitudes toward self, speaker, and the ideas presented.*

The Listener's Purposes.   Listeners always have one or more purposes when they come to a speech. No less than speakers, they're looking for something, whether it be information, confirmation of prior judgments about ideas or people, or simply to be entertained. As we note in more detail in the second section of this chapter, speakers must take listeners' purposes into account or risk rejection.

The Listener's Knowledge and Interest Levels.   In speaking situations, listeners' knowledge of and interest in the subject significantly affect how they respond to the message. One of your jobs is to figure out how much listeners know about your topic and whether they have any personal stake in it. Beyond assessing knowledge and interest, you also need to analyze cultural differences, if any, and how they will affect the audience's reception of your speech. For example, talking about "time" to a cultural group that does not place the same importance on "being on time" as your own requires an awareness of the difference. What shared experiences can you call on when talking with this audience?

The Listener's Command of Listening Skills.   As noted at the outset of this chapter, listeners vary in their abilities to process oral messages. Cultural differences may place greater responsibility on you as the speaker to ensure the ideas are clear, or the audience will "tune out." Further, even though college audiences have been listening to instructors for several years, they also want to know why they should listen to you. Motivating audiences to use the skills they have is as important as recognizing when they are not comprehending your message because of inadequate listening skills.

The Listener's Attitudes.   As our model suggests, listeners' attitudes toward themselves, the speaker, and the subject affect how they interpret and respond to speeches. Listeners with low self-esteem, for example, tend to be swayed more easily than those with stronger self-images. Listeners who feel their opinions are confirmed by the speaker also are more easily influenced than those holding contrary ideas. Moreover, as a rule, people seek out speakers whose positions they already agree with and retain longer and more vividly those ideas of which they strongly approve.[4] **Audience analysis** is one of the keys to speaking success, because you need to know much about people's attitudes before you can reach them.

Feedback

You may think of public speaking as communication flowing in one direction—from speaker to listener. Information, feelings, and ideas, however, flow the other way as well. **Feedback** is information that listeners return to you about the clarity and acceptability of your ideas.

Two kinds of information are provided through feedback. By looking for frowns or other signs of puzzlement or, in a classroom, seeing how well students do on tests, speakers can learn whether their ideas have been comprehended clearly. Speakers also can look for cues to the acceptability of their ideas; audiences may boo, look disgusted or antsy, and even leave the room. Being able to read feedback for signs of comprehension and acceptability is important, because this skill allows you to make mid-course adjustments in the speech.

For their part, listeners may provide **immediate feedback** in the form of verbal or nonverbal responses during an interaction. Some immediate feedback is *direct,* such as when questions are asked, whereas some is *indirect,* such as when speakers look for frowns, smiles, nodding heads, and other nonverbal cues to reactions.

FIGURE 3.2   The Types of Feedback

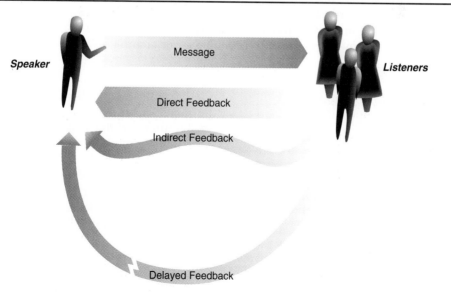

As noted earlier, however, some cultures consider it impolite to note their lack of acceptance through any feedback. Instead, they smile cordially, as if all is well, when in reality they really don't understand anything you say. Knowing in advance how different cultural values govern responsiveness will help you develop a sound perception of how effectively you have communicated your ideas. In some cases, you may not be certain until you have further concrete evidence through **delayed feedback,** which takes the form of oral, auditory, or visual signals received after the message has been transmitted. Examples include voice votes on matters a speaker has recommended, the sound of applause or boos, written evaluations from an instructor, or discovering that the person listening was unable to follow your instructions even though he or she never said anything was amiss (it may be embarrassing to admit lack of understanding in some cultural interactions).

The Channels

The public communication transaction occurs across multiple channels. The **verbal channel** carries words, society's agreed-on symbols for ideas. The **visual channel** transmits the gestures, facial expressions, bodily movements, and postures of the speakers and listeners, and these tend to clarify, reinforce, or give an emotional tone to the words or to transmit needed information about the audience's state of mind to the speaker. The visual channel sometimes is supplemented with a **pictorial channel** (visual aids such as diagrams, charts, graphs, sketches, and objects). The **aural channel**—also called the **paralinguistic channel**—carries the tone of voice and variations in pitch, loudness, and other vocal modulations; this channel carries cues to the emotional state of the speaker and the tone (ironic, playful, serious) of the speech.

Because these four channels are seen and heard simultaneously, the overall message really is a combination of several messages flowing through all of the pathways. Communication via multiple channels is what makes public speaking such a rich and subtle **transactional experience.** You must learn to shape and control the messages moving through all four channels.

The Situation

What you say and how you say it are affected significantly by the situations in which you're speaking. You don't talk the same way at work as you do at a party. Your speech is affected by the physical setting and the social context in which it occurs.

Physical Setting.   The physical setting influences listeners' expectations as well as their readiness to respond to your speech. People waiting at the convocation center for graduation ceremonies to begin have very different expectations from people attending a local politician's announcement of defeat at what might have been a victory party.

Even furniture and decor make a difference. Soft chairs and muted drapes put discussants at ease and promote productive exchange. The executive who talks to an employee from behind a massive walnut desk in the middle of an opulently decorated room with large windows looking down from the twenty-fifth floor gains a communication advantage from a setting, which connotes power, authority, and command over others. The professor who has soft chairs and a lamp table in the corner of her office for interacting with students creates a different atmosphere than the professor who remains seated behind a desk while leaving the student standing.

Social Context.   Even more important to message reception than physical setting is the social context in which speeches are presented. A **social context** is a particular combination of people, purposes, and places interacting communicatively. In a social context, *people* are distinguished from each other by factors such as gender, age, occupation, power, degree of intimacy, ethnicity, and knowledge. These factors in part determine how you "properly" communicate with others. You've learned not to talk in class while the instructor is talking. In other settings, you're expected to speak deferentially to your elders, your boss, a judge, or a high-status politician. Some settings have created formal conventions for engaging in communication (a court of law), while others are far more informal (a social gathering at a local restaurant).

Certain *purposes* or goals are more or less appropriately communicated in different social contexts: a memorial service is not the context for attacking a political opponent, but a "meet the candidates" night is. Some *places* are more conducive to certain kinds of exchanges than others: Public officials often are more easily influenced in their offices than in public forums, where they tend to be more defensive; sensitive parents scold their children in private, but never in front of their friends.

Societies are governed by customs, norms, and traditions that become the bases for communication rules. **Communication rules** are guides to communication behavior, specifying who talks to whom about what, in what style, and under what conditions. Some communication rules tell you what to do: "An audience will better remember what you have to say if you break your subject into three to five main points." Others tell you what to avoid: "Don't wander aimlessly across the stage while talking, because it will distract your audience." Such rules, of course, can be broken; some wandering speakers *are* listened to, probably because they have so many other virtues. Occasionally, rule breaking is inconsequential. Sometimes, however, it determines success or failure, and it always involves a certain amount of risk. The key is to determine the level of risk acceptable to you—and then act accordingly.[5]

The Cultural Context

Finally, elements of communication may have different meanings depending on the **culture**—the social understandings within which the communication is taking place. Each society has its own rules for interpreting communication signals. Some societies frown on taking second helpings of food; in others, it's a supreme compliment to the host or hostess. Negotiating the price of a T-shirt is unheard of at a Sears store in Atlanta, yet it's a sign of active interest in an Istanbul bazaar or a Cleveland garage sale. Communication systems operate within the confines of cultural rules and the expectations of the members of any given society.

Cultural rules and expectations become important in two situations: during *intercultural contact,* and during *cross-cultural presentations.* When talking to members of other societies on your home turf, you might offend them by violating some rule that they bring with them to your speech. A common violation during intercultural contact is too much familiarity or informality with a new acquaintance. To call people by their first names in public, for example, is simply not acceptable in many countries.

Your problem may be even greater, of course, if you attempt to speak in public in another country. During such cross-cultural presentations, you risk violating not only personal standards of interaction but the rules of the situation operating at that particular time and place. Americans soon learn they cannot joke publicly about royalty in Sweden in the same way they can about the president's family in the United States. If you are going to speak in various countries, you have to learn the communication rules governing how to introduce a person to an audience, to quote appropriate authorities, and to refer to yourself and audience members correctly. Rules for such communication situations tend to vary from country to country. To tap into the cultural context for public speaking is to grapple with the most fundamental questions of diversity and sociality—how people in various countries interact with each other and transact public business. For example, dog meat is considered a delicacy in some parts of the world, while in the United States, eating dog meat would be considered almost criminal—if not abhorrent. A speech that blames the Taiwanese, who do consider it a delicacy, for their "backward ways" would be inappropriate whether any Taiwanese were in the audience or not.[6] This is not to say that one cannot be against such a choice; rather, one can argue against a cultural practice without at the same time devaluing the people for whom that practice is considered normal. Nor would it be true that all Taiwanese believe the same way about a specific diet, any more than it would be to assume that because some Americans eat venison, all Americans approve of hunting deer. Cultural stereotypes have the distinct disadvantage of labeling all persons with the same characteristics. Speaking in a way that recognizes stereotypes for what they are—often misleading guides to individuals beliefs and values—will go a long way toward maximizing success.

The cultural context for public speaking is the ultimate source of the communication rules you've been taught. Because speeches almost always represent transactions whose appropriateness is determined by cultural rules or expectations, you'll find throughout this book explicit pieces of advice—do's and don't's. It's not really "wrong," for example, to skip presenting a summary at the end of your speech, but most audiences expect one. If you omit it, the audience might question your **communication competence**—your ability to construct a speech in accordance with the audience's expectations. A male speaker who pulls a handkerchief out of his back pocket, blows his nose, and crumples it up and puts it back—all in the middle of his speech—may be considered rather odd in this country, but in Japan, the act would be seen as "grotesque."[7] These sorts of expectations do not have to be followed slavishly, because conditions—and even speaker talents—vary from situation to situation. You should follow the rules of communication most of the time, however, because you want listeners to evaluate your ideas, not your communication skills. A consistent theme of this book is the supreme importance of developing communication competence—the possession and execution of speech skills.

Speakers and listeners, messages and feedback, channels, context, and culture are the primary elements of the public speaking process. As you strive to refine your skills in managing all of them, consider the following points:

- *A change in one element usually produces changes in others.* During a speech on learning to use the campus computer system, for example, your attitude will affect your language and delivery, your listeners' attitudes toward you, and even the feedback that you receive from them.
- *No single element controls the entire process.* You may think the speaker controls the entire process, but of course, the speaker does not. Listeners can tune in or tune out, and cultural expectations often affect the listeners' perceptions of the speaker's talents.

Overall, therefore, public speaking is a transaction or exchange: You prepare a speech to give your listeners, and in turn, they give you their attention and reactions or feedback. From all of the things you could say, you select only a few and tailor them to the listeners' interests, wants, and desires so they can absorb and accept your message. Just as you assert your right to speak, they assert their right to listen—or not to listen. *Public speaking is a communication transaction, a face-to-face process of mutual give and take.*

The preceding model of the speechmaking process will be given greater attention later. For now, the main goal is to initiate some thought about what is important in the process and how you may gain more control over those elements that are open to change. In the next section, we examine one element of the model in greater detail: the task of active listening.

CRITICAL LISTENING: THEORY AND PRACTICE

George called his neighbor Frank, who ran a trucking business. "I want to ship three sows and seven sheep to market tomorrow," George said. "Fine, I'll be there at 6 A.M.," replied Frank. At 5:50 A.M., George looked out his kitchen window to see a fleet of semis. Frank climbed out of the front cab, came to the door, and said, "We're ready." "Ready?" said George. "Why all those trucks?" "Well," replied Frank, "I figured that if you had 3,007 sheep to ship, I'd need every truck I have."

In your daily life, you spend more time listening than you do reading, writing, or speaking. Although you may assume you're a good listener from all that practice, you usually don't know about problems you might have until you miss something important. The fact is, you've probably never had any training in listening, especially for situations such as class lectures, where you're expected to acquire technical or abstract materials aurally. Just ask Frank and George about the problems that can result from mishearing numbers!

Hearing is the first step in the listening process. To listen to a message, you first must hear it. Hearing loss, which can result from any number of physiological or neurological dysfunctions, of only 15 decibels is enough to create problems in learning. Moreover, hearing loss contributes to listening difficulties.[8]

Listening, on the other hand, is "the process of receiving, constructing meaning from, and responding to spoken and/or nonverbal messages."[9] Just how important is listening? One study of who gets promoted and who doesn't in corporations reports that "the common factor that differentiated the successful candidates for promotion was this: the executive was *seen* as a person who *listens.*"[10]

In the remainder of this chapter, after more fully introducing the idea of listening, we focus on practical listening techniques you can use in almost any situation in which someone else is doing most of the talking. We finish by suggesting how you can put new listening skills to work in your classes.

Knowing Purposes: An Orientation to Listening Behaviors

There are many ways to categorize appropriate and inappropriate behaviors when it comes to listening (see Figure 3.3). The following approaches are not meant to be exhaustive but to orient you to the complexities involved in approaching audiences—and in asking them to listen to what you have to say. Knowing their purposes will assist you in gaining a hearing.

The RRP Listening Styles.   This approach suggests that when you approach an audience, you should consider whether they need to know the reasons, results, or processes most relevant to your message. The **reasons-oriented listener** wants to know why the idea is a good one—he or she will approach your speech looking for the rationale behind your idea or proposal. The **results-oriented listener** wants to know the bottom line—what is it that you are going to do? He or she will be impatient if you take too long getting to the bottom line.

FIGURE 3.3   The Styles of Listening

People may vary between and among these various approaches to listening—knowing in advance what the person is listening for *will assist you in developing your message.*

RRP	VAT	SUR
Reasons	Visual	Self-Absorbed
Results	Auditory	Unfocused
Processes	Tactile	Rules-Driven

The **process-oriented listener** checks when you begin to talk about how you went about making the decision, who will be affected by it, and how you will manage people's lives if they are unhappy with your choices. Stressing how your ideas will benefit the listener will help this person focus on your message.[11] In adapting to these listening styles, look for immediate feedback from your audience. If they appear to be impatient as you go over the reasons for your proposal in painstaking detail, you may want to cut it shorter ("cut to the chase") and move to the bottom line. Another strategy, especially if the audience contains people who also are more focused on process, is to present the bottom line, develop the rationale in brief comments, and then illustrate the benefits and consequences at the close. In this manner, you cover the interests of all three listening styles, without adversely turning off any one listener.

The VAT Listening Styles. Another way to think about how listeners approach your presentation is to consider whether they are primarily *visual, auditory,* or *tactile* listeners. **Visual listeners** need something they can see; as the old saying from Missouri goes, "show me." In this instance, visual aids become essential in drawing listeners into your presentation and getting them more involved in attending to your message. The kind of response you are looking for is "I can see what you mean." **Auditory listeners,** on the other hand, focus on what is said rather than on what is shown. These listeners are the "ideal" in terms of an audience that will critically evaluate what is being said. The response they will give is "I hear what you are saying," where "hear" means they have processed your message. **Tactile listeners** want to become involved in some way; they want not only to see but get a "hands-on" exposure to your message. If you are demonstrating how to do something or how a process works, asking for volunteers may bring forth those who like to get involved with materials. Not only "seeing" but, in fact, "seeing for themselves" is important to this style of listener. If you ask them what they think of your ideas, they may well indicate "I need to get a handle on this" or something to that effect. What they are saying is that they need to be personally involved in ways that visual and auditory listeners do not.[12] In presenting speeches, attempt to balance the needs of each group of listeners. If you have visual aids and can hand something out after the presentation that the tactile-oriented listeners can see, that may be the best way to cover all the bases. Ignoring visual and tactile listeners, in particular, means that you miss a clear segment of your audience. See the information provided in Chapter 11 ("Using Visual Aids") for advice relevant to focusing on the needs of visual and tactile listeners.

The SUR Listening Styles. While the previous styles generally are helpful in terms of active listening, the **SUR listening styles** that people sometimes employ are not at all useful to you as a speaker—unless you can circumvent their influence. These styles can be called by many labels, but one study refers to these listeners as the self-absorbed, unfocused, and rules driven. **Self-absorbed listeners** are more interested in themselves and their view of the world than they are in you and your views. **Unfocused listeners** attend without regard to any plan or pattern, and without knowing what they are looking for, their attention soon wanders off—perhaps never to return. **Rules-driven listeners** are quite capable of listening, but their focus is so narrowly constructed around whether rules or guidelines are being adhered to or violated that once they find a violation, they tend to miss the rest of the "big picture." These are people who will focus on all the reasons for not doing something, missing in the interim the arguments you present that might otherwise dissuade them.[13] Dealing with such negative behaviors is difficult, unless you have the chance to interact one on one with such listeners. If they are part of a larger audience, however, and the opportunity is not present for a question-and-answer period or some other direct interaction, you may never know that they have been left on the sidelines. For those who may be self-absorbed, the best you can do is give them reasons to "hear you out" rather than focus on their own views. If you have knowledge of their specific views, however, then dealing with those explicitly will at least gain their attention—if not their agreement. Unfocused listeners need structure; using PowerPoint as a handy "outline" may help keep their attention focused on one idea at a time. Giving them the pattern and then reinforcing it often during the speech may be the best way to keep them along for the ride. The rules-driven segment of your audience is harder to deal with, because you may not know for sure which rules, in their view, are being broken. Generally, if you are changing what they are accustomed to, you will, as with the "reasons" listeners, want to spell out why the change is important and, as with the "process" listeners, how the change will benefit them.

Other Listening Styles.   As noted, these are not the only ways to characterize audiences in terms of their listening behaviors. A recent study of college-student behaviors provides similar perspectives on the issue: Daydreaming, being distracted by other events or the environment, thinking about other issues (often stimulated by something the speaker says), and simple lack of interest in what is being said were the predominant reasons for ineffective or poor listening.[14] People also do not listen all of the time, even when they are attempting to listen well. Referring to what he terms "leftover thinking space," Lundsteen suggests that because the mind works faster than people talk, we seldom use all of that time to attend cognitively to what is being said. Instead, we may engage in one or more patterns or behaviors in the time left over from attending. One pattern is that of "small departures from communication," in which one departs several times from the line of communication but drops in often enough to keep the story intact (like watching a soap opera over a week or two but missing a few episodes). A second pattern is to go off on a "tangent" stimulated by something that is said. This can be less productive, as it takes more time away from what the speaker is saying. A third pattern is to engage in private argument with the speaker: Rather than concentrating on her or his points, the listener parallels the speech with a running commentary opposing the central idea being raised. While this may be invigorating, it does little to attend to the actual content of your message. A final pattern is the least useful—extended departures from the message being conveyed—whether due to lack of interest or other factors; the listener tunes out and only occasionally drops back in. The message has continued moving forward, however, so the listener usually ends up confused as to what is happening and finds it easier to take another extended break.[15] Recognizing that your audience is not always going to be "with you" will help you remember to add internal summaries and other guideposts to make it easier for audiences to reposition themselves when they do return to active listening.

Sometimes what you think is an example of poor or inattentive listening is not really that at all. A college professor used to listen to competitive debaters while playing solitaire. Once they were finished debating—and convinced the judge had obviously not been paying the slightest attention (he never stopped and took notes)—they were amazed to find that his critique was sharp, incisive, and invariably on target in assessing the value of their respective arguments. While they might not agree with his decision, they had to respect the fact that he had, indeed, been listening all the while. If you were speaking before an audience of Japanese businessmen and some appeared to be sleeping, you should not automatically draw the conclusion you were boring them. You may well be, but because Japanese do not believe it appropriate to look you in the eye, they will look away or even cross their arms and appear to be asleep while listening.[16] Knowing why someone appears inattentive means more than just drawing natural inferences based on your own cultural experiences.

Critical Listening for Comprehension and Judgment

We now switch positions from focusing on strategies you may use as a speaker in adapting to various listening styles to focusing on you as the person listening. Keep in mind that, as a listener, you may fit into one or more of the preceding strategies at different times—and, as a college student, can identify with the common problems most students express in terms of adequate listening behavior. As you probably know, you've got to work hard to listen well. There's no alternative to brainwork if you're going to keep out of trouble when receiving oral messages. The good news, though, is that you can train yourself to listen better. You can attack the problems of listening well in four ways: *know your purposes when trying to listen, develop techniques that help you comprehend speeches, design questions that help you evaluate or assess speeches on criteria that matter to you,* and *sharpen your note-taking techniques.*

Why Are You Listening?   This may sound foolish, but the first thing good listeners do is figure out why they're listening. As noted, this may be for specific reasons, for results, or for processing information. Knowing in advance which is most important to you will prepare you to focus on what is being said. That's not really as silly as it sounds, because you listen differently on specific occasions. On any given day, for example, you may listen intently to your instructors to learn new concepts and facts, listen to your favorite music to relax, and listen to sales personnel in a stereo shop to make sure that the person isn't skipping over some essential feature of the machine's performance or the

Critical listening is active listening.

dealer's guarantee. After reviewing listening research, Wolvin and Coakley identified five kinds of listening that reflect purposes you may have when communicating with others: appreciative, therapeutic, discriminative, comprehension, and critical.[17]

Appreciative listening focuses on something other than the primary message. Some listeners enjoy seeing a famous speaker; others appreciate the art of good public speaking. On these occasions, you listen primarily to entertain yourself.

Therapeutic listening provides emotional support for the speaker. Although it is more typical of interpersonal than of public communication, therapeutic listening does occur in public speaking situations, such as when a sports figure apologizes for unprofessional behavior, a religious convert describes a soul-saving experience, or a classmate reviews a personal problem and thanks friends for their help in solving it.

Discriminative listening requires listeners to draw conclusions from how a message is presented rather than directly from what is said. In discriminative listening, people seek to understand what the speaker really thinks, believes, or feels. You're engaging in discriminative listening when you draw conclusions about how angry your parents are with you—based not on what they say but on how they say it. An important dimension of listening depends on your ability to draw relatively sophisticated inferences from messages.

Listening for comprehension occurs when you want to gain additional information or insights from the speaker. This probably is the form of listening with which you're most familiar. When you listen to radio or TV news, to a classroom lecture on the ethnic-religious factions involved in Yugoslavian-Bosnian fighting, or to a counselor explaining computerized registration procedures, you're listening to understand—to comprehend information, ideas, and processes.

Critical listening demands that you both interpret and evaluate the message, and it is the most sophisticated and difficult kind of listening. It demands that you go beyond understanding the message to interpreting it, judging its strengths and weaknesses, and assigning it some value. You'll practice this sort of listening in class. A careful consumer also uses critical listening to evaluate sales pitches, campaign speeches, financial advice, or arguments offered by controversial talk-show guests. When you're listening critically, you decide whether to accept or reject ideas and whether to act on someone's advice.

While the following distinction is not absolute, it may be helpful in assessing the advantages of selecting a specific purpose in listening. In general, appreciative, therapeutic, and discriminative listening require that you assess and respond to the emotive tone in the message. Listening for comprehension and with a critical frame of mind require that you assess and respond cognitively to the message, but focusing on the message to understand and critique it is not the end of the story. You also need to engage in what may be called **decentering**— the process of engaging the other's ideas on their terms rather than your own. Your values and beliefs need to be decentered to place the other's rationale for speaking at the center of your analysis. As Johnson points out, "decentering occurs during listening when the listener assumes the cognitive perspective of the speaker in order to understand the speaker's intended meaning."[18] The following questions may aid in cognitively assessing the speaker's meaning:

- Do I understand the ideas?
- What's the main thrust of the speech?
- Does the speaker's message coincide with other things I know to be true?
- Does the speaker provide supporting material and acceptable explanations?
- Do these explanations support the speaker's conclusions?

Any of these purposes may be the primary aim at a given time. Other purposes also may be present during a specific occasion (you may listen to see if the speaker is angry or find yourself impressed with the artful manner in which the speaker handles a controversial topic). However, they will not be the major reason for attending to what is said. Assuming that you are, for the most part, listening for comprehension and you are attempting to assess the value of the speaker's ideas or proposal, how do you employ decentering to make sure you can accomplish your objective? The next discussion focuses more precisely on these cognitive tasks, with the aim of assisting you in becoming a focused, active listener.

Comprehending and Critiquing the Message. Fully comprehending what's being said requires that you understand the three essential aspects of speech content: *ideas, structure,* and *supporting materials.* You must understand clearly what ideas you're being asked to accept, how they relate to each other, and

COMMUNICATION RESEARCH DATELINE

LISTENING AND YOUR CAREER

One approach to listening research has focused on "the relationship between listening skills and individual performance." In their study, Michael Papa and Ethel C. Glenn hypothesized that a listening training program would improve employees' ability to adapt to a new computer system. They concluded that there was "strong evidence that listening ability impacts on employee productivity levels with new technology" and that "the provision of listening training programs improves employee's ability to perform with new technology."

Beverly Sypher, Robert Bostrom, and Joy Hart Seibert examined the relationship between listening and factors associated with one's communication ability, job level, and upward mobility. Their conclusions regarding "short term listening" (STL) and "lecture listening" (LL) included the following observations:

1. Persons with persuasive ability and sensitivity to social contexts have higher levels of skill in both STL and LL.
2. There is some evidence that a person's listening skill has a positive impact on job level—the better the skill, the higher the job.
3. There also is some evidence to support the notion that better listeners are more upwardly mobile within an organization.

M. H. Lewis and N. L. Reinsch, Jr., examined behaviors contributing to effective and ineffective listening. In a study of listening behavior in a bank and a hospital, they found that the work setting did not influence the kinds of behaviors that people appreciated or disliked. Effective behaviors included maintaining eye contact when listening to others, generally appearing attentive to the person talking, and following directions to demonstrate that you did listen. Ineffective behaviors included not following directions, not reacting verbally or nonverbally to the message, talking to others while someone is speaking, and not recalling previous messages.

For Further Reading

Michael J. Beatty and Steven K. Payne, "Listening Comprehension as a Function of Cognitive Complexity: A Research Note," *Communication Monographs* 51 (1984): 85–89.

Michael J. Papa and Ethel C. Glenn, "Listening Ability and Performance with New Technology: A Case Study," *Journal of Business Communication* 25 (Fall 1988): 6–15.

Beverly Davenport Sypher, Robert N. Bostrom, and Joy Hart Seibert, "Listening, Communication Abilities, and Success at Work," *Journal of Business Communication* 26 (Fall 1989): 293–303.

Marilyn Lewis and N. L. Reinsch, Jr., "Listening in Organizational Environments," *Journal of Business Communication* 25 (1988): 49–67.

HOW TO

BE AN ACTIVE LISTENER

- *Review* what the speaker has said. Mentally summarize key ideas each time the speaker initiates a new topic.
- *Relate* the message to what you already know. As you bring more ideas to bear on what you're hearing, your ability to listen effectively will increase.

- *Anticipate* what the speaker might say next. Use this anticipation to focus on the content of the message. If your expectations are accurate, you know you're tuned in.

Using the **RRA Technique**—review, relate, and anticipate—you can keep your attention centered on the message.

what sorts of facts and opinions underlie them. Asking three questions will help you to comprehend the message:

1. *What are the main ideas of the speech?* Determine the central idea of the speech, and look for the statements that help the speaker to develop it. These main ideas should be the foundation on which the speaker builds the speech. The next time you listen to a political commercial, listen for the main ideas: are you encouraged to support a new candidate because of what she or he proposes to do? Or, are you encouraged to vote because the incumbent has failed in some specific way to support goals the candidate thinks should be supported? Does the commercial sell you on the candidate or negate the incumbent's value? Always know what ideas you're being sold.

2. *How are the main ideas arranged?* Once you've identified the main ideas, you should assess the relationships between them. If the speaker is recounting the events of the Clinton administration but leaves out references to the sex scandals, you should know to be on your guard. Is this a biased account that glosses over what some would say are the most important, if sordid, events of any presidency? Is there a sound reason for shaping ideas in this particular manner so that some of the history is not spoken? In a speech claiming credit for an accomplishment, are the causes and effects reasonably related to each other? Let your experience in the world guide you here, but keep an open mind. In other words, identify what the structure of ideas is, and then probe the speaker's use of that form.

3. *What kinds of material support the main ideas?* Consider the timeliness, quality, and content of the supporting materials. Are facts and opinions derived from sources too old to be relevant to today's problems? Is the

speaker quoting the best experts? Ask yourself whether the materials clarify, amplify, and strengthen the main ideas of the speech. For example, if someone tells you to protest next year's 3.5-percent tuition increase, consider the following: If your school charges $15,000 or more per year, which would increase costs about $525, the protest may well be justified; if it charges $25 per credit hour, protesting an overall $25 to $30 increase (assuming 32 credits across a year, such an increase would raise the cost by about $28) would not be worth the effort and ill will. Examine the fact's ability to support the conclusion, and be sensitive to the *types* of supporting materials used: Are you getting facts and figures or only some vague endorsements from self-interested parties?

In other words, to comprehend the content, make sure you've gotten straight what ideas, relationships, and evidence you're being asked to accept.

Assessing What You've Seen and Heard

Once you've figured out why you're listening, how the ideas are arranged, and what supporting materials are being presented to you, you're in a position to form some opinions. Is the speech good/bad, just/unjust, fair/unfair, or true/false? Making such assessments is the only way to protect yourself from inflated claims, dated information, and no-good cheats. Completely assessing a speech could include asking yourself all of the following questions:

The Situation

1. *How is the situation affecting this speech and my understanding of it?* Is this the featured speaker or a warm-up act? Is the speaker expected to deal with particular themes or subjects? Am I in tune with this speech occasion? Speeches in churches, at basketball games, and during Rotary lunches are very different from each other, and you must adjust your judgment-making criteria accordingly.
2. *How is the physical environment affecting the speaking and my listening?* Is it too hot or too cold? Is the room too big or too small? Are there other distractions? The physical environment can have an important effect on your listening, so you might have to compensate (e.g., lean forward, move up, listen more closely).

The Speaker

3. *What do I know about the speaker?* The reputation of this person *will* influence you whether you want it to or not. Are you being unduly deferential or hypercritical of the speaker just because of his or her reputation? Don't let such reactions get in the way of critical listening.
4. *How believable do I find the speaker?* Are there things about the person's actions, demeanor, and words that make you accepting or suspicious? Figure out why you're reacting positively or negatively, and then ask yourself whether it's reasonable for you to believe this person or not.

5. *Is the speaker adequately prepared?* Imprecise remarks, repetitions, backtracking, vague or missing numbers, and the lack of solid testimony are all signs of a poorly prepared speaker. For example, a talk about how audiences influence TV-programming decisions should discuss, among other things, the networks' use of focus groups. If the speaker doesn't discuss this, you'll know that he or she hasn't gotten very far into the topic. Similarly, if the speaker can't explain the difference between Arbitron and Nielsen rating systems, you should question the reliability of other information in the speech.

6. *What's the speaker's attitude toward the audience?* How is the audience being treated: cordially or condescendingly, as individuals or as a general group, as inferiors or as equals? Answering these questions will help you not only to understand your own experience but to form some questions for the speaker after the speech.

The Message

7. *How solid are the ideas being presented?* We've been hammering on this point throughout the chapter, because it's crucial to assess the ideas presented in terms of your own knowledge and experience. Just one warning: You could be mistaken yourself, so don't automatically dismiss new ideas. That's how you stagnate intellectually. Do, however, listen all the more carefully when ideas seem strange, and make sure that you understand them and that they're well supported.

8. *Are the ideas well structured?* Are important ideas missing? For example, anyone who talks about "surfing the Web" and only refers to using Excite as a search engine is missing several other important means of finding information. In addition, if they go back and forth between search engines and Internet service providers without clearly demarcating the difference, you will have problems following the internal logic of the presentation. Structural relationships between ideas are what give them their solidity and coherence as a package.

9. *Is sufficient evidence offered?* You can skip ahead to Chapter 15 and see some of the tests of evidence and reasoning that you should make when faced with crucial decisions based on a speech you're hearing. The world is filled with slipshod reasoning and flawed evidence. Bad reasoning and a refusal to test the available evidence, after all, are what led the U.S. high command to believe that Pearl Harbor was an absolutely safe port in 1941. Listen for evidence, and write down the key parts so that you can mull it over, asking yourself if it's good enough to use as a basis for changing your mind. Adopt a "show me" attitude.

You certainly won't ask all nine of these questions every time you hear a speech. Remember that your listening purposes vary considerably from occasion to occasion. You'll need all nine questions only when doing critical listening at times of significant decision, such as which candidate to vote for, what lifestyle to follow, which side to support when land developers fight over where to put an expensive municipal stadium. Tailor your listening practices to your purpose for attending a speech.

Taking Good Notes

What we said earlier bears repeating: You're going to have to *practice* your listening skills to *improve* them. You've got to train yourself, and one of the easiest ways to do that while in college is to work on note taking. As you become a better note taker, you'll also become a better listener. Here are some tips for improving your note-taking skills.

Get organized. Develop your own note-taking system, and refine it. Some people like loose-leaf notebooks so that they can add, rearrange, or remove notes; others like the tidiness of spiral-or glue-bound notebooks. Whichever you choose, use separate notebooks for different courses and life experiences to avoid confusion—and learn to file.

Set aside a few minutes each day to review the syllabi for your classes, scan your readings, and review the previous class session's notes. This will prepare you to ask questions while the lecture or readings are still fresh in your mind, and it will help you to keep oriented to the class. In turn, being oriented to what's going on helps you take notes on the most important materials.

Leave 2- to 3-inch margins when taking notes. When reviewing your notes later, that marginal area will provide space for making additional comments. A great way to review and study is to write critical comments about what you agree or disagree with, what you don't understand, what you think is significant, and what you've found to be confirmed or contradicted by another source. Such critical commentary is an important stage in merging the material in your notes with your own thoughts.

Develop a note-taking scheme that works for you. Consider the possibilities:

- *Outline form.* Making a conscious effort to outline a speech or lecture as you hear it will help you to isolate the important ideas, structure, and supporting evidence.
- *Abbreviations.* Some abbreviations you'll want to use are obvious: the ampersand (&) for *and,* and *w/o* for *without.* Some go with particular subject matters, as when business majors write *mgt* and *acctg* for *management* and *accounting* and when biology majors use the F and C symbols for male and female. Others will be your own. Just make sure that you can remember the ones you invent!
- *Textual space.* Leave enough space throughout your notes so that you can add facts, clarification, and other alterations after comparing your notes with other students' or after doing related reading.
- *Multicolors.* You'll probably profit from color-coding—for example, black or blue for the main notes, red for questions or disagreements, and green for additional content.

By taking these actions, you're no longer a couch or a desk potato, a passive listener. You're an engaged, active listener who's demonstrating how public speaking should work as a two-way channel. The more you practice, the more effectively that channel will carry two-way traffic.

Special Needs for Critical Listening in the Classroom

Your speech classroom is set up to teach you multiple listening skills that will be of great use in the rest of your life. If you don't think it will be important, others do. The American Management Association, for example, advertises a seminar called "Listen Up! A Strategic Approach to Better Listening" for sales professionals; this 2-day seminar costs only $1235 for non members and $1075 for members.[19] It is evident that the business world takes the issue seriously.

Your classrooms are excellent settings for practicing new listening skills and for refining old ones. Use the Speech Evaluation Form on page 41 as a checklist when listening to speeches. It will sharpen your skills, forcing you to consider a full range of speechmaking dimensions. During this term, you also can improve your listening skills in the following ways:

1. *Practice critiquing the speeches of other students.* Practice outlining techniques. Take part in postspeech discussions, and ask questions of the speaker. You can learn as much from listening well as you can from speaking yourself.
2. *Listen critically to discussions, lectures, and student-teacher interactions in your other classes.* You're surrounded with public communication worth analyzing when you're in school. You can easily spot effective and ineffective speech techniques in those classes.
3. *Listen critically to speakers outside of class.* Attend public lectures, city council meetings, and political or religious rallies. Watch replays of presidential or congressional speeches on C-SPAN. You'll be amazed by the range of talent, techniques, and styles exhibited in your community every week.
4. *Examine the supporting materials, arguments, and language used in newspapers and magazines.* Refine your critical listening skills by practicing critical reading. Together, they represent the skills of critical thinking that you need to survive in this world. **Critical thinking** is the process of consciously examining the content and logic of messages to determine their bases in the world of ideas and to assess their rationality. Critical thinking is the backbone of evaluation. It's what happens when you listen and when you read the messages of others with your brain fully engaged. Don't leave home without it.
5. *Consider the role culture plays in the speaker's crafting of his or her ideas.* Not everyone will speak as you do, even if you agree with each other. Taking cultural differences into account and, through decentering, taking the position of the other to assess the intended meaning will go a long way toward minimizing erroneous interpretations.

Overall, then, listening makes public speaking a reciprocal activity. Listeners seek to meet their diverse needs, ranging from personal enjoyment to critical decision making, through specialized listening skills designed for each listening purpose. When both speakers and listeners work at making the speech transaction succeed, public speaking reaches its full potential as a medium of human integration and social identity.

CHAPTER SUMMARY

We began this chapter with an overview of the basic elements of the speechmaking process. The model stressed the importance of the images of self and others in the process of fashioning messages to communicate ideas clearly and effectively. The elements of that model—Speaker, Listener, Message, Feedback, Situation, Channel, and Cultural Context—were then discussed in more specific terms. Developing community within a culturally diverse world means that you must integrate the elements of the model in such a way as to enhance your effectiveness as a member of that community. The second major section of this chapter focused on the role of listening. Developing an awareness of the manner in which people seek to learn from you makes it easier to adapt your message to gain their attention and, potentially, their support. In addition to knowing how listeners approach the speech situation, it also is important to understand the role of comprehending and critiquing messages when you are in the role of listener. In fact, that knowledge helps you evaluate the adequacy of your own message. If you can satisfy your own understanding and critique, you've made progress toward meeting the expectations of others, as you often are your own worst critic. Assessing what you hear becomes a talent you will take virtually for granted through constant awareness of how to evaluate messages. Taking good notes also will increase your listening ability and have a positive impact on your academic performance. Practicing and refining your listening skills in your speech class and other classes will help you to acquire improved tools for success in the worlds of college, business, politics, and social life.

KEY TERMS

appreciative listening (p. 62)

audience analysis (p. 53)

auditory listeners (p. 59)

aural channel (p. 54)

communication competence (p. 56)

communication rules (p. 55)

content (p. 50)

credibility (p. 50)

critical listening (p. 63)

critical thinking (p. 69)

culture (p. 55)

decentering (p. 63)

delayed feedback (p. 54)

discriminiative listening (p. 62)

ethos (p. 00)

feedback (p. 53)

hearing (p. 00)

immediate feedback (p. 53)

listening (p. 52)

listening for comprehension (p. 62)

model of the process: speaker, listener, message, feedback, situation, channels, cultural context (p. 48)

paralinguistic channel (p. 54)

pictorial channel (p. 54)

process-oriented listener (p. 59)

reasons-oriented listener (p. 58)

results-oriented listener (p. 58)

RRA technique (p. 65)

RRP listening styles (p. 58)

rules-driven listeners (p. 60)

therapeutic listening (p. 62)

transactional experience (p. 54)

self-absorbed listeners (p. 59)

self-images (p. 49)

social context (p. 55)

SUR listening styles (p. 59)

tactile listeners (p. 59)

unfocused listeners (p. 59)

VAT listening styles (p. 59)

verbal channel (p. 54)

visual channel (p. 54)

visual listeners (p. 59)

ASSESSMENT ACTIVITIES

1. To learn to assess your own and other's speeches, watch a speech on videotape. Pause each time something strikes your attention, and jot down notes as you watch and listen. After viewing the speech several times, answer the following questions:

a. Does the speech seek to define community, share information, take a position in a debate, or call for social change? Does it have more than one of these general purposes? If so, which predominates? Why do you think so?

b. How does the choice of channel influence the speaker's approach to this audience? Is this the most appropriate channel to use in conveying the speaker's message? Why, or why not?

c. Does the speaker appear to be rhetorically sensitive to the situation and the audience? Given the content, structure, and style of the speech, what is the image the speaker appears to have of the audience? Does the speaker view listeners as passive consumers or as active, intelligent critics of the message?

d. What attitudes might the audience bring to this speech? Why would they be listening to the speaker?

e. How would you rate the speaker's skills and competencies? Does the speaker seem knowledgeable, self-assured, and trustworthy? Does the speaker's use of verbal and nonverbal communication result in a message that is clear, forceful, and compelling? Why, or why not?

f. List at least three ways the speaker could improve on this particular speech. Refer to the model discussed in this chapter as you formulate your answer.

2. Keep a listening log. For 2 days, record your oral communication interactions, noting to whom you were speaking, what your listening purposes were, and how effectively you listened given your purposes. Include talks with roommates, class meetings, coffee shop or lunchroom conversations, and evening activities. After completing the log, do a self-assessment: What are your strengths and weaknesses as a listener? What changes do you need to make to become a better listener?

REFERENCES

1. The word *transaction* is being used to indicate that public speaking is not a one-way mode of communication. Just as the speaker offers a message, so the listeners offer messages in the form of feedback. Speakers and audiences have mutual obligations to be forthright and honest in their appraisal and treatment of each other. Thus, each plays complementary roles during public speeches; hence, the word *transaction* clearly applies to this sort of communication exchange. For a more complete discussion of this concept, read the classic essay by Dean C. Barnlund, "A Transactional Model of Communication," *Language Behavior: A Book of Readings*, ed. Johnny Akins, et al. (The Hague: Mouton, 1970), 53–71.

2. On the interrelationships between self-concept and communication, see Joseph DeVito, *Messages: Building Interpersonal Communication Skills*, 3rd ed. (New York: HarperCollins, 1996), ch. 2, "The Self," 26–55.

3. Peggy Noonan, "Why the Speech Will Live in Infamy," *Time Special Report*, August 31,

1998, p. 36. The statistics quoted are reported on pp. 30–31.

4. For more information on such matters, see James B. Stiff, *Persuasive Communication.* (New York: Guilford Press, 1994), ch. 7, "Receiver Characteristics," 132–152.

5. For a fuller discussion of physical and social context, see Sarah Trenholm, *Persuasion and Social Influence.* (Englewood Cliffs, NJ: Prentice-Hall, 1989), ch. 8, "The Persuasive Environment." A good overview on social context is provided in Joseph DeVito, *Messages: Building Interpersonal Communication Skills,* 3rd ed. (New York: Harper-Collins, 1996), ch. 6, "Nonverbal Messages," 108–139. The best review of research on communication rules is found in Susan B. Shimanoff, *Communication Rules: Theory and Research* (Beverly Hills, CA: Sage, 1980).

6. Kazuo Nishiyama, *Japan-U.S. Business Communication.* (Dubuque, IA: Kendall-Hunt, 1995), 105.

7. Terri Morrison, Wayne A. Conaway, and George A. Borden, *Kiss, Bow, or Shake Hands. How to do Business in Sixty Countries.* (Holbrook, MA: Adams Media Corporation, 1994), 207.

8. Billie M. Thompson, "Listening Disabilities: The Plight of Many," *Perspectives on Listening,* eds. Andrew D. Wolvin and Carolyn Gwynn Coakley. (Norwood, NJ: Ablex Publishing Company, 1993), 124–169. Information cited is on p. 138.

9. The quotation comes from the International Listening Association's Web page; available online at http://www.listen.org.

10. Peter Meyer, *"So You Want the President's Job . . ." Business Horizons* 41 (1998); 2.

11. Rosemary V. Wood and Ruth T. Bennett, "Effective Communication via Listening Styles," *Business* 39 (1989); 45–48.

12. Jackie Taylor, "Learning Styles: A Practical Tool for Improved Communications," *Supervision* 59 (1998); 18–19.

13. Herbert Greenberg and Jay J. Avelino, "Can You Improve Someone's Listening Skills?" Available online at http://www.aednet.org/ced/dec96/listen.htm.

14. Mary Alice Griffin, Donnie McGahee, and John Slate, "Effective Listening Skills." Available online at http://www.bvte.ecu.edu/ACBMEC/p1998/griffin.htm.

15. Sara W. Lundsteen, "Metacognitive Listening," *Perspectives on Listening,* eds. Andrew D. Wolvin and Carolyn Gwynn Coakley. Information cited is on pp. 113–15. (Norwood, NJ: Ablex Publishing Company, 1993), 106–134.

16. Kazuo Nishiyama, *Japan-U.S. Business Communication.* (Dubuque, IA: Kendall-Hunt, 1995), 112.

17. Andrew Wolvin and Carolyn Coakley, *Listening.* (Dubuque, IA: William C. Brown, 1982), 3–11.

18. Jack Johnson, "Functions and Processes of Inner Speech in Listening," *Perspectives on Listening,* eds. Andrew D. Wolvin and Carolyn Gwynn Coakley. (Norwood, NJ: Ablex Publishing Company, 1993), 170–181. Information cited is on pp. 178–79.

19. American Management Association. Available online at http://www.tregistry.com/s0112271.htm.

Chapter 4

Public Speaking and Cultural Life

At its simplest, a **culture** is a social group's system of meanings. We can think of "culture" as the sorts of meanings that a given people attaches to persons, places, ideas, rituals, things, routines, and communication behavior. You've been taught since you were an infant, who is powerful or not (persons), how to act at home and in public buildings (places), what's true and false about the things you encounter in the world (ideas), how to greet family and strangers (routines), and the most effective—and ineffective—ways to get favors from your boss (communication behavior). Your culture thus is comprised of pieces of social knowledge that represent how you've been taught to comprehend and act successfully within the world of human beings.

All of this is true for everyone else as well. We've all been taught about persons, places, rituals, ideas, and the rest. Unfortunately, the meanings for those entities that you've been given may not be the same as the meanings someone else has learned—your experiences are different from those of others. This happens not only on an individual basis but on a group basis as well. Men and women in some important ways have been given different social educations. So have whites and Hispanics, poor and rich folk, and those who hear and those who cannot. All of our differences in psychological, social, political, economic, and behavioral—which is to say cultural—education can cause speakers some serious problems.

Barbara was distraught. "I can't go out there!" She was a delegate from her sorority house about to speak at a gathering of the campus African-American, Hispanic, and international students' associations on working together to make the city council reconsider a rezoning decision, one that would wipe out two blocks of student apartments and student-oriented stores. "Here I am, a white sorority sister born in Iowa, a state that's ninety-seven-and-a-half-percent white. And there they are, from the ghettoes of Chicago and New York, from foreign countries totally different from mine. They'll resent me.

What do we have in common?" "That's the question you must answer," replied her best friend, Glenda. "What do you have in common? You're all students here, you all live in proximity to the neighborhood about to be destroyed, you all enjoy gathering at those stores and shops on Becker Street—you have a lot in common!" "Well, I guess we do, but . . ." "But nothing!" said Glenda. "Quit emphasizing your differences. Sure you have them, but think of what you share and of your ways differences will become a strength in front of the city council. That's what to talk about."

Training in public speaking is in part a matter of learning about the cultural expectations of one's audience. Speakers must learn what those expectations are in order to be seen as socially competent and ideationally relevant to others. Speakers who want to affect audiences must learn to be exceptionally good at phrasing ideas and engaging the feelings of others within the communication traditions of the others' cultural traditions.

Learning about the cultural expectations of one's listeners, however, is easier said than done, because the doing—meeting those expectations—can be a most difficult task. There is always, perhaps, a tension between the self and society, between the individual and the collectivity, especially in the United States, where almost all children have been taught to maximize their potentials and to be their own persons. On the one hand, you are you, a unique individual with your own life experiences and your own thoughts about the world. On the other hand, you always are marked by social categories. You are an individual, yes, but you also are reminded regularly that you're gay, of Polish descent, twentysomething, an atheist, a junior in college who works as a sales clerk, and so on. You are an individual—a "listener," as we've discussed such people—but part of your self-identity, and certainly a major part of others' perception of you, is socially and culturally determined.[1]

In a world where identities are both individually and collectively constructed, you must answer some difficult questions as you prepare to talk publicly:

- Can you respect individual differences and cultural diversity while attempting to get a group of people to think alike and work together?
- Can you recognize the diversity of your audience's experiences, even their ideological schisms, while you nonetheless attempt to enact a public image that is credible?
- Can you be true to yourself and your commitments while adapting to others?
- Can you successfully negotiate the differences between what audiences expect of you and what you expect of yourself?

These are not easy questions to answer, and you certainly don't think of them every time you rise to say a few words. When you face audiences as different from you as Barbara felt her audience was from her, however, you'll want to follow her friend Glenda's advice and look for the **common ground**—the shared beliefs, attitudes, values, goals, and desires that turn a group of listeners into a people unified in thought and action.[2]

In this chapter, we discuss relationships between public speaking and cultural life by first examining the components of "culture" more specifically. Then, we review some strategies that you can use to unify and direct your listeners' thoughts and actions, even when they come from diverse cultural backgrounds.

UNDERSTANDING CULTURAL PROCESSES

We've defined *culture* generally. Before you can think about strategies for responding to key points of cultural diversity in your speeches, however, you'll want to think more about how it affects your everyday life.

The Dynamics of Culture

If **culture** is a concept broad enough to include all of a society's meanings for ideas, things, and activities, then we need a systematic vocabulary to break it down into units for analysis and study. This vocabulary is a bit abstract, but it's easier to understand if you focus on three dimensions of social life: *culture as lived, culture as thought,* and *culture as performed.*

Culture as Lived: Demographic Categories of Social Organization.   One way to examine cultural life is via the social categories through which others define us. You've learned that others sometimes define you by gender (male, female, transsexual), ethnic background (Swedish American, Asian American), age (young, middle-aged), sexual orientation (straight, gay, bisexual), nationality (Croat, Tibetan), educational background (high-school dropout, college grad), reference group (Girl Scout, Disabled American Veteran), religion (Sufi, Presbyterian), disability (hearing impaired, visually challenged), socio-economic status (underclass welfare recipient, upper-class taxpayer). Insofar as you think about yourself or others via such categories, those social markers become amazingly important in your relationships. In the story of Barbara, for example, she thought about herself in terms of race, gender, and reference or organizational group. Such markers can become determinative of **culture as lived.**[3]

FIGURE 4.1   The Dimensions of Culture

Culture is multifaceted and intermixed—living, thinking, and performing culture becomes "taken for granted" within your own community of friends.

Culture as Lived: social categories (gender, race) of identity

Culture as Thought: ideas and values given to you by others

Culture as Performed: ways you are taught to act publicly

Gender identification, for example, begins at a young age. Little boys and little girls generally learn to play differently from one another; those differences become more and more important as they mature, governing personal identity (straight or gay), social relations (the dating game), extracurricular activities (different high-school sports for females and males), and even work (women paid an average of 41 percent less for comparable work than men). Ethnic backgrounds produce similar ranges of identities, especially because, other things being equal, whites tend to have easier access to social-economic-educational institutions than people of color. Of course, other things are not equal, so one's economic status can neutralize or exacerbate racial differences. Age can enter in as well, because racial differences tend to harden with age. Reference groups also differ; African Americans and white Americans often gather in different clubs and churches. The question here is not, of course, whether any particular girl or African American has an identity totally separate from that of a boy or a white person. Rather, the question is this: when reminded of their gender or race (or another demographic category), how does an individual think about his or her identity, loyalties, and social expectations?

And so it goes: culture as lived, especially as you move out of your immediate neighborhood (i.e., away from the people who know you most intimately as an individual), becomes increasingly focused on cultural differences. Those differences have always been around, though the Black, Hispanic, gay/lesbian, and women's empowerment movements of the 1960s and 1970s, the growing emphasis on **cultural diversity** in the 1980s, and passage of the Americans with Disabilities Act in 1991 have sensitized most of us to their roles. **Multiculturalism**—the recognition that a country such as the United States possesses not a unitary culture with several **subcultures** but rather **co-cultures** that interpenetrate yet are separate from one another—is a fact of life.[4]

Culture as Thought: Ideology and Hegemony.   Not only have you been acculturated to act in particular ways through your experiences with others in everyday life, you've also been conditioned to think in particular patterns as well. You've been conditioned to think, perhaps, that love is worth dying for, that lettuce greens taste better than collard greens, that your personal safety is affected by what country you're in, that living the virtuous life pays off in the end, and maybe even that "blood is thicker than water." That is, others have taught you to think that certain values (e.g., love) are highly positive whereas others (e.g., dislike or hate) are highly negative, that personal tastes (e.g., in foods) are grounded in real differences between things rather than in mere preference, that people can be usefully stereotyped by such accidental characteristics as national origin, that rules for succeeding in your society (play by the rules to win) hold true everywhere, and that folk wisdom (often captured in aphorisms) contain eternal verities.[5]

A system of thought that embodies social values and perceptual orientations to the world is called an **ideology**. Ideologies have a power in your life that is naturalized,[6] that is, thought of as "what everyone knows" or "how things are

Jesse Jackson epitomizes the role of public speaking in the creation of diverse communities, whether in Chicago or the hills of Appalachia.

done around here." Ideologically grounded values and perceptions of the world are rooted in cognitions that always have been part of your environment, unquestioned and regularly reinforced by people important in your life—parents, siblings, friends, and authority figures in your community, church, and schools. A person in your locale who doesn't believe in love will be thought deviant, someone who prefers collard greens to lettuce will be regarded as a little strange. Someone who leaves his or her family (blood ties) to join a Hari Krishna community might even by chased down by deprogrammers.

Ideologies are powerful not only because familial, religious, social, and political institutions reinforce them but because of your own volition. You seldom question fundamental tenets of living with like-minded others; you even reinforce them in your own talk to others. For example, you're liable to rein in a child running away from the lunch table without having first been excused by adults and say, "That's not the way things are done around here, kid." In your own past, when a bigger and older bully pushed in front of you in the line for the drinking fountain, you likely thought that's simply the way the world is—that the bigger and older folks rule the roost. If you were raised in an urban neighborhood where Sunday afternoon block parties occurred almost weekly in the summer, you probably assumed that working class families were pretty much alike. In all of these instances, you internalized a series of cultural rules and beliefs, and you made them parts of your perceptual and valuative equipment.

Hegemony is a word for relationships between more powerful and less powerful people that are maintained, either in part or in whole, through complicity of the less powerful people. Hegemonic relationships often are signaled by phrases such as "That's the way we do things," "That's the way it goes," or "That's a fact of life." Relationships between classes (rich and poor), racial groups (e.g., white and non-white), and even the sexes (male and female) often are maintained as much by complicitous acceptance of one's status as by direct force. The idea of hegemony in part accounts for why it's so difficult to change social relations quickly. Even when women or Hispanics or gays have been "liberated" from some dimensions of their oppressions by others, not all of them join in the chorus of "Free at last! Free at last! Thank God Almighty, we're free at last!" There still are women who sneer at feminist thought, Mexican Americans who don't look forward to the revolution, and gays, lesbians, and bisexuals who haven't come out of the closet. Naturalized attitudes and social relations resist alteration. **Culture as thought** has a lock on many minds thanks to the forces of ideology and hegemony.[7]

Culture as Performed: Embodiment and Enactment. The rules and thoughts governing life can be put into words, such as when you recite the Pledge of Allegiance, promise to tell the truth in court testimony, or decline to loan a friend money by saying "Neither a borrower nor a lender be." More usually, however, cultural rules and the social roles that we come to accept—or at least live out—are not only heard but also seen. **Embodiment** is the process whereby ideas, attitudes, values, and social character are given corporeal existence in communication acts.[8]

You come to understand what a "senator" is by watching your own senator's news conferences and reading his or her newsletters. A television show such as *Everyone Loves Raymond* exaggerates husband-wife and parent-child talk; the acting out in comedic ways of gender and generational roles serves to critique the relationships between too many husbands and wives and too many parents and children. In addition, on *Chicago Hope,* we see how the personal and professional aspects of people's lives actually are inseparable. You come to understand what education is by watching people teach. The idea of police brutality was understood by one generation of Americans through watching the use of night sticks and cattle prods on civil rights demonstrators in the 1960s and by another generation viewing the capture of Rodney King in the 1990s. You learn many—perhaps even most—of the cultural rules you know because particular people embody them in face-to-face or mass-mediated activities.

In turn, then, you work to enact them. **Enactment** is a communication process whereby a person behaves in a manner consistent with society's cultural rules. Lawyers go to school to learn to interview clients and present cases in court; in short, they learn to think and then act like lawyers are expected to in their country. Individual athletic achievements often are recounted with opening phrases such as "I couldn't have done this without my teammates, who . . . ;" such modest behavior is consonant with rules for sports etiquette. In this course, you practice giving speeches with introductions, bodies, and conclusions on the assumption that such an arrangement for public talks is expected. Rules for speaking are grounded in audience expectations, which you try to enact so you'll be judged a competent speaker.[9]

Culture as performed, therefore, takes us to the heart of this book—how it is that members of a society communicate with each other. The forms of public talk (introductions, bodies, conclusions), the substance of public talk (accepted ways of reasoning), the relationships between speaker and audience (grounded in lived experiences), and even the outcomes of public speeches (who will listen to whom) are affected by your skills in "performing" those speeches in culturally sensible and accepted ways. In different societies, you'll likely have to learn different forms of talk.[10]

Performance should not be thought of here as a theatrical term, as acting out a script in such a way as to become someone else. In communication studies, the idea of performance is tied to life roles and cultural rules, not to artistic license.[11] Theatrical performance is judged by aesthetic standards; speech performance is judged by community or pragmatic standards, by whether people accept you, by what you have to say, and by how you say it. You learn these standards by seeing others embody them, and then you enact them yourself in hopes of affecting the beliefs, attitudes, values, and behaviors of others.

The Challenge of Cultural Diversity

Earlier we raised this question: can you respect individual difference and cultural diversity while attempting to get a group of people to think alike and work together? Yes, we think that you can. You can embody in your public oral presentations some generally accepted cultural standards for public interpersonal relationships. What those standards are and how you can embody them are the next topics of discussion.

UNIFYING DIVERSIFIED AUDIENCES: POSSIBLE STRATEGIES

One of any speaker's primary jobs is to acknowledge relevant cultural experiences or expectations affecting listeners' reception of a message, even while calling for unified thought and action. *Relevancy* is an important concept here. If you're giving a speech on how to etch glass, for example, your audience's racial background probably is irrelevant, but if you're talking about federal programs for low-income housing, race can easily become a relevant issue. If you're discussing affirmative action, race is central. So, how can you recognize

ETHICAL MOMENTS

ADAPTING TO CULTURAL ORIENTATIONS

The stated theme of this chapter is simple: You must learn to adapt your ways of talking to the cultural orientations of your listeners to achieve your goals as a speaker. What, however, are the ethical limits of that requirement?

1. Must you use profanity if talking about opponents to your position just because members of your audience do?
2. Is it ethical to play to the fears a Jewish audience might have of Arabs in a speech on the evils of population control?
3. When talking to an audience of West Africans about the importance of teenage growth and development, must you confront the practice in some of those countries of circumcising young teens, especially girls?
4. What sorts of appeals to motivation and hard work should you use when talking to an audience of people whose unemployment rate has been about 40 percent for the last 15 years?
5. What if you want to talk about a subject that is taboo (i.e., unspoken) in some country?

Set up some discussions in class where you tackle these and similar problems that members of your group have encountered. Ethical judgments become even more difficult to render when the participants have significantly different cultural backgrounds.

sociocultural difference or diversity while seeking to get people to work together? Consider the following strategies the best speakers have used regularly over the last few years.

Recognizing Diversity

When cultural differences between and among audience members are likely to come to people's minds when you're speaking, you should probably recognize them. Even in their differences, after all, members of a group must learn to think and act together. A famous example of this challenge in recent years was the so-called Million Man March on Washington organized by Minister Louis Farrakhan of the Black Muslin Nation in the fall of 1995. In fact, nearly 1 million people came, including many non-Muslims. Minister Farrakhan had to recognize his listeners' diverse backgrounds so that all, not just Black Muslims, would respond to his message. First, he read from a speech given by a white slaveholder in 1712 who advocated using fear, distrust, and envy to fracture the slave community. Then, he noted:

FIGURE 4.2 Strategic Choices

These strategies are not mutually exclusive or necessarily as ordered here. Paying attention to each, however, will assist you in developing messages that are adapted to the cultural context.

And so, as a consequence, we as a people now have been fractured, divided and destroyed, filled with fear, distrust and envy. Therefore, because of fear, envy and distrust of one another, many of us as leaders, teachers, educators, pastors and persons are still under the control mechanism of our former slave masters and their children.

And now, in spite of all that division, in spite of all that divisiveness, we responded to a call and look at what is present here today. We have here those brothers with means and those who have no means. Those who are light and those who are dark. Those who are educated, those who are uneducated. Those who are business people, those who don't know anything about business. Those who are young, those who are old. Those who are scientific, those who know nothing of science. Those who are religious and those who are irreligious. Those who are Christian, those who are Muslim, those who are Baptist, those who are Methodist, those who are Episcopalian, those of traditional African religion. We've got them all here today.[12]

Minister Farrakhan's reputation as a black militant almost demanded that he include a message of reconciliation between and among the various branches of African-American culture; if the Million Man March was to succeed, he had to argue that African-Americans regardless of cultural diversity had to commit themselves to common goals: "Black man, you don't have to bash white people, all we gotta do is go back home and turn our communities into productive places. All we gotta do is go back home and make our communities a decent and safe place to life."[13] In this case, the speaker recognized diversity but stated his goals in terms of the actions of individuals, not groups. Thus, diversity didn't turn into the kind of divisiveness advocated by the ancient slaveholder of 1712.

Inventorying the diversity of cultures in one's audience is a technique that you can quickly learn to use. For example, in a speech on why students in your school's Study Abroad Program should consider going to school in Malta, you might say:

Malta has earned its reputation as "The Crossroads of the Mediterranean," and for that reason, it can provide a wonderful social and educational experience for all of you. Those of you who want to learn in English will find classes taught in your mother tongue; those with ears for foreign languages will discover a score of them spoken in apartment complexes and restaurants. Churchgoers can find Catholic, Protestant, and Islamic houses of worship. White Eurocentric people and Black Afrocentric people work and play together on Malta. You can take sidetrips to nearby sites reflecting a variety of cultural experiences: you can eat scampi in Italy, cous cous in Morocco, goulash in Croatia, tapas in Spain, or lamb in Sicily. Your palate—and your mind—will be opened to a dozen cultures on Malta, allowing all of you to find a niche for comfortable living in a foreign land.

Even if the topic doesn't seem inherently multicultural, you'll want to be sensitive to diversity all of the time. For example, if you plan to mention dating in a speech on teenage urban lifestyles, think about whether you can assume everyone in your audience practices only heterosexual relationships. When talking about the crisis in health care, don't unnecessarily gender the professions by calling doctors "he" and nurses "she."

Negotiating Diverse Values

Because audiences often form into groups based on the diverse characteristics of the individuals comprising them, it's likely that different segments see the world in different ways—use some of the same words as others but mean quite different things. This is because people's **value orientations**—their habitual ways of thinking about positive and negative grounds for human thought and action—tend to become materialized in highly idiosyncratic ways. Consider, for example, how the phrase "family values" has been talked about in the 1990s. Everyone supports family values, but varied valuative orientations—we can call them liberal, middling, and conservative ideologies—lie underneath different people's use of that label (see Table 4.1).

These, of course, are simplified versions of people's political positions, but when most people argue about a governmental policy toward family values, they deal in such simplifications. That "family values" can mean such different things to people shouldn't be surprising, because the issue is a strongly divisive one in American society today. The differences are so great that you can't ignore them when talking about this topic, either. Rather, you're better advised to recognize the differences and define the phrase "family values" carefully, so that your listeners know exactly what you're talking about. Even then, you may well want to negotiate among the varied definitions. You might have to say, "All right, then, on what do we agree? How far can we go together in helping parents raise their children?" It was precisely this kind of thinking that got liberals, conservatives, and middle-of-the-roaders together in 1993 to form a coalition in Congress. That coalition passed the Family Leave Act in the name of both fostering traditional families (by requiring businesses to pay a parent while staying at home with an infant) and recognizing a child's needs (by guar-

TABLE 4.1   The Diversity of "Family Values"

Conservative Ideology	America is in moral decline and must return to older family values. We've become a permissive society characterized by divorce, illegitimacy, juvenile crime, and spoiled children. We must bolster the traditional, two-parent, heterosexual family as the best environment for children and eliminate governmental (including school) interference with the family's operations.
Liberal Ideology	America has to give parents more aid in raising their children. Everyone, not just parents, has a stake in making sure that children are cared for, supported, and raised to be good citizens. Because financial resources are so varied in this country and so many families are troubled, government at the local, state, and national levels must help parents with child care, health care, paid parental leave when children are infants, and other forms of financial assistance. It is better to help all forms of family—single- and dual-parent, traditional and nontraditional—with their children than to deal with juveniles in prisons later.
Middle-of-the-Road Ideology	Raising children should primarily be a matter of parental responsibility but with governmental safety nets in place. Parents must be made more responsible for the growth and actions of their children yet should have help available in the form of family planning agencies, subsidized adoption and abortion services, and sex education in the schools. If parents fail or abuse their children, the state should rescue children from such situations, but if not, parents should be made to take responsibility for their children's care, feeding, and nurture.

anteeing him or her parental support in the earliest stages of social life). The middle-of-the-roaders saw this act as a perfect example of family-business-government cooperation and so were equally supportive.

The tricky part of negotiating across valuative differences is to make sure that negotiations don't turn into *erasure*. If you try articulating Rodney King's theme—"Can't we all just get along?"—you might be interpreted as saying that everyone should think like you do—that women should think like men, that African Americans should think like whites, and that the underclass should accept their lot. Getting along doesn't mean becoming the same but rather looking for actions or activities that respect differences yet achieve aims common to multiple groups in society.

Accepting Multiple Paths to Goals

A still more difficult challenge often is to convince people that there are many ways to reach a shared goal. Thus, for example, some colleges and universities allow students to meet a foreign-language requirement in varied ways, such as a demonstration of skills (oral or written test), life experiences (having grown up in a household that spoke the language), and in-class instruction (taking enough classes to become proficient). Likewise, smoking-cessation programs often allow smokers to try different approaches to quitting, such as hypnosis, psychotherapy, the patch or nicotine gum, group therapy, and cold-turkey regimes.

Suppose you're in a situation, however, where people tend to say, as some parents do to their children, "There's only one way to do this: the *right* way!" In such situations, how can speakers create a sense of tolerance and acceptance of multiple paths leading to common goals? Metaphors and allegories (see Chapter 10) are useful ways for letting people see the utility of allowing multiple paths to shared goals. In his speech at the Atlanta Exposition in 1894, black social activist Booker T. Washington used the metaphor of the hand, whereby individual ethnic groups (i.e., the fingers) were depicted as attached to and a part of the same social system (i.e., the hand). In urging the U.S. Forest Service to hire a more culturally diverse workforce, Native-American Henri Mann Morton used the metaphors of a former chieftain to argue that multiple paths can lead to the same goal:

> Finally, I would like to leave you with the words of one of our Cheyenne philosophers, High Chief, who said:
>
> In this land there are many horses—red, white, black, and yellow. Yet, it is all one horse.
>
> There are also birds of every color, red, white, black, and yellow. Yet, it is all one bird. So it is with living things.
>
> In this land where once there were only Indians, there are difference races, red, white, black, and yellow. Yet, it is all one people.
>
> It is good and right.
>
> High Chief was a wise man. He knew that cultural uniquenesses have a strength of their own. At the same time he recognized our common humanity.
>
> You, too, know this, as indicated by your powerful theme of "Strength Through Cultural Diversity."[14]

The metaphor of colors—even Jesse Jackson's political group of the 1980s was called the Rainbow Coalition—is useful. It suggests how differences can be focused into a whole, just as the color spectrum is blended together to make "light." Historical examples also are useful, such as pointing to the success of multinational forces in times of war (the Allies of World War II or the Persian Gulf War), multinational forces in times of peace (UNICEF programs in the United Nations), interpersonal and group efforts in times of disaster (people-to-people support programs in Southeast Asia), and the overcoming of differences in times of celebration (the building of the multiracial South African Olympic team for the first time in 1996). Teaching people to accept multiple paths or cooperative arrangements to shared goals is a technique you must learn to use almost daily in your speech if you're going to successfully get past those matters that divide listeners into distrustful groups.

COMMUNICATION RESEARCH DATELINE

LANGUAGE IS NOT TRANSPARENT

Stephen Tyler has written that "Nothing so well marks the modern urge as [a] utopian dream of transparent language, of language so perfectly fitted to the world that no difference could insinuate itself between words and things."[15] Since the 1920s and 1930s, when many scholars tried to explain World War I as a war of misunderstanding—of propaganda, of evil manipulators of large institutions (especially governments)—we have hoped almost desperately that we could wipe out disagreements and conflict by using a "transparent language," in which the things that words point to are clear or a "neutral language," in which only descriptions are presented to others. By now, we know that both goals are impossible to meet. This is because:

1. Language cannot be neutral, because its meaning depends in part on context. Yelling "Fire!" in a theatre and on a firing range produces two different meanings.

2. Even neutral-sounding language can have strong evaluative force. "All men are created equal" seems to be a descriptive statement, but of course, it was used in governmental documents that decreed women and slaves had no civil rights.

3. Language is a human, not a natural, phenomenon. Thus, language expresses human orientations and attitudes toward the world, not the "true" characteristics of that world itself.

We have come to understand through studies of language in use during the last fifty years that we'll never find a transparent or a neutral language. We'll have to adapt to the language we have—and do everything we can to use it humanely.

Working Through the Lifestyle Choices of Others

An old saying recommends that "When in Rome, do as the Romans do." Often, you do. You might eat with chopsticks and a flat-bottomed spoon when in a Thai restaurant, remove your shoes when entering the home of a Finn, kiss Romanians on both cheeks when greeting them, or take a *siesta* after lunch in Spain. Urging people to accommodate to the lifestyles of other cultures is something you'll need to do on occasion, particularly if that's the only way to come together and coming together is important to you.[16]

A classic Western story of accommodation, of surrender to another's lifestyle, comes from the Book of Ruth in the Old Testament. Ruth, a Moabite, had been married to Mahlon, an Israelite from Judah. Mahlon and his brother died, so their mother Naomi decided to return from Moab to Judah. Ruth pleaded with Naomi to take her to Judah. Naomi kept thinking of reasons for Ruth not to move to what, for her, would be a foreign land. Ruth finally gave a short speech:

> Entreat me not to leave you or to return from following you; for where you go I will go, and where you lodge I will lodge; your people shall be my people, and your God, my God; where you die I will die, and there will I be buried. May the Lord so do to me and more also if even death parts me from you.[17]

The Book of Ruth records: "And when Naomi saw that she was determined to go with her, she said no more."[18] Furthermore, Ruth's actions led her future husband, Boaz, to notice her accommodation:

> All that you have done for your mother-in-law since the death of your husband has been fully told me, and how you left your father and mother and your native land and came to a people that you did not know before. The Lord recompense you for what you have done, and a full reward be given you by the lord, the God of Israel, under whose wings you have come to take refuge![19]

Here, we see an extraordinary effort at persuasion built around a full surrender to the lifestyle of others. In offering to engage in a series of acts reflective of another's lifestyle—living (lodging) with Naomi, dwelling among her people, worshipping her deity, and being buried with her—Ruth was able to enter into a complete and (apparently) mutually satisfying relationship with Naomi and all of Israel. Indeed, as a result of these promises, Ruth became the great-grandmother of the most famous of Israel's kings, David. Obviously, such a strategy of accommodation can have great personal consequences; one's own lifestyle may well be sacrificed. That very sense of personal sacrifice, perhaps, is why it's such a powerful approach to the transcendence of difference: if you're willing to give up part of your own identity, you are demanding to be taken with the utmost of seriousness.[20]

So, in urging your classmates to pressure Congress to pass a more aggressive policy on protecting gays in the military, you might say:

> Now, for many—probably even most—people in this class, the issue of gays in the military seems irrelevant. You're not gay, right? So, why worry? Well, there are plenty of reasons to worry. If the military can dictate sexual lifestyle, then it can dictate other aspects of lifestyle as well. If the military drives out gays "who tell," then it's weakening civil rights in this country as well as closing employment doors to about 10 percent of our population. If the military drives out gays, it prejudices the remaining military personnel against them. Even those of you who are straight, therefore, should have important social

and legal questions on your mind. Your life's not directly affected by the "don't ask, don't tell" policy, but you sacrifice little or nothing by trying to help a marginalized group in society find self-respect and legal standing in this country.

In this kind of argument, you work through a lifestyle difference that's not experienced by most members of the audience yet in a way that asks them to see how it's relevant to their own.

Maintaining Self-Identity When Facing Difference

Most of the time, you probably won't be willing to surrender your self-identity—your own life experiences and culture—to others. This creates a quandary: how can you be true to yourself while managing to work effectively with others?

One technique is to recognize your similarities with others even while maintaining your own identity. This is what President Lyndon Johnson did in 1965 when urging Congress to pass civil rights legislation: "There is no Negro problem. There is no Southern problem. There is no Northern problem. There is only an American problem. And we are met here tonight as Americans—not as Democrats or Republicans—we are met here as Americans to solve that problem."[21] Johnson was searching for a transcendent identity with which, he hoped, all in his audience could associate.

Identity also can become a complicated issue when speakers see themselves as having multiple identities that sometimes seem to conflict. Speaking to the

Every culture includes subcultures and co-cultures that must be taken into account when communicating.

1996 Republican National Convention, Mary Fisher had a potential identity problem. She had AIDS and was speaking as an AIDS advocate, yet she was speaking to an audience in which the more conservative members especially wanted little to do with AIDS patients or with federal programs for help. Fisher phrased the potential identity problem early in the speech: "I mean to live, and to die, as a Republican. But I also live, and will die, in the AIDS community—a community hungry for the evidence of [political] leadership and desperate for hope." To make use of that distinction—and to overcome it—Fisher chose to strip away the conservative political culture of her listeners to demand their action: "The question is not political. It's a human question, sharpened by suffering and death, and it demands a moral response." Thus, she could argue, by the end of her speech, that political action should be undertaken not for ideological reasons but for social and cultural ones. Hugging a 12-year-old, African-American girl named Heidia, who was born with AIDS, Fisher concluded her speech as follows:

> The day may come when AIDS will have its way with me, when I can no longer lift my sons to see the future or bend down to kiss away the pain. At that moment Max and Zack will become the community's children more than my own, and we will be judged not through the eyes of politics but through the eyes of children. I may lose my own battle with AIDS, but if you would embrace moral courage tonight and embrace my children when I'm gone, then you and Heidia and I would together have won a greater battle, because we would have achieved integrity.[22]

To find ways of affirming your own self—your own *ethos*—while also recognizing and complementing your listeners' sense of self is a search that you'll continue throughout your lifetime when you speak publicly. Finding ways of achieving unity in the midst of social diversity is a central challenge to all who would inform and persuade others. You'll often find yourself saying such things as:

- "Well, now, I'm not a Mexican American, but I think I can understand something of the community's concern about racial stereotyping in *The Return of Zorro*, because . . ."
- "The underclass in this country deserves more than a pat on the head, a dime in the tin cup, and a little contribution to your local Salvation Army shelter, though the financial support obviously is needed. The underclass deserves your attention—to its social and psychological as well as to its economic needs. You may not be poor, but your life is directly affected by your relationships with this part of American society."
- "Consider the daily life of a football player during the season. You may think that the idea of the student athlete is a crock, yet for football players every fall, it's a lifestyle they've got to learn to handle if they're going to survive both football and their class schedules. They need not your jealousy and disdain but your understanding and personal support."

One final point: just as you'll often maintain your own identity in the face of different others, so also will you want to urge others to act from a conviction that their own cultural identities provide the grounds for action. Karl Marx began his treatise on the proletarian revolution with the call, "Workers of the world, unite!" That very first sentence signaled his argument that workers, as a class, had to take control of their own destinies, because the upper (bourgeois) classes certainly weren't serving their interests. The phrase "Sisterhood is powerful" likewise was a rallying cry in the 1960s for that gender to recognize their own ability to influence their social, economic, and political relationships with others. Similarly, in that same period, the rallies around notions of "Black Power" and "Black is beautiful" asserted that race was a positive—not a negative—attribute of people. So, occasionally you will affirm not only your own but also others' identities as the bases of thought and action.

This is *not* to say that you'll always accept the lifestyle choices of others. There will be times you'll find it important to confront the socially dangerous or personally destructive behaviors of, for example, a drug addict or an alcoholic. There may be lifestyle choices that others have made that don't appeal to you, and you may find it impossible to accept appeals for cultural consistency, such as appeals to male bonding or sisterhood, to your whiteness or brownness, to your youth or status as an elderly person. Some questions will transcend cultural practices in your mind, and you'll be forced to assault them, such as what happens when most Americans are confronted by white supremacists. Even then, however, it's vitally important to understand all you can about culture as lived, thought, and performed so that you can select confrontational strategies with a chance of actually moving listeners to change their life patterns.

Throughout much of this book, you'll find us returning to questions of cultural life, multiculturalism, and the search for social unity. We do not approach what is essentially the cross-cultural dimensions of social life for political reasons. Although multiculturalism assuredly has strong political dimensions, our focus is cultural, not political. If you don't understand that speakers must adapt to their listeners' cultural moorings, you'll have great difficulty speaking to any but your own close circle. Social life—and, hence, public communication—is rooted in cultural practices.[23] Thus, it becomes your job to understand and to adapt your public speaking strategies to those practices.

CHAPTER SUMMARY

Culture is a social group's system of meanings. Thinking about culture as lived puts an emphasis on demographic or social categories for classifying people into groups. Cultural diversity represents differences in systems of meaning possessed by different groups in a society. Multiculturalism is a recognition that a country possesses not a unitary culture with several subcultures but a series of co-cultures that interpenetrate yet are separate from one another.

Culture also is a way of thinking. An ideology is a system of thought that embodies social values and perceptual orientations to the world. Hegemony is a concept that defines relationships between more powerful and less powerful people; those relationships are maintained in part by the complicity of the less powerful people.

Culture also is performed; you can see culture only when it is embodied. Embodiment is the process whereby ideas, attitudes, values, and social character are given corporeal existence in communication actions. Once you learn culturally significant behavior, you enact that culture when you speak. Enactment is a communication process whereby a person behaves in a manner consonant with a society's cultural rules.

The central cultural challenge that public speakers face is this: can you respect individual difference and cultural diversity while attempting to get a group of people to think alike and act together?

At least five primary strategies for communicating unity through diversity are available to public speakers: recognizing diversity while calling for unity, negotiating among diverse values, accepting multiple paths to shared goals, working through the lifestyle choices of others, and maintaining self-identity in the face of cultural difference.

KEY TERMS

co-cultures (p. 76)

common ground (p. 74)

cultural diversity (p. 76)

culture (p. 73)

culture as lived (p. 75)

culture as performed (p. 78)

culture as thought (p. 76)

embodiment (p. 78)

enactment (p. 78)

hegemony (p. 78)

ideology (p. 76)

multiculturalism (p. 76)

subcultures (p. 76)

value orientations (p. 82)

ASSESSMENT ACTIVITIES

1. Do a demographic profile of your speech classroom: have everyone anonymously record their sex, age, economic status of their family, religious background, place of birth or home state, and ethnic background. Your instructor will tabulate the results and then distribute them to everyone. Write down the central idea or claim for your next speech, and ask yourself: in what ways should the cultural backgrounds of my listeners as seen in the demographic profile affect how I handle this idea or claim? Turn it in for your instructor's comments.

2. Take one of the following topics and, by yourself or in class discussion, identify three or more valuative positions that might be held by ideologically liberal, conservative, and middle-of-the-road people. Then, suggest at least two shared goals you think might be acceptable to most people in all three groups. Work with one of the following topics:
   a. Undocumented (illegal) aliens.
   b. Equal Rights Amendment.
   c. Juvenile crime.
   d. Control and financing of public higher education.
   e. Environmental protection.

REFERENCES

1. To explore the role of social categories of human beings is to begin dealing with the "consequences of difference and divergences, boundaries and borders," in the words of Angie McRobbie (*Postmodernism and Popular Culture* [New York: Routledge, 1994], 6). Differences and divergences should not be considered as modes of

shattering society, as so often happens when scholars begin thinking about "the postmodern," but rather as challenges to individuals (speakers) who want to affect their world in positive ways.

2. What is here called, informally, "common ground" is called "radical categories" by cognitive scientist George Lakoff. A radical category is a variation of some central model. So, in one of his examples, the category "mother" can have different radicals or variations in interpretation: "(1) The birth model: the mother is one who gives birth. (2) The genetic model: the mother is the female from whom you get half of your genetic traits. (3) The nurturance model: your mother is the person who raises and nurtures you. And (4) The marriage model: your mother is the wife of your father" (*Moral Politics: What Conservatives Know That Liberals Don't* [Chicago: University of Chicago Press, 1996], 8). Radical categories are important rhetorically, because a motivational appeal to, say, "avoiding harm" may be interpreted by listeners in many ways: financial harm, physical harm, psychological harm, etc. Those are radicals or variations that allow people with quite different understandings of concepts to believe they are united with others in thought or action (in this case, united to avoid harm).

3. Some classic essays on speaking and lived culture are Gerry Philipsen, "Speaking 'Like a Man' in Teamsterville: Culture Patterns of Role Enactment in an Urban Neighborhood," *Quarterly Journal of Speech*, 61 (1975): 13–22; and his "Places for Speaking in Teamsterville," *Quarterly Journal of Speech*, 62 (1976): 16–25. Cf. D. N. Maltz and R. A. Borker, "A Cultural Approach to Male-Female Miscommunication," *Language and Social Identity*, ed. J. J. Gumperz (Cambridge, England: Cambridge University Press, 1982), 196–216. Those who pursue relationships between communication processes and lived culture often define "culture" in the way Richard Campbell does, as "the symbols of expression that individuals, groups, and societies use to make sense of daily life and to articulate their values" (*Media and Culture: An Introduction to Mass Communication* [New York: St. Martin's Press, 1998], 5).

4. For a discussion of co-cultures, see the introduction and essays in Alberto González, Marsha Houston, and Victoria Chen, eds., *Our Voices: Essays on Cultural Ethnicity and Communication*, 2nd ed. (Los Angeles: Roxbury Press, 1996). On multiculturalism's impact on public relationships and decision making, see Todd Gitlin, *The Twilight of Common Dreams: Why America is Wracked by Culture Wars* (New York: Metropolitan Books, 1995); for its history, see Stanley Aronowitz, *Roll Over Beethoven: The Return of Cultural Strife* (Hanover, NH: Wesleyan University Press, 1993).

5. For discussions of relationships between thought/speech and culture, see Donal Carbaugh, "'Soul' and 'Self': Soviet and American Cultures in Conversation," *Quarterly Journal of Speech* 79 (1993): 182–200; Randall A. Lake, "Between Myth and History: Enacting Time in Native American Protest Rhetoric," *Quarterly Journal of Speech* 77 (1991): 123–151; and Albert González, "'Participation' in WMEX-FM: Interventional Rhetoric of Ohio Mexican Americans," *Western Journal of Speech Communication* 53 (1989): 398–410. On the relationships between thought/speech and moral codes in particular, see Lakoff (n. 2), ch. 4, "Keeping the Moral Books," 44–64.

6. On the naturalization of myths and ideologies in our lives, see the classic work by French cultural theorist Roland Barthes, *Mythologies*, translated by A. Lavers (London: Paladin, 1973), especially the last chapter, "Myth Today."

7. For summaries of much work on ideology and hegemony, see the writings of John

Fiske, e.g., *Television Culture* (New York: Methuen, 1987) and *Media Matters: Everyday Culture and Political Change* (Minneapolis: University of Minnesota Press, 1994).

8. Marking places or even oneself culturally is a popular communication practice. See Dwight Conquergood, "Homeboys and Hoods: Gang Communication and Cultural Space," *Group Communication in Context: Studies of Natural Groups*, ed. Lawrence R. Frey (Hillsdale, NJ: Lawrence Earlbaum Associates, 1994), 23–55; and Dan Brouwer, "The Precarious Visibility Politics of Self-Stigmatization: The Case of HIV/AIDS Tattoos," *Text and Performance Quarterly* 18 (1998): 114–136. For an overview of embodiment, see Elaine Scarry, "The Merging of Bodies and Artifacts in the Social Contract," *Culture on the Brink: Ideologies of Technology*, ed. Gretchen Bender and Timothy Drucker (Seattle: Bay Press, 1994), 85–97.

9. For interesting studies of enactment, see Y. Griefat and Tamar Katriel, "Life Demands Musayara: Communication and Culture Among Arabs in Israel," *Language, Communication, and Culture*, ed. Stella Ting-Toomey and Filipe Korzenny (Newbury Park, CA: Sage, 1989), 121–137; and Cheryl R. Jorgensen-Earp and Lori A. Lanzilotti, "Public Memory and Private Grief: The Construction of Shrines at the Sites of Public Tragedy," *Quarterly Journal of Speech* 84 (1998): 150–170.

10. The Western linear logic to idea development is quite different from the emotion- or pathos-centered approach in classical Chinese rhetorical practice. See Mary M. Garrett, "Pathos Reconsidered from the Perspective of Classical Chinese Rhetorics," *Quarterly Journal of Speech* 79 (1993): 19–39. African Americans likewise draw from different cultural resources. See Patricia A. Sullivan, "Signification and African-American Rhetoric: A Case Study of Jesse Jackson's 'Common Ground and Common Sense' Speech," *Communication Quarterly* 42 (1993): 1–15.

11. For a discussion of these ideas, see Dennis Brissett and Charles Edgley, eds., *Life As Theatre: A Dramaturgical Sourcebook*, 2nd ed. (New York: Aldine de Gruyter, 1990).

12. From "Transcript from Minister Louis Farrakhan's remarks at the Million Man March," October 17, 1995, p. 4, available at CNN's website, http://cnn.com/US/9510/megamarch/10-16/transcript/index.html.

13. Ibid., p. 15.

14. Henri Mann Morton, "Strength Through Cultural Diversity," keynote address at the Northwest's Colville and Okanogan National Forest conference on cultural diversity, March 23, 1989, reprinted in Bruce E. Gronbeck, et al., *Principles and Types of Speech Communication*, 12th ed. (New York: Longman's, 1994), 327.

15. Stephen A. Tyler, *The Unspeakable: Discourse, Dialogue, and Rhetoric in the Postmodern World* (Madison: University of Wisconsin Press, 1987), 7.

16. On lifestyle choices, see Victoria Chen, "*Mien Tze* at the Chinese Dinner Table: A Study of the Interactional Accomplishment of Face," *Research on Language and Social Interaction* 24 (1990-1991): 109–140; and Shohana Blum-Kulka and Tamar Katriel, "Nicknaming Practices in Families: A Cross-Cultural Perspective," *Cross-Cultural Interpersonal Communication*, ed. Stella Ting-Toomey and Filipe Korzenny (Newbury Park, CA: Sage, 1991), 58–78.

17. Ruth 1:16–17, *Holy Bible*, Revised Standard Version.

18. Ruth 1:18, *Holy Bible*, Revised Standard Version.

19. Ruth 2:11–12, *Holy Bible*, Revised Standard Version.

20. The refusal to surrender one's ethnic or other lifestyle characteristic led in the 1990s to the rise of multiculturalism—the maintenance of differences in the face of pressures to eliminate them. To help you consider the impacts of surrendering or not, see

Gitlin (n. 4) or the crusty new introduction to a reissued 1972 book, Michael Novak, *Unmeltable Ethnics: Politics & Culture in American Life,* 2nd ed. (New Brunswick, NJ: Transaction Publishers, 1996), "Introduction to the Transaction Edition."

21. President Lyndon Baines Johnson, "We Shall Overcome," delivered to a joint session of Congress, March 15, 1965, reprinted in Theodore Windt, ed. *Presidential Rhetoric (1961–1980),* 2nd ed. (Dubuque, IA: Kendall/Hunt, 1980), 67.

22. Mary Fisher, address to the Republican National Convention, August 12, 1996, transcript done from the C-SPAN broadcast of the address.

23. This point is driven home in John C. Hammerback and Richard L. Jensen, "Ethnic Heritage as Rhetorical Legacy: The Plan of Delano," *Quarterly Journal of Speech* 80 (1994): 53–70. For a complete and quite compact introduction to the cultural study of human communication, see Stuart Hall, "The Work of Representation," *Representation: Cultural Presentations and Signifying Practices,* ed. Stuart Hall (Thousand Oaks, CA: Sage Publications, 1997), ch. 1, 13–17.

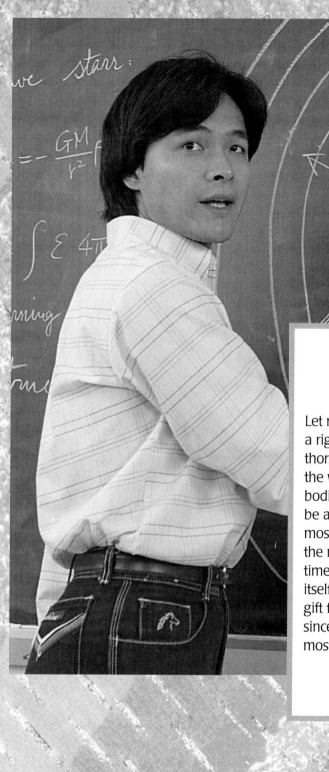

Part Two
PREPARATION

Let no one however demand from me a rigid code of rules such as most authors of textbooks have laid down. . . . If the whole of rhetoric could be thus embodied in one compact code, it would be an easy task of little compass: but most rules are liable to be altered by the nature of the case, circumstances of time and place, and by hard necessity itself. Consequently, the all-important gift for an orator is a wise adaptability since he [sic] is called upon to meet the most varied emergencies.

Quintilian
Institutio Oratoria I. xiii. 1–2

Chapter 5

Analyzing the Audience and Occasion

Public speaking is **audience** and **occasion centered.** You always speak to affect the informational repertoire, psychological state, or behavior of others, and you always speak where people (usually) have spoken before and where audience members expect particular kinds or ranges of speeches. The audience and the occasion act as guides to and constraints on speechmaking. In the words of Donald C. Bryant, since ancient Greece, the essence of public rhetoric has been that of "adjusting ideas to people and people to ideas."[1] Without engaging a particular audience at a particular time and place, you're just talking, not speaking.

A primary theme will be stressed throughout this chapter: *The goal of audience analysis is to discover which facets of listeners' demographic and psychological characteristics are relevant to your speech.* When you understand who your listeners are and which of their characteristics need to be taken into account when you talk on a specific topic, you can adapt your ideas to those characteristics. You also need to be sensitive to the demands of the occasion on your choice of themes and language. *An "occasion" includes a time and place set aside for particular events and activities; speakers must learn what people expect on those occasions and meet those expectations as fully as possible.* Where and when you speak should have concrete influences on what you say and how you say it. So, in this chapter, we first discuss the demographic and psychological features of listeners. We then take apart the rules governing speech occasions and indicate some of the specific moves you should be making while constructing your speeches to maximize your chances for rhetorical success.

ANALYZING AUDIENCES DEMOGRAPHICALLY

A **demographic analysis** is a study of the social and physical traits people hold in common. People often group themselves by such traits. For example, your gender has affected the way you play since you were a child, the young and the old often bring very different ways of thinking to bear on topics under discussion, and your level of education can affect what jobs you can apply for. Phrases such as "All women agree that . . . ," "White America is . . . ," or "The better-educated voter will . . ." signal that some group trait is particularly important to a subject under discussion. Such claims may well be exaggerated— "White America" is not really a monolithic body of people—yet they often characterize enough people to be a significant way to analyze some situation.

Many of these analyses are available publicly (e.g., public opinion polls distinguishing between men's and women's attitudes toward a set of presidential candidates), and many others can be located through research (e.g., government studies of the comparative costs of health care by age). Because you can directly observe many demographic characteristics of an audience just by looking at them, it's a good idea to begin an audience analysis with demographic factors. For most audiences, you can identify certain traits, at least generally; age, gender, education, some group memberships, and cultural and ethnic background.

Analyzing Demographic Categories

The competent speaker asks questions about the demographic characteristics of audiences to see which, if any, are relevant to the speech he or she is delivering. Consider the following categories:

- *Age:* Will the expected listeners primarily be young, middle-aged, or elderly, or will the group more likely be of mixed ages? Is there a special relationship between age groups, such as parent/child or teacher/student? Is your speech likely to be more familiar and interesting to one age group than to another?
- *Gender:* Will the listeners primarily be male or female, or will the group be split? Is this a topic likely to divide the audience along gender lines?
- *Education and experience:* How much will the listeners already know about the subject? Will their educational or experiential backgrounds allow them to grasp easily the essential ideas you want to convey?
- *Group membership:* Will the listeners belong to groups that represent specific experiences, attitudes, or identifiable values? Think how varied your answer to this question would be if you were talking to the Future Farmers of America, a Rotary International chapter in downtown Chicago, a League of Women Voters political platform meeting, or a social hour sponsored by the American Association of Retired Persons.
- *Cultural and ethnic background:* Will the listeners predominantly belong to specific cultural or ethnic groups? Are those group identifications likely to be raised by your speech? A speech arguing that English should be designated the only language spoken in elementary schools will make cultural-ethnic background relevant, because some school districts use Spanish as a primary language. A speech on where to find wild flowers for a fall bouquet, however, will not.

Using Demographic Information

The importance of demographic analysis for you as a speaker doesn't lie in simply answering these questions. Rather, *the key is to decide if any of these demo-*

graphic factors will affect your listeners' ability or willingness to understand and accept what you want to say. That is, does a particular group affiliation, age, or gender have any relevance in the situation you face? Does it influence the rhetorical choices you make in selecting a subject and developing a central idea or claim?

If you're addressing a group of citizens gathered to oppose the rezoning of an old neighborhood to stop its demolition and replacement by large apartments, for example, you should consider all of these questions. You might well assume that some of these listeners will be young married couples who can only afford cheaper, older housing. Others in the audience will be elderly, living on fixed incomes, who are unable to afford more expensive housing. If you know something about the neighborhood, you also may assume that they belong to one or more specific ethnic groups and that you'll have to relate to them in terms of their cultural backgrounds. You even might assume that some tenants in the rental properties will be on Aid to Families with Dependent Children, some employed in low-paying jobs, some unemployed, and still others in job-training programs. Overall, these are some of the demographic characteristics of many people who live in older, urban, inner-city neighborhoods. With these demographic characteristics in mind, you might adapt your speech to your listeners by using the following strategies:

- Avoid technical jargon.
- Give examples demonstrating that you understand the audience members want to maintain less expensive housing both by necessity and by choice.
- Recognize that a cross-section of urban society is banding together to save another neighborhood from being gentrified.

Demographic analysis can help you select and phrase your key ideas, and it sensitizes you to crucial factors that may influence your choice of themes, examples, and other supporting material. If your analysis is cursory or incomplete, you decrease your chances of being understood and of reaching agreement. Even when you're aware of the demographic characteristics, however, you still may create problems with your choice of language. Speaking to a group of African Americans, for example, and referring to them as "you people" and "your people" will demonstrate your lack of sensitivity and judgment—as Ross Perot discovered to his dismay when he addressed such an audience during the opening weeks of his 1992 presidential campaign. Appropriate use of demographic information can help you avoid such problems and convey a sensitive and caring attitude toward your listeners.

ANALYZING AUDIENCES PSYCHOLOGICALLY

Dividing audience members into **psychological profiles** on the basis of their beliefs, attitudes, and values also helps you adapt to their needs and interests. This is especially important if you intend to influence your listeners' thinking on issues. You need to know what ideas they already accept before you try altering their thoughts and actions. Sometimes careful demographic analysis will create such groupings naturally and provide clues about what your audience members think. For example, at a gathering of farmers who still farm a quarter-section (160 acres) or less, you can assume that most will strongly oppose so-called macroswine production facilities, where 2,000 or more hogs are raised at a single location. This demographic group likely will be worried about the smell, the fouling of the air when liquid manure is sprayed over fields to dispose of it, the possibility of polluting the local watershed, and the arrival of other signs of corporate farming. You can be pretty sure that they'll have great interest in legislation controlling the size of swine production facilities and the positions of gubernatorial candidates on such issues. When you have a more diversified audience, however, you might need to work on psychological profiling without much help from demographics; you'll have to explore beliefs, attitudes, values, and desires or fantasies in other ways.

Beliefs

The first task of psychological profiling is to understand an audience's beliefs. **Beliefs** are convictions about what is true or false. They arise from firsthand experience, public opinion, supporting evidence, authorities, and even blind faith. For example, you might believe that Anatomy is a difficult course based on your own experience. At the same time, you may believe that anatomy is important because it's required for the pre-med sequence, which you want to pursue as a concentration. So, although each belief is held for different reasons, both are considered true. Beliefs come in many different forms:

1. Beliefs that can be demonstrated and held confidently are called **facts.** Generally, facts are supported by strong external evidence. When you

FIGURE 5.1   The Varieties of Belief

	Beliefs of Fact	Beliefs of Opinion
Fixed Beliefs	Vegetarians live longer, healthier lives.	Broccoli tastes good.
Variable Beliefs	The quality of life I live depends on eating no meat.	It might be fun to learn to cook vegetarian meals.

say, "Research has proven that smokers can clear almost all damaging materials out of their bodies by not smoking for 10 years," you're very sure of that belief. You hold facts with certainty, because you have hard evidence to support them (in this case, many scientific studies).

2. **Opinions** are personal beliefs that may not be supported by strong external evidence. You may think that all cats are nasty animals, either because you've been scratched by cats or because you're allergic to them. However, your experience is limited. Many people like cats even if you don't. An opinion is a personal belief supported with less compelling external evidence than a fact. Sometimes many people hold the same opinion—that President Clinton was or was not guilty of "high crimes and misdemeanors" in the Lewinsky affair, or that the use of tanning booths is safer than direct exposure to sunlight—though they may not have a lot of strong, independent verification of the truth of that opinion. No matter how many hold it, it's still an opinion, not a fact.[2]

3. Some beliefs are variable, or relatively open to change, while others are fixed. **Fixed beliefs** are those that are highly resistant to change; they have been reinforced throughout a lifetime, making them central to one's thinking. Many childhood beliefs, such as "Bad behavior will be punished," "If you work hard, you'll succeed," or "Rich people cheated to get where they are" are fixed beliefs. The problem with stereotyped beliefs is that rich people may pay the taxes they owe and that sometimes bad people win. **Stereotypes** ignore individual differences and exceptions to rules, fixed beliefs often can be too rigid.

4. **Variable beliefs** are less well anchored in your mind and experiences. You might enter college thinking that you want to be a computer programmer; however, after an instructor praises your abilities in a speech class, you may consider becoming a speech writer. Then, you take a marketing class and find you're good at planning advertising campaigns. This sort of self-discovery continues as you take additional classes. Your beliefs about your talents change with your personal experiences. The same is true, of course, for members of your audience. One of your jobs in assessing beliefs is figuring out which of the listeners' beliefs relevant to your speech are variable. That is, which of their beliefs can you change to get them to go along with your central idea or claim?

Fact or opinion, fixed or variable, beliefs are those parts of people's psychological profiles that you should assess first, because they'll determine what kinds of supporting materials you'll want to use in clarifying a central idea or defend a claim.

Attitudes

The second task of psychological profiling is to identify audience attitudes. **Attitudes** are tendencies to respond positively or negatively to people, objects, or ideas. Attitudes are emotionally weighted as well. They express individual preferences and feelings such as, "I like my public speaking class," "Classical music is better than rap music," and "Cleveland is a beautiful city."

As a speaker, you should consider the dominant attitudes of your listeners. Audiences may have attitudes toward you, your speech subject, and your purpose. Your listeners may think you know a lot about your topic, and they may be interested in learning more. This is an ideal situation. If they think you're not very credible and they resist learning more, however, you must deal with their attitudes. For example, if a speaker says that you can earn extra money in your spare time by working at a telemarketing company, you might have a complex set of attitudinal reactions: You feel good about earning extra money, but you don't know enough about telemarketing to have an opinion on the topic. You also didn't especially care for the speaker when you talked with that person in the cafeteria last week, which affects how you feel about the proposal. Relationships among your attitudes toward the speech topic, purpose, and speaker can be complex, and how you trace out those relationships in your own mind will influence your final decision about telephoning strangers.

Attitudes express people's orientations toward the world—and even the factual conditions existing in the world. No matter how rational and fundamentally sound your analysis of some problem, therefore, you need to deal with attitudes. They're the keys to human reactions and, hence, to people's willingness to accept or reject ideas.

Values

The third component of psychological profiling is understanding audience values. **Values** are relatively enduring conceptions of ultimate goods and evils in human relationships as well as of the best and worse ways of pursuing those goods and evils. According to Milton Rokeach, such a definition recognizes that human beings have both **terminal values** and **instrumental values**—values toward which they aspire as well as values about the best ways of living out those aspirations.[3] Because values are the "big" concepts that we use to organize our beliefs and attitudes, they become central to rhetorical decision making.

Suppose that you and a friend might agree that economic gain is the primary goal worth pursuing in your first job yet disagree about how to best go after it. You might hold "efficiency" as a value and, hence, look for ways to gain salary and raises quickly and with the least effort. Your friend might hold "stability" as an important value and, hence, want to make more money only within a conservative company that offers good benefits. Both of you can cite popular wisdom guiding your action—you, "A stitch in time saves nine," and your friend, "Haste makes waste"—so it's not as though one of you is legitimated by society and the other is not. Rather, you hold conflicting instrumental values while pursuing the same terminal value.

Values are more foundational than beliefs and attitudes, because they represent the broad conceptual categories that help attitudes and beliefs cohere. Values serve as the foundations for the beliefs and attitudes that cluster around them. For example, a person may hold a value such as "Life is sacred." That value can be expressed in multiple attitudes, including "Abortion is wrong" or "Hunting is immoral." That value also may be expressed in beliefs such as "A fetus is a living human being with human rights" or "Hunting animals in the wild causes them cruel suffering."

Values, then, underlie an individual's particular attitudes and beliefs. Notice how billionaire entrepreneur George Soros works from common economic values to argue for "the decisive role that international financial capital plays in the fortunes of individual countries":

> The system is very favorable to financial capital, which is free to go where it is best rewarded. This has led to the rapid growth of global financial markets. The result is a giant circulatory system, sucking capital into the financial markets and institutions at the center and then pumping it out to the periphery either directly, as credits and portfolio investments, or indirectly through multinational corporations. . . . Until the Thai crisis in 1997, . . . [4]

Notice that Mr. Soros argued that "financial capital" is valued by its ability to travel easily around the world. He makes factual assertions about the rapidity of capital growth, going to the analogy of the circulatory system to make the belief statements more clear. Then, he begins an example to show that his valuing of financial capital over other economic factors can explain the operation of the real world—Thailand in 1997.

Because values exist in broad mixtures for most of us—as for Mr. Soros—they're often thought about collectively as **value orientations** or **ideologies.** Value orientations are aggregations of values shared by large numbers of people. Over the last decade, Americans have discussed neoconservatism, welfarism, the New World Order. Perot conservatism (and liberalism), "me"-ism, personal responsibility commitments, and a multitude of other value orientations or ideologies. They organize a great range of attitudes and serve as what Kenneth Burke called "terministic screens"—sieves that let some ideas through while filtering out others.[5] Being able to refer to value orientations held by audience members is a great advantage for speakers.

Desires, Visions, and Fantasies

Closely related to value orientations are **desires** and **fantasies.** We live in an era when desire, pleasure, and fantasy are understood less as escape mechanisms—a lecture often given by parents to their children—and more as vehicles for cultural identity and even political statements. At least since Dick Hebdige in 1978 offered his study of "style," we have realized that items of art, literature, music, dress, and expressed attitudes are both identity markers—showing the world who we are—and political statements. The fans of reggae who wear dreadlocks as a style and relive Bob Marley's music as political statements are exploring desire, pleasure, and fantasy as means of self-definition and political persuasion.[6]

Ernest Bormann calls group fantasies "rhetorical visions." A **rhetorical vision** is "the unified putting-together of the various scripts which give the participants a broader view of things."[7] That putting-together may occur around a master analogy, such as Franklin Roosevelt's "New Deal" or Bill Clinton's "New Covenant." Even more potent, perhaps, is the narrative center of such visions: the story of the New Israel that the Puritan used to envision the society they

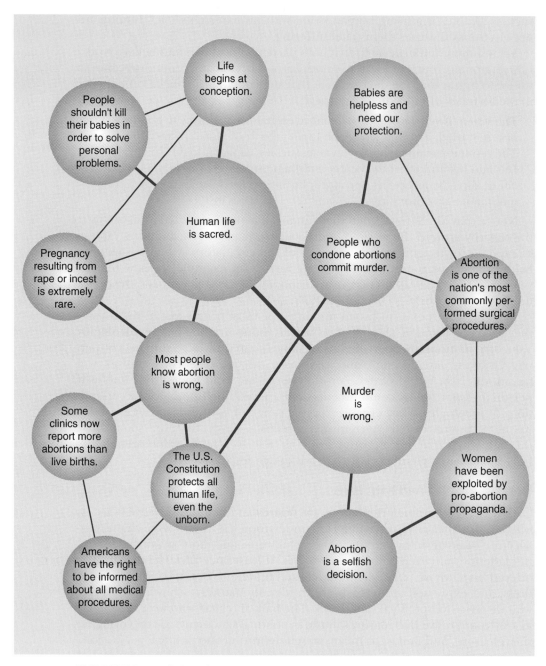

FIGURE 5.2   Belief, Attitude, and Value Clusters

were building in seventeenth-century America; the story of the proletarian revolution and upheaval of the social world that lay at the base of Marxism; and the vision of a new society created in love, creative suffering, and soul force that Martin Luther King, Jr., regularly described for his audiences. When all of an audience's existence is captured in such depictions, Bormann calls them "life-style rhetorical visions."[8]

Expressions of collective desire commonly are found in the conclusions of speeches, when speakers hope to leave listeners in a state of agreement and a frame of mind to work to achieve that which has been agreed on. It was just such a hope for common desire that Abraham Lincoln tried to articulate at the end of his first inaugural address:

> We are not enemies, but friends. We must not be enemies. Though passion may have strained it must not break our bonds of affection. The mystic chords of memory, stretching from every battlefield and patriot grave to every living heart and hearthstone all over this broad land, will yet swell the chorus of the Union, when again touched, as surely they will be, by the better angels of our nature.[9]

Rhetorical visions of society and of listeners' lives within that society also are regularly built by powerful speakers to renew or redirect an audience's political energies, to justify traditional courses of action, and to articulate new motivations for moving down new paths. They become the lenses through which group members are asked to view the world and to act within it. For example, notice the use of a rhetorical vision in the following quotation from Henri Mann Morton, a Native-American woman addressing the Colville and Okanogan National Forest conference on cultural diversity:

> I share your 1995 vision of a racially, culturally, gender-based, and humanistically representative workforce in which attitudes of respect, acceptance, and understanding are all pervasive.
>
> The vision I see is dedicated to a love of life, to a love of people, and love of the environment, particularly the land—the earth, she who is our grandmother, who must be revered and protected; she upon whom we walk and live; she who supports our feet and gives us life; she who nurtures us, her children. We all share this bond and as culturally diverse people we can draw strength from our rich cultural diversity.
>
> I would like to share with you this Cheyenne philosophical belief: "A nation is not conquered until the hearts of its women are on the ground. Then it is done, no matter how brave its warriors nor how strong its weapons."
>
> This shows the acceptance of, and respect for, the power of women. As equal partners of men, who too, have their own power, we then can see why the most powerful of all pairs in the universe are men and women working together.[10]

Notice how she intertwines a general vision of cultural diversity with a specific depiction, through quotation, of male-female union. The source of social life is seen in a feminine image of the grandmother and then is elaborated in the Cheyenne aphorism. This allows Morton's rhetorical vision to have breadth yet a unitary focus—on grandmother earth as the center of her dream.

If beliefs, attitudes, and values have a strongly cognitive or reasoned core to them, then matters of desire, vision, and fantasy are more emotional—separated from the external world and a part of people's worlds of feelings and psychological well-being. Trying to understand the desires, visions, and fantasies of audience members is tricky business; by asking some listeners beforehand, however, "What do you hope will come out this discussion?" you might get some clues to how you can tap into the power of feeling-states in your speeches.

Using a Psychological Profile

After you've developed a profile of your audience's beliefs, attitudes, values, and rhetorical visions, how can you use this information? Three ways are obvious:

1. *Understanding your audience's beliefs, attitudes, values, desires, and visions will help you frame your ideas.* For example, if an audience generally believes that childhood is crucial to human development, you might persuade them to volunteer for a day-care cooperative. If they espouse family values, your job should be even easier. If you have no indication that they're particularly interested in child development, however, you'll have to establish the crucial nature of youth and its development before you can ask for volunteers.

2. *Understanding your audience's beliefs, attitudes, values, desires, and fantasies will help you select your supporting materials.* Statistics generally work well with highly educated audiences but less well with those having little education. People who are attitudinally and valuatively involved with a topic are much more likely to scrutinize the evidence you use than people who are not.[11] Churchgoers, for example, are likely to understand and appreciate a rhetorical vision in which divine intervention in human life is described.

3. *Understanding your audience's beliefs, attitudes, values, desires, and rhetorical visions allows you to set realistic expectations as you plan your speech.* Not all audiences are equally amenable to change. You must always look for signs of resistance—deeply anchored beliefs and values, deep feelings of distrust or fear—when designing a speech. It's not likely that you'll convert a Christian to Islam or a Muslim to Judaism in one shot. In a group of college sophomores, however, several people are likely to be looking for a new major and probably are anxious about the process, in which case a speech on the usefulness and value of majoring in technology studies might prove most provocative.

ANALYZING THE SPEECH OCCASION

Sometimes analyzing the speech occasion is simple: You know you're attending a National Communication Association Speech Club meeting, you've been there often, and you know what's expected from you when asked to present a 5- to 10-minute report on public relations internship possibilities in local medical organizations. At other times, the occasions are complex, with rules and traditions governing what can be said, who can talk, how and when people can talk, and in what manner you must treat other people. While you may not have thought much about it, "an occasion" can control how you behave when talking to others.

As we've suggested, an **occasion** is a set of activities that occurs in a time and place set aside expressly to fulfill the collective goals of people who have been taught the special meanings of those activities. Let us unpack this definition.

In a time and place . . . Regular occasions, such as religious services, usually occur at special times (Fridays, Saturdays, Sundays) and in special places (mosques, synagogues, churches). Special events, such as political conventions, happen at specific times in halls designed to accommodate the people present and decorated to capture the value orientation and rhetorical vision of the party. These times and places take on special meanings of their own. Sunday morning in the United States is such a special time that many activities are scheduled around church services. The places where justice is handed down—courtrooms—are specially designed to emphasize permanence (made of marble), spaciousness (high ceilings in oversized rooms), elevation (the bench is raised above all other chairs so the judge looks down on everyone else), and impartiality (a black robe hides the individual features of the judge). As such, courtrooms have come to be known as quiet, decorous places where respect is shown to all parties.

Fulfilling collective goals . . . Most important, perhaps, people design occasions to meet the particular needs of particular groups, such as worship (church), justice (courts), passage to adulthood (bar mitzvahs, confirmations, debutante balls, commencement ceremonies), remembrance of basic values or heroes (monument dedications, holidays such as Memorial Day), and recognition of leadership and power (inaugurals, coronations). These are all activities in which individuals tend to participate as part of a group; a one-person ceremony or dedication doesn't mean much.

Special meanings . . . You don't enter the world knowing how to pray, cheer, dedicate, mourn with others, or inaugurate. Those are *social* activities that you must learn, either through instruction or through imitation.[12] Knowing and understanding what is expected of you and others are signs of belonging to a particular group. Outsiders do not possess this knowledge; insiders do.

The purposes, complexity, and even formality of occasions vary widely. A presentation to your public relations club may be an informal yet an important occasion; funerals and political conventions are much more formal. No matter what their formality, however, all occasions are governed by *rules* (do's and don't's), *roles* (duties or functions that different people perform), and judgments of *competency* (assessments about how well people play their parts). Occasions normally involve rather precise expectations of what will happen, to whom it will happen, who will participate, and how they will take part.[13]

A speech occasion is thus every bit as demanding as any other social or political event. Like other occasions, speech occasions are characterized by rules, expected roles, and judgments of competency—in other words, by audience expectations. Those expectations take two forms. **General audience expectations** are those associated with any public speaker working in a particular society. In the United States, this includes such rules as speakers shouldn't mumble; the larger the room, the larger your gestures should be; trusted speakers look audience members right in the eyes; and an excessive number or random gestures detracts from your message. Not all of these rules hold in every society, they're the products of this society. The second form, **specific audience expectations,** arise from habitual speaking practices in particular settings. Politicians on the campaign trail are expected to be enthusiastic, celebrate their own virtues, and attack their opponents. In some churches, preachers are expected to be even more excited and to deliver speeches filled with divine energy. Insurance salespeople are trained to ask questions of their listeners in the middle of their presentations ("How does this sound to you?" "Are these problems you face?" "Doesn't this make sense, given how young your children are?"). In some situations, you're expected to be an informer (orientation meeting), in others a comic (an after-dinner speech honoring a close friend), and in others, a persuader (a real-estate office).

As you face such audience expectations, you have three choices:

1. *Ignore the rules.* Sometimes a free spirit—a David Letterman or a Howard Stern—can ignore the usual rules for public speech and get away with it. Most of us, however, aren't nearly as interesting as they are. If you break too many rules, you can be broken—by your audience who thinks you don't know or care about their traditions.
2. *Cave in.* Equally dangerous is to accept all the rules, even if they go against your beliefs and backgrounds. If you visit a family with an overbearing mother who no one ever crosses and you feel insulted by something she says about you, do you cave in and say nothing? If so, the rules for speaking have stifled you.
3. *Adapt to the rules.* There are good ways, of course, for disagreeing with the mother just described. You can verbally recognize her place in the family but then note the injury her remark has done to you, defending yourself from an unfair attack. You can work within the aura of her family position while making your point if you're very, very careful.

Audience expectations, in other words, should be seen as opportunities to find ways into people's minds, not as barriers that stop communication. For that to happen, you must learn to read occasions—to interpret their effect on your speaking.

USING AUDIENCE ANALYSIS IN SPEECH PREPARATION

Neither demographic analysis nor psychological profiling is an end in itself, nor will merely thinking about the speech occasion produce foolproof speech preparation strategies. Rather, you perform these twin analyses to discover what might affect the reception of you and your message. You're searching for relevant factors that can affect the audience's attitudes toward you, your subject, and your purpose. In turn, these factors should guide your rhetorical choices regarding subject matter, themes covered, language used, and the appropriateness of visual aids in the speech setting.

Audience Targeting: Setting Realistic Goals

There are few occasions in which the choice of general speech purpose—to inform, to persuade or actuate, to entertain—is problematic. Once you've passed beyond this step, you need to determine what you can accomplish with a particular audience in the time available. As you think about **audience targeting,** five considerations are relevant: *your specific purpose, the audience's areas of interest, their capacity to act, their willingness to act,* and *the degree of change you can expect.* While what appears to be a reasonable or realistic aim may fall short of your actual goal, working within these parameters will make it far easier for you to obtain audience support for your ideas. Moving too far beyond what is realistic will, in general, increase the risk that your listeners won't follow you— even if they're sympathetic to the thrust of your remarks.

Your Specific Purpose.   Suppose that you have a part-time job with your college's Cooperative Education Office. You're familiar with its general goals and the programs, and you have sufficient personal interest to speak about these to other campus groups. What you have discovered about different audiences should help you determine appropriate, specific purposes for each. If you were to talk to a group of incoming first-year students at new student orientation, for example, you would know these things beforehand:

- They probably know little or nothing about the functions of a cooperative education office (they have few, if any, fixed beliefs about the office).
- They probably are predisposed to look favorably on cooperative education once they know how it functions (given their own career aspirations).
- They probably are, at their current stage of life and educational level, more concerned with practical issues such as selecting their courses, seeing an advisor, registering, and learning about basic degree requirements (whether a foreign language is required for English majors, whether a calculus course is required for business majors). While they want to be well-positioned to make the most of their junior or senior year, learning specifics about what they can do "if and when" is not a high priority at this time. Hence, they may require external motivation (provided by your arguments and illustrations) to develop interest in the subject.
- They are likely to see you as an authoritative speaker, especially if you're introduced—(or you introduce yourself)—as a staff member from Cooperative Education, and they likely are willing to listen to what you have to say.

Given these audience considerations, you probably should keep your presentation fairly general. Explain the principal functions of Cooperative Education, and review the prerequisites that must be met to be qualified (e.g., having

HOW TO

ANALYZE THE SPEECH OCCASION

- *What is the nature and purpose of the occasion?* Make sure the subject and purpose of your speech relate to the purpose of the meeting. If your speech is part of a series or will follow other speeches, find out the other speakers' approaches and decide how you will distinguish yours. If you are facing a **captive audience** (a group that is forced to attend), make an extra effort to show the significance of your subject to them.

- *What are the prevailing rules or customs?* Find out what customs are accepted in the speech situation: Is there a fixed program into which your speech must fit? Will listeners expect a formal speaking manner? An expression of respect for a tradition or concept? Also, find out whether there are more specific rules. For example, the audience at the Friars Club in New York expects the speaker to mercilessly "roast" (verbally abuse) the object of the specch—but in a good-natured way.

- *What are the physical conditions?* Will you speak outdoors or indoors? Will the audience sit or stand? How large will the room be? Will you need to bring your own audiovisual equipment? If the conditions will negatively affect your presentation, consider moving your audience closer together or helping them change locations to avoid excessive heat or moisture. If outside noise interferes, speak more loudly and distinctly than you normally would.

- *What events precede and follow your speech?* If you will speak right after a meal or at the end of a long program, acknowledge your listeners' reduced interest and potential drowsiness. Give them time to stretch and otherwise get comfortable. If you are the "warm-up" speaker, be careful to follow the customs and rules of the occasion. Consider the character of any other items on the program to get a sense of how the group functions, perhaps even getting clues about its basic values.

- *Have I figured out ways to target specific appeals to each significant segment of the audience?*

- *Can I create a rhetorical vision that will encompass both my purpose and my listeners' understandings of the world?*

selected a major and completed a set number of courses). Stress how a cooperative education experience can give them an early start on a possible career or introduce them to new career possibilities, all while earning academic credit. You might phrase your specific purpose as follows: "To brief incoming first-year students on the range of service offered by the Cooperative Education Office." That orientation would include a basic description of each service and a general appeal to use these services to make some curricular decisions.

Were you instead to talk about this subject to a group of college juniors, you would address the audience differently. You also would know these things beforehand:

- They are more likely to be aware of the general goals and programs of the Cooperative Education Office, but they may be misinformed—or even uninformed—about details.
- They generally have positive feelings about the advantages of cooperative education, but some may be unsure of whether it's well suited to their major or career interest or of whether they meet the prerequisite conditions for enrollment.
- They tend to value education pragmatically, that is, for how it's prepared them to earn a "decent living."
- They may view your qualifications with somewhat more skepticism, because you're one of their peers.

Given these factors, you should be much more specific in some areas. You should describe your own recent experience as a co-op student or, if you have yet to enroll in a co-op program, those of students who have completed the experience. First-person stories will help convince the audience that a wide variety of students can profit from co-op education—and that all they need do is check with the office to see if they qualify. In addition to fleshing out particulars about the "what" of cooperative education, you'll need to spend time on the "how": What steps should students take if they're interested in enrolling? Should they pursue employers on their own? If they know an employer, can he or she be involved?

You might phrase your dominant specific purpose in this way: "To inform juniors about the benefits gained by enrolling in Eastern University's Cooperative Education Program." Your subordinate purposes might include "Demonstrating the ease with which students can enroll in the program" and "Illustrating that almost every student may be served."

Areas of Audience Interest.   You can use both demographic analysis and psychological profiling to help you decide what ideas will interest your listeners. This is critical in narrowing your topic choice and in choosing specific ideas to develop. Suppose that you know something about communicating with people from diverse cultures. An audience of new management trainees for an international firm would be very interested in hearing how communication may differ as one moves from a Japanese to a Latin American market. An audience of mid-level managers for the same company could want to know more, if only to assess for themselves whether a new training program should be put online. An audience of vice-presidents and regional managers would want to know how insensitivity to communication across cultures may affect employee morale as well as company productivity and profits.

Sometimes, however, you will want to create a new set of interests in an audience. For example, you might want to inform a group of college students about southwestern cooking. Some audience members already may have more than a passing interest in the culinary arts, while others may be relatively uninformed and uninterested. For those already interested, you can draw connections between traditional midwestern, meat-and-potatoes flavors and those of southwestern cuisine. For those not already interested, you should work from backgrounds in southwestern food they already have. You could show how southwestern cuisine is built around some flavors they already know from fast-food Mexican restaurants and how easy it is for them to broaden their taste by learning how to order different courses. For this speech, you might phrase your central idea as "Knowing more about southwestern cooking will open up whole new, exciting, food-preparation and eating experiences." Phrasing the central idea in this way ties the subject to both segments of your audience.

The Audience's Capacity to Act.   As noted in the section on narrowing speech subjects, limit your request to an action that lies within your listeners' range of authority. Don't ask them to accomplish the impossible. To demand that a group of college students take direct action to stop the netting of tuna is unre-

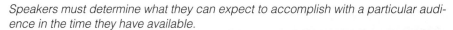

Speakers must determine what they can expect to accomplish with a particular audience in the time they have available.

alistic, for example, especially if you're in the corn belt of the United States. However, you can ask them to boycott tuna and other products associated with tuna harvesting that are not marked as "dolphin safe." You also can urge them to write their local congressional representatives to implore their support for more stringent fishing regulations and put them in touch with larger organizations already lobbying on this problem.

Sometimes an audience analysis reveals that different segments of your audience have varying capacities to undertake actions. If so, you'll want to address those segments separately in the action step of your speech. For example, in addressing an open meeting of the city council on why the city should sponsor a major fund-raising road race, you'll want to target different subgroups with different calls to action:

- *Council members:* "Pass a special appropriation to the recreation services budget that funds a part-time race director and publicity chair."
- *Potential race sponsors:* "Support the race by contributing money, food, and prizes for the various race categories."
- *Runners:* "Use your contacts at other marathons, 10K and 5K races, and charity walks to bring out-of-towners to this event."

By using this method, each call for action is suited to the range of authority and talents possessed by each subgroup of listeners.

The Audience's Willingness to Act.   Not only must you be concerned with audience authority but also with audience will. You'll need to assess the degree to which listeners are willing to put themselves on the line for your ideas or proposals. For example, a speech urging students to upgrade their CPR training has a better chance of success when given at a fraternity or sorority meeting about service projects than it does in your speech classroom. People attending the meeting are committed to the idea of public service—or they wouldn't have come to listen. On the other hand, people in your classroom are strongly aware that you're "practicing" public address; hence, they're usually more distanced from you, more attuned to the quality of your appeals and style of speaking, and less caught up in the spirit of advice-following. They are difficult listeners to reach, because they hear so many appeals from fellow students during the term.

Your assessment of an audience's will or desire may influence the wording of your claim. Addressing a fraternity, sorority, or a panhellenic council comprising both groups, you might phrase a claim in this fashion: "Running a campaign to upgrade students' CPR skills is the best service project our organization can undertake this semester." In your speech classroom, you might phrase this same claim differently. "You should upgrade your CPR training as a matter of personal commitment to human beings in need." The first version acknowledges both the purpose of the meeting (identifying a service project) and the willingness of the listeners to act on some project. The second version plays down or ignores the occasion (a classroom speech), because that occasion doesn't encourage listeners to take your advice. Instead, the wording personalizes the subject, allowing the speaker to tug on at least a few heartstrings.

Degrees of Change.   Finally, as suggested earlier, you must be realistic in targeting the degree of change you can reasonably hope to obtain. In an informative context, there is a natural limit on how much information you can present about the topic due to the time limits and the complexity of the subject. For instance, it would take more than a 5-minute speech to do justice to the controversy surrounding changes in traffic beltways. Demographic factors such as age, work location, and educational development will influence how much change you can effect. In addition, deciding whether the information is new or already known will influence how much material you can cover in a single speech. Talking to a group of people who commute to work in a city is one thing; talking to people who live in a small, relatively uncrowded town of 40,000 is another.

In other words, audience analysis should help you determine how to phrase your specific purpose, central ideas, and claims for maximum effectiveness. The understanding you gain about your audience in this manner also gives you a more realistic expectation of the degree of change in behavior, beliefs, attitudes, values, and commitments to action that is possible.

Audience Segmentation: Selecting Dominant Ideas and Appeals

The preceding discussion of demographic analysis and psychological profiling of relevant beliefs, attitudes, values, and desires or fantasies focused on targeting your audience as a group. Keep in mind, however, that no matter how people are crowded together, arranged in rows, or reached electronically, they're still individuals. Although influenced by culture and society, each person holds unique beliefs, attitudes, values, and aspirations. You also function as a unique individual when approaching the audience as a speaker.

Ideally, approaching each listener one-on-one would be most effective. Sometimes you can, but such communication is time-consuming and inefficient in matters of broad public concern. Imagine an evangelist such as Billy Graham talking to each one of us individually. If you assume 160 million adults and five minutes per person, it would take 300 million minutes—or more than 570 years of nonstop talking! Rather than take that approach, it's no wonder that religious leaders have resorted to broadcasting their messages simultaneously to millions of television viewers. They have found that they can simulate the atmosphere of personal conversation through their delivery and choice of language. In so doing, they can begin to think of listeners as individuals hearing the message in the privacy of their own homes.

These evangelists and their advisers have adopted a technique long familiar to advertisers: audience segmentation. **Audience segmentation** is a matter of dividing a mass audience into subgroups—or "target populations"—that hold common attitudes, beliefs, values, or demographic characteristics. The earlier illustration of addressing city council members, sponsors, and runners in

Effective persuasion on the speaker's analysis of both demographic and psychological profiles of the audience.

terms of their different capacities to act is an instance of such segmentation. A typical college-student audience might be segmented by academic standing (freshmen through seniors), academic majors (art through zoology), classroom performance (A through F), and even extracurricular activities (officer training programs, varsity sports, recreational clubs, political groups). It is up to *you* to decide which segments make the most sense for your speeches.

Accurately Identifying Subgroups/Segments. The process of identifying subgroups must be accurate and relevant to the speech purpose and occasion. This will not only allow you to better phrase your appeals, it will help you avoid irritating your listeners unnecessarily. A speaker who begins with "Now you girls are going to have to realize that we guys are more interested in your bodies than your minds" probably would alienate three subgroups in the audience. The female members probably would be irritated at being called "girls" and identified as mere bodies. The male members who, in fact, are attracted to females who are literate, smart, and capable of clever conversation also would be offended by having been excluded. Gay and lesbian members would see once again the heterosexual parts of the world getting all of the attention. The appeal would be better phrased as "Because we're all interested in establishing satisfying interpersonal relationships, . . ." This appeal aims at the proper audience segments—all people interested in various kinds of relationships—and allows audience members to fill in the individual relationships about which they're worried.

Selecting Relevant Psychological Statements.   Audience segmentation also should help you identify statements of belief, attitudes, values, and desire to include in your speech. If you can accurately identify the relevant subgroups, you can include psychological appeals for each in your speech, thereby greatly increasing the personal appeal and potential effectiveness of your message.

Suppose that you were invited to an agricultural gathering of interested parties to talk about the Freedom to Farm Act, which removed federal price supports for agricultural products and deregulated many parts of agribusiness. If you were defending the claim that "The Freedom to Farm Act will, in the long run, greatly improve the working and business conditions for agriculture," you'd want to suggest factual and valuative benefits for various segments of the audience:

- *Farmers:* "You'll be able to use the futures markets, crop insurance, and individualized contracts with buyers to better control your own destiny." (Appeal to freedom and profitability.)
- *Government representatives:* "You'll no longer have to handle the problem of price support legislation, but instead will be able to concentrate on developmental research and negotiations for opening up new markets for American agriculture." (Appeal to excitement, new challenges.)
- *Marketers of farm products:* "You're now able to negotiate your own prices with suppliers and your own contracts with domestic and foreign buyers." (Appeal to financial flexibility.)
- *Insurance companies:* "You'll see great growth in your agricultural business now that you, rather than the federal government, will be safeguarding farmers' investments." (Appeal to growing financial prosperity.)
- *Consumer advocates:* "Without the federal government serving as the major player in farming and marketing, you'll be fulfilling your watch-dog functions by examining the principal players' actual transactions, for which they alone are responsible." (Appeal to control and effectiveness.)[14]

Although this segmentation has not used every conceivable value term, the procedure should be clear: think through possible reasons people might accept your claim because of values they hold, and use a value-sensitive vocabulary to phrase your actual appeals for acceptance. Thus, audience analyses—in combination with audience segmentation—are valuable tools for selecting your main lines of appeal and argument.

Choosing Among Valuative Appeals.   Finally, as you might guess, audience segmentation will help you select a valuative vocabulary for your speeches. Even informative speeches must contain appeals to audience interests. You can use a **valuative vocabulary** to motivate different segments of the audience to listen to and accept your information. For a class demonstration, for example, you might introduce your speech in this way:

Gardening with raised beds has become all the rage. And today, I want to show you how you can do it, even with a small plot. Raised-bed gardening produces more flowers and vegetables per square yard than conventional gardening [*efficiency value*], cuts the time spent weeding to a minimum [*pragmatic value*], and gives you the satisfaction of having designed and executed a beautiful addition to your window boxes or yard [*personal satisfaction value*].

With that statement, you give your audience three different reasons for listening and have a good chance of appealing to every listener. If you want, you also can tell them the growing flowers and vegetable plants will be beautiful, thereby adding an *aesthetic value* as well.

Creating a Unifying Vision or Fantasy

Ultimately, an audience must act together. Therefore, although you can individualize appeals to particular segments, ideally you should find a vision—a big picture—that brings all the segments back into a whole. One of two approaches is traditionally used. When addressing the 1988 Democratic National Convention, Jesse Jackson used the *additive method*, reassembling the segments but allowing each sub-audience to keep it own identity. After describing how his grandmother in Greenville, South Carolina, sewed together old, mismatched pieces of cloth to make blankets, he admonished his audience to do likewise:

> Now, Democrats, we must build such a quilt. Farmers, you seek fair prices and you are right, but you cannot stand alone. Your patch is not big enough. Workers, you fight for fair wages. You are right. But your patch, labor, is not big enough. Women, you seek comparable worth and pay equity. You are right. But your patch is not big enough. Women, mothers, you seek Head Start and day care and prenatal care on the front side of life, you're right, but your patch is not big enough.
>
> Students, you seek scholarships. You are right. But your patch is not big enough. Blacks and Hispanics, when we fight for civil rights, we are right, but our patch is not big enough. Gays and lesbians, when you fight against discrimination and for a cure for AIDS, you are right, but your patch is not big enough. Conservatives and progressives, when you fight for what you believe, right-wing, left-wing, hawk, dove—you are right, from your point of view, but your point of view is not enough.
>
> But don't despair. Be as wise as grandmama. Pool the patches and the pieces together, bound by a common thread. When we form a great quilt of unity and common ground, we'll have the power to bring about health care and housing and jobs and education and hope to our nation. We the people can win.[15]

Jesse Jackson thus added the segments of his audience together, sewing their patches into a large, Democratic quilt. Using the additive method, he enabled each segment to retain its identity in the rhetorical vision.

The *integrative method* for constructing a vision strips the individual segments of their identities, attempting to make everyone feel like everyone else. When using such a technique, the speaker hopes to make the audience members feel as one. This was the tactic used by Louis Farrakhan at the Million Man March to Washington, D.C., in the fall of 1995. He built his final appeal around a pledge, asking the audience to forget about their former activities and become new men, committed to each other and their society. The pledge was long. Here is the opening:

> Now, brothers, I want you to take this pledge. When I say I, I want you to say I, and then say your name. I know that there's so many names, but I want you to shout your name out so that the ancestors can hear it.
>
> Take this pledge with me. Say with me please, I, say your name, pledge that from this day forward I will strive to love my brother as I love myself. I, say your name, from this day forward will strive to improve myself spiritually, morally, mentally, socially, politically, and economically for the benefit of myself, my family, and my people. I, say your name, pledge that I will strive to build businesses, build houses, build hospitals, build factories, and then to enter international trade for the good of myself, my family, and my people. I, say your name, pledge that from this day forward I will never raise my hand with a knife or a gun to beat, cut, or shoot any member of my family or any human being, except in self-defense.
>
> I, say your name, pledge from this day forward I will never abuse my wife by striking her, disrespecting her for she is the mother of my children and the producer of my future. I, say your name, pledge that from this day forward I will never engage in the abuse of children, little boys, or little girls for sexual gratification. But I will let them grow in peace to be strong men and women for the future of our people.[16]

When visions are well crafted, they surround an audience, helping it feel like an integrated group. When listeners are caught up in the same vision, they can be forged into a working unit.

SAMPLE AUDIENCE ANALYSIS

In this chapter, we have surveyed various factors that you will consider as you analyze your audience and occasion. If you work systematically, these choices will become clearer. Suppose you belonged to a citizens' action group that was fighting against giant hog lot or confinement operations in your state—a member of Citizens for Clean Air and Water. You decide to talk at a public hearing in your county being held by the state Senate Agricultural Committee. You might prepare the following comprehensive analysis of your audience as you prepare your speech:

SAVING IOWA'S AIR AND WATER

I. General description of speech.
  A. *General purpose:* To persuade.
  B. *Specific purpose:* To persuade the Senate Agricultural Committee to adopt a 2-year moratorium on giant hog lots (macro-swine production units).

II. *General description of the audience:* At this public hearing are several representatives of your citizens' action committee; three members of the Iowa Pork Producers Association (who also will speak); about five small-farm farmers; two farmers with 2,000-hog, macro-swine production units; most local newspaper, radio, and television operations; and about three dozen people who have come to listen.

III. Audience analysis.

A. Demographic analysis.

1. *Age:* Most individuals attending the meeting are between 25 and 65. The age range means that I'm facing experienced adults, all of whom can vote and pressure their legislators if I can get through to them. My own age (19) will be a factor only when I urge them to think about air and water quality for future generations.

2. *Gender:* The caucus is a mixed group, with slightly more men than women. I want to make sure that I recognize the role of women in farm operations and, generally, in protecting their families.

3. *Education:* This is a well-educated community, and among members of this audience are many people who know much about the highly publicized lagoon break of last year and other relevant issues. I can assume enough knowledge so that I don't have to detail particular aspects of the problem, though I'll want enough details to get major stories in the press.

4. *Group membership:* All listeners are politically active and registered voters. I can assume that most are ready to act (or to oppose actions).

5. *Cultural and ethnic background:* Ethnic background is primarily European and not a factor here. Culturally, almost all people attending have a sense that Iowa's economy—even its manufacturing—is tied tightly to agriculture (an agribusiness economy). Iowans generally envision themselves as "heartland" people, with courtesy, common sense, civic pride, and neighborliness values that are spoken of often. In Iowa's culture, the business and rural myths of agrarian life come into conflict. I must deal with that conflict.

B. Psychological profile.

1. *Factual beliefs:* For years, most Iowans have believed that large-scale agricultural operations can be—and have been—regulated successfully by the state. Everyone in this audience also knows that some environmental problems have surfaced in recent years, leading to the present Senate Agricultural Committee hearings. These problems mean that beliefs should be variable—capable of being altered.

2. *Opinions:* The idea that a "man's home [farm] is his castle" and loyalty to one's community also are in conflict: Should a farmer be able to do what he or she wants with the land, or are there community responsibilities that need to be taken into account? Opinions vary. I must address them.

3. *Attitudes:* Listeners probably consider me naive and idealistic. I must demonstrate that I know what I'm talking about. Enough Iowans buy into "Think globally, act locally" so that I can exploit local issues.

IV. *Values:* Listeners are committed to the democratic process and take pride in community political involvement at the state and national levels. They see themselves as common people—"the heart of America"—fulfilling the American dream. They value common sense and compromise, protecting the individual while celebrating community.

With this prespeech audience analysis completed, the next steps in preparing the speech are clearer. The audience analysis points to the kinds of supporting materials needed. For instance, for the Senate committee members, you need facts on the size of problem in the state and the nation. Also useful would be information about other states (e.g., North Carolina) that have acted to slow the development of macro-swine production units. For the press, spectacular, specific instances are attractive pieces of testimony. To blunt your opponents' counterarguments, know the details of who built the lagoons that broke and sent pig manure into wells and streams. To locate this information, do the following:

1. Use the library's computerized database to investigate "macro-swine production units" and "hog farming."
2. Obtain a copy of the University of Iowa's three-year study on giant hog operations.
3. Access electronic versions of the *Des Moines Register* for 1997 and 1998 to inventory its stories on hog farming and, if possible, interview at least one of the reporters involved.
4. E-mail Ken Silverstein, who wrote the article on "meat factories" in the January/February 1999 issue of *Sierra,* at counterpunch@erols.com tp see if he has additional sources you should check.[17]
5. If possible, convince Senator Tom Harkin (D-Iowa), who sits on the national Senate Agricultural Committee and commissioned a report on hog farming in December 1997, to come or send a representative to the hearing.
6. Interview at least two small-operation farmers who live near a macro-swine production unit to talk about their concerns for air and water quality.
7. Find out what you can about the North Carolina moratorium on new macro operations.
8. Interview local environmental experts to get measures of local air and water quality.

While this list may seem extensive, it is likely to yield useful information, because it is a *specific* rather than a *general* search for facts on meat factories. Then, with the demographic and psychological profile of the audience completed and your research compiled, you can adapt your ideas and appeals to your audience. You might include the following main ideas in your speech:

1. Stress the openness and fairness with which Iowans typically address problems facing the state. Make it clear that you understand these decisions are not necessarily easy, because the state's economic base is as important as the right of citizens' to protection from dangerous, state-controlled practices. Point out that "the Iowa family farmer"—as that person typically is mythified—is not a player in this game; rather, what's being investigated are corporate farms with direct ties to hog slaughtering and marketing companies.

2. Make it clear that this is not simply a moral issue. Air and water quality are very real, pragmatic considerations; the health of Iowans is at stake. Aim these issues particularly at the senators and the family people in the audience.

3. Point out that other states have faced the same problems: economic development versus environmental safety, and the right to earn a living versus the desirability of living in a neighborly way. In particular, talk about the state with the second-largest hog production, North Carolina, and what it's doing to protect itself and its citizens. Make sure that the senators understand much can be learned from thinking of North Carolina as a parallel case.

4. Push to create an open forum for continued discussion to keep the press and citizens involved.

5. Recognize the area's excellent efforts at political reform in local projects. In addition, because you're talking near a university population, stress the need for continued study. All of this points not to the dismantling of macro-swine production units but to a moratorium—a 2-year moratorium, you advocate, to commission additional studies of both operating giant hog operations and air/water quality in the areas of those operations.

CHAPTER SUMMARY

Public speaking is audience centered and occasion centered. The primary goal of audience analysis is to discover the aspects of listeners' demographic and psychological backgrounds that are relevant to your speech purposes:

- *Demographic analysis:* the age, gender, education, group membership, and cultural as well as ethnic background of the audience.
- *Psychological analysis:* the beliefs, attitudes, values, desires, visions, and fantasies of the audience.

Once you can profile your listeners, you can adapt your speech purposes and ideas to them. Analysis of the occasion complements analysis of the audience. An *occasion* is a set of activities that occurs in a time and place set aside for the express purpose of fulfilling collective goals for and by people who have been taught the special meanings of those activities. You should attempt to analyze your speech occasion's rules for speaking, habitual roles played by both speaker and audience, and the standards of competency that will be applied to your speech.

The analysis of both audience and occasion will help you with audience targeting: deciding on realistic specific purposes, areas of audience interest, the audience's capacity and willingness to act, and the degree of change you can expect. Your analysis also will aid you in audience segmentation: creating basic appeals that accurately identify subgroups, applying psychological statements that are relevant to their lives, and using appropriate valuative appeals.

The ability to adapt your speech to the needs of a particular audience and occasion is the mark of a competent public speaker.

KEY TERMS

attitudes (p. 101)

audience centered (p. 97)

audience segmentation (p. 114)

audience targeting (p. 109)

beliefs (p. 100)

captive audience (p. 110)

demographic analysis (p. 97)

desires (p. 103)

facts (p. 100)

fantasies (p. 103)

fixed beliefs (p. 101)

general audience expectations (p. 108)

ideologies (p. 103)

instrumental values (p. 102)

occasion (p. 107)

occasion centered (p. 97)

opinions (p. 101)

psychological profiles (p. 99)

rhetorical vision (p. 103)

specific audience expectations (p. 108)

stereotypes (p. 101)

terminal values (p. 102)

valuative vocabulary (p. 116)

value orientations (p. 103)

values (p. 102)

variable beliefs (p. 101)

ASSESSMENT ACTIVITIES

1. Using the Sample Audience Analysis outline on pages 118–119 as a checklist, respond to each item for your next speech, and turn it in two class periods before you're due to speak. Your instructor will examine and comment on it before you speak to be sure that you've maximized your chances of success.

2. Study the occasion of presenting a speech in your classroom. Working either in groups or alone (depending on your instructor's instructions), answer the following questions:
   a. What are the prevailing rules and customs you must follow in this classroom?
   b. What physical conditions affect the way you speak?
   c. How do speech days work? (What will precede and follow your speech? Are there any special challenges presented in the ways speech days are run in this class?)
   After you've answered the questions, write down three things you will do to adapt to this situation.

3. Secure a copy of Minister Louis Farrakhan's speech, either from the Information Arcade at the University of Iowa Libraries or from CNN U.S. News (cnn.org). (Both are on the Internet.)
   a. Identify beliefs, attitudes, values, and visions that you think are hostile to those of the white viewers of that day.
   b. Note how, if at all, Minister Farrakhan narrows the gaps between his beliefs, attitudes, and values and those of his white audience.
   c. Name or label the tactics he used, and discuss briefly in what kinds of situations you can use them.

REFERENCES

1. Donald C. Bryant, *Rhetorical Dimensions of Criticism* (Baton Rouge: Louisiana State University Press, 1973), 19.

2. For more discussion, see David L. Bender, ed., *American Values* (San Diego, CA: Greenhaven Press, 1989); and Milton M. Rokeach, *Beliefs, Attitudes, and Values: A Theory of Organization and Change* (San Francisco: Jossey-Bass, 1968).

3. Milton Rokeach, *The Nature of Human Values* (New York: Free Press, 1973). Cf. the discussion of polarized policy warfare be-

cause of contraposed, extreme values in Deborah Tannen, *The Argument Culture: Moving from Debate to Dialogue* (New York: Random House, 1998), especially ch. 2.

4. George Soros, "The Crisis of Global Capitalism," excerpted in *Newsweek,* 7 December 1998, 78.

5. See Kenneth Burke's ideas on terministic screens in his *Language as Symbolic Action: Essays on Life, Literature, and Method* (Berkeley: University of California Press, 1966). For a clear discussion of value orientations, see Malcolm O. Sillars, *Messages, Meanings, and Culture: Approaches to Communication Criticism* (New York: Addison-Wesley-Longman, 1991), ch. 7, "Value Analysis: Understanding Culture in Value Systems."

6. Dick Hebdige, *Subculture: The Meaning of Style* (London: Methuen, 1979). This is a large topic: exploring the social force and politics of desire, pleasure, and fantasy takes you into many worlds, such as the music of Madonna (especially during the late '80s and early '90s) advertising, political statements such as Martin Luther King, Jr.'s, "I Have a Dream" speech of 1963, dressing-for-success or for expressions of self-identity, and the like. For some basic theoretical reading, see Roland Barthes, *The Pleasures of the Text* (New York: Hill and Wang, 1975); and Jean Baudrillard, *The Ecstasy of Communication,* trans. Bernard and Caroline Schutze, ed. Sylvère Lotringer (New York: Semiotext[e], 1988). For applications, see overviews in Stuart Hall, ed., *Representation: Cultural Representations and Signifying Practices* (Thousand Oaks, CA: Sage, 1997). On the "aesthetization" or "fashioning" (p. 5) of social identities and political attitudes, see Paul du Gay, ed., *Production of Culture/Cultures of Production* (Thousand Oaks, CA: Sage, 1997). For summaries of current advertising theory and analysis, see Katherine Toland Frith, ed., *Undressing the Ad: Reading Culture in Advertising* (New York: Peter Lang, 1997); and for discussions of the politics of pleasure and other feeling-

states, see John Fiske, *Media Matters: Everyday Culture and Political Change* (Minneapolis: University of Minnesota Press, 1994), and Roderick P. Hart, *Seducing America: How Television Charms the Modern Voter,* rev. ed. (Thousand Oaks, CA: Sage, 1999).

7. The idea of rhetorical vision was introduced in Earnest G. Bormann, "Fantasy and Rhetorical Vision: The Rhetorical Criticism of Social Reality," *Quarterly Journal of Speech* 58 (1972): 396–407. All of his ideas as well as his analysis of the history of rhetorical visions in political speechmaking are found in his book *The Force of Fantasy: Restoring the American Dream* (Carbondale, IL: Southern Illinois University Press, 1985), with this quotation coming from p. 8.

8. Bormann 1985 (n. 7): 8. See also Bruce E. Gronbeck, "Rhetorical Visions from the Margins, 1963–1988," *Retoriska Frågor: Texter on tal och talare från Quintilianus till Clinton tillägnade Kurt Johannesson,* ed. Christer Åsberg (Stockholm: Nordstedts Förlag, 1995), 267–281.

9. Abraham Lincoln, "First Inaugural Address [4 March 1961]," *The American Reader: Words that Moved a Nation,* ed. Diane Ravitch (New York: HarperCollins, 1990), 143.

10. Morton's speech, "Strength Through Cultural Diversity," was reprinted whole in Bruce E. Gronbeck, et al., *Principles and Types of Speech Communication,* 12th ed. (New York: Addison-Wesley-Longman, 1994), 319–327; the quoted paragraphs are from pp. 326–327.

11. Topic involvement and rational message analysis are discussed by R. E. Petty and J. T. Cacioppo, *Communication and Persuasion: Central and Peripheral Routes to Attitude Change* (New York: Springer-Verlag, 1986).

12. Edward Hall argues that you learn about culture and social expectations in three ways: formally (when someone tells you what to do), informally (when you imitate what others are doing), and when you are older, technically (when you learn why

members of a society do certain things and not others through explanations). See Hall, *The Silent Language* (Greenwich, CT: Fawcett, 1959), ch. 4, "The Major Triad," 63–91.

13. For a broader discussion of occasion, see Elihu Katz and Daniel Dayan, *Media Events: The Live Broadcasting of History* (Cambridge, MA: Harvard University Press, 1992).

14. Material taken from "Freedom to Farm Victory," *Des Moines Sunday Register,* 13 December 1998, J1–J2.

15. Jesse Jackson, "Common Ground and Common Sense," *Vital Speeches of the Day* (15 August 1988), 54 (21):651.

16. Louis Farrakhan, "Transcript from Minister Louis Farrakhan's Remarks at the Million Man March, October 17, 1995," orig. from CNN U.S. News, copyright © 1995 Cable News Network, Inc., and distributed on the World Wide Web by the Information Arcade, University of Iowa Libraries, 1995 (www.arcade.uiowa.edu).

17. Ken Silverstein, "Meat Factories," *Sierra,* January/February 1999, 28–35, 110, 112.

Chapter 6

Developing Ideas: Finding and Using Supporting Materials

Consider the student who wanted to do a speech on the Clinton-Lewinsky affair of 1998. She accessed the World Wide Web, pulled up the Yahoo! search engine, typed in "Lewinsky," and got 1,226 hits. Stunned, she thought about returning to her library's electronic card category to access *Reader's Guide* instead, but then she stopped, knowing that there's probably even more hits in the popular press.

This student's experience reflects a paradox that you'll surely encounter as a speaker: on the one hand, as you prepare your speeches, you'll want to make them substantive and worthwhile for your audience. You need to have materials that are concrete, reasonably connected to claims you are making, and convincing. On the other hand, knowing what you need—some statistics, some testimony from reliable sources, some explanations, and so on—is only half the battle, because as you search for such materials, you'll probably find yourself overwhelmed by the volume of information available. The search tools of today—such as the World Wide Web, where you can access libraries and home pages from around the globe, electronic card catalogues, CD-ROM search technologies for major newspapers and special indexes—will deluge you with enough information not just for a six-minute speech of explanation but for dozens of such speeches.

In this chapter, we explore the kinds of supporting materials speeches demand. A good speech burns supporting materials like jet fuel, and this chapter discusses the various kinds of energy that fuel speeches. We then tackle the questions of where to find those fuels and how to burn them. We discuss electronic, print, face-to-face, and mailed forms of supporting materials, and we look at some strategies for putting them together to achieve maximum power and effectiveness.

Thinking through the kinds of material you need before you actually hit the library or an http:// command on your computer is a habit you must cultivate. Searching for supporting materials purposively is the key to success—and to sanity.

WHAT TO LOOK FOR: FORMS OF SUPPORTING MATERIALS

Five types of supporting materials are regularly used by competent speakers: explanations, comparisons and contrasts, examples and narratives, statistics, and testimony.

Explanations

An **explanation** is a description or expository passage that makes a term, concept, process, or proposal clear or acceptable. Explanations tell what, how, or why, and they show relationships between a whole and its parts. They also may make it easier to understand concepts that are difficult to grasp. As with other forms of support, explanations must be presented clearly and attached explicitly to the central ideas of your speech to be useful.

An explanation tells an audience what something is by offering defining and clarifying details. So, when vice-chairman of the board of AT&T Randall

FIGURE 6.1 **The Forms of Supporting Materials**

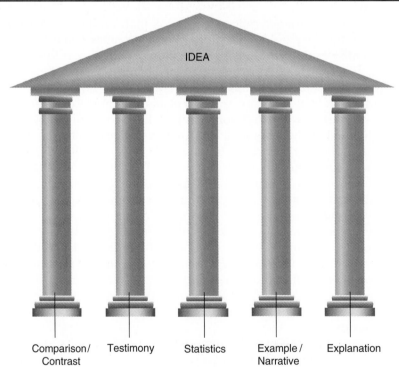

Tobias introduced an audience at West Virginia University to fiber optics communication, he first made sure they understood what "fiber optics" was:

> Fiber optics systems combine lasers as small as grains of sand with glass fibers as thin as strands of hair. Unlike ordinary glass, it's ultra-pure. If oceans were made of this glass, you could see to the bottom.
>
> In fiber optics systems, lasers transmit billions of light pulses each second as bits of data through these glass strands. The bits represent conversations, computer data or images. Currently we transmit about 3.4 billion bits a second, equal to 50,000 simultaneous phone calls on a pair of fibers. But within not-too-distant developments in the technology, we expect to transmit one trillion bits per second, or about 70 million simultaneous conversations on a single pair of wires.[1]

Notice that the explanation begins with a little analogy; Tobias hopes that references to sand and hair will help the audience visualize fiber optics. Then, he launches the explanation with descriptive material.

Explanations are good ways to clarify ideas. They should not be too long or complicated, however, and they should not have to carry the weight of the argument. For example, Tobias' explanation was clear, but by itself, it didn't point to a problem or idea worth considering. Explanations clarify but seldom prove anything.

Comparisons and Contrasts

Comparisons and contrasts are useful verbal devices for clarifying ideas—to make them distinctive and focused. Pointing out similarities and differences helps listeners comprehend your ideas and opinions.

Comparisons.   **Comparisons** are kinds of analogies that connect something already known or believed with ideas a speaker wishes to have understood or accepted. Comparisons, therefore, stress similarities. During the darkest days of the U.S. Civil War, Lincoln answered critics who attacked the administration's policies by comparing the plight of the government with that of the famous tightrope walker, Blondin, attempting to cross the Niagara Falls:

> Gentlemen, I want you to suppose a case for a moment. Suppose that all the property you were worth was in gold, and you had put it in the hands of Blondin, the famous rope-walker, to carry across the Niagara Falls on a tightrope. Would you shake the rope while he was passing over it, or keep shouting to him, "Blondin, stoop a little more! Go a little faster!"? No, I am sure you would not. You would hold your breath as well as your tongue, and keep your hands off until he was safely over. Now the government is in the same situation. It is carrying an immense weight across a stormy ocean. Untold treasures are in its hands. It is doing the best it can. Don't badger it! Just keep still, and it will get you safely over.

Contrasts. **Contrasts** help to clarify complex situations and processes by focusing on differences. A speaker explaining arena football would want to contrast it with the more familiar rules governing interscholastic football. To clarify the severity of the 1996 drought, the news networks contrasted average rainfall for normal summers with the rainfall that year. Contrasts not only can clarify unfamiliar or complex problems but also can strengthen the arguments you wish to advance. When H. Ross Perot spoke at the Reform Party Nominating Convention in 1996, he used the following contrast to show why private enterprise works better than government: "In business, you can promote people based on their performance. In politics, you get promoted based on your acting ability."[2]

Perot's contrast was clear and pointed in its references. Helping an audience reason along with you by visualizing differences is an excellent strategy for getting them to accept your ideas.

Comparisons and Contrasts Used in Combination. You can use comparisons and contrasts together to double your audience's ability to see. For example, a student once was speaking about the messages one finds in cartoons. To help his listeners see that cartoons provide social-political commentary, he compared and contrasted *Rocky and Bullwinkle* with *Beavis and Butthead:*

> Both cartoons have stirred up considerable public controversy. In the 1960s, some people boycotted *Rocky and Bullwinkle* just as some refuse to watch *Beavis and Butthead* today. There were major differences, however. *Rocky and Bullwinkle* episodes pitted the pair against Boris and Natasha mimicking the Cold War conflict between the U.S. and the Soviet Union. *Beavis and Butthead,* on the other hand, avoids political commentary while focusing on the struggle of the main characters with adolescence. *Rocky and Bullwinkle* was action-oriented; *Beavis and Butthead* is talk-oriented, offering a running social commentary on American attitudes and values.

Whenever using comparisons and contrasts, make sure that one of the items is familiar to listeners. Comparing arena football and interscholastic football will make no sense to listeners from Ireland, for example, who probably don't know anything about either one. You'd have to compare and contrast arena football and European soccer to clarify the arena game for them.

Examples and Narratives

A detailed example of an idea you wish to support is either an *illustration* or a *narrative.* If the example describes a concept, condition, or circumstance, it's called an **illustration;** if it's in story form, it's called a **narrative.** An illustration or narrative is always, however, a big "for instance"—something concrete that makes abstract or general ideas easier to comprehend. Illustrations share many characteristics with explanations, with the difference being that an illustration is always a "for instance" while explanations can take different forms. If the illustration is undeveloped or set up as string of quick examples, it's called a **specific instance.**

Some illustrations and narratives are hypothetical (made up); others are factual—recitations of actual events or references to persons, places, and things. If you were giving a speech on why students should move out of dormitories and into apartments, you might narrate a "typical" evening in a dorm: loud music, a constant flow of pizza delivery people through the hall, a traveling party, a false fire alarm, nonstop card games, illegal alcohol, and an engagement shower. Although not all of these may occur on the same night, asking listeners to imagine what life would be like if they did would help you convey the intensity of your antidormitory feelings through a made-up narrative.

For many audiences, fact-based illustrations and narratives are more potent. President Ronald Reagan was famous for his reliance on homey little narratives. Equally well-known for stories is Black Muslim Minister Louis Farrakhan. Notice how he uses a story to drive the argument he's advancing:

> We are a people, who have been fractured, divided and destroyed because of our division [and who] now must move toward a perfect union. But let's look at a speech delivered by a White slave holder on the banks of the James River in 1712.
>
> Sixty-eight years before our former slave masters permitted us to join the Christian faith. Listen to what he said. He said, "In my bag I have a foolproof method of controlling black slaves. I guarantee everyone of you, if installed correctly, it will control the slaves for at least 300 years. My method is simple. Any member of your family or your overseer can use it. I have outlined a number of differences among the slaves and I take those differences and I make them bigger. I use fear, distrust, and envy for control purposes."
>
> I want you to listen. What are those three things? Fear, envy, distrust. For what purpose? Control. To control who? The slave. Who is the slave? Us.[3]

Minister Farrakhan's story was plausible, short, and powerful.

Specific instances are undeveloped illustrations or examples; usually, they are grouped into a list so that they pile one upon the other to drive the speaker's point home. The Roman orator Cicero was the first advocate of "filling the mind" with examples. He called the technique *accumulatio,* or accumulation, in Book III of his treatise on rhetoric *De Oratore.*[4] They're undeveloped because their power comes from cumulative effect rather than from vivid detail.

Sometimes, you can use a single specific instance if all you need is a quick example: "You're all familiar with the windows in this classroom, but you might not have noticed their actual construction. I want to talk about windows like the ones around you—these double-glazed, low-emissivity, gas-filled windows—and how the use of such seemingly expensive windows contributes to reduced energy consumption on campus and in your life." More often, though, speakers pile on instances either to clarify their point or to prove it. That's what Mary Fisher did when speaking to the Republican National Convention about AIDS. She said to the delegates, "[T]he AIDS virus is not a political creature. It does not care whether you are Democrat or Republican, it does not ask whether you are White or Black, male or female, gay or straight, young or old." She continued with even more specific instances:

Tonight, I represent an AIDS community whose members have been reluctantly drawn from every segment of American society. Though I am White, and a mother, I am one with a Black infant struggling with tubes in a Philadelphia hospital. Though I am female, and contracted this disease in marriage, and enjoy the warm support of my family, I am one with the lonely gay man sheltering a flickering candle from the cold wind of his family's rejection.[5]

With these accumulated instances, Fisher was trying to bridge the gap between her own existence as an AIDS-infected white, Republican mother and the groups of citizens she feared her political party was ignoring.

Statistics

Statistics are numbers that show relationships between or among phenomena—relationships that can emphasize size or magnitude, describe subclasses or parts (segments), or establish trends. By reducing large masses of information into generalized categories, statistics can clarify situations, substantiate potentially disputable central ideas, and make complex aspects of the world clear to listeners.

Magnitudes. We often use statistics to describe a situation or to sketch its scope or seriousness—its size or **magnitude.** Especially if one statistical descrip-

A speaker can use statistics to describe a situation or to sketch its scope or magnitude. By reducing large masses of information into general categories, statistics can clarify and substantiate a claim.

tion of the size of a problem is piled upon others, the effect on listeners can be strong. So, a speech dealing with President Clinton's relationship with the public during the 1998 impeachment process could cite three, four, even five polls that all showed him with the support of 55 to 65 percent of the public even as the House Judiciary Committee and the full House worked on articles of impeachment.

Not all uses of magnitudes, of course, need such piling of instances. Simple, hard-hitting magnitudes sometimes work even better. For example, arguing that there is "very little nutritional value in a hamburger, chocolate shake, and fries," Brenda Theriault of the University of Maine simply noted that "of the 1,123 calories in this meal, there are 15 calories of carbohydrates, 35 calories of protein, and 1,073 calories of fat."[6] These were all the numbers the listeners needed to understand the nutrition in a typical fast-food meal.

Segments.   Statistics also are used to isolate the parts of a problem or to show aspects of a problem caused by separate factors; parts or aspects can be treated as statistical **segments.** In discussing the wisdom of renovating the University of Iowa's student union, for example, a speaker might point to a survey indicating that 54 percent of the student body said it would pay $60 per student for the renovation; 21 percent, $45; 6 percent, $30; and 20 percent, nothing.[7] You then could say, "In other words, four out of five students are willing to help finance the renovation out of their own funds." Another student did precisely this kind of move when talking about how people shop on the World Wide Web:

> In 1996, people spent a total of $518 million dollars on products and services they found via the Web. Computer products sales comprised 27% of this total and travel $243 million dollars, making up over half of all Web sales. The remainder of the sales is divided almost equally among adult entertainment, general entertainment, food/drink, gifts/flowers, and apparel.[8]

As the Iowa example indicates, be sure to point out the significance or importance of those segments. Don't expect listeners to do your work for you.

Trends.   Statistics also often are used to point out **trends**—indicators that tell us where we were, where we are now, and where we may be heading. The comparison of statistical representations across time allows you to say that a particular phenomenon is increasing or decreasing (see Table 6.1). An interesting use of a trend argument can be seen in testimony given before the U.S. House Subcommittee on Human Resources by Hortense Hunn, Executive Director of the California Preschool Services Department in San Bernadino County. She presented the following trend in spending on the Head Start program:

> There are numerous official fact sheets documenting Head Start's growth and development since its inception in 1965. I do not intend to reiterate the litany of glowing statistics which are readily available; suffice it to say that the National Head Start Program has grown from an "embryonic" program enrolling 561,000 children for about $96 million in the summer of 1965 to an

TABLE 6.1   Types of Statistics

In a speech to inform, a speaker might use three types of statistics to describe students at Central University. What other forms of supporting material could complement these numbers?

Magnitudes	Segments	Trends
"Three fourths of all Central University students come from the state."	"Sixty percent of all Central University students major in business; 25 percent are humanities majors; the remaining 15 percent are in fine arts."	"Since 1975, enrollment at Central University has increased by 20 percent every 5 years."

"adolescent" program serving over 721,000 children and families for $1.7 billion in this year.[9]

Notice Ms. Hunn's adaptation to her audience. She mentioned "glowing statistics" to ask her audience to see them positively. She used growth metaphors ("embryonic," "adolescent") to project not only a sense of accomplishment but also the need for further growth, and she emphasized the program's services to children rather than some of its more controversial aid to families. Listeners have a much harder time rejecting children than their parents.

Using Statistics.   When you use statistics to indicate magnitude, divide phenomena into segments, or describe trends, you can help your listeners by making the numbers more user-friendly:

1. *Translate difficult-to-comprehend numbers into more immediately understandable terms.* In a speech on the mounting problem of solid waste, Carl Hall illustrated the immensity of 130 million tons of garbage by explaining that trucks loaded with this amount would extend from coast to coast three abreast.[10]
2. *Don't be afraid to round off complicated numbers.* "Nearly 300,000" is easier for listeners to comprehend than "296,454." "Just over 33 percent" or, better yet, "about a third" is preferable to "33.5 percent."
3. *Use visual aids to clarify complicated statistical trends or summaries whenever possible.* Hand out a photocopied sheet of numbers, draw graphs on the chalkboard, or prepare a pie chart on an overhead transparency. Such aids allow you to concentrate your words on explaining the significance of the numbers rather than on making sure the audience understands and remembers them.
4. *Use statistics fairly.* It's easy to mislead with statistics—even if you don't exactly lie. Arguing that professional women's salaries increased 8.3 percent last year may sound impressive to listeners until they ask how much professional men's salaries increased and realize women are still

ETHICAL MOMENTS

THE NUMBERS GAME

The rise of science in this century has been accompanied by the rise of numerical data—and its public exhibition. By now you've been told by one poll that the public favors a liberalization of abortion laws by two-to-one but by another poll that the public favors tightening abortion laws by an equal percentage. You know that four out of five dentists surveyed recommend a particular brand of toothpaste. You've heard that a brand of cigarettes has the lowest level of tar and nicotine—from more than one manufacturer. As both listener and speaker, you have to make some ethical calls when encountering such data:

1. Contradictory polls such as those on abortion usually result when questions are asked in slanted ways. "Do parents have to right to know when their underaged kids seek a dangerous abortion?" tends to encourage a positive answer, whereas "Ought women have the right to control their own bodies without external interference from others?" also encourages a positive answer—but one in favor of a very different public policy than the first. Questions can be loaded in favor of opposing public policies. You're wise to report the actual questions when quoting poll results.

2. Who were those "four out of five dentists surveyed?" Is it ethical to cite statistics without reviewing how they were gathered and calculated?

3. If your favorite brand of cigarettes is one of five brands that all have the same low tar and nicotine content, then technically, of course, yours has the lowest—and so do the other four brands. Is it ethical, however, to claim your brand is "the lowest," or must you say that it is "one of the lowest"?

It's easy to fiddle with numbers: to round up or down, to compare only parts rather than wholes, and to ignore key details that would properly contextualize information for listeners. If you play fast and loose with numbers, however, you might get caught. Learn to play the numbers game honestly so as to protect your reputation.

paid more than a quarter less than men on comparative jobs. Provide fair contexts for your data.[11]

Testimony

When you cite the opinions or conclusions of others, you're using **testimony.** Testimony sometimes merely adds weight, clarity, or impressiveness to an idea, as when you quote Mahatma Gandhi or a clever turn of a phrase by Rosie O'Donnell. So, when Richard Reeves wanted to conclude a speech about important women in the twentieth century, he offered as an epitome of his central claim the words of the first woman elected to Congress, Jeannette Rankin: "You take people as far as they will go, not as far as you would like them to go."[12]

All testimony should meet the twin tests of pertinence and audience acceptability. When used to strengthen a statement rather than merely to amplify or illustrate an idea, testimony also should satisfy four more specific criteria:

1. The person quoted should be qualified, by training and experience, to speak on the topic being discussed. Athletes are more credible talking about sports equipment or exercise programs than endorsing breakfast food or local furniture stores.
2. Whenever possible, the authority's statement should be based on first-hand knowledge. An Iowa farmer is not an authority on a Mississippi drought unless or he or she has personally observed the conditions.
3. The judgment expressed should not be unduly influenced by personal interest. Asking a political opponent to comment on the current president's performance will likely yield a self-interested answer.
4. Listeners should perceive the person quoted as being an actual authority. An archbishop may be accepted as an authority by a Roman Catholic audience but, perhaps, not by a Protestant or Hindu audience.

When citing testimony, don't use big names simply because they're well known. The best testimony comes from experts whose qualifications your listeners recognize.

Finally, always acknowledge the source of an idea or particular phrasing. Avoid *plagiarism*—claiming someone else's ideas, information, or phraseology as being your own. Plagiarism is stealing. Give your source credit for the material, and give yourself credit for having taken the time to do the research (see the section "Using Source Material Ethically" later in this chapter).

WHERE TO LOOK: SOURCES OF SUPPORTING MATERIALS

So, you may know what kinds of materials you want for your speech—some solid numbers, a nice list of specific instances, a well-developed illustration or story, testimony from credible people, a hard-nosed explanation, and some clarifying comparisons and contrasts. Now, where do you find such materials? You'll find those materials exactly where you find all ideas in this world: in electronic networks and storage technologies, in print, in interaction with others, and in information-gathering instruments that you construct yourself.

The Electronic World

You've seen the ads: AT&T promising you access to information from everywhere, the Pentium III chip bringing you sounds and images from every imag-

TABLE 6.2   Checklist for Supporting Materials

You should evaluate your supporting materials when you plan your speeches. Answer the questions on this checklist as you plan your supporting materials.

General Considerations

_____1. Have I included sufficient supporting material?
_____2. Are my supporting materials distributed throughout my speech?
_____3. Do I provide extra support for confusing or controversial ideas?
_____4. Are my supporting materials interesting and clear?
_____5. Do I adequately credit the sources of my supporting materials?

Explanations

_____1. Are my explanations short and direct?
_____2. Do I provide other forms of support in addition to explanations?

Comparisons and Contrasts

_____1. Is at least one of the items in a comparison or contrast familiar to my listeners?
_____2. Is the basis of the comparison clear?
_____3. Is the contrast distinct enough?

Examples and Narratives

_____1. Is the illustration or narrative clearly related to the idea it's intended to support?
_____2. Is the illustration or narrative typical?
_____3. Is the illustration or narrative vivid and adequately detailed?
_____4. Have I provided enough specific instances?
_____5. Can listeners easily recognize or understand the instances I mention?

Statistics

_____1. Are my statistics easy to understand?
_____2. Have I rounded off complicated numbers?
_____3. Am I using statistics fairly?
_____4. Should I use visual materials to clarify complicated numbers?
_____5. Have I adequately interpreted the statistics I've cited for my listeners?

Testimony

_____1. Is the authority qualified to speak on the topic being discussed?
_____2. Is the authority's statement based on firsthand knowledge?
_____3. Is the authority's opinion subject to personal influence or bias?
_____4. Do my listeners know the authority's qualifications?
_____5. Will my listeners accept this person as an authority?

inable society, and your own college or university linking you with other institutions of learning and ideas throughout the world. Working your way through government, commercial, and educational networks takes a few skills, though probably not as many as the novice might think. At most schools and through an increasing number of inexpensive commercial services, you now can surf the Internet, upload information from CD-ROMs in libraries, and search your own library electronically with relative ease.

The Electronic Card Catalog.   Most college and university libraries either have or will soon install a computerized search system for their holdings and also for journals or magazines in general. If you have access to such a system, it should be your first stop. For example, the University of Iowa uses the Oasis system, which is popular among larger research libraries. It allows you to search the university's card catalog, that of a consortium of libraries, the Humanities and Social Science Indexes and several versions of *Psychological Abstracts.*

Suppose you want to do a speech on the financing of home health care for the terminally ill through hospice organizations. In early 1999, if you entered "death" at the University of Iowa, you'd pull up 1,521 hits—far too many. If you entered "hospice," you'd still have 78 items—an overpowering number. If you then dropped to the subcategory "hospice-costs," however, you'd come to down to four books. That much you can handle.

Learning to narrow through precise specification of topic or subcategorization will make your searches less frustrating. Many systems offer you **Boolean searching,** where you use words such as "and," "or," and "not" to control the subject matter. So, "medieval *or* architecture" gets you all references with either word, "medieval *and* architecture" pulls up references with both words, and "medieval *and* architecture *not* England" highlights medieval architecture everywhere except England. Also knowing authors, titles, and the like will help you even more. Take time to look at the pamphlet or online help menu, and make sure you use your local electronic card catalog with maximum efficiency.

One last point: Find out what databases you have access to through your library system. ERIC (Educational Resources Information Center) will help you locate scholarly papers in the humanities. MEDLINE will get you into psychosocial and physiological studies of disease and associated medical problems, and LEXIS-NEXIS will give you access to a staggering number of public and commercial information sources.

CD-ROM Searches.   We're living through a great explosion in the use of the **CD-ROM**—a technological device that uses the CD as a storage vehicle for computer data. CDs hold much more information than floppy disks, hence are used to store and to retrieve data from multiple volumes' worth of materials. Check to see what your local libraries have, perhaps *The New York Times Index, The Oxford English Dictionary on CD-ROM, The Modern Language Association Indexes,* or the *Table of Contents to Communication Journals* (which includes all articles published in National Communication Association journals since 1990).

The world of supporting materials now at your fingertips is still subject to the requirements of proper citation.

As more and more databases become available on CD-ROM, you'll be able to link electronically with the actual articles you want.

The World Wide Web. The **Information Superhighway** was the great metaphor of the 1980s and early 1990s—a system allowing everyone to access information electronically from around the globe. Today, you can use a variety of search tools to access unlimited information sources, yielding truckloads of data. You also can link pages of data together, and with a mere click of a mouse or tap of an "enter" key, access the **World Wide Web.** The Highway is transportation; the Web is a way of reading many assembled sources at once. The Web is an access protocol that allows you to enter the maze of computerized language, pictures, and sounds from any point in that maze—and then to move from site to site simply by clicking on a word or a symbol. A little vocabulary will help you work through the Web:

- *Telnet:* A command that takes you to remote sites.
- *HTTP: Hyper Text Transport Protocol,* which is a command to your computer to take you to some site.
- *FTP:* A *File Transfer Protocol* that lets you retrieve information.
- *Usenet:* Interactive accounts that link you to newsgroups or interactive discussions.

- *Archie, Gopher, Veronica, WAIS (Wide Area Information Servers):* Multiple tools for accessing information sites in useful ways.
- *HTML: HyperText Markup Language,* which is a script used to create the main or home page of a Web site.
- *FAQ:* Computerese for *Frequently Asked Questions*—check it when you're unsure about something.
- *Hypertext:* Highlighted words that, when clicked, transport you to other texts (if you're on the Web).
- *URL: Uniform Resource Locator,* that is, the address of some site. Addresses include .com=commercial company; .edu=an educational institution; .net=a company that connects you to the Internet; .gov=a governmental site; .org=a nonprofit organization; .mil=a military group; .us=someone in the United States who doesn't fit into another category; and specific codes for other countries (e.g., uk for the United Kingdom, se for Sweden, fi for Finland, etc.).
- *World Wide Web:* The network of servers (computers online) that provides hypertext searches on the Internet, usually with the abbreviation "www" in them.[13]

Speech Research on the Web. By now, you probably cannot tune into a sports broadcast, a news hour, or even a prime-time television show without being told you can use a "www" command to get to its home page, such as ESPNET's sports scores for the day, CNN International's informational background on big stories, *USA Today* online, National Public Radio's discussion group, or propaganda from the Republican and Democratic parties. You soon discover you can go to Mississippi State University for the Internet Movie Database, to SCREENsite for links between the Library of Congress and directories on film and television resources, to the Harvard-MIT-Tufts consortium on negotiation and conflict resolution, to the University of Maryland's site full of resources and simulations for high-school students, and to state and federal government sources through ".gov" locations. Taking time to discover how to draw on such information will make your time for speech preparation not only well spent but even fun. Here is a sample of useful sites for speech research:

FIGURE 6.2   Metasearching the Web: Search Engines

AltaVista / LinkStar / WebCrawler / InfoSeek / OpenText / Galaxy Einet / Lycos /
CUI / AccuFind / Yellow Pages / Yahoo / WWW Yellow Pages / Apollo / Starting Point /
ComFind / What's New Too / BizWiz / Nurd World Media / Metro / Walla / Excite /
DejaNews / WWWW / Cortex Group / Virtual tourist / GNN Select / IBM InfoMarket /
Inktomi / G.O.D. / UK Wellow Web / ALiWeb / All in One / Magellan / Point / A2Z / HotBot /
SurfPoint / Maven / GTE SuperPages / On'Village / Top10 / BigYellow / BigBook /
Rescue Island / Israel Business Connection / SwitchBoard / Inso / FTP Search /
InfoHighway / Sivuv / PathFinder / Fish-Search / Harvest Broker / The Israeli Machine /
Snoopie File Search / Dewa/

Subject	Site
Genealogy	http://www.genealogy.org/~ngs
Health (disease control)	http://www.cdc.gov/cdc.htm
Electronic newspapers	http://www.enews.com
USA Today	http://www.usatoday.com
City networks	http://www.city.net
Maps	http://www.mapquest.com/
Links to people	http://www.bigfoot.com
Sports	http://www.wwcd.com/hp/sports.html
White House	http://www.whitehouse.gov
U.S. House of Representatives	http://www.house.gov
U.S. Senate	http://www.senate.gov

When telneting to Web sites around the world, you'll discover utterly amazing places, such as where the Aryan (white power) women hang out, individuals' home pages paying homage to Marilyn Monroe or Nostradamus, full texts of song lyrics, places to watch election returns from many countries, sites with sound bites and video clips, and even sites where you can shop for John Deere tractors or find parts for your 1948 9N Ford tractor. Because almost anyone can put up a Web site, you must learn to evaluate them both for quality of information and for importance of opinion. Here are some of the tests as outlined by Esther Grassian of the UCLA College Library:[14]

Content and Evaluation

1. How complete and accurate are the information and the links provided by this source?
2. How good is this site vis-à-vis other sites or print sources? (A librarian can help answer this question.)
3. What are the dates on the site and its materials?
4. How comprehensive is the site? Is the site-builder interested only in certain aspects of a topic (e.g., the Arab side of the Arab-Israeli conflict)? Does he or she attempt to cover everything available—and if so, how? Are evaluations of links to other sources provided?

Source and Dates

1. Who produced the site? Why? What authority or knowledge does the site-builder have? Is there a sponsoring organization with a vested interest in what results from people using the site?
2. Is there evident bias in the materials you find?
3. When was the site mounted, and when was it last revised? How up-to-date is it?
4. Is it easy to contact the site-builder with questions?

Structure

1. Does the site follow good graphics principles? Is the use of art purposive or decorative?

2. Do the icons clearly represent what is intended?

3. Does the text follow basic tenets of good grammar, spelling, and composition?

4. Can the text be used by both line-mode (text-only) and multimedia (words/sound/pictures) users?

5. Are links provided to Web "subject trees" in directories—lists of Web sources arranged by subject?

6. How usable is the site? Can you get through it in a reasonable time?

Other

1. Is appropriate interactivity available?

2. Can you transfer secure information to and from the site?

3. Are links to search engines provided?

Search Help.   Grassian's last point also is ours: You need to be able to use **search engines** to help you through the maze of material available electronically. A search engine is an online database that allows you to explore broad subjects and find specific information by being directed to a source. It's like the bibliographies in a library's reference area, and some—the "super" engines—are like the bibliographies of bibliographies. They come with different virtues as well. *Large databases* include Yahoo!, Alta Vista, HotBot, Northern Light, Excite, InfoSeek, and Lycos. *Advanced search features* on InfoSeek and Alta Vista allow you to easily search within your results or refine your questions; *annotated directories* that tell you how to get into searches as you search include AlphaSearch and the University of Iowa Gateway (both guides to especially academic search), the Britannica Internet Guide, LookSmart, Snap!, and The Mining Co. *Business directories* include Livelink Pinstripe, Dow Jones Business Directory, SearchZ, and Northern Light Industry Search. A nice online guide to search engines, *Guide to Meta-Search Engines* by Jian Liu, will help you even further with these and other tools.[15] See Table 6.3 for advice on which search engines to use for which approaches to information finding and retrieving.

The Print World

Most teachers and experts will tell you to watch out when you use information from the Web and to do your final research, when possible, in the print world. There simply are more controls on print than electronic sources, generally speaking. The trick for using traditional print competently is to look for the different kinds and qualities of information in different places.

Newspapers.   Newspapers obviously are a useful source of information about events of current interest. Moreover, their feature stories and accounts of unusual happenings provide a storehouse of interesting illustrations and examples. You must be careful, of course, not to accept everything in a newspaper as true, because the haste with which news must be gathered sometimes makes complete accuracy difficult. Your school or city library undoubtedly has copies of one or two highly reliable papers, such as the *New York Times,* the *Observer,* the *Wall Street Journal,* or the *Christian Science Monitor,* as well as of the leading

TABLE 6.3 Internet Search Engines

Information Needed	Characteristics of the Search Engine
Overview of topic	Yahoo! organizes information in "trees," from general to specific topics.
Relevant hits only	Excite has excellent summaries, and you can ask for "more documents like this one."
Review of what's available on the Internet	MetaCrawler works across search engines; Inference Find searches engines, merges the results, and removes redundancies.
Pinpoint research	AltaVista is massive yet has a fast indexer of full texts; good for very specific searches.
Common words	HotBot is fast and powerful, and ranks results and other options for searches.
Have a date	HotBot Super Search limits by date.
Scientific information	AltaVista has the best rating among general engines.
Proper name searches	AltaVista and InfoSeek are sensitive to capital letters; HotBot can search names in regular or reversed order (Sam Jones; Jones, Sam).
Images, sounds, media types (Java, VRML), extensions (jpg; .gif)	Try Lycos Media, HotBot Super Search, The Amazing Picture Machine, Yahoo! Computers and Internet, or Multimedia:Pictures.
E-mail discussion groups	LISZT is a directory of listservs and those (majordomos) who run them.
Quotations	Go to The Quotations Page, Bartlett, or Land of Quotes.
Titles	Use Hytelnet to search telnet sites by title.
Lyrics	See the International Lyrics Server.
Browse sites	Both A2Z and Yahoo! use subject trees directories with short descriptions of files.
All search engines at once	Got to All-In-One or Mamma (the "mother of all search engines"). To stir in directories, Usenet news sites, and FTP sites, use Dogpile or WebTaxi.

Source: Information taken from material prepared by Debbie Abilock (1996), updated 6/13/98, at http://www.nueva.pvt.k12.ca.use/~de . . . library/adviceengine.htm, with some help from Kathy Schrock. See endnote 13.

newspapers in your state or region. If your library has the *New York Times Index,* you can locate that paper's accounts of people and events from 1913 to the present. Another useful and well-indexed source of information on current happenings is *Facts on File,* which has been issued weekly since 1940. (Some newspapers also can be accessed and searched on the Web or on CD-ROMs from your library.)

Magazines.   The average university library subscribes to hundreds of magazines and journals. Some, such as *Time, Newsweek,* and *U.S. News & World Report,* summarize weekly events. *The Atlantic* and *Harper's* are monthly publications that cover a wide range of subjects, both of passing and of lasting importance. *The Nation, Vital Speeches of the Day, Fortune, Washington Monthly,* and *The New Republic,* among others, publish commentary on current political, social, and economic questions. More specialized magazines include *Popular Science, Scientific American, Sports Illustrated, Field and Stream, Ms., Better Homes and Gardens, Byte, Today's Health, National Geographic,* and *The Smithsonian.*

   This list is, of course, just the beginning. Hundreds of periodicals are available that cover thousands of subjects. To find specific kinds of information, use the *Readers' Guide to Periodical Literature,* which indexes most of the magazines you'll want to consult in preparing a speech. If you'd like more sophisticated material, consult the *Social Sciences Index* and the *Humanities Index,* which now are computerized in most libraries. Similar indexes are available for publications in technical fields and from professional societies; a reference librarian can show you how to use them.

Yearbooks and Encyclopedias.   The most reliable source of comprehensive data is the *Statistical Abstracts of the United States,* an annual publication covering subjects ranging from weather records and birth rates to steel production and election results. Information on Academy Award Winners, world records in various areas, and the "bests" and "worsts" of almost anything can be found in the *World Almanac, The People's Almanac, The Guinness Book of World Records, The Book of Lists,* and *Information Please.* Encyclopedias such as the *Encyclopaedia Britannica* and *Encyclopedia Americana* attempt to cover the entire field of human knowledge and are valuable chiefly as initial references or for background reading. Refer to them for important scientific, geographical, literary, or historical facts; for bibliographies of authoritative books on a subject; and for ideas you don't need to develop completely in your speech.

Documents and Reports.   Various government agencies—state, national, and international—as well as many independent organizations publish reports on special subjects. The most frequently consulted governmental publications are the hearings and recommendations of congressional committees in the publications from the U.S. Department of Health and Human Services or Department of Commerce. Reports on issues related to agriculture, business, government, engineering, and scientific experimentation also are published by many state universities. Endowed groups such as the Carnegie, Rockefeller, and Ford Foundations and special interest groups such as the Foreign Policy Association, Brookings Institution, League of Women Voters, Common Cause, and the U.S. Chamber of Commerce also publish reports and pamphlets. Though by no means a complete list, *The Vertical File Index* serves as a guide to some of these materials. Also search "newsletters" with LEXIS-NEXIS.

Books.   Most subjects suitable for a speech have been written about in books. As a guide to these books, use the subject-matter headings in the card catalog of your local library. Generally, you'll find authoritative books in your school library and more popularized treatments in your public library. You now can access your and other libraries' card catalog electronically. This often makes your search more efficient and productive.

Biographical Dictionaries. The *Dictionary of National Biography, Dictionary of American Biography, Who's Who, Who's Who in America, Current Biography,* and more specialized works organized according to field contain biographical sketches especially useful in locating facts about famous people and in documenting the qualifications of authorities whose testimony you may quote.

The Face-to-Face World

As you become a more proficient oral communicator during this course, you should not forget that you can use the skills you're gaining in speech preparation and analysis to help you acquire information as well. You can prepare and conduct interviews with people who can supply you with facts, opinions, background information, and leads to other sources.

Conducting Informational Interviews. The goal of an **informational interview** is to obtain answers to specific questions. In conducting the interview, you hope to elicit answers that can be woven into your speech. These answers also can increase your general understanding of a topic so that you avoid misinforming your audience or drawing incorrect inferences from information obtained through other sources. The interviewee may be a content expert or someone who has had personal experience with the issues you'll discuss. If you are addressing the topic of work at absolute zero, who better to help you than a physicist? If you are explaining the construction of farm ponds, you might contact a local civil engineer.

You should observe the following general guidelines when planning an informational interview:

- *Decide on your specific purpose.* What precise information do you hope to obtain during the interview? One caution: If you are interviewing controversial figures, don't attack them. Even if you disagree with the answers being given, you're not someone from *Law and Order,* seeking to win a jury's vote by grilling the witness. This does not mean that your purpose cannot encompass tough questions or those that seek further clarification of answers that seem "not right." You can raise such questions without provoking an argument.
- *Structure the interview in advance.* The beginning of an interview clarifies the purpose and sets limits on what will be covered. You also can use this time to establish rapport with the person being interviewed. The middle of the interview comprises the substantive portion: information being sought is provided. Structure your questions in advance so that you have a rough idea of what to ask and when. Finally, the list will be useful as you summarize your understanding of the major points; this will help you avoid misinterpreting the meaning given to specific points by the person

interviewed. The following format is an example of one you might follow in an informational interview:

  I. Opening
    A. Mutual greeting
    B. Discussion of purposes
        1. Reason information is needed
        2. Kind of information wanted
 II. Informational portion
    A. Question #1, with clarifying questions as needed
    B. Question #2, with clarifying questions as needed
    C. [and so on]
III. Closing
    A. Summary of main points
    B. Final courtesies

- *Remember that interviews are interactive processes.* There is a definite pattern of "turn-taking" in interviews that allows both parties to concentrate on one issue at a time and also assists in making the interview work for the benefit of both. This interactive pattern requires that both parties be careful listeners, because one person's comment will affect the next comment of the other. Should you forge ahead or ask intervening questions to clarify or elaborate on a previous response? Constantly ask yourself that question.

Communicative Skills for Successful Interviewers.   It should by now be clear that adept interviewers must have certain communicative skills.

- *A good interviewer is a good listener.* Unless you take care to understand what someone is saying and interpret the significance of those comments, you may misunderstand that person. You can achieve clarification only if you are a good listener (see Chapter 3 on listening for comprehension).
- *A good interviewer is open.* Many of us are extremely wary of interviewers. We are cynical enough to believe they have a hidden agenda—unstated motives or purposes—that they are trying to pursue. Too often, interviewers have said they "only want a little information" when actually they were selling magazine subscriptions or a religious ideal. Frankness and openness should govern all aspects of your interview.
- *A good interviewer builds a sense of mutual respect and trust.* Feelings of trust and respect are created by revealing your own motivation, getting the person to talk, and expressing sympathy and understanding. Sometimes, of course, your assumptions of integrity and goodwill can be wrong, but to start with suspicion and distrust is to condemn the relationship without giving it a fair chance.

The Snail-Mail World

Even as you acquire e-mail and other computer-based electronic communication skills, you should not neglect "snail-mail"—the mail that travels in semis, little white Jeeps, and the leather bags that postal carriers bring to your front door daily. You may get enough junk mail to realize there's still profit to be made in writing to people the old fashioned way—through letters of inquiry and questionnaires.

Letters of Inquiry.   Sometimes a simple letter requesting information from an institutional source is all you need to gain some useful material. You might want to write to your college president and ask for a copy of her fall convocation speech; to Bennetton for the Web address of their home page so that you can get pictures to their TV ads, or to the U.S. Government Printing Office for their latest catalog of consumer-protection pamphlets. When writing such a letter, follow a few simple rules:

1. *Keep it short.* Explain why you're writing and what you want as specifically as you can. Three to four short paragraphs—certainly less than two-thirds of a page—are enough. Don't say "where can I find out about your ads?" but rather "where can I locate the text for the first Neon ad that was broadcast during the 1994 Super Bowl?"
2. *Keep it easy.* If you need only minimal information—say, an address—leave room at the bottom of your letter where your correspondent can reply and then return the same letter to you.
3. *Include a stamped, self-addressed envelope.* OK, so Frito-Lay could afford to put a stamp on a letter, but if you save them typing an envelope and make them feel a little guilty by stamping it, it'll be harder for them to simply toss it aside without replying.

Let's now look at an example of a short letter of inquiry:

A Letter of Inquiry

Customer Service Representative

ABC Beverage Distributing Company

Local Address

Re: Posters for Current Advertising Campaign

Dear Customer Service Representative:

I am a student at Middle College, taking a course in public communication. As part of a class assignment, I have decided to give a speech analyzing the current imaginative advertising campaign for Drink-a-billy Root Beer. I would like to include as visual aids for my speech some posters that have been prepared for this campaign. I have seen them locally and find them even more effective than the TV ads.

Could you please send me one or two of the posters that have been distributed to local grocery stores? I will be needing them by November 16 to show them during my speech. If there's any cost associated with sending the posters, let me know and I'll be happy to reimburse you.

If you cannot send the posters, please indicate so on the enclosed postcard. Thank you for your help in this matter.

Sincerely yours,
Shirin Hasian

In this letter, Hasian has explained what she needs and used positive language so the distributor does not think she's going to attack the product. She also has specified the date by which she needs it so the process doesn't drag on forever and has sent along a card so she won't be expecting something that's not going to come. (If the ABC representative wants to tell her she has to write somewhere else for the posters, that also can be written on the card and mailed to her with minimal effort.)

Questionnaires.   On other occasions, you may wish to discover what a group of people knows or thinks about a subject. If, for example, you wanted to give a speech on a proposed halfway house for people with disabilities, you might survey residents in the vicinity. You could send a questionnaire to people chosen randomly from the phone book or to all residents within a three-block radius from the proposed site. If you're seeking information on a new college advising program, you could survey dormitory residents or members of several classes. With the results, you then may construct your own statistical summaries for presentation as part of your speech.

When developing a questionnaire, keep the following guidelines in mind:

- Be sure the form explains the exact purpose of the questionnaire and the procedures to follow in responding to the questions.
- Keep the form short and focused on the specific points for which you wish to have responses.
- For ease of summarizing, use closed questions (e.g., ask for "yes/no" responses where appropriate, use categories such as "strongly agree/agree/disagree/strongly disagree" if you want ranges of opinion).
- Phrase questions in clear, neutral language. Do not use loaded terms (e.g., "Do you wish to see mentally unbalanced, unpredictable people living next to your children?").
- Pilot-test the form with a few people to see if the instructions are clear and determine if any need to be rephrased.
- If mailing the questionnaire, include a stamped, self-addressed envelope to encourage returns.

Recording Information in Usable Forms

When you find the information you've been looking for, either photocopy it or take notes. Whether you use 4- by 6-inch notecards or a notebook, it is helpful to have an accurate, legible record of the materials you wish to consider for your speech. An incomplete source citation makes it difficult to find that information again if you need to recheck it; hurried scribbles are hard to decipher later as well.

Many people find that notecards are easier to use than a notebook, because they can be shuffled by topic area or type of support. If you use a notebook, however, try recording each item on half a page. Most of your information will not fill a page, so this will save paper. Cutting the sheets in half will make it easier to sort your data or to adopt a classification scheme and relate information to particular themes or subpoints of your speech.

USING SOURCE MATERIAL ETHICALLY

Now that we've discussed locating and generating material for your speeches, we come to a major ethical issue—plagiarism. **Plagiarism** is defined as "the unacknowledged inclusion of someone else's words, ideas, or data as one's own."[16] One of the saddest things an instructor must do is cite a student for plagiarism, because in speech classes, students do occasionally take material from a source they've read and present it as their own. Many speech teachers and members of audiences habitually scan the library periodicals section. Even if listeners have not read the article, it soon becomes apparent that something is wrong: the wording differs from how the person usually talks, the style is more typical of written than spoken English, or the speech is a patchwork of eloquent and awkward phrasing. In addition, the organizational pattern of the speech may lack a well-formulated introduction or conclusion or not be one normally used by speakers. Often, too, the person who plagiarizes an article reads it aloud badly—another sign that something is wrong.

Plagiarism is not, however, simply undocumented verbatim quotation. It also includes undocumented paraphrases of others' ideas and undocumented use of others' main ideas. For example, if you paraphrase a movie review from *Newsweek* without acknowledging that staff critic David Ansen had those insights or use economic predictions without giving credit to *BusinessWeek,* you are guilty of plagiarism.

Suppose you ran across the following idea while reading Neil Postman's *Amusing Ourselves to Death: Public Discourse in the Age of Show Business:*

> The television commercial is not at all about the character of products to be consumed. It is about the character of the consumers of products. Images of movie stars and famous athletes, of serene lakes and macho fishing trips, of elegant dinners and romantic interludes, of happy families packing their station wagons for a picnic in the country—these tell nothing about the products being sold. But they tell everything about the fears, fancies and dreams of those who might buy them. What the advertiser needs to know is not what is right about the product but what is wrong about the buyer. And so, the balance of business expenditures shifts from product research to market research. The television commercial has oriented business away from making

products of value and toward making consumers feel valuable, which means that the business of business has now become pseudo-therapy. The consumer is a patient assured by psycho-dramas.[17]

Imagine that you wanted to make this point in a speech on the changing role of electronic advertising. Of course, you want to avoid plagiarism. Here are some ways you could use these ideas ethically:

1. *Verbatim quotation of a passage.* Simply read the passage aloud word for word. To avoid plagiarism, say, "Neil Postman, in his 1985 book *Amusing Ourselves to Death: Public Discourse in the Age of Show Business,* said this about the nature of television advertisements." You then quote the paragraph.

2. *Paraphrasing of the main ideas.* Summarize the author's ideas in your own words: "We've all grown up with television advertising, and most of the time we endure it without giving it much thought. In his book *Amusing Ourselves to Death: Public Discourse in the Age of Show Business,* Neil Postman makes the point that instead of selling us on the virtues of a product, advertisers sell us our own fears and dreams. Advertisements are more about us than about the products being sold."

3. *Partial quotation of phrases.* Quote a brief passage, and then summarize the rest of the author's ideas in your own words: "Postman suggests that the shift from product research to market research indicates a shift in emphasis away from the product being sold and to the consumer. He says that business now focuses on making the consumer feel better through 'pseudo-therapy. The consumer is a patient assured by psycho-dramas.'" Be sure to pause, however, and say "quote" to indicate when you are quoting the author's words.

Plagiarism is easy to avoid if you take reasonable care. Moreover, by citing such authorities as Postman, who are well educated and experienced, you add their credibility to your own. Avoid plagiarism to keep from being expelled from your class—or even from your school. Avoid it for positive reasons as well: to improve your *ethos* by associating your thinking with that of experts.

Finding and using supporting materials expertly give your speeches power and drive. As we noted at the beginning of this chapter, supporting materials are the fuel—have plenty along for the journey!

CHAPTER SUMMARY

Competent speakers use five primary forms of supporting materials to clarify, amplify, and strengthen their presentations:

- *Explanations,* which answer the questions "what," "how," or "why."
- *Comparisons and contrasts,* which explain the similarities and differences between

ideas and processes familiar and unfamiliar to listeners.

- *Examples and narratives,* which provide detailed illustrations, undeveloped specific instances, or stories.
- *Statistics,* which show the numerical relationships between or among phenomena.

- *Testimony,* which cites the opinions or conclusions of qualified experts.

These materials can be assembled from the electronic world (electronic card catalog, CD-ROM indexes, World Wide Web searches), the print world (newspapers, magazines, yearbooks and reports, books, biographical dictionaries), the face-to-face world (informational interviews), and the snail-mail world (letters of inquiry, questionnaires). Record information from any source both fully and accurately, either on notecards or notebook pages. Avoid plagiarism.

KEY TERMS

Boolean searching (p. 136)

CD-ROM (p. 136)

comparison (p. 127)

contrast (p. 128)

explanation (p. 126)

illustration (p. 128)

Information Superhighway (p. 137)

informational interview (p. 143)

magnitude (p. 130)

narrative (p. 128)

plagiarism (p. 147)

search engines (p. 140)

segments (p. 131)

specific instance (p. 128)

statistics (p. 128)

testimony (p. 133)

trends (p. 131)

World Wide Web (p. 137)

ASSESSMENT ACTIVITIES

1. Read one of the speeches in this textbook, and identify the forms of its supporting material. Down the lefthand side of the page, record the idea or assertion being made. Across from it, on the righthand side, indicate the type(s) of supporting materials used to clarify, amplify, or strengthen it. Then, assess the speaker's use of supporting materials: Were good choices made (or not)? In other words, was the material adequate to clarify, amplify, and strengthen ideas? What could have been done better? How?

2. Work in groups of two to four students, trying to make sure at least one member of the group has access to the Internet (though all of this information can be found in a good library). Work in pairs, with each pair assigned four items to find—one student working in print resources and the other electronically, if possible. (If that's not possible, students should work together in the print resources.) When the pairs turn in their reports, they should include a careful citation of where they found the information:

   a. Weekly or daily summary of current national news.

   b. Daily summary of stock market action.

   c. Text of Bill Clinton's grand jury testimony of August 17, 1998.

   d. Text of Bill Livingstone's first speech as House Majority Leader in January 1999.

   e. A mission statement for the National Rifle Association.

   f. At least three different meanings for the word "wit" and dates when those meanings came into use.

   g. Current status of California legislation on educational reform.

   h. Description of a recent traffic accident, locally or nationally reported.

   i. A list of CDs by Paula Cole.

   j. Brief sketch of the Big Ten's basketball schedules.

REFERENCES

1. Randall L. Tobias, "In Today Walks Tomorrow," *Representative American Speeches, 1992–1993,* ed. Owen Peterson, Vol. 65, No. 6 (New York: H. W. Wilson, 1993), 105.
2. H. Ross Perot, CNN Coverage of the Reform Party Nominating Convention, Long Beach, CA, 11 August 1996.
3. Minister Louis Farrakhan, "Transcript from Minister Louis Farrakhan's Remarks at the Million Man March," 17 October 1995, from cnn.com/US/9510/megamarch/10-16/transcript/index.html.
4. To examine Cicero's own use of *accumulatio,* see Donovan J. Ochs, "Rhetorical Detailing in Cicero's Verrine Orations," *Communication Studies* 23 (1982): 310–318.
5. Mary Fisher, "A Whisper of AIDS," *Women's Voices in Our Time,* ed. Victoria L. DeFrancisco and Marvin D. Jensen (Prospect Heights, IL: Waveland Press, 1994).
6. Brenda Theriault, "Fast Foods," speech given at the University of Maine, Spring 1992.
7. "Union Needs Make-Over, Students Say," *The Daily Iowan,* 16 December 1998, 1.
8. Material from John Simons, "The Web's Dirty Secret," *U.S. News & World Report* 121 (19 August 1996): 51.
9. Hortense Hunn, "Testimony Before House Subcommittee on Human Resources," 8 April 1993. *Oversight Regarding the Head Start Program,* House of Representatives Hearing, 103 Congress (Washington, DC: U.S. Government Printing Office, 1993), 88.
10. Carl Hall, "A Heap of Trouble," *Winning Orations, 1977.*
11. Go to http://literacy.kent.edu/Midwest/Math/refsites.html to pursue many works on how to use statistics. Such a study area is called the study of numeracy.
12. Richard Reeves, "The Woman of the Century," *American Heritage,* December 1998, 12.
13. For a larger vocabulary, find a good basic book on the Web or check out *Kathy Schrock's Guide for Educators* at http://www.capecod.net/schrockguide/yp/iypsrch.htm.
14. Esther Grassian, "Thinking Critically about World Wide Web Resources," http://www.library.ucla.edu/libraries/college/instruct/web/critical.htm, 1997.
15. Found at http://www.indiana.edu/~librcsd/search/sla.html. Because IBM helped Indiana University put its library online, it has become a most important research source.
16. Louisiana State University, "Academic Honesty and Dishonesty," adapted from LSU's Code of Student Conduct, 1981.
17. Neil Postman, *Amusing Ourselves to Death: Public Discourse in the Age of Show Business* (New York: Viking Penguin, 1985), 128.

Chapter 7

Adapting the Speech Structure to Audiences: The Motivated Sequence and Patterns of Internal Organization

For his first major classroom speech, Tom decided to talk about a subject he was interested in—doing research at the Library of Congress. Because he had just been there, he wouldn't need to do any more work in preparing the speech; he could just tell the audience how much he learned while there. When his turn came, he walked confidently to the lectern and simply began telling his story. Midway through the speech, he thought he sensed disinterest on the part of the audience. "What could be wrong with them?" went through his mind as he moved on to the most exciting part of the speech—looking up sources on the computerized catalog. When he finished, the instructor asked for any comments from his listeners. Their comments shocked him: "What was the reason for that speech?" "Do you always ramble when you speak?"

Tom's experience is not far off the mark when one speaks without considering the audience. Tom had assumed that because students wrote research papers, they would automatically find his descriptions worthwhile. He had given no thought to the audience's interests or needs; hence, he didn't even bother to think about ways to motivate interest in his topic. He also hadn't bothered to structure his speech to keep the flow of events clear in the audience's mind. If he forgot to mention something, he just circled back and filled in the missing information. ("When I talked about bringing your laptop into the building, I forgot to tell you", "Oh, you also need to make sure that . . .", "Lastly, but before I get to that, you should also realize that . . ."). Personal familiarity with a topic is not the same as spending time making sure the audience can follow the development of ideas, as Tom discovered. Audiences dislike rambling, unconnected, incoherent patterns as they listen. Structuring ideas provides direction for the audience; it lets them follow the development of your message so that by the time you conclude, they know the central idea or claim and how it was explained or supported.

In this chapter, we explore organizational patterns that assist you in arranging your materials in the most effective manner. Before examining specific patterns, however, it is important to consider using language to structure ideas and how listeners perceive your speech structure. The *motivated sequence* is a well-known, general-purpose approach that approximates how audiences think as they respond to your message—the questions they ask themselves that need to be answered as you move through each phase of your presentation.

USING LANGUAGE TO ORGANIZE IDEAS

People actively seek organization in their environment, imposing it if they cannot find it naturally. Watch young children: They learn early that one set of furniture goes in a bedroom, another in a kitchen, and a third in a living room. By elementary school, they can determine what is *foreground* in a picture and what is *background* or supporting detail. Such processes of differentiation lend coherence to their perceptions of objects and events. They also can complete or fill in missing elements in sequences or patterns of words or drawings. For example, if someone says "One, two, three, four," you almost automatically continue with "five, six, seven, eight." If a cartoonist draws a few pen lines of a well-known person, you probably can identify the individual. Or, if you see an unclosed circle, you'll likely perceive it as a circle because of its resemblance to complete ones you've seen.[1] Generally speaking, the principles of **differentiation** and **closure**—of sorting items into groups and completing pictures or experiences in your mind's eye—are central to our understanding of verbal organization or order.

The key idea underlying verbal organization is this: *People use language to structure and, thereby, make sense of their world.* Think of some language strategies you use to organize parts of your life:

- *Numerical order:* "In the first place . . ." Such language use establishes sequence.
- *Temporal order:* "Before I . . ." "After you do . . ." This language establishes when things might be done.
- *Physical space:* "In the middle"; "to the west, east, and, south." Establishing spatial relationships allows you to "see" physical order through language.
- *Topics or types:* "Executive, legislative, and judicial branches of government"; "animal, vegetable, and mineral"; "past, present, and future." Dividing a subject into manageable—and memorable—topics helps clarify relationships.
- *Narrative order:* "Once upon a time"; "I heard a story the other day"; "I awoke with a start that morning." Turning a series of events into a story—with a beginning, middle, end, and even a "moral" or message—is a way of making disorganized experiences coherent and giving them a point or application.
- *Logical inference:* "Because of this . . . , therefore . . ."; "As evidence for this assertion"; "I believe that because." These phrases show connections between ideas, thereby indicating what follows from what.

- *Hierarchies:* "Higher, lower"; "inside, outside"; "under class, middle class, upper class"; "important, unimportant"; "main points, secondary points." We often build hierarchies out of social or intellectual judgments to help us understand or argue for what is more or less central to our lives.

These are just some of the language devices used in organizing or ordering life experiences. These phrases show relationships among ideas, events, and objects, and as we convey our perceptions to others, these phrases become indispensable aids in making ideas clear.

As listeners, we depend on a speaker's use of specific phrases to cue us as to the sequencing or patterning of ideas—what comes first, where are we, etc. As listeners, we look for the same sense of order in a speech as the speaker moves from central idea to explanatory points or from claim to supporting reasons. There is a convenient orientation to how listener's process structure that has become known as **Monroe's Motivated Sequence.** The next section is devoted to this holistic structure for organizing messages.

THE FIVE BASIC STEPS OF THE MOTIVATED SEQUENCE

The steps of the motivated sequence conform to a listener's desire for coherence and order. As a holistic way of organizing speeches, it is responsive to the thought processes listeners often follow when receiving new information or solving problems. When you find yourself listening to a classroom speech, you probably experience a predictable series of reactions: "Why should I listen?" "Ok, what do you mean? Why is that true?" "How does this affect me?" "So, what do you want from me as a result of this speech?" These and other questions are typical responses by audience members as they listen to an informative or persuasive presentation.

From the listener's perspective, the major reasons for listening can be reduced to two broad classes: reasons serving the person's *biological* needs, and reasons supporting the person's *social* desires or intent.[2] The motive to eat when hungry or sleep when tired results from biologically determined needs or drives. External stimuli such as a stuffy room also can affect your physiological state. Providing reasons to listen when the audience is hot, tired, hungry, or all three is essential if you want your ideas heard. Social motives are individual goals, desires, or behaviors that result from acting in accordance with your understanding of what others expect or value. Your desires to achieve success on a speech, to feel wanted or needed by others, and to be the kind of person others admire are examples of personal, social motives. From your listeners' perspective, the same social motives direct and guide their response to you. They wish to be seen as attentive, interested, cooperative members of your audience (for the most part). Presenting your ideas in a manner that maximizes their ability to adhere to these common social motives enables them to attend to the entirety of your speech rather than just to a few minutes of it.

The motivated sequence provides a template of sorts, arranged in five basic steps, for this natural progression of audience queries. As a starting place, you

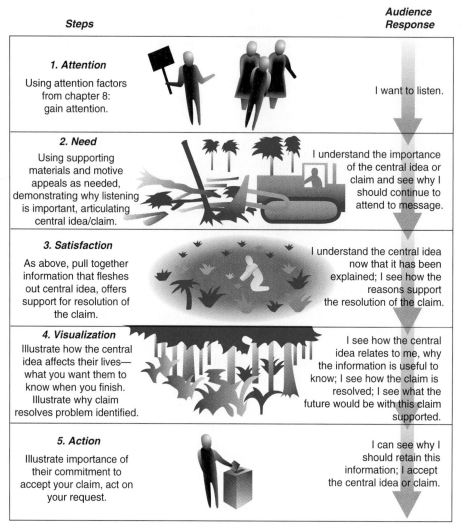

Steps

Audience Response

1. Attention

Using attention factors from chapter 8: gain attention.

I want to listen.

2. Need

Using supporting materials and motive appeals as needed, demonstrating why listening is important, articulating central idea/claim.

I understand the importance of the central idea or claim and see why I should continue to attend to message.

3. Satisfaction

As above, pull together information that fleshes out central idea, offers support for resolution of the claim.

I understand the central idea now that it has been explained; I see how the reasons support the resolution of the claim.

4. Visualization

Illustrate how the central idea affects their lives— what you want them to know when you finish. Illustrate why claim resolves problem identified.

I see how the central idea relates to me, why the information is useful to know; I see how the claim is resolved; I see what the future would be with this claim supported.

5. Action

Illustrate importance of their commitment to accept your claim, act on your request.

I can see why I should retain this information; I accept the central idea or claim.

FIGURE 7.1   The Motivated Sequence

must get people to *attend* to a problem or feel strongly enough to want to hear more about the deficiency you want them to help correct. Then, you can address more specific needs or desires in relation to an individual's personal sense of *need*. Once these have been established, you can attempt to *satisfy* them by showing what can be done to solve the problem or alleviate its impact on their lives. Simply describing a course of action may be insufficient to move an audience to act, move to *visualizing* what the situation would be like if the action were carried out or, conversely, what it would be like if the action were not taken. With these motivational tasks completed, you can appeal to the audience members to *act*—to put into practice the proposed solution to the problem. The sequential patterning of these steps—from attention to action—is not a hard and fast rule; you will need to adapt the pattern to the rhetorical situation you face. The key: use this pattern as a template in asking yourself what questions will the audience be likely to ask, and in what order? Do they need a strong "attention" step, or are they already keyed into the topic's importance? Will they ask to be "satisfied," and at what point? As a holistic organizational tool, the motivated sequence can be used to structure many different sorts of speeches on many different topics.

Now that we've briefly introduced the motivated sequence, we examine more closely the individual steps. In particular, we note their internal structuring, the methods for developing them, and the kinds of materials that can be used effectively in each.

The Attention Step

As a speaker, your first task is to gain attention. In planning this stage, you need to read ahead and examine the nine factors of attention discussed in Chapter 8: activity, reality, proximity, familiarity, novelty, suspense, conflict, humor, and the vital. In general, you always need to begin your speech with something more innovative than "Today I'd like to . . ." or "My speech today is on . . ."

Your manner of delivery also affects the attentiveness of your audience. The vigor and variety of your gestures and bodily movements and the flexibility and animation of your voice are important determinants of audience enthusiasm and interest. Your credibility—or *ethos*—as it is judged by your listeners also assists you in securing their attention. If they already have high regard for you, they're more likely to be attentive as you begin your presentation. The color and impressiveness of your language and style also affect the audience's willingness to attend to your message. For example, a lackadaisical delivery, coupled with a colorless and uninteresting style, is counterproductive. Fundamentally, however, you capture and hold your listeners' attention through the types of ideas you present. Your ideas must resonate with their biological or their social interests and personal needs before they will feel compelled to listen. Gaining attention is an initial step in bringing your ideas to an audience, but remember that keeping their attention also is vitally important. Use the same attention devices (see Chapter 8) as you develop the remaining steps of the motivated sequence; in particular, these devices can be used to heighten attention during the need and visualization steps.

The Need Step

Assuming the audience is attending to you and your message, you must set forth reasons for their being concerned about the issue you're discussing: Why is the information or viewpoint vital to their interests? Why should they think the problem is urgent? To provide answers, the **need step** can be set up effectively like this:

1. *Statement.* Offer a clear statement of the need. State the central idea or claim, and even phrase it in more than one way to make the point clear.

   Among people of color, there is a growing need for social and political activism on the part of young adults—activism that makes a difference.[3]

2. *Illustration.* Present one or more illustrations or specific instances to give listeners an initial idea of the problem's seriousness and scope— its importance or significance.

   Mary Kay Penn, 32, is president of the Institute of African American Folk Culture in Harlem; she recently raised $50,000 for the Institute and convinced an Hispanic organization to donate a photo processing lab.

   The New Progressive Party in Wisconsin, largely African American and Latino, has elected 22 officials from its ranks.

   The Black Student Leadership Network, a college-based arm of the Children's Defense Fund, aided more than 2,000 children this past summer; its southern region coordinator is only 23.

3. *Ramification.* Using the types of supporting materials discussed in Chapter 6, clarify your statement of need and justify the concern you're expressing. Add more examples, additional statistics, testimony from experts, and other forms of support to drive your analysis forward.

   Nationally, there are four reasons why such activism must continue: First, proposed cuts in student aid may affect as many as 1.5 million students; people of color will be among those affected. Second, historically black colleges and universities, such as Howard University, which depends on federal subsidies for 55 percent of its budget, will be adversely affected by reductions in federal aid to education. Third, court-ordered changes in voting districts may adversely affect communities of color, thereby changing, literally, the complexion of Congress. Fourth, the transition to block grants to states, with state caps on spending for programs like Aid to Families with Dependent Children, will mean lessened flexibility in meeting needs. To the extent people of color are recipients, they, along with others, will find it more difficult to receive needed assistance.

4. *Pointing.* Impress upon your listeners the issue's seriousness, scope, and significance to them. Tie it to their health, happiness, security, or other interests.

   Given the national deficit, it is clear that some cuts, especially in the social areas just noted, will be coming. What can you do? Lamont Harris, 27-year-old founder of a center devoted to giving people survival skills, Reality Plus One, says this in response: "It's gonna make people fight back. Maybe this time we won't stop short like we did in the 70s." Are you ready to fight back—to organize on your own and provide services where shortages and the absence of assistance will occur?

In the need step, you have two primary goals: to make your subject clear, and to relate your subject to the concerns and interests of your audience. Although you may not need to use all four tactics every time you discuss some need, you at least should think about them. For example, when arguing for the end of an armed conflict in a distant region of the world, you wouldn't need to do much with illustration and ramifications; on the other hand, the statement of the need—how does the problem affect listeners in Two Dot, Montana, or Corea, Maine—is of critical importance. Adjust the development of the need step to your topic, the audience's knowledge base, and their concerns.

The Satisfaction Step

The purpose of the **satisfaction step** is to help your listeners understand the information you're presenting or to obtain their assent to the action you're proposing. The structure of this step varies depending on whether your purpose is primarily informative, entertaining, or persuasive. Consider this step for each type of speech.

The Satisfaction Step in a Speech to Inform. Giving your listeners a clear understanding of a topic is the key to meeting this step. Consider a speech on the need for social and political activism. If cast as an informative speech, it does not include a well-developed plan for how to respond to such activism, as would a speech to persuade or actuate, but you certainly would want your listeners to know that activism is alive and well in communities of color.

In the satisfaction step of a speech to actuate, a speaker can explain the new action, belief, or attitude that will remedy the problem.

1. *Initial summary.* Briefly state the main ideas you'll cover.

   Responding to the challenge will not be easy; it will take personal commitment and hard work. But, as the following examples suggest, it can be done. . . .

2. *Detailed information.* Discuss the facts and explanations pertaining to each of the main ideas. For our speech on activism among people of color, give further examples of the social service work being done and the political organizing going on in communities of color.

3. *Final summary.* Restate the main ideas you've presented together with any important conclusions you want to leave with your listeners. If your purpose in this speech is informative rather than persuasive, this step would fall short of actually asking them to act on their own.

   In this speech, I've given you a number of examples of social service and political activity currently being carried out by young people of color. As students, we need to be concerned about the effects of funding cuts on our and others' lives; we can learn from the examples set by our sisters and brothers.

The Satisfaction Step in a Speech to Persuade or Actuate.   In these types of speeches, the satisfaction step is developed as a major subdivision of the speech. The following elements usually are included:

- *Statement.* Briefly state the attitude, belief, or action you wish the audience to adopt.
- *Explanation.* Make sure your statement is understood by the audience. Diagrams or charts may be useful in explaining a complex proposal or plan.
- *Theoretical demonstration.* Show how this belief or action logically meets the problem illustrated in the need step.
- *Workability.* If appropriate, present examples showing that this solution has worked effectively in the past or that this belief has been supported by experience. Use facts, figures, and expert testimony to support your claim about the workability of your proposal or idea.
- *Meeting objections.* Forestall opposition by answering any possible objections that might be raised.

These elements may not be needed in every speech to persuade or actuate, and they also may not appear in this order. For instance, if workability is key to the success of your proposal and the audience already is well informed, you can shorten the preceding steps and spend most of your time persuading the audience your idea can work.

Conversely, if workability is not the central issue but an explanation of how your solution solves the problem is in order, you may spend more time on this facet. In any case, the elements—in sequence—offer a useful framework for presenting a solution to a problem: briefly state what you propose to do, explain it clearly, show how it remedies the problem, demonstrate its workability, and answer any objections.

The Satisfaction Step in a Speech to Entertain.   When your purpose is to entertain—to present a useful thought or sentiment in a lighthearted, humorous manner—the satisfaction step can constitute the major part of your speech. Your goal is to satisfy the audience that the speech is, in fact, entertaining and has conveyed an idea or sentiment worth their time and attention. When developing the satisfaction step in a speech to entertain, follow these guidelines:

1. *Initial statement of theme.* Briefly indicate the sentiment or idea you will discuss.
2. *Humorous elaboration.* Develop the theme with particular attention to hypothetical and factual illustrations and specific instances that convey a lighthearted—yet meaningful—message to the audience.
3. *Final summary.* Restate your main theme by connecting your illustrations to the point you wish to make.

The Visualization Step

The **visualization step** most commonly is included in speeches to persuade and actuate. The function of this step is to intensify the audience's desire or willingness to act—to motivate listeners to believe, feel, or act in a certain way. The primary strategy is to project listeners into the future and illustrate vividly the results of accepting or denying the proposed belief or of acting or failing to act as the speaker directs. The step may be developed in one of three ways:

1. *Positive method.* The **positive method of visualization** describes the favorable conditions that will prevail if the audience accepts your beliefs or proposals. Use specific examples and illustrations to give audience members a clear sense of what they can look forward to by their agreement.
2. *Negative method.* The **negative method of visualization** describes the adverse conditions that will prevail in the future if the audience does *not* adopt your ideas or proposal. Graphically describe the danger or unpleasantness that will result from their denial or inaction.
3. *Contrast method.* The **contrast method of visualization** combines both positive and negative perspectives on the future. Forecast the negative possibilities first and then introduce the positive attributes that can be expected if the audience embraces your ideas or acts upon your proposal. By means of such contrast, the bad and good effects—the disadvantages and advantages—are more striking than if they were presented in isolation from one another.

Whichever method you use, realize that the visualization step must always stand the test of reality—the conditions you picture must appear believable and probable. In addition, you must make every effort to put your listeners into the picture; use vivid imagery to create mental images that allow the audience members to see, hear, feel, taste, or smell the advantages or disadvantages you describe. The more real you make the projected situation, the greater your chances of getting a significant, positive response from your audience.

HOW TO USE THE VISUALIZATION STEP THROUGH CONTRASTIVE EFFECTS: AN ILLUSTRATION

Suppose you enter the university, as nearly 40 percent of our students do, as an "undecided"—either with few interests and even less sense of your educational goals or with many ill-defined, poorly focused interests. How will you select courses? You might approach the problem in one of two ways: either you "go with the flow," or you seek early advice and plan systematically to ensure graduation after four years./1

First Approach

If you use the first approach, you begin by taking only courses that meet specific requirements (e.g., English, speech, math, science courses). In your second year, you start experimenting with some electives—courses that will not meet specific requirements. You find yourself listening to and accepting your friends' recommendations— "Take Speech 124 because it's easy," "Take Photography 102 because it's cool," or "Take Art 103 because you get to draw what you want." Now comes your junior year. You're nowhere near a major, and you're getting close to the three-quarter mark in your education. Your advisor, parents, and friends all nag you. You even get down on yourself. In your senior year, you sample some social work courses, finally discovering something you really like. Only then do you realize it will take three or four more semesters—if you're lucky—to complete a B.S.W. degree./2

Contrasting Approach

In contrast, suppose you're one of the other half of the "undecided"— those who seek career and personal advisement early. You enroll for the no-credit "Careers and Vocational Choices" seminar in your first semester. While meeting your liberal arts requirements, you take classes in several different departments to test your interests. During your sophomore year, you work within three or four areas of possible interest; you take more advanced courses in these areas to ascertain your interest and ability. Near the end of your sophomore year, you talk with people in Career Planning and meet frequently with your advisor. By your junior year, you get departmental advisors in two majors, find out you don't like one subject as much as you thought, and consult only the second advisor after midyear. You go on to complete the major, take a summer course between your junior and senior year to catch up because you are a little behind, and obtain your degree "on time."/3

Closing Visualization

Carefully planning, experimenting with possible interests, reasoning thoughtfully about your reaction to different areas of study, and rigorously analyzing your own talents are actions that separate the completers from the complainers four years later, so

. . . [*move into the action step at this point*]./4

The Action Step

The only speech that *always* requires an **action step** is one that seeks specific action on the part of the audience. With other speech purposes, such as to inform, persuade, or entertain, you seek in this step to answer the question: "So, what do you want me to do with this information or as a result of being entertained?" Urging further study of the topic, illustrating a moral point through humor, or seeking to strengthen a belief or attitude in meeting a persuasive purpose are ways the action step is used naturally to answer this question.

The action step should be relatively brief. Two adages apply: "Stand up, speak up, shut up," and "Tell 'em what you're going to tell 'em, tell 'em, and then tell 'em what you told 'em." In the case of the social activism speech discussed earlier, an action step might be phrased as follows:

> In this speech, I've claimed that young sisters and brothers need to act on behalf of our own communities. I've presented four reasons why we must continue, as cuts in student aid, education aid, changes in representativeness in Congress, and reductions in social service support will adversely affect communities of color. We can either bury our heads in the sand and hope this crisis will pass, that it won't hurt too much, that our brothers and sisters will not suffer too much, or we can take matters into our own hands, and act. Whether your own interests lead you into social service or political organizing, Tammy Johnson, a member of the New Progressive Party, says it best: "There are those of us who have been doing community work for a while, and we decided that we could establish ourselves through our closeness to the community. If you really want to do the democracy thing, you have to do it block by block."

USING THE MOTIVATED SEQUENCE TO ORGANIZE SPEECHES

As an overall pattern of development, the most obvious use of the motivated sequence is in persuasive or actuative situations, but it also can be easily adapted to informative situations. Having reviewed the steps or stages of the motivated sequence, the following illustrations will make it much easier for you to use this overall pattern. These illustrations also represent each of the main types of speeches you're likely to experience as part of a classroom assignment or later in your career or community involvement. (See Chapters 13 and 14 for more detailed information on using the motivated sequence.)

Using the Motivated Sequence to Inform

Generally, informative speeches concentrate on the first three steps of the motivated sequence. Of course, you need to elicit the listeners' initial attention and then sustain it throughout the rest of the speech. You also must motivate them to listen, approaching the need step in this way: Why should anyone want to know the information you're about to present? Then, to satisfy this need, you actually supply the material on the subject of your speech. Sometimes an action step is added in response to the "so what?" question: What should your listeners do with this information?

You don't emphasize the action step in an informative speech, but it can provide a nice conclusion. All five steps of the motivated sequence are applied in the following overview of the steps in an informative speech.

Specific Purpose: To Inform people about how AIDS is transmitted.

Attention Step	I. Does the prospect of getting AIDS frighten you?
Need Step	I. If we are to be less frightened by this insidious disease, we all need to be better informed about the ways we can be infected and about the myths concerning how it can be acquired.
Satisfaction Step	I. AIDS can be acquired through specific sexual practices by both males and females and through sharing needles used for drug intake; it cannot be acquired from kissing, toilet seats, or sitting across from a person with AIDS.
Visualization Step	I. With this information, I hope to have allayed any irrational fears you may have by being very specific about when you are and are not at risk."
Action Step	I. This information can be useful as you consider the meaning of "safe sex" as well as when you encounter people who are HIV positive.

The following outline fleshes out in more detail how the motivated sequence can be used in an informative speech. In this case, the visualization step is omitted.

USING THE MOTIVATED SEQUENCE IN AN INFORMATIVE SPEECH
SLEEP APNEA

Attention Step	I. Do you snore, or do you know someone who does?
	II. If you snore, do you find yourself falling asleep at odd times during the day even though you're not tired?
Need Step	I. For most of us, snoring is simply a laughing matter.
	II. For one out of ten snorers, it may not be.
	A. These snorers suffer from sleep apnea.
	B. This disease causes the person to stop breathing for short periods of time.
Satisfaction Step	I. Snoring, when severe enough to cause apnea, produces negative effects on one's health.
	A. Apneic snorers suffer from short moments of oxygen deprivation accompanied by higher-than-normal levels of carbon monoxide, which affect the heart, brain, and other vital organs.
	B. Apneic snorers develop hypertension (i.e., chronic high blood pressure) at a much faster rate than nonsnorers.
	C. Apneic snorers have a much higher incidence of depression and headaches than nonsnorers.
	D. Apneic snorers experience social problems, such as job instability, marital difficulties, inability to concentrate, irri-

tability, and even aggressive behavior at a higher rate than nonsnorers.

II. You can assess the possibility of sleep apnea through a number of methods.
  A. Monitor your own snoring with a tape recorder; listen for pauses that last between 10 seconds and 1 or 2 minutes.
  B. Have a sleep partner monitor your snoring pattern; time the actual breathing lapses characteristic of snoring behavior.
  C. Daytime sleepiness is a major clue to the existence of apnea.

Action Step

I. The next time your rest is interrupted by someone's snoring, remember that it may not be a laughing matter for that person.[4]

Using the Motivated Sequence to Persuade

The following outline urges listeners to reconsider the policies governing state lotteries. It is not a complete outline, but its detail shows how supporting material is integrated into the various stages and the overall speech is developed.

INTEGRATING SUPPORTING MATERIAL INTO THE MOTIVATED SEQUENCE

THE COST OF LOTTERIES

Specific Purpose: To convince listeners we need to reconsider the policies governing state lotteries.

Attention Step

I. Yesterday, thousands of men and women in our state stepped up to the cashier at their local convenience stores and purchased lottery tickets. Many of these men and women went home with a chance on a dream instead of the basic necessities of life. It's time we reconsidered this form of institutionalized gambling—our state lottery.

Need Step

I. The state lottery has two hidden costs.
  A. It encourages gambling.
  B. It is a regressive tax on the poor.

Satisfaction Step

I. We can offset these costs in three ways.
  A. We can fund a program to help compulsive gamblers.
  B. We can limit advertising for lottery tickets.
  C. We can limit the number of tickets any one person can purchase.

Visualization Step

I. We would realize specific benefits if these steps are adopted.
  A. We would help more compulsive gamblers than currently.
  B. Reducing advertising would reduce the media mania surrounding the event.
  C. The chance that some would spend beyond their means would be curtailed.
  D. These three steps would not affect the current revenue associated with state lotteries.

Action Step

I. We need to understand the true, hidden costs of state lotteries.

    A. We need to pay attention to the needs of those most affected: compulsive gamblers, and the poor.

    B. We need to urge the adoption of the proposals I've presented.

Using the Motivated Sequence to Actuate

All five steps of the motivated sequence are used in a speech to actuate. The audience is asked to go beyond a change in belief or awareness of new information to actually behaving in new ways. The following overview illustrates how the steps lead naturally to an action step.

Specific Purpose: Urging classmates to join a blood donors' group being formed on campus.

Attention Step	I. If you had needed an emergency transfusion for a rare blood type in Choteau County on December 23, 1998, you might not have received it.
Need Step	I. Blood drives seldom collect sufficient quantities of blood to meet emergency needs in a rural area such as this one.
Satisfaction Step	I. A blood donors' association guarantees a predictable, steady supply of needed blood to the medical community.
Visualization Step	I. Without a steady supply of blood, our community will face needless deaths; with it, emergencies like yours can be met with prompt treatment.
Action Step	I. You can help by filling out the blood donors' cards I am handing out.

As another example, consider the previous speech on gambling; if you were to move from a persuasive to an actuative speech, you would simply add the following argument as a closing point:

Action Step	I. What do I want from you?
	A. I want you to join me in signing this petition to our state legislature, urging acceptance of the proposals I've outlined.
	B. I also want you to join with me in creating a chapter of Gamblers Anonymous in our community.

Using the Motivated Sequence to Entertain

The speech to entertain may exist for humor in its own right, but more often, it uses humor to make a serious point. When you expect the audience only to sit back and enjoy the presentation (e.g., at a comic revue), the attention step is the only one required. When you want to both entertain your audience and make a serious point, however, additional steps are needed. In the following outline, all steps of the motivated sequence are appropriate to the "moral" that the speaker draws from the discussion of optimism versus pessimism and the concluding appeal for acting as an optimist.

USING THE MOTIVATED SEQUENCE IN A SPEECH TO ENTERTAIN

A CASE FOR OPTIMISM

Attention Step	I. Perhaps you've heard the expression "The optimist sees the doughnut, the pessimist, the hole."
Need Step	I. To the pessimist, the optimist is a fool: the person who looks at an oyster and expects to find pearls is engaging in wishful thinking. II. To the optimist, the pessimist is sour on life: the person who looks at an oyster and expects to get ptomaine poisoning is missing out on the richer possibilities life can offer.

Satisfaction Step	I. The pessimist responds to every event with an expectation of the worst that could happen.
	II. The optimist, on the other hand, looks for the bright side.
	   A. The day after a robbery, a friend asked a store owner about the loss. After acknowledging that he had indeed suffered a loss, the store owner quipped, "But I was lucky; I marked everything down 20 percent the day before—had I not done that, I would have lost even more."
	   B. The optimist is one who cleans her glasses before she eats grapefruit.

Visualization Step	I. When you look on the bright side, you find things to be happy about.
Action Step	I. Be an optimist: "Keep your eye on the doughnut and not on the hole."[5]

Before going on to more specific organizational patterns, the following sample speech exemplifies use of the motivated sequence. Read it by focusing on how the structure of the speech leads the audience toward a specific conclusion.

ASSESSING A SAMPLE SPEECH

As you read the following speech, prepared by Maria Lucia R. Anton of the University of Guam, note that the attention step (paragraphs 1–4) creates initial curiosity as to the general purpose of the speech and then identifies the source and meaning of the statement in relation to sexual assault policies.[6] In paragraph 5, Maria introduces the *need* (that not all campuses have such policies in place). In a series of paragraphs (6–9) Maria *satisfies* the need as presented and then moves to *visualizing* what a solution (a policy) would bring (paragraphs 10–18). The *action* step is introduced in the final two paragraphs.

SEXUAL ASSAULT POLICY A MUST

Maria Lucia R. Anton

Attention Step	"If you want to take her blouse off, you have to ask. If you want to touch her breast, you have to ask. If you want to move your hand down to her

genitals, you have to ask. If you want to put your finger inside her, you have to ask."/1

What I've just quoted is part of the freshman orientation at Antioch College in Ohio. In the sexual offense policy of this college, emphasis is given to three major points: (1) If you have a sexually transmitted disease, you must disclose it to a potential partner, (2) To knowingly take advantage of someone who is under the influence of alcohol, drugs and/or prescribed medication is not acceptable behavior in the Antioch community, (3) Obtaining consent is an on-going process in any sexual interaction. The request for consent must be specific to each act./2

For those who engage in sex, the goal is 100% consensual sex. It isn't enough to ask someone if they would like to have sex, you have to get verbal consent every step of the way./3

This policy has been highly publicized and you may have heard it before. The policy addresses sexual offenses such as rape, which involves penetration, and sexual assault, which does not. In both instances, the respondent coerced or forced the primary witness to engage in nonconsensual sexual conduct with the respondent or another./4

Need Step

Sexual assault has become a major problem in U.S. campuses today. However, in spite of increased sexual assaults on campuses, many still go without a policy to protect their students. The University of Guam, where I am a senior, is one example./5

Sexual Assault has become a reality in many campuses across the nation. Carleton College in Northfield, Minnesota, was sued for $800,000 in damages by four university women. The women charged that Carleton was negligent in protecting them against a known rapist. From the June 3, 1991, issue of *Time Magazine:*

> Amy had been on campus for just five weeks when she joined some friends to watch a video in the room of a senior. One by one the other students went away, leaving her alone with a student whose name she didn't even know. "It ended up with his hands around my throat," she recalls. In a lawsuit she has filed against the college, she charges that he locked the door and raped her again and again for the next four hours. "I didn't want him to kill me, I just kept trying not to cry." Only afterwards did he tell her, almost defiantly, his name. It was on top of the "castration list" posted on women's bathroom walls around campus to warn other students about college rapists." Amy's attacker was found guilty of sexual assault but was only suspended.
>
> Julie started dating a fellow cast member in a Carleton play. They had never slept together, she charges in a civil suit, until he came to her dorm room one night, uninvited, and raped her. She struggled to hold her life and education together, but finally could manage no longer and left school. Only later did Julie learn that her assailant was the same man who had attacked Amy./6

Ladies and gentlemen, the court held that the college knew this man was a rapist. The administration may have been able to prevent this from happening if they had expelled the attacker, but they didn't. My campus has no reports of sexual assault. Is the administration waiting for someone to be assaulted before they formulate a sexual assault policy? This mistake has been made elsewhere, we don't have to prove it again./7

Perhaps some statistics will help you understand the magnitude of the problem. According to *New Statesman & Society,* June 21, 1991, issue:

> A 1985 survey of sampled campuses by *Ms. Magazine* and the National Institute of Mental Health found that 1 in every 4 college women were victims of sexual assault, 74 percent knew their attackers. Even worse, between 30 to 40 percent of male students indicated that they might force a woman to have sex if they knew they would escape punishment. In just one year from 1988–1989, reports of student rape at the University of California increased from 2 to 80./8

These numbers are indeed disturbing. But more disturbing are the effects of sexual assault. A victim feeling the shock of why something this terrible was allowed to happen. Having intense fears that behind every dark corner could be an attacker ready to grab her, push her to the ground and sexually assault her. Many waking moments of anxiety and impaired concentration as she remembers the attack. Countless nights of reliving the traumatic incident in her sleep. Mood swings and depression as she tries to deal internally with the physical hurt and the emotional turmoil that this attack has caused./9

Satisfaction Step   Many campuses are open invitations for sexual assault. The absence of a policy is a grand invitation. I have never been sexually assaulted so why do I care so much about a policy? You know why, because I could be assaulted. I won't sit and wait to be among 1 out of every 4 women on my campus to be assaulted. The first step to keep myself out of the statistics is to push for a sexual assault policy on my campus. One way to do this is through a petition to the university./10

Although the Antioch policy sounds a little far-fetched and has been the target of criticism in comedy routines such as "Saturday Night Live," although students feel this is unnatural, many campuses are taking heed and revisiting their own policies. Campuses like mine don't have a sexual policy to revisit. Does yours?/11

By far the most controversial policy today is that of Antioch. I'm not saying that we need one as specific as theirs, but every university has a responsibility to provide a safe environment for its students. Universities have an obligation to provide a sexual assault policy to protect its students./12

The following points are fundamental to the safety of the students and need to be addressed by universities:

1. Every campus should have a sexual assault policy that is developed with input from the students, faculty, staff and administration. The policy then needs to be publicized in the student handbook. The school newspaper should print and campus radio broadcast the policy periodically to heighten awareness.

2. Campuses must institute programs to educate students and other campus personnel. Examples of these include discussing the sexual assault policy during mandatory student orientation and conduct special workshops for faculty and other staff.

3. Outline a step-by-step written procedure to guarantee that sexual assault victims are assisted by the university. It is pertinent that they are not without support at this very critical time./13

Visualization Step   My vision is a campus where there is no place for any sexual assault. I want to leave my classroom at night knowing that my trip from the building to the car will not be one of fear for my personal safety./14

You may be saying to yourself that there are laws to handle crimes like these. From *The Chronicle of Higher Education*, May 15, 1991 issue, Jane McDonnell, a Senior Lecturer in Women's Studies at Carleton, says colleges cannot turn their backs on women. "We'd be abandoning victims if we merely sent them to the police," she says. "The wheels of justice tend to grind slowly and rape has one of the lowest conviction rates of any crime."/15

Without a policy, most institutions lack specific penalties for sexual assault and choose to prosecute offenders under the general student-conduct code. In cases such as Carleton College, Amy's attacker was allowed back on campus after his suspension and consequently he raped again./16

Although the policy may not stop the actual assault, would be offenders will think twice before committing sexual assault if they knew they would be punished. In addition, it guarantees justice for victims of sexual assault. We need to make it loud and clear that sexual assault will not be tolerated./17

Yes, universities have a big task in the struggle to prevent sexual assault./18

Action Step   You and I can actively assist in this task and can make a giant contribution to move it forward. On my campus students have not only voiced their concerns but we have also started a petition demanding that the university formulate a sexual assault policy./19

The bottom line is, we need to prevent sexual assault on campus. The key to prevention is a sexual assault policy. If you don't have a policy, then you need to petition your administration to have one. I know I won't stop my advocacy until I see a policy on my campus./20

DEVELOPING PATTERNS OF INTERNAL ORGANIZATION WITHIN THE STEPS OF THE MOTIVATED SEQUENCE

The motivated sequence gives you a solid overall structure, but it doesn't really help you with some of the complicated structural problems you'll face—especially in the need, satisfaction, and visualization steps.

For example, suppose you're building a speech about why criminal penalties for the crimes need to be strengthened. You can think of several reasons that would support a need for this kind of change: the increase in hate crimes over the past few years, the apparent inability of present laws to deter such crime, and the specific problems certain groups have as victims of such crimes. As you think about that range of needs, you realize that satisfaction—plans for change—are equally complicated: Some would argue that singling out hate crimes makes other crimes seem less serious—murder is murder, they would argue. So, how can you satisfy the "need" in a way that does not denigrate the value of lives lost in crimes not motivated by "hate"?

The same sort of thing could be said about the visualization step. Usually, it's organized chronologically: "If we don't act today, the situation will be worse tomorrow and, sooner or later, become disastrous." Yet, if your need and satisfaction steps are complicated, visualization will become equally difficult. On the issue of strengthening hate crime laws, you must ask yourself, "How will things be different if my solution is put into effect, and what will that mean for all citizens?"

The attention and action steps usually can be handled pretty easily, the three middle steps often demand a lot of organizational work. Five key criteria for communicating ideas to an audience should be met as you think about speech organization:

1. *The organization of* **main points** *must be easy for the audience to grasp and remember.* Listeners find it easier to track your ideas if they see relationships among the main points. If the structure is clear, they even *anticipate* your next point through the pattern.

2. *The pattern must allow full, balanced coverage of the material it organizes.* When making three arguments in support of a claim, you usually want to spend roughly the same amount of time on each, because the first point might be important for some listeners, while the second and third points appeal to others. Audiences usually can sense *proportion,* and they may well wonder why you spend far more (or less) time on one point or another.

3. *The pattern should be appropriate to the occasion.* As noted, on some occasions you're expected to observe group traditions. Political fund-raising speeches, for example, almost always are built around a problem-solution format—with a call for contributions as the action step. Audiences on this and other occasions expect certain topics and even certain organizational patterns.[7]

4. *The pattern should be adapted to the audience's needs and level of knowledge.* The motivated sequence is based on listeners' fundamental thought processes, whereas patterns of internal organization depend upon other aspects of audience awareness of an issue or problem. If listeners are not well informed, an historical chronology that contextualizes the issue may be needed for them to understand the evolution of events. If they are knowledgeable, a cause-effect pattern that compacts such an analysis in the need step—but then develops a more complicated satisfaction step—probably will work better. Start where the audience is, and take them where you want to go.

5. *The speech must move forward steadily toward a complete and satisfying end.* Keeping the audience with you is easier if they have a clear idea of where you're heading during the speech. Repeated backtracking to pick up lost points confuses and aggravates your listeners. Using clear transitions between main points—"Now that we've seen why we must change, what are we going to do?"—will assist audiences in tracking your ideas.

These are the primary criteria that should guide development of the body of material going into your speeches. Keep these in mind as you review the common types of organizational patterns that work best for people delivering oral messages.

PATTERNS OF INTERNAL ORGANIZATION

The four most useful patterns for structuring the bodies of speeches are *chronological, spatial, causal,* and *topical.*

Chronological Patterns

The defining characteristic of a **chronological pattern** is the temporal structuring of happenings or events. Chronology can be used in a temporal sequence to orient listeners who know little about a topic, or it may be used to unfold a story or narrative.

Subjects often suggest their own organizational pattern—a chronological pattern is well suited to explaining a process or sequence of events.

Temporal Sequence.   To use a **temporal sequence,** you begin at some period or date and move forward (or backward) systematically to provide background information. So, for a speech on why the United States has devoted so much more time and money to manned rather than unmanned space flights, you'd do well to use a temporal sequence, examining the unmanned rocket flights of the 1950s and 1960s, the Kennedy era commitment to manned flights to the moon, and the Nixon era commitments to a manned space station and shuttle technology, which continued even after the *Challenger* disaster of 1986. Such a selection and sequencing of events—both of which are strategic moves made by a speaker who uses a temporal sequence—allows you to use the past to explain the present.

Narrative Sequence.   If you want to do more than explain or provide background for some problem, however, a *narrative* (story) allows you to draw conclusions about a series of events. For example, Aesop's fables are narratives with morals about human motivations and actions; lawyers, too, tell stories in arguing for their defendant's guilt or innocence. In a **narrative sequence,** therefore, stories are the source of supporting material for some claim.[8] Suppose you want to argue that the image of Gypsies in this country does not do justice to their persecution in Eastern Europe. A narrative sequence, wherein the story comprises the need step and the lessons-to-be-learned as part of the satisfaction step, would work well.

USING NARRATIVE SEQUENCE: AN ILLUSTRATION

THE PERSECUTION OF EASTERN EUROPEAN ROMA (GYPSIES)

Claim: The Roma of Eastern Europe are a persecuted people.

Attention Step   [Review the romanticized version of Gypsies that generally is given in this country; contrast that with a specific illustration of their actual life conditions in Eastern Europe.]

Need Step

I. Continue the review of specific illustrations of their life; end with the question: "How did they come to be treated this way?"

II. Perhaps the best way to answer this is to explain the story of their heritage.

A. The Roma are, as best we know, originally from India—they migrated to Eastern Europe around 800–950 A.D.

1. Their language (Romani) is a derivative of Sanskrit and is close to Hindi.

2. Although not all groups today communicate in some dialect of their original language, the Roma of the southern Balkans use Romani as well as Slavic, Turkish, Albanian, or Greek languages.

3. They were firmly established in Europe in the mid-fourteenth and fifteenth centuries, with reports of Roma in Serbia by 1348, in Germany by 1407, and in Spain by 1425.

B. True to their nomadic culture, they have not established, as have Serbs, Croats, Albanians, etc., a specific homeland.
1. This has caused them to be seen as "outsiders" even though they and their descendants have lived in areas for 500 years.
2. The absence of a homeland means no one country or nationality speaks for them or defends their interests.
C. Their persecution is not a recent phenomenon.
1. They were slaves in two Romanian principalities from the fourteenth to the nineteenth century (slavery was abolished in 1864).
2. Considered outcasts, they were expelled from other areas, furthering their image as nomads.
3. When not sold into slavery, there were bounties "for their capture, dead or alive, and repressive measures included confiscation of property and children, forced labor, prison sentences, whipping, branding, and other forms of physical mutilation."
4. During the Nazi regime, more than 600,000 were exterminated.
D. Programs of assimilation have been the recent experience of the Roma.
1. Czechoslovakia banned nomadism in 1958.
2. Poland banned nomadism in 1964.
3. In Hungary and in the Balkans, assimilation meant working in the most dangerous, lowest paid jobs.
4. In Czechoslovakia, a policy of monetary incentive for sterilization of women was disproportionately applied to Roma women (in one city in 1989, half the women sterilized were Roma; Roma women also were often sterilized without their consent).
5. Education for Roma children often was in what, for them, was a second language; hence, they were considered "retarded and tracked into special classes."
6. Because they lacked legal status as a minority, they were regarded as "a socially degraded stratum," a "disadvantaged social stratum," or as "other nationalities" in several Eastern European countries without recourse to human rights afforded other peoples.
7. In Bulgaria, from the early 1970s forward, Roma language, music, musical instruments, and dress were banned.

Satisfaction Step
I. From this story, we can clearly see that the Roma are a persecuted people.

Visualization/Action Step Combined
I. From this characterization of the Roma, and more could be said about their perceived status as a "socially unacceptable population," I hope to have altered your conception of the life Gypsies experience today in Eastern Europe. A romantic story this is not![9]

Spatial Patterns

Generally, **spatial patterns** arrange ideas or subtopics in terms of their physical proximity or relationship to each other. A specialized form of spatial patterns are **geographical patterns,** which organize materials according to well-known regions or areas. So, the evening weather forecast reviews today's high-pressure dome over your area, then the low-pressure area lying to the west, and the arctic cool-air mass that seems to be coming in behind that low-pressure area from Canada. The notion of geography, however, need not be applied only to land-masses; you can use it to talk about physical spaces, such as the different services available on the four floors of a university library. In an age when travel is highly popular and comparatively inexpensive, you might well find yourself giving a speech using a geographical pattern, as in the following speech.

USING SPATIAL PATTERNING: AN ILLUSTRATION

ENSURING CULTURAL SURVIVAL: EMPOWERING THE LIVES OF INDIGENOUS PEOPLES

Central idea: Around the globe, projects are being undertaken to ensure that the customs and language of people in remote regions survive.

Attention Step	[Opening story about the Native American experience regarding a loss of cultural heritage in the United States; note that the process of assimilation and loss of culture does not stop at our borders.]
Need Step	[Discussion of why loss of culture is an important issue—why should we be concerned with other peoples' loss?]
Satisfaction Step	I. As we move outside our borders, we can travel to specific regions and learn about projects aimed at restoring or maintaining a peoples' identity. A. We can begin by moving just south of our own border, to Mexico, where the San Jtz'ibajom project in the Mayan Chiapas community is working to preserve oral history as well as improve literacy in their mother tongue. B. We move further south to the Amazon, where the Amazonian Peoples Resources Initiative is working to improve conditions among Peruvian Amazonians. C. Changing continents, and moving what seems a world away, we travel next to Afghanistan, where the Afghan Refugee Weavers' Project has been undertaken.
Visualization Step	[Visualize what it means to each of these communities as they seek to maintain their local culture.]
Action Step	[Note that the trip they have taken with you has given them some sense of the need for—and the activity occurring to ensure—cultural survival.][10]

Giving your audience a sense of physical relationship through spatial ordering also works with single arguments or ideas. A speech on the effects of nuclear fallout could organize damage assessments from "ground zero" (the point of impact) through areas one mile away to regions ten, fifty, and a hundred miles out.

The great utility of spatial patterns is their visual component. Helping audiences *see* ideas is a virtue for someone using an oral medium of communication.

Causal Patterns

As the name implies, **causal patterns** of organization move either from a description of present conditions to an analysis of the causes that seem to have produced them or from an analysis of present causes to a consideration of future effects. Because ideas are developed in direct relationship with each others, a sense of coherence is communicated to listeners. When using a *cause-effect pattern,* you might first point to the increasing number of closed courses (i.e., too few places) in your college each semester and then show the result—it takes students longer to graduate. Or, using an *effect-cause pattern,* you could argue that everyone knows how long it takes students to graduate, and then argue that closed classes are the cause (at least in part).

USING CAUSE-EFFECT AND EFFECT-CAUSE PATTERNS
REQUIRING COMMUNITY SERVICE FOR HIGH SCHOOL GRADUATION (OPTION 1)

Claim: Requiring that high school students engage in community service as a condition of graduation (cause) leads to an erosion of the very volunteer spirit it is designed to promote (effect).

Attention Step   [Draw attention to the importance of the issue.]

Need Step   I. Several students have forced the issue by appealing to the courts.
          A. Students in Bethlehem, Pennsylvania, who already were active refused to report their activities to school authorities.

FIGURE 7.2   Developing a Causal Pattern

Note how one specific cause is identified as the "force" behind specific effects—what kind of support would be necessary to illustrate the connection between the cause and each effect?

Purpose: *To argue that deforestation of the Amazon Region must stop.*

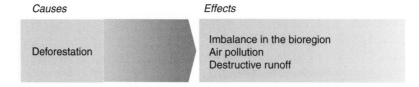

        1. They lost in court.
        2. The school denied their diplomas.
    B. Students in Chapel Hill, North Carolina, filed suit.
        1. As one student, already an Eagle Scout, suggested, requiring what should be a volunteer activity leaves "no heart" for the activity.
        2. The case has not been completed.

Visualization Step   [Indicate what the long-range consequences will be if we ignore the problem.]

Action Step   [Appeal to listeners' self-interest—what is done at the high school level could gravitate to becoming a college requirement—to hold their attention on this issue as something to follow in the future.]

REQUIRING COMMUNITY SERVICE (OPTION 2)

Claim: An enriched understanding of others, and a sense of fulfillment (effects) can result from requiring students to engage in community service (cause).

Need Step   I. Students are enriched through their exposure to community service.
    A. In Hebbville, Maryland, an elementary teacher regularly incorporates visits to nursing homes.
        1. Students get to practice their reading in the presence of an eager audience.
        2. In the process, they gain a greater understanding of and empathy for the elderly.
    B. Young veterans of the Hebbville program are quiet testimony to its success.
        1. One fourth grader who came back to help the younger class prepare for their experience played a garbled tape, and then pointed out that this is how many elderly might hear the students if they are almost deaf.
        2. As another fourth grader noted, it is fun to make people happy.[11]

Both outlines share a common characteristic: each starts with the aspect of the situation *better known* to audience members and then develops more fully the lesser-known facets of the problem. As a guiding principle, *use a cause-effect sequence when listeners are generally well acquainted with the cause, but use an effect-cause sequence when the effect is better known.* Note also that each option illustrates a different view of the same issue. Such events are rarely one-sided; depending on your personal beliefs, this example illustrates how you can construct speeches supporting your views—even though another person may take the opposing option as his or her choice.

Topical Patterns

Some speeches on familiar topics are best organized in terms of standardized subject-matter divisions. Financial reports customarily are divided into assets and liabilities; discussions of government into legislative, executive, and judicial matters; and comparisons of telescopes into celestial and terrestrial models. In these instances, the topic suggests its own pattern of development. **Topical patterns** are useful in speeches that enumerate aspects of persons, places, things, or processes. Your coverage of these aspects may be a **complete enumeration** of a subject, as in an analysis of the "who-what-when-where-how-why" scheme that encompasses any story you wish to report on or a **partial enumeration,** as in coverage of the most common types of World Wide Web search engines.

USING THE TOPICAL PATTERN OF PARTIAL ENUMERATION

THE BASIC TYPES FOR WEB SEARCHES

Central Idea: Knowing the basic search engine types can help you discover information on the World Wide Web.

Attention Step   [Elicit interest through the usual devices.]

Need Step   [Point out how the audience can use this information.]

Satisfaction Step
    I. There are three basic types.
        A. Subject directories: Yahoo!—www.yahoo.com—a general, all-purpose search engine.
        B. MetaSearch Engines: Dogpile—www.dogpile.com—searches 25 different smaller search units, three at a time.
        C. Netnews groups: DeJaNews—www.dejanews .com—a means of locating news groups on the web.

Visualization Step   [After encouraging them to experiment with each one, illustrate the kinds of information your own search uncovered.]

Action Step   [Review the key points you want listeners to take away from your speech, and encourage them to start using these resources.]

Topical patterns are among the most popular and easiest to use in organizing your speech. Given the usual practice of a partial rather than complete enumeration of topics, you may need to justify your limitations by indicating why you're not talking about other facets. If someone asks, "Why didn't you talk about Alta Vista?" they are telling you that they don't think your limitation of the topic was reasonable. Thus, you'd better be ready to answer, "Because the similarity between Yahoo! and Alta Vista is fairly close, as they both depend on subject categories for searches." All that's required is that the audience understand why some items were included and others weren't. That understanding can come either from your logical development of the topic or from an explicit statement about its scope.

INTEGRATING PATTERNS INTO THE MOTIVATED SEQUENCE

Having looked at some internal patterns, you now may consider the relationship between the motivated sequence and the chronological, spatial, causal, and topical patterns:

- *Attention Step—Introduction to Speech:* As introductory devices, you might use chronological or spatial methods in beginning a hypothetical story; overall, organize the introduction to satisfy the functions discussed in Chapter 8.
- *Need Step—Body of Speech:* Use chronological, spatial, causal, or topical patterns to relate the main points to one another. You may even use one pattern for main points and another to organize subpoints (see the next section on organizing main points and subpoints).
- *Satisfaction Step—Body of Speech:* Use any of the patterns to organize this step; you even may use one pattern for main points and another for subpoints. Whatever pattern is used should be tied to needs, however, because the relationship between the need step and the satisfaction step is key to the body of your speech.
- *Visualization Step—Body or Conclusion of Speech:* You can highlight the positive or negative benefits, or you can contrast these to illustrate why your proposal is worth considering. A chronological pattern running from past to future or a geographical pattern illustrating effects in different regions also might be employed in creating a visual picture for the audience.
- *Action Step—Conclusion of Speech:* A specific pattern is not needed. Conclusions can call for specific actions or review the main ideas to give listeners a sense of what they could do with the information, ideas, and proposals you've presented.

Organizing the Main Points and Subpoints

The relationship between the **main points** needs to be clear to the audience. In the following example, spatial ordering connects the two main points of comparison—(the United States and Germany). Underneath each main point, the ordering of **subpoints** also must follow some kind of ordering pattern. In this case, each point is arranged in a topical pattern, with direct contrasts (I. A–II. A . . .) between the subpoints. In addition, the sequence of main points allows the audience to consider the more familiar scene (the United States) before moving to the less familiar one (Germany).

Building Easy-to-Follow Arrangements of Your Ideas.   There are several easy ways to organize main and subpoints to make the relationship between ideas clear to the audience. The first is illustrated here by combining main and subpoints; the second is illustrated through causal patterning.

HOW TO

CHOOSE ORGANIZATIONAL PATTERNS

- Does your *subject matter* guide you toward a particular pattern? For example, to explain basic principles of professional flower gardening, a spatial pattern would be a natural choice.
- Does your *specific purpose* suggest which pattern is most serviceable? For example, to explain changing definitions of rape and the social effects of these definitions, a chronological pattern for the main points and cause-effect units for the subpoints would be logical choices.
- Do the needs or expectations of *your audience* call for specific topical patterns?

For example, an audience listening to a speech urging the rerouting of three creeks to make room for a new highway might expect you to address particular points: positive impacts of the highway, environmental impact of the rerouting, and costs of the project.

- Does *the occasion* call for specific topical patterns? For example, every presidental inaugural address *must* mention the historicity of the occasion, the binding up of wounds after an ugly political campaign, domestic problems, foreign-policy problems, and a call for citizens' help.

COMBINING PATTERNS WITH MAIN AND SUBPOINTS

CONTRASTS BETWEEN UNITED STATES AND GERMAN MANAGERS

Main Subpoint	I. The U.S. managers' expectations are as follows:
	A. Communication between colleagues is task centered and impersonal.
Subpoint	B. The need to be liked by others is a prime motivating factor influencing communicative behavior: more informal address/tone.
Subpoint	C. Assertiveness, direct confrontation, and fair play dominate in the approach to decision making, but there is low level of logical analysis with a usually low level of language sophistication.
Main Subpoint	II. The German managers' expectations are as follows:
	A. Communication between colleagues combines socioemotional and task features; hence, it is not as impersonal.
Subpoint	B. The need to be seen as credible and establish one's place in a corporate hierarchy is a prime motivating factor in influencing communicative behavior: more formal address/tone.

Subpoint   C. Also assertive and directly confrontative, but with a higher
                level of logical analysis and more sophisticated language.[12]

Causes and effects are often developed in main point/subpoint sets, where the
causes appear in the main points and the effects appear as sub-subpoints.

USING CAUSAL ORDERING OF MAIN AND SUBPOINTS

OUR DISAPPEARING SALMON

Causal Claim   I. Industrial pollution has caused a decline in the U.S. salmon
                population.
Main Point   A. Dam construction has severely affected salmon.
Subpoint   1. There are 14 barriers on a major salmon river.
Subpoint   2. Eleven of the 14 barriers are hydroelectric facilities.
Sub-subpoint   a. These facilities produce high water temper-
                    atures.
Sub-subpoint   b. Estimates of fish loss from excessive temper-
                    atures are as high as 16 percent.
Main Point   B. Chemical and industrial pollution also have harmed the salmon.
Subpoint   1. Discharge of chemicals such as PCB has hurt the salmon
                population.
Subpoint   2. PCB kills salmon roe (i.e., eggs), thus limiting the future
                population even further.

This lesson is important: *Developing your ideas in parallel forms makes them more coherent and clear and, hence, more memorable and powerful.* Controlling the structure of ideas is a key means of getting an audience to see the world as you see
it—and if they see as you see, they're more likely to think and act the way you
want them to.

Using PowerPoint to Help You Organize the Main Points

Although we discuss operating principles associated with Powerpoint in another chapter (see Chapter 9), this is a good place to mention its value in organizing ideas. Because PowerPoint uses a logical indentation format for
each succeeding level, it is easy to see whether your points belong under a
main heading or at the same level as the main heading. Once you have constructed your slides, you can move to Outline View and see, at a glance, how
your ideas are structured.[13] You also can use the editing function in Outline
View to make specific changes in the slides. You can replace words or rearrange their placement to better reflect the logical structure of your presentation. You also can view all of your slides in sequence—and move those slides
around as needed to combine ideas in different ways. You even can isolate all
the "slide titles" to see how the overall structure of the presentation looks.
These techniques can assist in controlling the flow of the presentation and
give you a chance to see, much like a typed outline, how the presentation will
unfold. You also can ask a friend to look at the screen list of titles and see
whether he or she has any trouble understanding the internal logic of your
speech's structure.

CHAPTER SUMMARY

The human need to find or create order in the world is the basis for the need to organize public presentations. Listeners need speakers to provide emphasis via distinctions between foreground and background differentiation and via a sense of completeness that provides closure to messages. Monroe's Motivated Sequence was introduced early in this century as a means of combining problem- and motivated-centered structures for ideas. It provides an orderly approach to problem solving within a motivational framework. Its five steps—attention, need, satisfaction, visualization, and action—can be used to structure any speech, whether informative, entertaining, persuasive, actuative.

Building a conceptually clear structure for your major ideas is crucial. Listeners need to see and comprehend a pattern in your ideas if they're to make sense of them. As long as the pattern you select is sensitive to your topic, purpose, and the expectations of the audience and occasion, your message should be received as a logically coherent approach to some idea or problem. Five criteria should guide you toward some pattern:

- The organization of the main points must be easy for the audience to grasp and remember.
- The pattern should allow full, balanced coverage.
- The pattern should be appropriate to the occasion.
- The pattern should be adapted to the audience's needs and level of knowledge.
- The speech must move steadily forward.

The four classes of internal organizational patterns include chronological (temporal, narrative), spatial (as well as geographical), causal (effect-cause, cause- effect), and topical (complete and partial enumeration). Different patterns can be combined, especially by ordering main points in one pattern and subpoints in another.

KEY TERMS

action step (p. 160)

attention step (p. 155)

causal patterns (p. 174)

chronological pattern (p. 170)

closure (p. 152)

complete enumeration (p. 176)

contrast method of visualization (p. 159)

differentiation (p. 152)

geographical patterns (p. 173)

main points (p. 169)

Monroe's Motivated Sequence (p. 153)

narrative sequence (p. 171)

need step (p. 155)

negative method of visualization (p. 159)

partial enumeration (p. 176)

positive method of visualization (p. 159)

satisfaction step (p. 157)

spatial patterns (p. 173)

subpoints (p. 177)

temporal sequence (p. 171)

topical patterns (p. 176)

visualization step (p. 159)

ASSESSMENT ACTIVITIES

1. Choose a social controversy as a topic for a speech, and specify two audiences, one opposing the issue and the other supporting it (e.g., a speech on the need for additional day care facilities presented to a liberal audience and a conservative audience). Using the motivated sequence as a pattern, specify how you would develop each step so it is appropriate to each audience. Write a concluding paragraph that explains the differences between the speeches as adapted to the differing audiences.

2. Develop brief outlines for an informative and a persuasive speech using the samples in this chapter as guides. What are the major differences between the outlines? Which steps are included in or deleted from the analysis? What do you do differently in each step when orienting your speech toward presenting information or persuading an audience? Following these outlines, write your response to these questions. Then, hand in your outlines and response for evaluation by your instructor.

3. Prepare a five- to seven-minute speech on a subject of your choice for presentation in class. Before you present the speech, critically appraise the organization you have used and write a brief paper defending your approach in organizing the main points and subpoints. Immediately after presenting the speech—and taking into account comments from the class—write a brief addendum on the experience of presenting your speech. Did it work the way you anticipated? Would you change your approach in any specific area of the speech? Hand in the analysis to your instructor.

4. Working in small groups in class, suggest how, assuming the end product is to be a short in-class speech, the main points can be organized in each of the following topics:

Why many small businesses fail

Developments in laser technology

Digging for sapphires, gold, or opals

Eat wisely, and live long

Problems of the part-time student

Racquetball for the beginner

Appreciating impressionist art

Computer literacy

REFERENCES

1. The concept of closure is one of the Gestalt principles of perception. The term *gestalt* (meaning "wholeness") is used to refer to a group of psychologists who have researched these aspects of cognitive processes. For a brief review of basic Gestalt principles, see John R. Anderson, *Cognitive Psychology and Its Implications* (New York: W. H. Freeman, 1980), 53–56; and Philip G. Zimbardo, *Psychology and Life*, 13th ed. (New York: HarperCollins, 1992), 266–268.

2. Katherine Blick Hoyenga and Kermit T. Hoyenga, *Motivational Explanations of Behavior: Evolutionary, Physiological, and Cognitive Ideas* (Monterey, CA: Brooks/Cole, 1984).

3. Information for this speech is derived from Raoul Dennis, "Retroracism," *Young Sisters and Brothers* (September 1995): 80–86.

4. Information cited in Steve Kaplan, "Snoring," *World and I*, 2 (July 1987): 298–303.

5. Based in part on information from *Friendly Speeches* (Cleveland: National Reference Library). See Chapter 16 for a full text.

6. Maria Lucia R. Anton, "Sexual Assault Policy a Must," *Winning Orations 1994.* Reprinted by permission of Larry Schnoor, Executive Secretary, Interstate Oratorical Association, Mankato State University, MN.

7. See the case studies of the presidential inaugural address in Herbert W. Simons and Aram A. Aghazarian, eds., *Form, Genre, and the Study of Political Discourse* (Columbia, SC: University of South Carolina Press, 1986), especially the essays by Karlyn Kohrs Campbell and Kathleen Hall Jamieson, 203–225; Bruce E. Gronbeck, 226–245; and Robert P. Hart, 278–300. See also Roderick P. Hart, *The Sound of Leadership* (Chicago: University of Chicago Press, 1987); and Karlyn Kohrs Campbell and Kathleen Hall Jamieson, *Deeds Done in Words: Presidential Rhetoric and the Genres of Governance* (Chicago: University of Chicago Press, 1990).

8. Walter R. Fisher goes so far as to argue that narrative persuasion is the most powerful kind of speaking. See his *Human Communication as Narration: Toward a Philosophy of Reason, Value, and Action* (Charleston, SC: University of South Carolina Press, 1987). See also Kathleen Hall Jamieson, *Eloquence in an Electronic Age: The Transformation of Political Speechmaking* (New York: Oxford University Press, 1988).

9. Information for this outline taken from Carol Silverman, "Persecution and Politicization: Roma (Gypsies) of Eastern Europe," *Cultural Survival Quarterly* (Summer 1995): 43–49.

10. Information taken from "Special Projects Update," *Cultural Survival Quarterly* (Summer 1995): 8–9.

11. From Suzanne Goldsmith, "The Community Is Their Textbook," *The American Prospect* (Summer 1995): 51–57.

12. From Robert F. Friday, "Contrasts in Discussion Behaviors of German and American Managers," *Intercultural Communication: A Reader,* 7th ed., ed. L. A. Samovar and R. E. Porter. (Belmont, CA: Wadsworth, 1994), 274–285; originally published in *International Journal of Intercultural Relations* 13 (1989): 429–445.

13. Robert H. Blissmer and Roland H. Alden, *Working with Microsoft PowerPoint 4.0* (Boston: Houghton Mifflin, 1995).

Chapter 8

Maintaining Audience Attention and Involvement

So, you stayed up late the night before your speech was due, finding one last statistical trend to help you demonstrate the second point and locating an awfully nice quotation from William Shakespeare to use as a summary of the third point. You worded each argument carefully so that it was clear and forceful. Then you went to bed. . . . A mistake! You forgot to think about ways to gain **audience attention** in the **introduction** of your speech so that your listeners will, in fact, decide to listen. You also forgot about how your information would maintain their attention throughout the speech and how you would structure a **conclusion** that reminds listeners of what you said and why they should believe or act on your words. Audiences need more than your information and arguments to stay with you. As suggested, you don't just start; you introduce a speech. You also don't just quit; you conclude a speech. How you accomplish these tasks makes a major difference in whether the audience will listen attentively to your ideas.

In this chapter, we first consider strategies for gaining and maintaining attention. Then, with these as a basis, we can discuss ways you can orient your listeners to what you have to say. Orienting listeners through an astute introduction can spell the difference between an audience that "merely listens" and one that intently seeks to learn what you have to say. The overarching concept that we introduce is that of **rhetorical orientation:** the art of framing your presentation in a way that lets the audience know what is expected from them as listeners. Leaving an audience with a clear understanding of what you want them to know, believe, or do also takes more than a "well, that's it" type of ending. The strategies that we review, coupled with those for introducing a speech, will give you the advantage you need to keep the audience tuned into your message. Finally, we show you how introductions and conclusions can be easily integrated into a speech built around the motivated sequence: Introductions fulfill the attention step, and conclusions are tied to either the visualization or the action step. We also concentrate on making beginnings and endings fit around speeches organized in other ways, because it is in those other cases that genuine rhetorical orientation is occurring.

CAPTURING AND HOLDING ATTENTION IN AMERICAN CULTURE

The strategies discussed here are specifically attuned to how American audiences may react to presentations. We are an active, busy people, with little time to "stop and smell the roses." In fact, "Time is money" is a favorite saying, and the more time you are asking from your listeners, the more money they may well feel they are losing. Thus, making your presentation worth their time is critical. Essentially, your listeners need reasons for *wanting* to listen. Even when you have their attention, it tends to ebb and flow. So, you must constantly watch for lapses. James Albert Winans, a twentieth-century pioneer in public-speaking instruction, expressed the problem succinctly: *Attention determines response.* If the audience does not attend, they cannot respond as you wish. By gaining their attention—and striving to maintain it throughout the presentation—you have a better chance they will still be there with you at the conclusion of your presentation.

What is **attention?** For our purposes, it can be thought of as a *focus* on one element in a given environment, with other elements fading from the conscious perception as a result.[1] To give attention, then, is to perceive "in relation to a goal [either] internally or externally motivated."[2] The link between attention and motivation—understood here in the general sense of "a reason for listening"—is illustrated in the following example: In 1968, Martin Luther King, Jr., went to Memphis, Tennessee, to support striking African-American sanitation workers in their demands for improved wages. The evening of April 3, he spoke in a hot, crowded church about the history of civil rights, his joy to be living "just a few years in the second half of the twentieth century,"[3] the tense times in his life, his upcoming Poor People's Campaign that was planning a March on Washington, and Christian injunctions to social action. Videotapes of the speech show an audience interacting with King, moving and jostling, laughing and talking. The audience became quiet and transfixed, however, as he moved through the conclusion of the speech:

> We've got some difficult days ahead. But it really doesn't matter with me now because I've been to the mountaintop. And I don't mind. Like anybody I would like to live a long life. Longevity has its place, but I'm not concerned about that now. I just want to do God's will, and He's allowed me to go up to the mountain, and I've looked over and I've seen the Promised Land. I may not get there with you, but I want you to know tonight that we as a people will get to the Promised Land. So I'm happy tonight, I'm not worried about anything. I'm not fearing any man. Mine eyes have seen the glory of the coming of the Lord.[4]

That crowd had talked and shouted through the speech, then quieted as it focused intently on King's prophetic, concluding words. As King finished, they

The forceful delivery and use of language by Dr. Martin Luther King, Jr., combined to capture and hold the attention of his audiences.

exploded in joy and appreciation as his concluding religious image broke through their focus and returned them to the church, Memphis, the strike, and the interracial problems of the United States in 1968. King blended internal and external motives to listen in focusing their attention on his message.

Few of us will ever rivet onto ourselves the undivided focus of an audience the way King did just before his assassination, yet we can work to gain and hold attention. A vigorous and varied delivery helps. Likewise, your reputation as a trustworthy and honest person (positive *ethos*) can command respect—and attention. Lively and picturesque language shows audiences word-pictures and makes it easier for them to stay with you. Think of lectures you've listened to in the past or in the current semester or quarter, what strategies did the lecturer use that made you stay tuned? What strategies should he or she have used? Consider the following **attention gaining/maintaining strategies**—which of these might the lecturer have used to better involve you in the presentation?

Activity

Suppose you have two TV sets, side by side. One shows Brandy performing motionless behind a microphone, the other carries one of her music videos—a fully choreographed production number. Which one will you look at? Nothing is so boring as talk that seems to stand still, providing far too much detail on a minor point. Instructions and demonstrations, in particular, demand orderly,

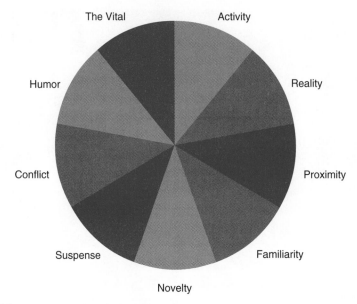

FIGURE 8.1   The Factors of Attention

systematic progress. Nothing is worse than a lecturer who stands still, locked in place, delivering ideas in a monotone. You need to create a sense of movement in the presentation that shows the audience you are alive and active.

Reality

The earliest words you learned were names for tangible objects—"Mama," "milk," "dog." While the ability to abstract or generalize is one mark of human intelligence, there persists in all of us an interest in concrete **reality**—the here-and-now of sense data. American audiences are attuned to "the real;" we didn't call Ronald Reagan the "Great Communicator" because he was always on top of his facts. We called him that because, whether we agreed with his ideas or not, he had an astute ability to relate events in a way that became real. Human-interest stories spark attention and gain audience involvement in the ideas being presented. Being abstruse and abstract may work in a written essay, but live audiences need a touch of realness to latch onto as they listen.

Proximity

Consider the following:

> Do you realize how much fast food is consumed on this campus? Within four blocks of this classroom are nine restaurants, including a McDonald's, a Wendy's, and a Pizza Hut. Two are local submarine houses. Even the student union runs a fast-food bar. A key question we face is this: What are our lunch habits doing to our nutrition—to our body and mind?

Such an example, whether used as an introduction or later in the speech, brings the topic close to home, thus providing **proximity.**

Familiarity

Especially in the face of new or strange ideas, references to the familiar sustain attention. One way to use **familiarity** to your advantage is to employ *analogies:* Noting, for example, that the London postal or zip codes are arranged like directions on a compass (the initial letters indicate directions and the next set of numbers represent degrees or positions) uses something familiar to explain something unfamiliar. Another positive use of familiarity is to begin a speech with references to proverbs or well-known slogans, such as "A stitch in time saves nine" or "Just do it." Within American culture, audiences are responsive to what they already know. When such a reference is used in a unique or appropriate way, it brings the audience into the presentation and incites them to listen further.

Novelty

As the old adage has it, when a dog bites a man, it's an accident; when a man bites a dog, it's news. Two special types of novelty are *size* and *contrast.* In a speech on the high cost of national defense, one speaker caught the attention of his audience with this sentence: "Considering that it costs more than $5000 to equip an average soldier for combat, it is disquieting to learn that in a year his equipment will be 60 percent obsolete."[5] In a speech entitled "Common Ground and Common Sense," Jesse Jackson employed the following historical contrast:

> Twenty-four years ago, the late Fanny Lou Hamer and Aaron Henry—who sits here tonight from Mississippi—were locked out on the streets of Atlantic City, the head of the Mississippi Freedom Democratic Party. But tonight, a black and white delegation from Mississippi is headed by Ed Cole, a black man, from Mississippi, 24 years later.[6]

In using novel materials, be careful not to inject elements that are so different or unusual as to be unfamiliar. **Novelty** gains its strength from an initial familiarity with the allusion; using the familiar in new and unique ways gives it added punch.

Suspense

Much of the interest in mystery and detective stories arises from the uncertainty about their outcome. When giving a speech, you also can create **suspense** by structuring stories so they build to a surprising climax. For example, you might begin a speech on mental retardation with the scenario of a developmentally disabled child; then, after describing the causes of and care for those who are developmentally disabled, you reveal that you've been talking

HOW TO

GET YOUR AUDIENCE'S ATTENTION

- Keep it moving! Ideas that "move" tend to attract attention; like ideas, the speech should march or press forward (activity).
- Keep refocusing on the here and now. Refer to specific events, persons, and places. Audiences can hang abstract ideas on specific details (reality).
- Bring the topic close to home. A direct reference to something nearby in time and space often orients an audience who may be wondering what you're talking about (proximity).
- Show how the unfamiliar is like the familiar. People generally are more comfortable when you refer to familiar ideas (familiarity).
- Introduce novelty. New and unusual developments attract wide notice. Just be careful that your audience can relate what you're saying to things they know about (novelty).

- Add suspense. Create uncertainty by pointing to puzzling relationships or unpredictable forces. Use suspense in stories you use to illustrate your ideas, building up to a surprising climax (suspense).
- Note conflicts or controversies. Controversy compels attention. Like suspense, controversy suggests uncertainty, and like activity, controversy is dynamic (conflict).
- Share humor. Listeners pay attention when they're enjoying themselves. Humor allows listeners to participate actively, diffuses tension, and revives a tired audience (humor).
- Personalize your speech. People pay attention to matters affecting their health, reputation, property, or employment. Make your speech unavoidably relevant (the vital).

about your brother. If your speech runs long, however, you need other strategies to keep the audience's attention—they will not follow you to the "surprising end" if they tire of listening in the meantime.

Conflict

Controversy compels attention. Just consider the ratings of prime-time TV soap operas that emphasize extremely strong interpersonal **conflict** in their plots. Over 30 years ago, Malcolm X gave voice to the frustration of African

Americans in that generation with his now-classic words: "If you never see me another time in your life, if I die in the morning, I'll die saying one thing: the ballot or the bullet, the ballot or the bullet."[7] The contrast was vivid, and the implication of conflict was equally vivid.

Humor

Listeners usually pay attention to a speech when they're enjoying themselves, and **humor** provides a chance for listeners to participate more actively in the transaction by sharing their laughter. When using humor to capture or hold attention, follow three guidelines:

- *Be relevant.* Beware of wandering from the point. Don't tell a joke just for the sake of telling a joke. If the humor doesn't reinforce an important idea, leave it out.
- *Use good taste.* Consider the occasion. You don't want to tell a knee-slapper during a funeral, for example. You should avoid off-color stories as well, because they will offend most—if not all—audience members.
- *Be quick.* A long, drawn-out story loses its value as listeners struggle to figure out where you are going—and what the story has to do with the point you've been making. A short, concise, "humorous anecdote," however, can be very helpful in reducing audience tension while making your point.

The Vital

People nearly always pay attention to matters that affect their own well-being. When you hear "Students who take an internship while in college find jobs after graduation three times as fast as those who don't," you're likely to pay attention. Appealing to **the vital,** therefore, is a matter of *personalizing* your speech, of making it unavoidably relevant not just to the group but to specific individuals in your audience.

Although these nine generic strategies do not exhaust the ways in which you can obtain and hold attention, they do provide an easy-to-use repertoire of ways to enliven your presentation. Keep these in mind not only for introducing and concluding your speech but for maintaining attention throughout. Focusing only on openings and closings, while critically important, is not sufficient in itself to maintain audience attention as you develop your central idea or claim with evidence and illustrations. As the next section illustrates, however, by considering the overall strategy of orienting your listeners, you can adapt these attention strategies at the start and continue using them all the way to the conclusion of your speech.

FRAMING THE SPEECH: RHETORICAL ORIENTATION

Rhetorical orientation is a process of effectively positioning listeners in relation to the substance of your speech—to the central idea or claim you are advancing, the arguments you are making, and the supporting materials you've assembled. The new homeowner is likely to say to an admiring visitor, "Here. Stand here so you can see the effect we were going for when we designed this house for this lot." Likewise, the effective introduction says, "Look at my central idea in this way. If you do, you'll see that it's interesting and relevant to your life." The successful conclusion says, "Look at the speech in this way. If you do, you'll see that the ideas I've talked about are important, significant for you and your life, and compelling."

Competently built introductions accomplish three goals:

1. The well-framed introduction orients the listeners' *attention*. It gets them to focus on the subject matter at hand, and it piques their interest. The strategies for gaining and maintaining attention discussed earlier are relevant here, but you must find ideas that will convince an audience your speech is important to their lives.

2. The well-framed introduction orients the listeners to the speaker's qualifications. The audience must believe that you know what you're talking about (good sense), that you're a straight shooter (good morals), and that you've got their best interests in mind (good will). These are the three grounds—good sense, good morals, and good will—that Aristotle identified as being central to a speaker's **ethos** or credibility.

3. The well-framed introduction orients listeners to the speech's ideas and their development. An audience must come to understand what you're talking about, why you're talking about it, and how you'll develop those ideas. At least in part, this aspect of rhetorical orientation usually takes the form of a good **forecast**:

HOW TO

FRAME A SPEECH

In your introduction:
- Focus on gaining your audience's attention, especially if listeners aren't likely to be interested in your topic.
- Establish your expertise, particularly if the audience isn't aware of your qualifications.
- Satisfy any special demands of the occasion; if you depart from custom, justify your departure.
- Work to create goodwill when the audience isn't sympathetic to you or your ideas.

In your conclusion:
- Signal the audience that the speech is about to end by refocusing them on the message.
- Answer the question "So what?" for your listeners.
- Influence the audience with your own enthusiasm and interest to help keep them involved in the message.

So today, yes, I want to talk to you about the "people's musical instrument," the lowly harmonica. First I'll talk about its development through the first half of the nineteenth century in Germany. Then, I'll say something about the coming of Mattias Hohner and his company for manufacturing harmonicas, which set off a craze in harmonica playing during the 1920s. Third, I'll get to the heart of this speech: an explanation of the roles harmonicas have played in the development of country-western, blues, and even rock music in the United States. And finally, if you've paid attention, I'll finish with a little demonstration of why this musical instrument has been called "the heart's horn."

Notice this forecast sets up the three main points of the speech and even promises the audience a little entertainment by the end (if it's been paying attention) as an inducement to stay with the speaker.

In speech introductions, therefore, rhetorical orientation situates listeners to best see the potential of the speech: *why* they should listen, *to whom* they're listening, and *how* they should go about following the speech. You also need to adopt a similar rhetorical orientation strategy in ending the speech, because a good conclusion has focus, flair, and a sense of finality:

- Even average speakers remind listeners what they've been talking about—the focus of the speech—and why listeners should be interested—the focus of their attention.
- Better speakers also show a bit of their rhetorical talents during conclusions by wording ideas in compelling ways, finding just the right quotation or final appeal that captures the tone of the speech—thus reengaging the listeners' needs and interests—and by pacing their oral delivery to capture the sense of an ending.
- All speakers must be able to create a sense of **The End,** the feeling that the speech, in fact, is over, which is to say that nothing else needs to be said at this time on this topic by this speaker. You want to end speeches in such a way that listeners say "Amen!"—which means "Yes, it shall be so." Seeking that sort of affirmation of you and your ideas should become the dominant purpose in your conclusions. The three F's—focus, flair, and finality—represent the dimensions of your conclusion's orienting work: orienting listeners to your ideas, your talents, and areas of expertise—and to The End of their listening experience.

With attention and rhetorical orientation strategies as a solid foundation, you'll find it easy to create introductions and conclusions that accomplish your primary objective—an audience listening to what you have to say.

TYPES OF SPEECH INTRODUCTIONS

Although you will use attention strategies throughout your speech, you have some special requirements in this regard during those first few seconds. Your listeners are making judgments about you and the speech in that first half-minute:

- Interesting or boring?
- Relevant or irrelevant?
- Knowledgeable or dumb?
- Forceful or limp?
- Prepared or just running at the mouth?
- Clear or muddy?
- Confident or unsure?
- Made for me or for someone else?

With all these questions to answer, listeners actually give you their attention readily—but only for a few seconds. Once most of the questions are answered, they're ready to tune in, tune out, or graze: the grazers are constantly shifting their focus from you to a person sitting a row ahead to a sound outside to this evening's activities and back to you, their minds working like remote control devices, zipping from channel to channel. It's your job to make sure they tune you in—and stay long enough to want to come back. You need to draw them into your world. As noted, you need to tie your speech to listeners' needs and interests to hold their attention, to convince them you know what you're doing, and to help them comprehend your main ideas and their development. The following techniques aim at one or all of these functions.

Referring to the Subject or Occasion

If your audience already has a vital interest in your subject, you need only state that subject before presenting your first main point. The speed and directness of this approach signals your eagerness to address your topic. Professor Russell J. Love used this approach when discussing rights for people with severe communication problems: "My talk tonight is concerned with the rights of the handicapped—particularly those people with severe communication disabilities. I will be presenting what I call a bill of rights for the severely communicatively disabled."[8]

Although such brevity and forthrightness may strike exactly the right note on some occasions, you should not begin all speeches this way. To a skeptical audience, a direct beginning may sound immodest or tactless; to an apathetic audience, it may sound dull or uninteresting. When listeners are receptive and friendly, however, immediate reference to the subject often produces a clear, engaging opening.

Instead of referring to your subject, you may sometimes want to refer to the occasion that has brought you and your audience together. When Pope John Paul II addressed the United Nations General Assembly on its fiftieth anniversary, he certainly was aware of the occasion as being historic and, therefore, recognized it:

> *Mr. President, Ladies and Gentlemen.* It is an honour for me to have the opportunity to address this international Assembly and to join the men and women of every country, race, language and culture in celebrating the fiftieth anniversary of the founding of the United Nations Organization. In coming before this distinguished Assembly, I am vividly aware that through you I am in some way addressing *the whole family of peoples living on the face of the earth.* My

Conveying belief in your ideas and sincere interest when speaking assists in maintaining audience attention throughout your presentation.

words are meant as a sign of the interest and esteem of the Apostolic See and of the Catholic Church for this Institution. They echo the voices of all those who see in the United Nations the hope of a better future for human society.[9]

In thus elevating the speaking occasion, the Pope made his speech—and the audiences listening to it—seem more important. Grand occasions demand serious listening.

Using a Personal Reference or Greeting

At times, a warm, personal greeting from a speaker or the remembrance of a previous visit or scene also serves as an excellent starting point. Personal references are especially useful when a speaker is well known to the audience. For example, Barbara Bush used a personal reference to a previous visit to Wellesley College as she addressed the senior class. She elaborated on her enthusiasm for the occasion when she added, "I had really looked forward to coming to Wellesley, I thought it was going to be fun; I never dreamt it would be this much fun. So thank you for that."[10]

If a personal reference is sincere and appropriate, it will establish goodwill as well as gain attention. Avoid extravagant, emotional statements, however, because listeners are quick to sense a lack of genuineness. At the other extreme, avoid apologizing. Don't say, "I don't know why I was picked to talk when others could have done it so much better." or "Unaccustomed as I am to public speaking." Apologetic beginnings suggest that your audience need not waste time listening. Be cordial, sincere, and modest, but establish your authority and maintain control of the situation.

Asking a Question

Another way to open a speech is to ask a question—or series of questions—to spark thinking about your subject. For example, Nicholas Fynn of Ohio University opened a speech about free-burning of timberland as follows: "How many of you in this room have visited a National Park at one point in your life? Well, the majority of you are in good company."[11] Such a question introduces a topic gently and, with its direct reference to the audience, tends to engage the listeners.

For those who do not really expect an actual audience response, rhetorical questions usually help forecast the development of the speech. Anne Wilfahrt of Mankato State University, Minnesota, was advocating the repeal of the 1872 General Mining Law, which grants individuals the mineral rights to their land, when she used a rhetorical question as a lead-in to her forecast in this manner: "Does the Mining Law of 1872 affect you and me, and is it in need of repair work? Yes, and such an opinion can be triggered by first briefly clarifying the original intent of the law; secondly, exploring the financial and environmental downfalls of this 1872 law in the 1990s; and finally, exposing proposed legislative measures that address these downfalls."[12]

Making a Startling Statement

On certain occasions, you may choose to open a speech with the shock technique—making a startling statement of fact or opinion. This approach is especially useful when listeners are distracted, apathetic, or smug. It rivets their attention on your topic. For example, the executive director of the American Association for Retired Persons (AARP), after asking some rhetorical questions about health care, caught his listeners' attention by following a strong claim with two startling examples:

> Given what we're spending on health care, we should have the best system in the world.
>
> But the reality is that we don't.
>
> Thirty-seven million Americans have no health insurance protection whatsoever, and millions more are underinsured.
>
> We are twentieth—that's right, twentieth—among the nations of the world in infant mortality. The death rate for our black newborn children rivals that of Third World countries. And poor children in America, like their

brothers and sisters in Third World nations, receive neither immunizations nor basic dental care.[13]

Avoid overusing shock techniques as they can backfire; your listeners may become angry when you threaten or disgust them.

Using a Quotation

A quotation may be an excellent means of introducing a speech, because it can prod listeners to think about something important and often captures an appropriate emotional tone. When Agnar Pytte, president of Case Western Reserve University, spoke to the Cleveland City Club on the topic of political correctness and free speech, he opened his speech with a quotation: "As Benjamin Cardozo said: 'Freedom of expression is the indispensable condition of all our liberties.'"[14] Pytte continued by using Cardozo's statement to investigate the current debate over political correctness on college campuses. The opening quotation provided the groundwork by effectively piquing the interest of the audience and inviting listeners to consider the impact of political correctness on free speech. Pytte could then proceed to discuss current examples of the political correctness debate, confident that his audience was paying attention.

Telling a Humorous Story

You can begin a speech by telling a funny story or relating a humorous experience. When doing so, however, recall the three earlier cautions in making sure that humor works for you rather than against you:

- *Be relevant.*
- *Use good taste.*
- *Be quick.*

Earnest Deavenport, chair and CEO of Eastman Chemical Company, observed all three of these rules when addressing the American branch of the Société de Chimie Industrielle:

> I want to begin with a story about a tightrope walker who announced that he was going to walk across Niagara Falls. Well, nobody believed that was possible, and the crowd that had gathered tried to talk him out of it. But to everyone's amazement, he made it safely across and everybody cheered. Then he asked, "Who believes I can do it blindfolded?" And everyone cried, "Don't do it, you'll fall!" But again, he made it safely across.
>
> Then he said, "Who believes I can ride a bicycle across?" And they all said, "Don't do it, you'll fall!" But he got on his bicycle and made it safely across.
>
> Then he said, "Who believes I can push a full wheelbarrow across?" Well, by that time, the crowd had seen enough to make real believers of them, and they all shouted, "We do! We do!" At that he said, "Ok . . . Who wants to be the first to get in?"

> Well, that's how many investors feel about companies who have adopted the philosophy that balancing the interests of all stakeholders is the true route to maximum value.
>
> They are skeptical at first, then believers after they see some solid results, but are very reluctant to get in that wheelbarrow.[15]

After telling that story and tying it to his topic, Deavenport was ready to develop a picture of Eastman Chemical Company's approach to balancing the interests of various groups who watch developments in the industrial world of chemicals.

Using an Illustration

A real-life incident, a passage from a novel or short story, or a hypothetical illustration also can get a speech off to a good start. As with a humorous story, however, an illustration should be interesting to the audience as well as relevant to your central idea. Deanna Sellnow, a then-student at North Dakota State University, used this technique to introduce a speech on private credit-reporting bureaus:

> John Pontier, of Boise, Idaho, was turned down for insurance because a reporting agency informed the company that he and his wife were addicted to narcotics, and his Taco Bell franchise had been closed down by the health board when dog food had been found mixed in with the tacos. There was only one small problem. The information was made up. His wife was a practicing Mormon who didn't touch a drink, much less drugs, and the restaurant had never been cited for a health violation.[16]

The existence of a problem with private credit-reporting bureaus is clear from this introduction. In addition, when listeners get involved with someone like John Pontier, who has encountered the problem, they become more attentive. When this happens, the illustration can have a powerful impact.

Building a Speech Forecast

As suggested several times, highly competent speakers always are careful to forecast the development of their speeches. The simplest forecast merely enumerates the sections of a speech, as Whitney Sugarman of Seton Hall University did when beginning her talk on the overuse of cesarean sections at birth:

> [The fact that so many cesarean sections are unnecessary] will become evident as we first, understand the process of a cesarean section and the detrimental effects to mother and child; then delve into the nonclinical factors leading to the rise of cesareans in this country; and finally, magnify steps that must be taken to decrease the number of cesareans performed each year in the United States.[17]

With a little more effort, a speaker can use the forecast to suggest the *coherence* of a speech and its development as well. So, in reminding his audience that the day of great oratory is dead but should be recovered, Dean

Willich of Wittenberg University offered a simple forecast that succeeded in making his speech feel like a complete unit of thought: "I would like to introduce you to the tradition of oratory, then look at the contemporary state of persuasive speaking; and finally, show you how a synthesis between the two will help us grow to be more effective persuasive speakers."[18] Just by talking about his third point as a synthesis of the first two, Willich left the impression that his speech would be a unified bundle of ideas; such a forecast undoubtedly helped the audience see and anticipate his developmental strategies.

TYPES OF SPEECH CONCLUSIONS

The best conclusions mirror good introductions by returning to the viewpoints articulated early in the speech, recapturing the tone with which it started, and reaffirming the speaker's goals for—and control over—the speech. A good speech often feels like a circle; an audience understands that it's entered a universe of thought and action at some point, taken a trip around that universe, and then returned to the place where it entered, now much wiser and more knowledgeable than when it came in. Creating a sense of having taken an interesting and worthwhile journey through important ideas requires careful attention to various types of speech conclusions.

Issuing a Challenge

You may conclude your speech by focusing directly upon the audience, hoping that you can inspire your listeners to get up and act in constructive ways. Such a conclusion attempts to involve listeners directly—intimately—with your speech. Jerry Junkins, president and CEO of Texas Instruments, used just such a technique when trying to convince fellow business executives to become more active in introducing new technologies to the nation's schools:

FIGURE 8.2   The Beginning and Ending of a Speech

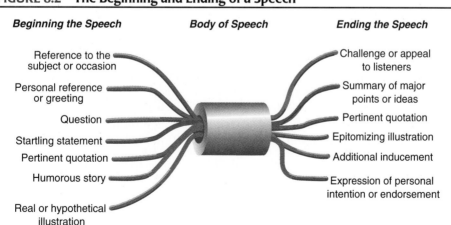

Beginning the Speech	Body of Speech	Ending the Speech
Reference to the subject or occasion		Challenge or appeal to listeners
Personal reference or greeting		Summary of major points or ideas
Question		Pertinent quotation
Startling statement		Epitomizing illustration
Pertinent quotation		Additional inducement
Humorous story		Expression of personal intention or endorsement
Real or hypothetical illustration		

> It's up to us . . . to bring the benefits of information technology not only to our companies . . . but also to America's communities and schools . . . so that our infrastructure can become and remain the equal of any in the world.
>
> It's up to us . . . to be sensitive and responsive to the social implications of our technology . . . and to be imaginative in our attempts to address those concerns.
>
> It's up to us . . . to do *all* of these things . . . and do them all at once . . . because the future won't wait. The technologies are here. They're already stirring the pot.
>
> Our challenge is not so much to harness those technologies . . . as it is to *unlock their potential.*[19]

Note here the combined use of repetition of a phrase ("it's up to us") and the direct challenge to the audience to act. Repetition can be an effective way to retain attention as you elaborate on the specific things the audience is to do, provided you keep the "listing" relatively short—had this run on to eight or nine repetitions, it would have started losing its impact on the audience.

Summarizing the Major Points or Ideas

In an informative speech, a summary allows the audience to pull together the main strands of information and evaluate the significance of the speech. In a persuasive speech, a summary gives you a final opportunity to present— briefly—the major points of your argument. For example, one student presented this summary of an informative speech on tornadoes:

> You've seen the swirling funnel clouds on the six-o'clock news. They hit sometimes without much warning, leaving in their paths death and destruction. Now you should understand the formation of funnel clouds, the classification of tornadoes on the Fujita scale, and the high cost of tornadoes worldwide in lives and property. Once you understand the savage fury of tornadoes, you can better appreciate them. Tornadoes are one of nature's temper tantrums.

If the student's purpose had been to persuade his listeners to take certain precautions during a tornado alert, the summary of the speech might have sounded like this:

> The devastation left in the path of a tornado can be tremendous. To prevent you and your loved ones from becoming statistics on the six-o'clock news, remember what I told you this afternoon. Seek shelter in basements, ditches, or other low areas. Stay away from glass and electric lines. And remember the lesson of the Xenia, Ohio, disaster: Tornadoes often hit in clusters. Be sure the coast is clear before you leave your shelter. Don't be a statistic.

In each case, summarizing the main ideas of the speech gives the speaker another opportunity to reinforce the message. Information can be reiterated in the summary of an informative speech, or the major arguments or actions can be strengthened in the summary of a persuasive speech.

Using a Quotation

You can cite the words of others to capture the spirit of your ideas in the conclusion of your speech. In fact, quotations often are used to end speeches. Poetry may distill the essence of your message in uplifting language and quoted prose—if the author is credible—may gather additional support for your central idea.

Using an Illustration

Illustrations engage your listeners emotionally, and a concluding illustration can set the tone and direction of your final words. Your illustration should be both inclusive and conclusive—inclusive of the main focus or thrust of your speech and conclusive in tone and impact. Sometimes a single illustration can even tie together a whole speech. This is what Michael Twitchell, a student in a speaking contest, did when talking about the causes and effects of depression. Here's his opening:

> Have you ever felt like you were the little Dutch boy who stuck his finger in the leaking dike? You waited and waited but the help never came. The leak became worse and the water rushed around you and swept you away. As you fought the flood, gasping and choking for air, you realized that the flood was inside yourself. You were drowning and dying in your own mind. According to the *American Journal of Psychiatry,* as many as half the people in this room will be carried away by this devastating flood. What is this disaster? Mental depression.

Now, notice how Twitchell's concluding words reinforce the illustration used in his introduction:

> Let's go back to my illustration of the little Dutch boy. He was wise to take action and put his finger in the dike, preventing the flood. In the case of depression, each one of us must be like the little Dutch boy—willing to get involved and control the harmful effects of depression.[20]

Supplying an Additional Inducement to Belief or Action

Sometimes you may conclude a speech by quickly reviewing the principal ideas presented in the body and then supplying one or more additional reasons for endorsing the belief or taking the proposed action. In the speech just described, Michael Twitchell spoke at length about the devastating effects of depression. After proposing numerous reasons for people to get involved in the battle, Twitchell offered in his conclusion an additional inducement:

> Why should you really care? Why is it important? The depressed person may be someone you know—it could be you. If you know what is happening, you can always help. I wish I had known what depression was in March of 1978. You see, when I said David Twitchell could be my father, I was making a statement of fact. David is my father. I am his son. My family wasn't saved; perhaps now yours can be.

Stating a Personal Intention

Stating your own intention to adopt the action or attitude you recommend in your speech is particularly effective when your prestige with the audience is high or you have presented a concrete proposal requiring immediate action. By professing your intention to take immediate action, you and your ideas gain credibility. In the following example, a speaker sets himself up as a model for the actions he wants his listeners to take:

> Today I have illustrated how important healthy blood is to human survival and how blood banks work to ensure the possibility and availability of blood for each of us. It is not a coincidence that I speak on this vital topic on the same day that the local Red Cross Bloodmobile is visiting campus. I want to urge each of you to ensure your future and mine by stopping at the Student Center today or tomorrow to make your donation. The few minutes that it takes may add up to a lifetime for a person in need. To illustrate how firmly I believe in this opportunity to help, I'm going to the Student Center to give my donation as soon as this class is over. I invite any of you who feel this strongly to join me.

SELECTING INTRODUCTIONS AND CONCLUSIONS

So far, we've talked about the functions of introductions and conclusions, about fitting them together to provide a solid rhetorical orientation to your speech, and about a variety of strategies to begin and end speeches. At this point, you should be able to build a generally serviceable opening and closing for a speech. Suppose you want to stretch yourself a bit farther, however, to move beyond the skills of the average speaker and into the world of highly competent speechmakers, of the kind we've been quoting throughout this chapter. What then? How do you become a superior opener and closer?

The answer—as always in this textbook—is that you must learn to assess yourself, your listeners, the subject matter, and the requirements of the occasion. The answers to four questions should help you construct high-quality introductions and conclusions:

1. *What are your own experiences and abilities?* The best source of powerful illustrations is your own life. Stories of your own experiences usually come across as natural and involving, especially if your own reactions to those experiences are like those your listeners would feel in the same situation. Anecdotes that you've gotten elsewhere, however, must be practiced and, at the very least, put into your own words to make them a part of you.

    Working from your own experiences also tends to increase the listeners' positive reactions to your qualifications. If you don't have first-hand experience, you need to show the audience, through explicit statements or the quality of your research materials, that you know what you're talking about.

Your abilities as a speaker also may constrain your choices. If you don't tell funny stories in a natural, relaxed manner, attempting a humorous anecdote may not be wise. On the other hand, if you're known as a clown and want to be taken seriously for a change, you need to set forth your qualifications explicitly and, when concluding, create a serious mood for the consideration of your views. Humor may not be your best vehicle under these circumstances.

2. *What is the mood and commitment of the audience?* If you're speaking on a subject already announced and known to be controversial, gaining attention through a startling statement or a humorous anecdote may be highly inappropriate. If the audience is indifferent or has already heard several presentations on the same subject, a direct reference to the subject may be perceived as dull and unoriginal. A rhetorical question that forces them to think for a moment or a startling statement that creates curiosity, however, may be appropriate, because both induce listeners to participate directly rather than listen passively.

3. *What does the audience know about you and your commitment to the subject?* If you're already known as an expert in an area, stating your qualifications would be repetitious and may even convey conceit. If your personal experience and depth of feeling generally are unknown, however you'll want to reveal these through personal reference or, as Michael Twitchell did, through an additional inducement at the close of your address. Either approach establishes both your knowledge and your personal involvement in the subject. Allow time to pass before you attempt to bring deeply felt experiences—especially those involving loss of life—before an audience. If you appear emotionally shaken or teary-eyed, the tension level will increase as the audience shares your personal discomfort, and the effectiveness of your personal revelation will correspondingly decrease. Finally, using a challenge or statement of personal intent also is an effective means of demonstrating your commitment to the subject.

4. *What constraints are imposed by the situation or setting?* A somber occasion (a funeral or dedication of a war memorial) is hardly the place for hilarious stories. On the other hand, some serious occasions (commencements) can be enlivened by humor. The student speaker who ended his high-school address by waving a beer bottle and proclaiming "This Bud's for you" quickly discovered that his attempt at humor was received well only by part of his audience; the faculty and parents did not react as pleasantly as his peers. Not everything goes—even when *you* see nothing wrong with the story or allusion. A reference to the occasion or personal greeting, however, may be an appropriate reminder to the audience that you, as well as they, appreciate the significance of the occasion. Pertinent quotations and epitomizing illustrations, whether at the beginning or the end, also may convey a sense of the event's meaning for everyone present.

This discussion of appropriate introductions and conclusions is not intended to be exhaustive. Rather, it illustrates the general approach to *thinking through* possible audience reactions as you select various means of introducing and concluding your speech. A "thought-through" speech will be perceived as being well prepared by your listeners—whether they ultimately agree with you or not.

SAMPLE OUTLINE FOR AN INTRODUCTION AND A CONCLUSION

An introduction and conclusion for a classroom speech on doing research using the World Wide Web might take the following form. Notice that the presentation begins with an illustration that will engage the listeners, as they've been 'there' before. The presentation then outlines in brief the development of the speech. In concluding, the short summary of key points serves to pull the ideas together as a final reminder, and then circles back to the opening illustration to provide a fitting closure.

Introduction

   I. It is 11PM, almost time to shut down for the night, when your eye catches a textbook leaning precariously on a stack of other texts—and then it hits you a paper is due at 11 tomorrow, and no, you didn't do the research you promised you'd do, much less start the paper

      A. What next—a few excuses run through your tired brain as you try to think of ways to dodge the inevitable late night—and finally you turn to the computer, and begin to settle in, but first, where do you find material at this time of the night?

      B. As many of you have already guessed, the prime resource for that late night crisis is none other than the World Wide Web—an all-night delicatessen, if only you know where to look for the right stuff.

  II. Knowing how and where to look for resources is the "trick"—and in this presentation, I will review the reasons the Web is an excellent resource, talk about specific search phases, and then provide some useful tips to assist in finding the right material.

Conclusion

   I. The search phases we have discussed—using meta-search engines, using the most powerful of the crawlers, and using sources with hyperlinks—make it possible to find the kind of materials needed in less time.

  II. The tips—using quote marks, using words such as 'not' and truncating words—also make the process more streamlined, and enhance your chances of finding the material you need.

 III. It is now midnight, and a brief half hour of searching the web provided the key materials needed for your research paper. In fact, you found more material than you could use!! The paper is now well underway, and it looks, with any luck, like you'll still get some sleep.

CHAPTER SUMMARY

Recall Winans' advice in noting that "attention determines response." The strategies for gaining and maintaining attention—Activity, Reality, Proximity, Familiarity, Novelty, Suspense, Conflict, Humor, and The Vital—provide ways to motivate your listeners to attend to your ideas. More specifically, introductions and conclusions provide a rhetorical orientation to your speeches, thus framing them in ways audiences can understand and appreciate. Well-framed introductions orient an audience's attention, show them your qualifications, and direct them to your ideas and their development. Well-framed conclusions demonstrate focus, flair, and a sense of finality for your talks. Useful ways of beginning a speech include referring to the subject or occasion, using a personal reference or greeting, asking a question, making a startling statement, using a quotation, telling a humorous story, using an illustration, and building a speech forecast. Speeches can be concluded by issuing a challenge, summarizing the major points or ideas, using a quotation, using an illustration, supplying an additional inducement to belief or action, and stating a personal intention. Your decision regarding which strategies you use, whether singly or in combination, should depend on you and your experiences, the mood and commitments of the audience, the audience's knowledge of you and your commitments, and any constraints imposed by the situation or setting. The most competent speakers carefully think through strategies for moving into and out of their speeches because of the importance of rhetorical orientation in making them successful behind the lectern.

KEY TERMS

activity (p. 185)

attention (p. 184)

attention gaining/maintaining strategies (p. 185)

audience attention (p. 183)

conclusion (p. 183)

conflict (p. 188)

ethos (p. 190)

familiarity (p. 187)

forecast (p. 190)

humor (p. 189)

introduction (p. 183)

novelty (p. 187)

proximity (p. 187)

reality (p. 186)

rhetorical orientation (p. 183)

suspense (p. 187)

The End (p. 191)

the vital (p. 189)

ASSESSMENT ACTIVITIES

1. Following the principles and guidelines presented in this chapter, prepare a three- to four-minute speech to inform. Narrow the subject carefully so that you can do justice to it in the allotted time, and concentrate on developing ways to gain and hold the audience's attention. Hand in an outline along with a brief analysis of the audience and the occasion when you present the speech. In your analysis, indicate why you think your approach to attention will work in this situation.

2. You've been asked to speak on a controversial issue. Assume that the setting for three versions of the speech will include three different occasions: a classroom at your school, where audience members are mixed in their support or rejection of the issue; a favorable ("pro") audi-

ence, highly sympathetic to you and your position; and an unfavorable ("con") audience, hostile to you and your position. Write three introductions, one for each setting. Include a brief paragraph explaining your rhetorical orientation to those three audiences, and then turn in the introductions and rationales to your instructor.

3. Devise one-minute introductions and conclusions for your next informative

speech. Deliver them to a small group in class, in round-robin fashion, so that everyone gets a crack at the group. Have each member of the group rate your introduction in terms of attention value, perception of your qualifications, and forecast of your speech's development and your conclusion in terms of focus, flair, and sense of finality. Collect the ratings from everyone, and use their feedback to refine your opening and closing.

REFERENCES

1. Psychologist Philip G. Zimbardo has likened attention to "a spotlight that illuminates certain portions of our surroundings. When we focus our attention on something and thus become conscious of it, we can begin to process it cognitively—converting sensory information into perceptions and memories or developing ideas through analysis, judgment, reasoning, and imagination. When the spotlight shifts to something else, conscious processing of the earlier material ceases and processing of the new content begins." *Psychology and Life.* 12th ed. (Glenview, IL: Scott, Foresman, 1988), 225.

2. Gibson E. and Rader, N., "Attention: Perceiver as Performer," *Attention and Cognitive Development,* ed. Gordon A. Hale and Michael Lewis (New York: Plenum 1979), 1–22). Cited in Russell A. Barkley, "Critical Issues in Research on Attention," in *Attention, Memory, and Executive Function,* ed. G. Reid Lyon and Norman A. Krasgegor (Baltimore, MD: Brookes Pub. Co. 1996)

3. Martin Luther King, Jr., "I've Been to the Mountaintop," *Contemporary American Voices: Significant Speeches in American History, 1945–Present,* ed. James R. Andrews and David Zarefsky (New York: Longman, 1992), 115.

4. King, 120. (See n. 3.)

5. Neal Luker, "Our Defense Policy," a speech presented in a course in advanced public speaking at the University of Iowa.

6. Jesse Jackson, "Common Ground and Common Sense," *Diversity in Public Communication: A Reader,* eds. Christine Kelly, E. Anne Laffoon, and Raymie E. McKerrow (Dubuque, IA: Kendall-Hunt, 1994), 140.

7. Malcolm X, "The Ballot or the Bullet," *Diversity in Public Communication: A Reader,* eds. Christine Kelly, E. Anne Laffoon, and Raymie E. McKerrow (Dubuque, IA: Kendall-Hunt, 1994), 138.

8. Russell J. Love, "The Barriers Come Tumbling Down," Harris-Hillman School Commencement, Nashville, May 21, 1981. Reprinted by permission.

9. Pope John Paul II, "Democracy and Christianity," *Vital Speeches of the Day,* 62 (November 1, 1995): 35.

10. Barbara Bush, "Choice and Change," Wellesley College, June 1, 1990. Manuscript available from the text's author.

11. Nicholas Fynn, "The Free Burn Fallacy," *Winning Orations 1989.* Reprinted by permission of Larry Schnoor, Executive Secretary, Interstate Oratorical Association, Mankato State University, Mankato, MN.

12. Anne Wilfahrt, "General Mining Law of 1872; Statute 17–90," *Winning Orations 1992.* Reprinted by permission of Larry Schnoor, Executive Secretary, Interstate Oratorical Association, Mankato State University, Mankato, MN.

13. Horace B. Deets, "Health Care for a Caring America: We Must Develop a Better System," *Vital Speeches of the Day,* 55 (August 1, 1989).

14. Agnar Pytte, "Political Correctness and Free Speech: Let the Ideas Come Forth," *Vital Speeches of the Day*, 57 (September 1, 1989).
15. Earnest W. Deavenport, "Walking the High Wire: Balancing Stakeholder Interests," *Vital Speeches of the Day*, 62 (November 1, 1995): 49.
16. Deanna Sellnow, "Have You Checked Lately?" *Winning Orations*. Reprinted by permission of Larry Schnoor, Executive Secretary, Interstate Oratorical Association, Mankato State University, Mankato, MN.
17. Whitney Sugarman, "Cesarean Sections: The Needless Scars of Profit," *Winning Orations 1992*. Reprinted by permission of Larry Schnoor, Executive Secretary, Interstate Oratorical Association, Mankato State University, Mankato, MN.
18. Dean Willich, "Traditional Oratory: Thoroughbred of Persuasive Speaking," *Winning Orations 1992*. Reprinted by permission of Larry Schnoor, Executive Secretary, Interstate Oratorical Association, Mankato State University, Mankato, MN.
19. Jerry R. Junkins, "Realizing the Promise: Our Role as Business Leaders," *Vital Speeches of the Day*, 62 (November 1, 1995): 57.
20. Michael A. Twitchell, "The Flood Gates of the Mind," *Winning Orations*. Reprinted by permission of Larry Schnoor, Executive Secretary, Interstate Oratorical Association, Mankato State University, Mankato, MN.

Chapter 9

Developing the Speech Outline

W hy outline a speech? Recall the opening story in the preceding chapter—had Tom taken the time to carefully outline his presentation, he still may not have made his listeners as impassioned about research as he, but at least they would have understood the purpose of his speech. An outline keeps you on track, allows you to concentrate on what needs to be said, and reminds you of points you otherwise may forget to mention. In addition, you can make side notes to remind you when to show a slide or pause so that audience members can focus on a graph or other visual aid you have presented. Although your past experiences with outlining may not have been the most pleasant (remember outlining in eighth or ninth grade?), the fact is that outlining is an important tool for the speaker. In addition to guidance, an outline helps you evaluate the coherence or cohesiveness of your ideas: You can discover what ideas you've overemphasized to the exclusion of other notions, can see more clearly what should be added, and can tell at a glance that you've buried your most important point as subpoint 3 under main point 2. Thus, while the outline is written for the speaking situation, it serves as an evaluative tool as well.

Speech outlines come in many forms, depending on the purpose for which they've been constructed. In this chapter, we review the elements of good outline form (in case you've forgotten those earlier lessons in eighth or ninth grade!). Then, we get into the heart of the matter: the process of moving from your initial ideas to an outline you can use in presenting a speech.

REQUIREMENTS OF GOOD OUTLINE FORM

There are many "good" outline forms, depending on the way you want to use them. The following four requirements are applicable to all outlines, regardless of their purpose or form. To facilitate recognition of the difference between sloppy and logical outlining, we alternate a "wrong" with a "right" illustration to make application of the rule easier to see.

1. *Each item in the outline should contain one main idea.* When two or more ideas are included in a main point, an audience has more difficulty tracking the development of the point.

Wrong

I. When you buy your eggs in the supermarket, you probably don't think about the fact that chicken farms may cause serious problems for those living in the surrounding area as the chickens produce manure, which in turn produces flies, beetles, and a maladorous odor that makes living in the area a constant battle with bugs and smelly air, but as we have learned, the larger the farming operation, the more clout it has with government, hence the lives of those in the area goes on without recourse to assistance.

By sketching the structure of your speech in advance of presentation, you can determine whether the major sections fit together smoothly.

This is a mess. It is hard to discern what the main point of the speech is from this sentence. It appears the speaker is angry about the presence of chicken farms (perhaps the speaker has personal experience?), but the series of examples and the unsupported allegation about big business makes this too large a "claim" to swallow whole.

Right

    I. Chicken farms need to be better regulated.
        A. Chicken farms produce tons of manure that needs to be managed in a way to reduce flies and other pests.
        B. Stricter regulations on the use of beetles to minimize the fly population also need to be implemented.

In this case, the claim is clearly focused on regulations. The initial points set forth the position that the speaker wants to establish and the evidence requirements. To support *A*, one would need statistics on the amount of manure and on the nature and extent of the insect infestation. To support *B*, the speaker needs to illustrate specifically what has happened in several instances to show this is as serious an issue as he or she claims.

2. *Less important ideas in the outline should be subordinate to more important ideas.* You already know this is true; the trick is to actually carry it out so that listeners will understand the rational structure of your arguments.

Wrong

    I. The cost of medical care has skyrocketed.
        A. Operating room fees can run to tens of thousands of dollars.
            1. Hospital charges are high.
            2. A private room can cost $1,500 a day.
        B. X-rays and laboratory tests are extra charges.
        C. Complicated operations may cost over $50,000.
            1. Doctors' charges constantly go up.
                a.   Office calls usually cost between $30 and $50.
                b.   Surgical costs have increased.
            2. Drugs are expensive.
            3. Most antibiotics cost from $2 to $3 per dose.
        D. The cost of even nonprescription drugs has mounted.

This outline is sloppily arranged. Listeners would feel bombarded by numbers and general references to hospitals and doctors—and probably would not be able to sort it all out. To help listeners grasp the main ideas, notice what happens when the material is sorted by cost in a topical outline:

Right

    I. The cost of medical care has skyrocketed.
Reason   A. *Hospital charges* are high.
Support   1. A private room may cost as much as $1,500 a day.

2. Operating room fees may be tens of thousands of dollars.

3. X-rays and laboratory tests are extra.

Reason   B. *Doctors' charges* constantly go up.

Support   1. Complicated operations may cost more than $50,000.

2. Office calls usually cost between $30 and $50.

Reason   C. *Drugs* are expensive.

Support   1. Most antibiotics cost from $2 to $3 per dose.

2. The cost of even nonprescription drugs has mounted.

The second form highlights the three main topics and *subordinates* the examples, which are the supporting materials, to the three main arguments. The key word here is *fit:* what example fits within or under what topic? Reasons (*A,B,C*) fit within or under claims; supporting materials (*1,2*) fit within or under reasons.

3. *A consistent set of symbols should be used.* Each indention should be designated by the same set of symbols. The most common set looks like this:

I. Main idea.

     A. Major subpoint or topic.

         1. Aspect of the subpoint or topic.

            a. Perhaps a statistic or quotation.

               (1) Perhaps bolstering support.

You can use other sets of symbols (*A., 1., a.* if you only need three levels). However, the primary concern is to be consistent so that the rational structure of your thoughts emerges clearly, both for evaluative and for guidance purposes.

4. *The logical relation of items in an outline should be shown by proper indention.* Why? Because this makes it easier to see what is subordinate to what. As noted earlier, reasons and supporting materials should not be on the same level. By indenting—and using a consistent format for the levels used in outlining—the process of evaluating your claim or central idea becomes much easier.

Wrong

I. Picking edible wild mushrooms is no job for the uninformed.

     A. Many wild species are highly toxic.

         1. The angel cap contains a toxin for which there is no known antidote.

         2. Hallucinogenic mushrooms produce short-lived highs, which are followed by convulsions, paralysis, and possibly, death.

     B. Myths abound regarding ways to choose "safe" mushrooms.

         1. Mushrooms easily peeled still can be poisonous.

         2. Mushrooms eaten by animals are not necessarily safe.

         3. Mushrooms that do not darken a silver coin in a pan of hot water could be toxic.

Right

I. Picking edible wild mushrooms is no job for the uninformed.

    A. Many wild species are highly toxic.
       1. The angel cap contains a toxin for which there is no known antidote.
       2. Hallucinogenic mushrooms produce short-lived highs, which are followed by convulsions, paralysis, and possibly, death.
    B. Myths abound regarding ways to choose "safe" mushrooms.
       1. Mushrooms easily peeled still can be poisonous.
       2. Mushrooms eaten by animals are not necessarily safe.
       3. Mushrooms that do not darken a silver coin in a pan of hot water could be toxic.[1]

DEVELOPING THE SPEECH: STAGES IN THE OUTLINING PROCESS

You should develop your outline—as well as the speech it represents—through a series of stages. Your outlines will become increasingly complex and complete as the ideas evolve and you move closer to the final form of your speech. We will examine each of the major stages, beginning with the *rough outline,* and then consider in sequence the *technical plot outline* and the *speaking outline.*

Developing a Rough Outline

Suppose your instructor has assigned an informative speech and allowed you to choose the subject. You decide to talk about World Wide Web (WWW) search strategies, these might be helpful to classmates looking for speech materials. In the six to eight minutes you have to speak, you obviously cannot cover such a broad topic adequately. After considering your audience (see Chapter 5) and your time limit, you decide to focus your presentation on the steps to be taken—and avoided—in finding useful information.

    As you think about narrowing your topic further, you jot down some possible ideas. You continue to narrow your list until your final ideas include the following:

1. General information about the Internet and WWW to set the scene.
2. Search phases: Moving through various search engines.
3. Search strategies that are useful.
4. Search strategies that are not as useful.

Your next step is to consider the best pattern of organization for these topics. Because searching is itself a sequential process, a **chronological pattern** would allow you to discuss the initial steps in preparing to search and then move forward in time to more sophisticated searching. Because you are not posing this as a problem, patterns such as **cause-effect** or **effect-cause** would not be as easy to work into the structure of this speech. After examining the alternatives, you finally settle on a **topical pattern,** which allows you to present four topics that are related to the search process:

1. Setting the context in terms of the WWW as a research resource.
2. Elaborating on search phases—moving from metasearch engines to more specific ones.
3. Discussing search strategies that further focus search.
4. Discussing search strategies that are not as useful.

These four topics form the basis for your rough outline:

  I. General discussion of the WWW.
    A. As a research resource.
    B. Familiarizing audience with key terms to be used.
 II. Search phases.
    A. Discuss metasearch engines and what they can do.
    B. Discuss more specific search engines: If you are looking for "x," use search engine "y."
III. Discuss search strategies or tips that will focus the research.
    A. Using quote marks.
    B. Using NOT or −.
    C. Using AND or +.
IV. Discuss search strategies that will not be as useful.

A **rough outline** identifies your topic, provides a reasonable number of subtopics, and shows a method for organizing and developing your speech. Notice that you've arranged the main points topically and used a "general to specific" ordering under main point II, which also suggests a sequential process for searching. Under main point II, you also have organized the subpoints topically. A word of warning: *As you refine your outline, make sure that the speech does not turn into a "string of beads" that fails to differentiate between one topic and the next.*

HOW TO PREPARE A GOOD OUTLINE

  I. Determine the general purpose of the speech for the subject you have selected.
    A. You need to limit the subject in two ways.
      1. Limit the subject to fit the available time.
      2. Limit the subject to ensure unity and coherence.
    B. You also need to phrase the specific purpose in terms of the exact response you seek from your listeners.
 II. Develop a rough outline of your speech.
    A. List the main ideas you wish to cover.
    B. Arrange these main ideas according to the methods discussed in Chapter 7.
    C. Arrange subordinate ideas under their appropriate main heads.
    D. Fill in the supporting materials for amplifying or justifying your ideas.
    E. Review your rough draft.

COMMUNICATION RESEARCH DATELINE

PERCEPTUAL GROUPING: THE ORGANIZATION OF SUBORDINATE POINTS

What basic principles do we use to organize information into meaningful patterns? Gestalt psychologists, who believe that organization is basic to all mental activity and reflects the way the human brain functions, provide some useful clues. As suggested in this chapter, psychologists argue that people learn by adding new bits of information to old constructs. Although the information that we encounter changes, the constructs remain constant. There are several relatively common constructs that people use to group new bits of information:

1. *Proximity:* We group stimuli that are close together.
2. *Continuity:* We tend to simplify and to find similarities among things rather than differences.
3. *Contiguity:* We connect events that occur close together in time and space.
4. *Closure:* We complete figures by filling in the gaps or adding missing connections.
5. *Similarity:* We group items of similar shape, size, and color.

You can use these constructs to enhance audience understanding of your ideas: The speech outline can be cast in a pattern of thinking that is familiar to your audience. Consider the constructs for organizing subordinate points shown in the accompanying table.

These constructs also may assist you as you evaluate your outline, especially as you develop the technical plot. Are your most important ideas near, or proximate, to each other? Do they advance a chain of thinking in a coherent manner implying continuity? Are they linked together or contiguous? Are they sufficiently comprehensive to permit accurate closure?

    1. Does it cover your subject adequately?
    2. Does it carry out your specific purpose?
III. Develop technical plot outline.
    A. Begin by reviewing the following questions.
        1. Are main ideas concise, vivid, and—insofar as possible—in parallel terms?
        2. Do the major heads directly address the needs and interests of your listeners?
    B. Are the subordinate ideas concise and clearly stated?
        1. Are they subordinate to the main idea they are intended to develop?

TABLE 9.1   Strategies for Organizing Speech Information

Organizing Strategy	Main Construct	Explanation	Example
Parts of a whole	Proximity	You help your audience perceive how the new information is all part of a whole.	"The grip, shaft, and head are the main parts of a golf club."
Lists of functions	Continuity	You show your audience the connections between pieces of new information.	"The mission of a police department consists of meeting its responsibilities of traffic control, crime detection, and safety education."
Series of causes or results	Contiguity	You show your listeners the precise relationship between pieces of new information.	"The causes of high orange juice prices may be drought, frost, or blight in citrus-producing states."
Items of logical proof	Closure	You connect separate items of information along a coordinated line of reasoning.	"We need a new high school because our present building (a) is too small, (b) lacks modern laboratory and shop facilities, and (c) is inaccessible to handicapped students."
Illustrative examples	Similarity	You help your audience accept your main point by grouping specific cases or examples.	Cite the outcome of experiments to prove that adding fluoride to your community's water supply will help prevent tooth decay.

Are they similar enough to suggest they belong together as main points?

For Further Reading

Jacob Beck, ed. *Organization and Representation in Perception* (Hillsdale, NJ: Lawrence Erlbaum, 1982); Stephen E. Palmer, "Gestalt Psychology Redux," *Speaking Minds,* eds. Peter Baumgartner and Sabine Payr (Princeton: Princeton University Press, 1995), 157–176; Barry Smith, ed. *Foundations of Gestalt Theory* (Munich: Philosophia Verlag, 1988); and Irvin Rock, ed. *The Legacy of Solomon Asch: Essays in Cognition and Social Psychology* (Hillsdale, NJ: Lawrence Erlbaum, 1990).

2. Are they coordinate with other items at the same level (that is, are all *A-B-C* series and *1-2-3* series roughly equal in importance)?
C. You now are ready to fill in the supporting materials.
  1. Are they pertinent?
  2. Are they adequate?
  3. Is there a variety of types of support?
D. Recheck the completed outline.
  1. Is it written in proper outline form?
  2. Does the speech, as outlined, adequately cover the subject?
  3. Does the speech, as outlined, carry out your general and specific purposes?

Developing a Technical Plot Outline

After completing your rough outline and learning more about your topic through background reading, you're now ready to assemble a **technical plot outline,** which is a diagnostic tool used to determine whether a speech is structurally sound. Use your technical plot outline to discover possible gaps or weaknesses in your speech. Begin this process by laying your current outline beside a blank sheet of paper. On the blank sheet, identify opposite each outline unit the corresponding supporting materials, types of motivational appeals, factors of attention, and other devices. For example, indicate on the blank sheet wherever you use statistics; you also might include a brief statement of the function of the statistics. Then, examine the list of supporting materials, motivational appeals, factors of attention, and so on. Is there adequate supporting material for each point in the speech? Is the supporting material sufficiently varied? Do you use motivational appeals at key points in the speech? Do you attempt to engage your listeners' attention throughout the speech? Answering these questions with your technical plot outline can help you determine whether your speech is structurally sound, whether there is adequate supporting material, whether you've overused any forms of support, and whether you have effectively adapted your appeals to the audience and content.

SAMPLE TECHNICAL PLOT OUTLINE

What follows typifies the kind of outline you will initially construct, as it mixes full sentences with phrases as needed to clearly indicate your thoughts. In most cases, however, you will use a more precisely phrased speaking outline—provided that will fulfill your instructor's goals regarding how detailed to make your outline.

SEARCH STRATEGIES FOR SUCCESSFUL RESEARCH ON THE WWW

[Introduction and conclusion are assumed—this is the "content" portion of the presentation.]

First topic	I. Conducting research on the WWW is an excellent tool in locating speech materials.
First subtopic	A. The Web is an amazing library resource.
Statistics	1. Alta Vista estimates more than 1.7 billion web pages as of mid-June 1998.
	2. None of the web search engines access all the pages available, including Alta Vista.
Second subtopic	B. The WWW is a convenient resource.
Motivational appeal	1. If you have an Internet connection where you live, you can log on any time day or night.
	2. Information never sleeps.
Transition topic	C. Before you start, some key terms to know.

Definitions [use black- 1. *HTTP:* Hypertext Transfer Protocol.
board, tripod, or Power- 2. *URL:* Uniform Resource Locater.
Point slides for terms] 3. *Hyperlinks:* links to relevant resources.
Second main topic   II. Search phases.
Specific instances   A. Phase one: Use metasearch engines.
[list on board or use   1. Inference find: http://www.inference.com/infind.
slides to make it easy   2. MetaFind: http://www.metafind.com.
for audience to see   3. MetaCrawler: http://www.metacrawler.com.
and copy the terms]   4. Dogpile: http://www.dogpile.com.
 B. Phase two: Use those with the most power to locate specific
 information.
Specific instances   1. Infoseek: http://www.infoseek.com.
[illustrate as above]   2. Alta Vista: http://www.altavista.com.
 3. Northern Light: http://www.northernlight.com.
 4. Hotbot: http://www.hotbot.com.
 5. For other search engines: http://www.home.co.il/search
 .html.
Third subpoint   C. Phase three: Use "webliographics" resources—focus on sites
 with hyperlinks to your subject area.
 1. Yahoo!: http://www.yahoo.com.
 2. Argus Clearinghouse: http://www.clearinghouse.edu.
 III. Search tips: Experiment with the search engine you are using in trying these features, because not all engines accept the same codes.
Explanation   A. Place more than one word in quotation marks.
Specific instance   1. Ex. "Web search engines."
Explanation   B. Use either NOT or – to eliminate hits on a specific word.
Specific instance   1. Ex. Rhetoric NOT speeches.
 C. AND or + also will assist in focusing the search.
 1. Ex. Rhetoric AND public spheres AND criticism.
 D. OR produces hits on both terms used in a search.
 1. Ex. Arguing OR conflict.
 E. Truncate words to find as many variations as possible.
 1. Ex. "Femini" – retrieves for feminist, feminism, feminine ...
Final main point   IV. Search strategies to avoid.
Explanation   A. Typing in a general subject term and seeing what pops up.
Explanation   B. Using "Subject Directories" within Search Engine Menu.[2]

Developing a Speaking Outline

As you probably realize, the technical plot outline is not intended for actual speaking use. It gives you a chance to see what is needed or how to make sure the audience understands the information, but it is not the kind of outline you actually would use in a speech on WWW search strategies. Compress the technical plot outline into a speaking outline, using the same indentation and symbol structure. The major difference in this compression of outlines is that each item in a **speaking outline** is referred to in shorthand—phrases or single key words. Developed in this manner, the previous technical plot outline looks like this:

SAMPLE SPEAKING OUTLINE

I. Conducting research on the WWW.
   A. The WWW as a library resource.
      1. Alta Vista—1.7 billion web pages as of mid-June 1998.
      2. None access fully.
   B. Convenience of the WWW.
      1. Modem/Internet connection.
      2. Information never sleeps.
   C. Key terms.
      1. *HTTP:* Hypertext Transfer Protocol.
      2. *URL:* Uniform Resource Locater.
      3. *Hyperlinks:* links to relevant resources.

II. Search phases.
   A. Phase one: Use metasearch engines.
      1. Inference find.
      2. MetaFind.
      3. MetaCrawler.
      4. Dogpile.
   B. Phase two: Specific engines.
      1. Infoseek.
      2. Alta Vista.
      3. Northern Light.
      4. Hotbot.
      5. Search Engine Listing.
   C. Phase three: "webliographics" resources.
      1. Yahoo!
      2. Argus Clearinghouse.

III. Search tips.
   A. Quotation marks.
   B. NOT or −.
   C. AND or +.
   D. OR.
   E. Truncate words.

IV. Search strategies to avoid.
   A. General subject terms.
   B. Subject directories.

What you use in writing out your speaking outline depends on your personal preference; some people like to work with small pieces of paper and others with notecards. Whatever your choice, however, your speaking outline should serve several functions while you're addressing your audience: (a) it should provide you with reminders of the direction of your speech—main points, subordinate ideas, and so on; (b) it should record technical or detailed material such as statistics and quotations, and (c) it should be easy to read so that it does not detract from the delivery of your speech. Each notecard or piece of paper should contain only one main idea.

I. Conducting research on the World Wide Web

A. The Web as a library resource
   1. AltaVista - 1.7 billion web pages as of
      mid-June, 1998
   2. None access fully
B. Convenience of the Web
   1. Modem/Internet connection
   2. Information never sleeps
C. Key Terms [SHOW POSTER]
   1. HTTP: hypertext transfer protocol
   2. URL: uniform resource locater
   3. Hyperlinks: links to relevant resources

II. Search phases

A. Phase One: Use meta-search engines
   1. Inference Find
   2. MetaFind
   3. MetaCrawler
   4. Dogpile

B. Phase Two: Specific engines
   1. Infoseek   **4.** Hotbot
   2. AltaVista   **5.** Search Engine Listing
   3. Northern Light

C. Phase Three: 'webliographics' resources
   1. Yahoo!
   2. Argus Clearinghouse

III. Search tips

   A. Quotation marks
   B. "Not" or "–"
   C. "AND" or "+"
   D. "OR"
   E. Truncate words

IV. Search strategies to avoid

   A. General subject terms
   B. Subject directories

FIGURE 9.1   Sample Speaking Outline on Notecards

Notecards for a speech on Web Search Strategies.

There are four main characteristics of properly prepared speaking outlines:

1. Most points are noted with only a key word or phrase—a word or two should be enough to trigger your memory, especially if you've practiced the speech adequately.
2. Ideas that must be stated precisely are written down fully, for example, "Information never sleeps."
3. Directions for delivery—for example, "SHOW POSTER"—are included.
4. Emphasis is indicated in a number of ways—capital letters, underlining, indentation, dashes, and highlighting with colored markers. (Find methods of emphasis that will easily catch your eye, show the relationship of ideas, and jog your memory during your speech delivery.)

Using PowerPoint to Integrate Verbal and Visual Outlines

As noted in the previous chapter, PowerPoint offers a highly useful tool in making sure both you and your audience know where you are as you present your ideas. The speech on WWW search strategies lends itself especially well to

FIGURE 9.2   PowerPoint Slides/Notes

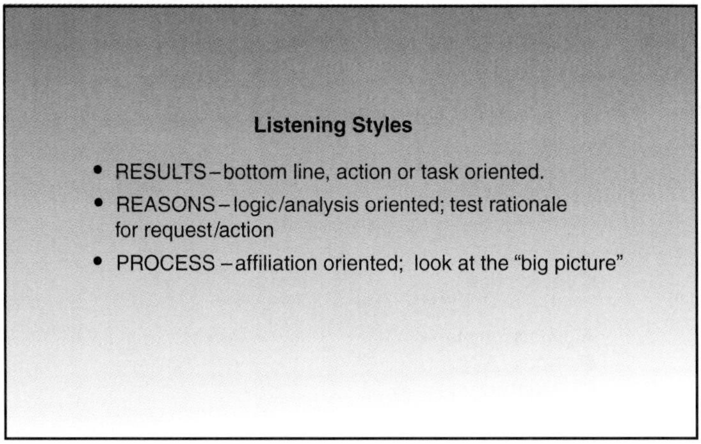

Listening Styles

- RESULTS–bottom line, action or task oriented.
- REASONS–logic/analysis oriented; test rationale for request/action
- PROCESS–affiliation oriented; look at the "big picture"

Listening Styles

RRP–Results, Reasons, Process
Results: Focuses on "what is to be done"
Reasons: Focuses on "why should this be done?"
Process: Focuses on "how has this recommendation been reached?"

the use of PowerPoint, as the listing of Web sites needs to be clear for the audience: simply hearing the names and addresses will not be a sufficient means of conveying useful information to the audience.

The primary advantage in using PowerPoint is that you can make notes on each slide shown. When you print your "Notes" file, you get a smaller version of the slide and your notes below, so you can stay on track with the information presented (see Fig. 9.2). Because PowerPoint also allows you to bring each subpoint to the screen as you refer to it, you also can manage the information given so that the audience focus is on each point as it is discussed. In this way, you integrate what you are saying to the audience as they are seeing the "evidence" for themselves on the projection screen.

CHAPTER SUMMARY

Arranging and outlining need not be tedious tasks. If you've understood the fundamentals presented in this chapter, you now realize that outlines are both diagnostic tools and guides to delivering ideas. You also are aware of the elements of a good outline:

- Each item should contain only one idea.
- Less important ideas should be subordinate to more important ones.
- Logical relationships should be shown through proper indentation.
- A consistent set of symbols should be used.

You also should be able to work through the logical progression involved in developing ideas, from the construction of a *rough outline,* followed by the addition of a *technical plot,* and then the drafting of a final *speaking outline.* Should you desire—or your instructor approve—you might take some short cuts in the actual process by eliminating the technical outline. You also could write out those comments that you want to make sure you say in a specific way and leave other material as key words or phrases. Whether or not you risk using an abbreviated method, you should be aware of the evaluative role that outlining can play in the speaking process.

KEY TERMS

cause-effect (p. 210)

chronological pattern (p. 210)

effect-cause (p. 210)

rough outline (p. 211)

speaking outline (p. 215)

technical plot outline (p. 214)

topical pattern (p. 210)

ASSESSMENT ACTIVITIES

1. Revise both (a) and (b) following the guidelines for correct outline form.
   a. The nuclear freeze concept is a good idea, because it allows us to stop nuclear proliferation and will help make us feel more secure.
   b. **I.** We should wear seatbelts to protect our lives.
   II. Studies indicate seatbelts protect children from serious injury.
   III. Studies indicate seatbelts reduce risk of head injury.
2. For a speech assigned by the instructor, develop a rough outline and a technical plot in accordance with the samples provided in this chapter. Hand in your speech outline in time to obtain feedback before presenting your speech.
3. Working in small groups, select a controversial topic for potential presentation in class. Brainstorm possible arguments that could be offered on the pro and the con sides. Using these as a basis, develop a rough outline of the main points to be presented on both sides.

REFERENCES

1. Information taken from Vincent Marteka, "Words of Praise—and Caution—About Fungus Among Us," *Smithsonian* (May 1980):96–104.
2. Information for this outline is taken from John A. Courtright and Elizabeth M. Perse, *Communicating Online: A Guide to the Internet*, (Mountain View, CA: Mayfield Publishing, 1998), http://www.lib.berkeley.edu/TeachingLib/Guides/Internet/FindInfo.html and http://freelance.co.nz/webpages.htm.

Part Three
CHANNELS

It may therefore be fairly concluded, that to neglect all or any part of the labour which constitutes correct delivery; whether it be the due management of the voice, the expression of the countenance, or the appropriate gesture, is so far an injury to the cause in which the speaker is engaged, and so far deprives his composition of its just effect.

Gilbert Austin
Chironomia:
Or a Treatise
on Rhetorical Delivery
(1806)

Chapter 10

Using Language to Communicate

When Neil Armstrong first set foot on the moon in 1969, millions of Americans heard him say, "That's one small step for man, one giant leap for mankind." It seemed an appropriate thing to say: a two-phrase speech that captured in a simple, eloquent way the realization that another ball-of-rock in the universe had been traversed by an earthling. Yet, as people thought about Armstrong's words, at least some noticed that they formed a tautology; the distinction between a "step for man" and a "leap for mankind" was not clear at all. After Armstrong heard the rebroadcast, he was quick to say that a key word—the word "a"—had been lost in transmission. The words that he had actually intoned were, "That's one small step for *a* man, one giant leap for mankind." Then the two phrases actually asserted two different actions—those of an individual, and those of the people for whom that individual acted. Within another year or so, however, the astronaut faced still another question: Why did he talk only about the male half of the population? While the astronauts (at this point) were all male, the NASA team included both males and females, and all of "humankind"—not just "mankind"—took that leap into the future in late July of 1969. Neil Armstrong had no answer to that question, probably deciding to quit explaining his speech while he was still a hero.

As Armstrong discovered, language functions on multiple levels of meaning. Language is a **referential, relational,** and **symbolic** medium of communication. Through its referential or pointing abilities, language refers to aspects of the world: "dog," "bagel," "man." Through its relational powers, it suggests associations or relationships between people; "Give me a bagel" not only points to bagels but indicates that one person has the power or authority to command another as well. Armstrong's little speech also asserted that he was not only an individual—a man—but also a representative of all others—(hu)mankind—and, thus, related to his audience in a particular way. As we noted in the moon shot example, Armstrong's selection of the words "man" and "mankind" were taken to be signs of a gendered focus—perhaps symbolic of the male's penchant for seeing his half of the species as being the achievers and the lords of society. So, it's not enough to know words and what they mean abstractly when preparing speeches. You also must understand how language-in-use reflects human relationships and shared senses of reality—your culture and your thinking. In other words, not only do words "mean," but the act of using some words rather than others can be crucial to successful (or unsuccessful) communication. *Both language and language use are symbolic processes.*

In the next three chapters, we turn our attention to the encoding of messages. **Encoding** is the activity of putting ideas into verbal and nonverbal codes so that an audience's **decoding,** or interpretative process, occurs in the ways you want. The codes you use—the channels through which ideas are communicated to listeners—include verbal language, visual aids, and bodily and vocal behaviors, and even movements, postures, and sound. In this chapter, we focus on word choices: using language strategically by how you select words and which words you use, when you use them, and where you use them as you talk with others publicly.

USING LANGUAGE ORALLY

Before we tackle the questions of choosing words and styles for effective speeches, we should stop and think about "speech" as a particular kind of language use. When you think of language, you probably think of printed words in magazines, books, and the like. The "language arts" that most people learn in school are those of written language—grammar, style, sentence structure, syntax, and the rational construction of paragraphs and whole essays.

Long before written language developed, however, there was speech—oral language. Written language is only about three thousand years old (give or take a century or two). Orality reaches into the unknowable preliterate ages; even with the coming of written language to the ancient world, it maintained its ascendancy in the language world for centuries. Scribes recorded speech, and speech still created ideas and guided human action. The power of oral rhetoric was at its greatest in ancient Greece precisely at the time—the fifth and fourth centuries B.C.E.—when Greek was being stabilized as a written language.

Why is all this important to you even now, at the dawn of a new millennium? *Speech still retains, at least ideally, many characteristics it acquired in those years before writing.* Taken together, we identify those characteristics as an **oral style**—language use recognizing that speech practices differ significantly from writing practices because of the kinds of social business people usually conduct through talk. We reviewed some of that business in Chapter 1 but go a bit further here. What determines how language should be used in face-to-face, oral communication? The following characteristics typify this sort of communication:

- Speech is *face to face*. It involves people physically oriented to each other. The words and actions flow from the behavior of one person into the sensory equipment of another. Thus, oral language always is specifically en-

Abraham Lincoln said, "Speak so that the most lowly can understand you, and the rest will have no difficulty."

veloped by actual persons who are aware of each other's presence and personages.

- Speech is strongly *social*. In other words, when speaking, individuals bond with each other into concrete relationships. Speech is especially relational in its force, because there is copresence—people who are directly apprehending each other and, thus, constructing or embodying relationships. Sometimes the relationship preexists, as when an employee talks with a boss; at other times, the relationship is built on the spot, as when two strangers start talking to each other on the bus.

- Speech is *ephemeral*, which is to say the words disappear into nothingness as soon as they are uttered. Some of the sound waves strike the tympannus (eardrum) of people, but the rest dissipate completely. You can reread a paragraph, but you cannot hear oral words again (unless you ask for a repetition). Speakers seldom repeat everything, so they must find other ways to help listeners remember, especially when the speakers are stringing together several ideas or arguments. This is why it's so important for oral language to be concrete or specific and why, as we shall see, connectives, metaphors, images, and so on are essential to public speaking.

- The best speech is *enthymematic*. It is built on ideas that the listeners generally accept. In ancient Greece, an **enthymeme** was an ideational structure, sort of like a syllogism, in which the audience was presumed to be able to supply the missing premise. So, when an orator argued "We should go to war with Sparta because the battle will make us rich [feared/admired/safe]," the argument would make sense—and work—only if the listeners believed that wealth was good, to be feared was a good thing for a country, the admiration of others was to be sought, or collective safety was a goal every government should pursue. Building speeches enthymematically—on audiences' preexisting beliefs, attitudes, values, and interests—is a key to success (as we've been noting all through this book).

The fact, then, that oral public speech is face-to-face, socially bonding, ephemeral, enthymematic communication means that stylistically, it is quite different from written language. When someone has written out a speech, it probably begins something like this:

> I am most pleased that you could come this morning. I would like to use this opportunity to discuss with you a subject of inestimable importance to us all—the impact of inflationary spirals on students enrolled in institutions of higher education.

Translated into an oral style, this speech might begin like this:

> Thanks for coming. I'd like to talk today about a problem facing all of us—the rising cost of going to college.

Notice how much more natural (to the ear) the second version sounds. The first is wordy, filled with prepositional phrases, complex words, and formal sentences. The second addresses the audience directly and contains shorter sentences and a simpler vocabulary that make it easier to understand aurally. Oral style has other characteristics as well when used by the most competent speakers, and we examine this style in three ways in this chapter. First, we look at different strategies for making word choices competently and ethically, then at appropriate style in general, and finally, at your social responsibilities in using language publicly to strengthen rather than destroy the social fabric of your country.

USING LANGUAGE COMPETENTLY

Because the language in speeches is spoken aloud in front of a group, it is **public speech**—language used by a group of people. You might have developed private speech for use with a tight group of friends or your siblings, but those private words and phrases will not mean the same things at all when you're talking to people from outside your reference groups or family. Therefore, you must be especially sensitive to what audiences in general will judge as being "good" or "competent" language use as well as "ethical" public speech.

Competent language use in speeches involves selecting words that make your public talk both clear and powerful. You should choose words that make your speech comprehensible and capable of affecting your listeners' beliefs, attitudes, values, and behaviors.

Effective Word Choice

Clear and effective word choice depends upon five features: *accuracy, simplicity, coherence, language intensity,* and *appropriateness.*

Accuracy. Pick words that help listeners understand precisely what you're talking about. If you tell a hardware store clerk that "I broke the dohickey on my hootenanny and I need a thingamajig to fix it," you'd better have the hootenanny in your hand, or the clerk won't understand you. Thus, when you speak, one goal is precision. You should leave no doubt about your meaning.

Words are symbols that represent concepts or objects, but your listener may attach a meaning to your words that's quite different from the one you intend. This misinterpretation becomes more likely as your words become more abstract. *Democracy,* for example, doesn't mean the same thing to a citizen in the suburbs as it does to a citizen in the ghetto. It also will elicit different meanings from Americans who belong to the Christian Coalition than it will from those who belong to the American Socialist Party.

Simplicity. "Speak," said Lincoln, "so that the most lowly can understand you, and the rest will have no difficulty." Because electronic media reach audiences more varied than Lincoln could have imagined, you have even more reason to follow his advice today. Say *learn* rather than *ascertain, try* rather than *endeavor, use* rather than *utilize,* and *help* rather than *facilitate.* Do not use a longer or less familiar word when a simple one is just as clear. Evangelist Billy Sunday illustrated the effectiveness of familiar words in this example:

> If a man were to take a piece of meat and smell it and look disgusted, and his little boy were to say, "What's the matter with it, Pop?" and he were to say, "It is undergoing a process of decomposition in the formation of new chemical compounds," the boy would be all in. But if the father were to say, "It's rotten," then the boy would understand and hold his nose. "Rotten" is a good Anglo-Saxon word, and you do not have to go to the dictionary to find out what it means.[1]

Simplicity doesn't mean *simplistic;* never talk down to your audience. Just remember that short, direct words convey precise, concrete meanings.

Coherence. People listening to you speak don't have the luxury of reviewing the points you have made, as they do with a written essay. Nor are they able to perceive punctuation marks that might help them distinguish one idea from another as you speak. To be understood, oral communication requires **coherence,** or the logical connection of ideas. To achieve coherence, you must use **signposts,** or words or phrases such as "first," "next," or "as a result," that help listeners follow the movement of your ideas. Signposts such as "the history of this invention begins in . . ." also provide clues to the overall message structure.

Summaries, like signposts, provide clues to the overall speech structure. Preliminary and final summaries are especially helpful in outlining the major topics of the speech. **Preliminary summaries** (also called *forecasts* or *previews*) precede the development of the body of the speech, usually forming part of the introduction; **final summaries** follow the body of the speech, usually forming part of the conclusion. Consider the following examples:

Preliminary Summaries	Final Summaries
Today I am going to talk about three aspects of . . .	I have talked about three aspects of . . .
There are four major points to be covered in . . .	These four major points— [restate them]—are . . .
The history of the issue can be divided into two periods . . .	The two periods just covered— [restate them]—represent . . .

In addition to these summarizing strategies, signposts may be **connectives**— or *transitions*—linking phrases that move an audience from one idea to another. The following are useful connective statements:

- In the first place . . . The second point is . . .
- In addition to . . . notice that . . .
- Now look at it from a different angle . . .
- You must keep these three things in mind to understand the importance of the fourth . . .
- What was the result?
- Turning now to . . .

You can improve the coherence of your speeches by indicating the precise relationships among ideas. Those relationships include parallel/hierarchical, similar/different, and coordinate/subordinate relationships. Here are some examples:

- *Parallel:* Not only . . . but also . . .
- *Hierarchical:* More important than these . . .
- *Different:* In contrast . . .
- *Similar:* Similar to this . . .
- *Coordinated:* One must consider X, Y, and Z . . .
- *Subordinated:* On the next level is . . .

Preliminary or final summaries and signposts are important to your audience. These summaries give listeners an overall sense of the coherence of your message.

Intensity. You can communicate your feelings about ideas and objects through word choices, and you can communicate your attitude toward your subject by choosing words that show how you feel. For example, consider these attitudinally weighted terms:

		Subject	*Verb*	*Object*
✚	**Positive**	A Doctor of Philosophy at an institution of higher learning	discussed	dialectical perspectives on life and living.
✚	**Neutral**	The philosophy professor at State U	outlined	Karl Marx's economic and social theories.
▬	**Negative**	An effete intellectual snob at the local haven for druggies	harangued our children with	Communist drivel.

FIGURE 10.1   Language Intensity Chart

Highly Positive	**Relatively Neutral**	**Highly Negative**
Savior	G.I.	Enemy
Patriot	Soldier	Baby-killer
Freedom fighter	Combatant	Foreign devil

These nine terms are organized by their intensity, ranging from the highly positive *savior* to the highly negative *foreign devil*. Notice the religious connotations in the extreme examples of language intensity.

How intense should your language be? Communication scholar John Waite Bowers suggested a useful rule of thumb: Let your language be, roughly, one step more intense than the position or attitude held by your audience.[2] For example, if your audience already is committed to your negative position on tax reform, then you can choose intensely negative words, such as *regressive* and *stifling*. If your audience is uncommitted, you should opt for comparatively neutral words, such as *burdensome*. And, if your audience is in favor of tax changes, you can use still less negative words, such as *unfair*.

Appropriateness.   Your language should be appropriate to the speech topic and the situation. Solemn occasions call for restrained and dignified language; joyful occasions call for informal and lively language. The language used at the christening of a baby would not work at a pep rally, and vice versa. Suit your language to the tone of the occasion, and watch your use of slang with audiences from different generations.

Definitions

Audience members need to understand the fundamental concepts of your speech. You cannot expect them to understand your ideas if your language is unfamiliar. As a speaker, you have several options when working to define unfamiliar or difficult concepts.

You're probably most familiar with a **dictionary definition,** which categorizes an object or concept and specifies its characteristics: "An orange is a *fruit* [i.e., category] that is *round, orange* in color, and a member of the *citrus family* [i.e., characteristics]." Dictionary definitions sometimes help you learn unfamiliar words, but they do not help an audience much.

Occasionally, a word has so many meanings that you need to choose one. In this case, use a **stipulative definition** to orient your listeners to your subject matter. A stipulative definition designates the way a word will be used in a certain context. You might say, "By *rich,* I mean . . ." or something like the following:

> By *mass media,* scholars of communication traditionally have referred to such public communication media as newspapers, magazines, films, radio broadcasting, and telecasting. I want to expand that concept this morning to include the Internet. While it's not "mass" in the usual sense of being only a one-to-many medium, in fact it's being used that way by marketers selling you books, cars, antiques, computer programs, and even pets and other personal services. So, by a "mass medium," I'll mean any communication technology capable of permitting a source to reach large numbers of people that the source has no personal contact with.

You can further clarify a term or concept by telling your audience how you are *not* going to use the concept—by using a **negative definition.** Chicago police Sergeant Bruce Talbot defined *gateway drug* in this manner:

> [F]or adolescents, cigarette smoking is a gateway drug to illicit drugs such as marijuana and crack cocaine. By gateway drug I do not mean just that cigarettes are the first drug young people encounter, alcohol is. But unlike alcohol, which is first experienced in a social ritual such as church or an important family event, cigarettes are the first drug minors buy themselves and use secretly outside the family and social institutions.[3]

Using a negative definition along with a stipulative definition, as did Sergeant Talbot, allows you to treat a commonplace phenomenon in a different way.

Sometimes you may want to reinforce an idea by telling your listeners where a word came from, and one way to do this is by using an **etymological definition.** So, you might want to talk about the fact that the words *communication, community,* and *communion* all have the same Latin root: *-com* (with) and *munis* (public work), suggesting that all three words involve working together for the public good. You then could argue that communicators have a shared obligation to communicate publicly to commune (i.e., share) with others the work of society (i.e., the community).

One of the best ways to define a term is by an **exemplar definition,** especially if the concept is unfamiliar or technical. Exemplar definitions are familiar examples; "The building we're in today, the Administrative Center, is a perfect example of what I want to talk about—Bauhaus art and architecture. This style of architecture represented a redefinition of aesthetics that has affected many buildings, paintings, and plays with which many of you are familiar."

A **contextual definition** tells listeners how a word is used in a specific context. For example, Professor Jonathan Mann argued that AIDS and other new diseases are changing our understanding of health—not as individuals but as a society—and he captured that change by defining the word *solidarity* in terms of health:

> Solidarity describes a central concept in this emerging perspective on health, individuals, and society. The AIDS pandemic has taught us a great deal about tolerance and nondiscrimination, a refusal to separate the condition of the few from the fate of the many. Solidarity arises when people realize that excessive differences among people make the entire system unstable. Charity is individual; solidarity is inherently social, concerned with social justice, and therefore also economic and political.[4]

Still another means of making technical or abstract notions easier to understand is the **analogical definition,** which compares a process or event that is unknown with ones that are known, as in "Hospitals and labs use cryogenic tanks, which work much like large thermos bottles, to freeze tissue samples, blood, and other organic matter." By referring to what is familiar, the analogical definition can make the unfamiliar much easier to grasp. You've always got to be sure, however, that the analogy—like the shoe—fits.

Overall, select a definitional strategy that makes sense for your subject matter, listeners, and purposes.

Imagery

A third kind of competent language use involves linguistic word pictures—imagery. People grasp their world through the senses of sight, smell, hearing, taste, and touch. To intensify listeners' experiences, you can appeal to these senses. **Imagery** consists of sets of sensory pictures evoked in the imagination through language. The language of imagery is divided into seven types, each related to the particular sensation it seeks to evoke: *visual* (sight), *auditory* (hearing), *gustatory* (taste), *olfactory* (smell), *tactile* (touch), *kinesthetic* (muscle strain), and *organic* (internal sensations).

Visual Imagery. Visual imagery describes optical stimuli. Mention size, shape, color, and movement, and recount events in vivid visual language. Consider the conclusion from a speech by former Federal Communications Commissioner Newton N. Minow to the Gannett Foundation Media Center in 1991. He envisioned a past event—a look at primitive TV in 1938—to reintroduce some timeless problems. He played off the "vision" of television as well as the imagery of light (or dark, in the case of the Gulf War of 1991). In his speech, *vision* became a wonderfully ambiguous word referring both to light and to what we learn to see in the world:

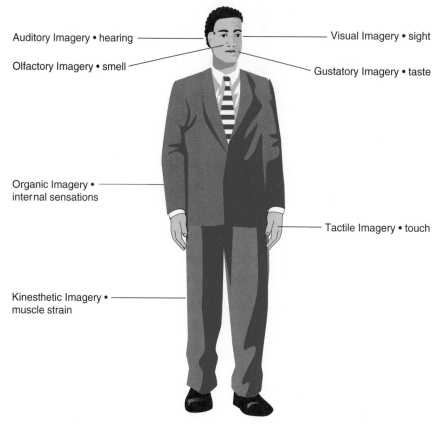

Auditory Imagery • hearing

Olfactory Imagery • smell

Organic Imagery •
internal sensations

Kinesthetic Imagery •
muscle strain

Visual Imagery • sight

Gustatory Imagery • taste

Tactile Imagery • touch

FIGURE 10.2   The Types of Imagery

I commend some extraordinary words to the new generation. F. B. White sat in a darkened room in 1938 to see the beginning of television, an experimental electronic box that projected images in the room. Once he saw it, Mr. White wrote:

"We shall stand or fall by television, of that I am sure. I believe television is going to be the test of the modern world, and that in this new opportunity to see beyond the range of our vision, we shall discover either a new and unbearable disturbance to the general peace, or a saving radiance in the sky."

That radiance falls unevenly today. It is still a dim light in education. It has not fulfilled its potential for children. It has neglected the needs of public television. And in the electoral process it has cast a dark shadow.

This year, television has enabled us to see Patriot missiles destroy Scud missiles above the Persian Gulf. Will television in the next thirty years be a Scud or a Patriot? A new generation now has the chance to put the vision back into television, to travel from the wasteland to the promised land, and to make television a saving radiance in the sky.[5]

Auditory Imagery.   To create auditory imagery, use words that help your listeners hear what you're describing. Auditory imagery can project an audience into a scene. For example, author Tom Wolfe described a demolition derby by recounting the chant of the crowd as it joined in the countdown, the explosion of sound as two dozen cars started off in second gear, and finally, "the unmistakable tympany of automobiles colliding and cheap-gauge sheet metal buckling."[6]

Gustatory Imagery.   Gustatory imagery depicts sensations of taste; sometimes you may even be able to help your audience taste what you're describing. Mention its saltiness, sweetness, sourness, or spiciness, and remember that foods have texture as well as taste. If demonstrating how to prepare homemade honey mustard, describe the bite on your tongue of the powdered mustard overlaid with the sweetness of the honey yet also with the savor of the salt. Detailed descriptions allow your listeners to participate in the experience through their imaginations.

Olfactory Imagery.   Olfactory imagery describes sensations of smell. Smell is a powerful sense, because it normally triggers a flood of associated images. You can stimulate this process by describing or comparing the odor with more familiar ones. Elspeth Huxley remembered her childhood trek to Kenya at the turn of the century by recalling its smells:

> It was the smell of travel in those days, in fact the smell of Africa—dry, peppery yet rich and deep, with an undertone of native body smeared with fat and red ochre and giving out a ripe, partly rancid odour which nauseated some Europeans when they first encountered it but which I, for one, grew to enjoy. This was the smell of the Kikuyu, who were mainly vegetarian. The smell of tribes from the Victoria Nyanza basin, who were meat-eaters and sometimes cannibals, was quite different; much stronger and more musky, almost acrid, and, to me, much less pleasant. No doubt we smelt just as strong and odd to Africans, but of course we were fewer in numbers, and more spread out.[7]

Tactile Imagery.   Tactile imagery is based on the sensations that come to us through physical contact with external objects. Let your audience feel how rough or smooth, dry or wet, or slimy or sticky modeling clay is (texture and shape). Let them sense the pressure of physical force on their bodies, the weight of a heavy laundry bag, the pinch of jogging shoes, or the blast of a high wind on their faces (pressure). Sensations of heat or cold are aroused by thermal imagery.

General Douglas MacArthur's great speech to the cadets of West Point on "duty, honor, and country" used vivid examples of tactile imagery as he described soldiers of the past, "bending under soggy pack on many a weary march, from dripping dusk to drizzly dawn, slogging ankle deep through mire of shell-pocked roads; to form grimly for the attack, blue-lipped, covered with sludge and mud, chilled by the wind and rain, driving home to their objective, and for many, to the judgment seat of God."[8]

Kinesthetic Imagery. Kinesthetic imagery describes the sensations associated with muscle strain and neuromuscular movement. Let your listeners experience for themselves the agonies and joys of running a marathon—the muscle cramps, the constricted chest, the struggle for air—and the magical serenity of getting a second wind and gliding fluidly toward the finish line.

Organic Imagery. Hunger, dizziness, nausea—these are organic images. There are times when an experience is not complete without the description of inner feelings. The sensation of dizziness as a mountain climber struggles through the rarefied mountain air to reach the summit is one example; another is how the bottom drops out of your stomach when the rollercoaster rattles down the steep decline. Because such imagery is powerful, you shouldn't offend your audience by overdoing it. If you call attention to sheer technique—to description for its own sake—your imagery will lose its power, and overdone organic imagery becomes gruesome, disgusting, or grotesque when you get too far into the description of blood and guts or cramps and nausea.

Combining Types of Imagery. The seven types of imagery—visual, auditory, gustatory, olfactory, tactile, kinesthetic, and organic—directly involve the listeners' sensory equipment in your speech. Sensations become avenues into their minds. Not every image will work with everyone, however, so use a variety throughout your speech to engage various segments of your listeners. Well-crafted narratives also can interweave multiple sorts of images in a single vision, as you can see here:

> The strangler struck in Donora, Pennsylvania, in October of 1948. A thick fog billowed through the streets enveloping everything in thick sheets of dirty moisture and a greasy black coating. As Tuesday faded into Saturday, the fumes from the big steel mills shrouded the outlines of the landscape. One could barely see across the narrow streets. Traffic stopped. Men lost their way returning from the mills. Walking through the streets, even for a few moments, caused eyes to water and burn. The thick fumes grabbed at the throat and created a choking sensation. The air acquired a sickening bittersweet smell, nearly a taste. Death was in the air.[9]

In this example, college student Charles Schaillol uses vivid, descriptive phrases to reach the senses of his listeners: visual—"thick sheets of dirty moisture"; organic—"caused eyes to water and burn"; and olfactory and gustatory—"sickening bittersweet smell, nearly a taste." In telling the story of Donora, Pennsylvania, Schaillol works hard to position his listeners squarely in the middle of that town during 1948.

To be effective, such illustrations must be plausible and keep the listeners' attention focused on the subject matter—not on the technique. When imagery is used well, listeners' feelings are engaged in an almost experiential way. Had Schaillol simply said, "Air pollution was the cause of death in Donora," he would not have been able to tie together his ideas and his audience's feeling-states nearly so well.

Metaphors

Images created by appealing to the senses often are metaphors. A **metaphor** is a piece of language used in an unusual way, normally to transfer the meaning of one person, place, thing, or process to something else. "The man was a lion in battle" transfers the characteristics we associate with lions—authority, power, commanding presence—to the person. Thus, *lion* is being used metaphorically in this sentence. We use metaphors when they'll help our listeners understand something more clearly; as rhetorical scholar Michael Osborn notes, good metaphors should "result in an intuitive flash of recognition that surprises or fascinates the hearer."[10] If the hearer is not jolted, informed, or given a clear orientation to whatever's being discussed, the metaphor probably is dead (as in "the legs of the table," where *legs* is a dead metaphor) or is just plain ineffective.

Once-fresh metaphors also can turn into **clichés**—metaphors so far gone they can have almost a reverse effect. Clichés can diminish your ideas rather than enhance or clarify them—unless they're used humorously, as in the advertisement for the book *The Dictionary of Clichés:* "Not to beat around the bush, or hedge the bet, this is a must-read for every Tom, Dick, and Harry under the sun!"[11]

Good metaphors can create new understanding and uplift an audience. Such metaphors even can be drawn from everyday experiences, which give them wide audience appeal. For example, relying on our common experiences of lightness and darkness, Martin Luther King, Jr., intoned a solemn message that was driven by metaphor:

> With this faith in the future, with this determined struggle, we will be able to emerge from the bleak and desolate midnight of man's inhumanity to man, into the bright and glittering daybreak of freedom and justice.[12]

This basic light-dark metaphor allowed King to suggest (a) sharp contrasts between inhumanity and freedom as well as (b) the inevitability of social progress (as "daybreak" inevitably follows "midnight"). The metaphor communicated King's beliefs about justice and injustice, and it urged others to action now that daylight was upon us.

As we wind to a close, remember that words are not neutral pipelines for thoughts flowing from one person to another. Words reflect the world outside the mind and also help shape and create perceptions of people, events, and social contexts—referentially, relationally, and symbolically. Language and its effective use enables you to move others to believe, think, and act.

USING LANGUAGE ETHICALLY

Competent public language use makes your ideas both clear and powerful. Ethical public language use makes them culturally acceptable and respectful of others' thinking. Some of the issues we discuss later (under the heading "Selecting Language that Communicates Civility and Care for Others") also have ethical dimensions, but here, we want to deal with three common uses of language that possess clear ethical dimensions: linguistic attacks upon others (ad hominem arguments), the refusal to mention groups of people who should be referenced (linguist erasure), and conspiratorial attacks on people and institutions (critiquing domination).

Ad Hominem Attack

The phrase "ad hominem" is Latin for "to the person" or, more usually, "to personal circumstances."[13] An **ad hominem attack** is an argument made against another person rather than upon the ideas that he or she espouses. *Argumentum ad hominem* was identified as a fallacy in reasoning by John Locke some three hundred years ago, because he was striving to ensure that arguments-about-the-world were conducted on a strictly reality- or idea-centered basis. He believed that attacks upon arguers deflected attention from the real issues.[14]

So, when you say that "You certainly can't believe that presidential candidate Bob Dole favors campaign finance reform—look at all of the political action committee money he took for his own campaign," you are offering an ad hominem argument. You're not attacking Dole's plan for finance reform but, rather, his truthfulness. Further, the attack is based upon past behavior, even upon the assumption that Senator Dole really was just another politician, not upon present circumstances or intentions.

Ad hominem attacks often are based on stereotypes of groups or collectivities. Thus, some think that African Americans cannot really be Republicans because they should favor a liberal agenda and a welfare state, that real men suppress their softer emotions and cannot be expected to be warm and caring, and that all Catholics oppose state-sponsored abortions or Protestant Irish people. It's the "Everyone knows that . . ." aspect to ad hominem attacks that makes them so powerful with some audiences.

Are they fair, however? Usually not. In fact, they may well represent the most common kind of unethical attack on others that you'll run into—or be tempted to use—as a speaker. Sometimes, of course, the personal circumstances of a counter arguer are relevant. In presidential campaigns, for example, it's impossible to have positions on all the issues, so most of us rely on some assessment of the candidates' character—evidence of their good sense, good will, good morals, vision, and caring for the electorate—to help us decide for whom to vote.[15] Generally speaking, however, always examine the ad hominem attack very, very closely to make sure it's just not a diversionary or ungrounded, stereotyped reaction to an opponent.

Linguistic Erasure

A concept that is difficult to explain but certainly also is important to public talk is **erasure,** or *not* labeling or talking about a person or group of people that "demands" to be mentioned. This language phenomenon is called the "third persona" by rhetorical theorist Philip Wander.[16] If a picture of the speaker constructed in words is the first persona and the picture of the audience built into the speech is the second, then people who are important to a speech but not actually mentioned in it comprise the third persona—and are erased.

Suppose you were giving a speech on the quincentenniary celebration in the United States of the arrival of Christopher Columbus. Suppose you also were talking about the heroism and faith that drove Columbus and his crew to venture into uncharted lands and found colonies for other Europeans in the New World. In this speech, you'd probably construct an image of yourself as someone interested in history—and good at it—by using multiple sources and good speechmaking techniques. That's the picture of the first persona built into the speech. The picture of the noble Italians and Spaniards who initiated the Age of Discovery at the end of the fifteenth century would be the second persona—a vision of European adventurers who made life on this continent possible for others. And the third persona? If you did not mention the coastal Indians awaiting the Pilgrims; the Cubans, Blacks, and Central American Indians whom Hernán Cortéz enslaved in the early sixteenth century; or the Florida Indians ravaged by European diseases when Sir Francis Drake tried to conquer Saint Augustine in the 1580s, then the natives of the American territories were the third personae.[17] They were not mentioned in your heroic tale yet obviously were extremely important players in that story: "What about the locals, the natives?" some in your audience would ask.

Linguistic erasure is a matter of eliminating someone's presence in a story or argument by simply not mentioning them. "The Final Solution" could be talked about in Hitler's Germany without actually saying the word "Jews": The metaphor of the "solution" made it unnecessary for believers in National Socialism to mention them. Speeches about "nuclear families" often ignore the needs of single-parent or nonheterosexual families. Talk about being pro-choice and granting women control over their own bodies and destinies often avoids references to the dead fetuses (that fill the talk of pro-life advocates).

Now, of course, there are times when you actually choose to concentrate only on part of a story. If you decide, for example, to talk only about the European explorers in the Age of Discovery because you're interested primarily in the effect of exploration upon Europe, then tell that to your audience. In that way, the listeners know there is a Native American side of the story but that it is not relevant to your speech. Thus, you'll not be questioned ethically for your lack of discussion regarding their fate.

Critiquing Domination

Another ethical question you face when selecting language has to do with a decision on whether or not to talk conspiracies. That may seem like an odd decision until you think about all the conspiratorial talk that floats through American media: talk that the CIA supplied drugs to the African-American community to keep it from rising up, references by Hillary Clinton in early 1998 to a vast right-wing conspiracy trying to drive her husband out of politics, discussions in the Middle East of a Euro-American conspiracy to keep the area destabilized to make our presence there necessary or let us keep our eyes on their oil, or arguments that the white community controls the standardized tests that get students admitted to college and that measure intelligence, thus keeping itself in a superior position.

The point is not whether any of these are true. Conspiratorial talk about dominant groups holding down others, controlling institutions, or enslaving different segments of society does not depend upon facts. After all, if the facts could be ascertained—if someone could prove that right-wingers have chased Bill Clinton systematically for two-and-a-half decades—then something could be done about the problem. In the 1950s, Senator Joseph McCarthy claimed he had a list of 208 Communists in the State Department. He never showed the whole list to anyone else, however, because then each person could have had a security check. No, conspiracies—and, indeed, domination of one group by another in general—depends upon fear and anger, upon shadows and not substance. Often, just enough facts are supplied to suggest the conspiracy to dominate is true; so Hillary Clinton actually mentioned three names in her appearance on the *Today Show* when she alleged this conspiracy. The charge of a conspiracy drew its power, however, from the audience's willingness to believe her—from their belief that evil-doers influence politics.[18]

Critiquing domination, thus, is a linguistic strategy of charging that some situation has been brought about by a widespread—usually society-wide—operation wherein a group or social segment suppresses the rights, chances to succeed, and even the identities of other groups.[19] So, when arguing that television helps establish the power of white—and especially male—America to dominate U.S. policy toward other countries, Kent Ono built this argument:

> One of the most obvious ways television has contributed to neocolonialist relations is by aiding the U.S. government in demonizing people of color worldwide, such as Saddam Hussein, Moammar Kadafi, Manuel Noriega, the Ayatollah Khomeini, and Fidel Castro. Whenever the U.S. government and military want to justify a military intervention to reestablish their domination over economically, technologically, and militarily less powerful peoples, they manufacture a demonic view of someone, almost always a swarthy male, as a psychopathic, uncontrollable, irrational, and fascistic leader.[20]

The point here, again, is not whether these charges are true—they may well be. Rather, the point is the entire rationale for economic, political, and military policy has been reduced to a conspiracy of the white world to control the world of color. The actual rationales for U.S. foreign policy have been flattened to a single dimension—the will to dominate—which Ono believes must be critiqued.

Is it ethical to reduce U.S. foreign policy to a single rationale? Should a speaker use such language as "demonizing," "establish their domination," or "manufacture a demonic view"? Such language, of course, is ad hominem attack, but it also is simplifying and reductionistic to a dangerous level: It may well stop thought about other aspects of U.S. foreign policy, and stopping thought is an ethical matter. Think carefully about your purposes and options before launching into conspiratorial arguments about domination. They may be satisfying to an audience—which, after all, then can say "Hey! It's not my fault! There's a conspiracy to hold me down!"—but they also may stop actual solutions to problems from being pursued.

Ad hominem attack, linguistic erasure, and critiquing domination are but three of the common ways in which language choices (or nonchoice, in the case of erasure) engage important ethical questions. We discuss other ethical decisions speakers must make in the following sections of this chapter as well.

SELECTING AN APPROPRIATE STYLE

Now, we can think more systematically about how not just words but also oral style generally should guide how you talk with other people or how you present yourself orally. The combination of stylistic decisions you need to make generally is called **tone,** which is the predominant effect or character of a speech. Tone is an elusive quality of speech, but we can identify four dimensions of tone that you should consider: serious versus humorous atmosphere; gendered versus gender-neutral language; speaker-, audience-, or content-centered emphases; and propositional versus narrative style.

Serious Versus Humorous Atmosphere

You cultivate the atmosphere of the speaking occasion largely through your speaking style. During a graduation speech or an awards banquet address, you want to encourage the personal reflection of your listeners, but during a fraternity gathering or holiday celebration, you want to create a social, interactive atmosphere.

Sometimes the atmosphere of the occasion dictates what speaking style should be used. You don't expect a light, humorous speaking style during a funeral; even so, sometimes a minister, priest, or rabbi will tell a funny story about the deceased. The overall tone of a funeral eulogy, however, should be somber. In contrast, a speech after a football victory, election win, or successful drive to change collegiate graduation requirements seldom is solemn. Victory speeches are times for celebration and unity.

Humorous speeches can have serious goals as well—even speeches designed to entertain have worthy purposes. These speeches can be given in grave earnestness. The political satirist who throws humorous but barbed comments at pompous, silly, or corrupt politicians aims to amuse the audience as well as urge political reform. Think of all the Clinton or Lewinsky jokes you heard in 1998: Some were offered just for fun, but many had serious political overtones.

The speaking **atmosphere** is the mindset or mental attitude that you attempt to create in your audience. A serious speaker urging future professors to remember the most important things in life might say, "Rank your values, and live by them." That same idea expressed by actor Alan Alda sounded more humorous:

We live in a time that seems to be split about its values. In fact it seems to be schizophrenic.

For instance, if you pick up a magazine like *Psychology Today,* you're liable to see an article like "White Collar Crime: It's More Widespread than You Think." Then in the back of the magazine they'll print an advertisement that says, "We'll write your doctoral thesis for 25 bucks." You see how values are eroding? I mean, a doctoral thesis ought to go for at least a C-note.[21]

ETHICAL MOMENTS

DOUBLESPEAK

Advertisers, politicians, and military spokespersons often are accused of using words that deceive or mislead. The Bush and Clinton administrations did not want to raise taxes, for example, and so instead pursued *revenue enhancement* through *user fees*. The rush to **doublespeak**—the use of a technical jargon that sidesteps issues or distorts meaning—was accelerated during the Vietnam War, when "we got *pacification* for eradication, *strategic withdrawal* for retreat, *sanitizing operation* for wholesale clearance, *accidental delivery of armaments* for bombing the wrong target, *to terminate with extreme prejudice* for a political assassination, and many, many others" (Bryson, 302). Advertisers have given us *real faux pearls* and *genuine imitation leather* and, of course, *virgin nylon*. The indiscriminate use of the phrases *low sodium, low cholesterol, low sugar,* and *low fat* has led to a governmental attempt to control the abuse of such labels. So, how about you?

1. Suppose you notice biased language in an article you're going to quote. Should you cite it as supporting material in your speech?

2. Do you ever use big words and unnecessary technical language just to impress your listeners? Should we call "football players" by that sanctimonious phrase "student athletes"? Do you feel better if someone calls a "test" an "hourly opportunity" or a "feedback session"? Is spanking a child any less onerous if it is called "corporal discipline"?

3. How about using language to avoid hurting someone or making them feel bad? Should you really call someone "vertically challenged" instead of "short" or "visually impaired" instead of "blind"? In these sorts of cases, do the new words actually call more attention to the person's difficulties than the old ones?

For Further Reading

On the matter of neologisms—new and often technical words coming into English—see Bill Bryson, *Made in America: An Informal History of the English Language in the United States* (New York: William Morrow, 1994). On language usage generally, see Joe Glaser, *Understanding Style: Practical Ways to Improve Your Writing* (New York: Oxford University Press, 1999).

Which atmosphere is preferable? The answer depends on the speaking situation, your speech purpose, and your listeners' expectations.

Gendered Versus Gender-Neutral Language

Words themselves are not intrinsically good or bad, but as noted at the beginning of this chapter, they communicate values or attitudes to your listeners and can suggest relationships between you and your audience. Gender-linked words—particularly nouns and pronouns—require special attention. **Gender-linked words** are those that directly or indirectly identify males or females, such as *policeman, washerwoman, waiter,* and *waitress.* Pronouns such as *he* and *she* and adjectives such as *his* and *her* also obviously are gender-linked words. **Gender-neutral words** do not directly or indirectly denote males or females—*chairperson, police officer,* or *firefighter.*

Since the 1960s and the advent of the women's movement, consciousness of gendered language has gradually surfaced. The question of whether language use affects culture and socialization still is being debated, but as a speaker, you must be careful not to alienate your audience or unconsciously propagate stereotypes through your use of language. In addition to avoiding most gender-linked words, you need to handle two more problems:

1. *Inaccurately excluding members of one sex.* Some uses of gendered pronouns inaccurately reflect social-occupational conditions in the world: "A nurse sees *her* patients 8 hours a day, but a doctor sees *his* for only 10 minutes." Many women are doctors, and many men are nurses. Most audience members are aware of this and may be displeased if they feel you're stereotyping roles in a particular profession.

2. *Stereotyping male and female psychological or social characteristics.* "Real men never cry." "A woman's place is in the home." "The Marines are looking for a few good men." "Sugar 'n spice 'n everything nice—that's what little girls are made of." Falling back on these stereotypes gets speakers into trouble with audiences—both male and female. In these days of raised consciousness, audiences are insulted to hear such misinformed assertions. In addition, these stereotypes conceal the potential in individuals whose talents are not limited by their gender.

These problem areas demand your attention. A speaker who habitually uses sexist language is guilty of ignoring important speaking conventions that have developed over the last several decades.

Ultimately, the search for gender-neutral expressions is an affirmation of mutual respect and a recognition of equal worth and the essential dignity of individuals. Gender differences are important in many aspects of life, but when they dominate public talk, they're ideologically oppressive. Be gender-neutral in public talk to remove barriers to effective communication.[22]

Speaker-, Audience-, or Content-Centered Emphases

Because you use speeches to conduct different kinds of personal, social, and professional business, you can end up emphasizing various aspects of the communication process in your message. Sometimes you're stressing *your* thoughts or *your* opinions—your position as a knowledgeable or sensitive person. On such occasions, much of the speech is constructed in the first person: "I." At other times, however, the focus is on the audience or things you and the audience can accomplish together; in those circumstances, you're likely to address the audience in the second-person ("you") or in the first-person plural ("we"). Then, there are times when the subject matter itself is the center of attention,

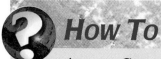

How To

AVOID SEXIST LANGUAGE

- *Speak in the plural.* Say, "Bankers are often . . . They face . . ." This tactic often is sufficient to make your language gender-neutral.
- *Switch to "he or she" when you must use a singular subject.* Say, "A student majoring in business is required to sign up for an internship. He or she can . . ." This strategy works well as long as you do not overdo it. If you find yourself cluttering sentences with "he or she," switch to the plural.

- *Remove gender inflections.* It's painless to say *firefighter* instead of *fireman, chair* or *chairperson* instead of *chairman,* and *tailor* instead of *seamstress.*
- *Use gender-specific pronouns for gender-specific processes, people, or activities.* It is acceptable to talk about a mother as *her* or a current or former president of the United States as *him.* Men do not naturally bear children, after all, and a woman has not yet been elected to the presidency.

such as in a class lecture, in which case references to "I" and "you" or "we" all but disappear.

Sometimes the emphasis of the whole speech is speaker-, audience- or content-centered, but the emphasis more often shifts from one section to another. This clearly happened in a speech given by Allen H. Neuharth, chair of the Freedom Foundation, when he accepted the DeWitt Carter Reddick Award for Outstanding Achievement in Communication given him by the College of Communication of the University of Texas at Austin. In this speech, Neuharth employed all three emphases:

"I" Directed:

In 1952, just two years out of the University of South Dakota, a classmate and I started a weekly statewide sports tabloid newspaper called *SoDak Sports.* We begged, borrowed and stole all the money we could—about $50,000. Two years later, we had lost it all, our venture went belly-up and we were bloodied and bowed. I ran away from home, went to Miami, found a job as a reporter for $95 a week.

There, when I wasn't working or having fun in the sun, I thought a lot about what went wrong with my plan to become rich and famous in South Dakota. Gradually, I got it. I didn't really have a plan. I only had an idea. I hadn't really considered the risk/reward ratio. I hadn't figured out how to pay the rent. My first venture went broke because of mismanagement. I had mismanaged it. Once you admit you're the one who screwed up, it's much easier to get up off the floor, dust yourself off and try again.

"You/We" Directed:

[W]e must overcome our reluctance to criticize ourselves or our co-workers or competitors. Most in the media are unbelievably thin-skinned. We spend most of our lifetime criticizing or analyzing everyone else—politicians, business people, academicians. But we seldom turn that spotlight on ourselves. Our egos are enormous.

"They/It" Directed:

The media, thanks to instant satellite communication, is the glue that is bringing this globe together. Without the satellite—and instant global communication—there would have been no Tiananmen Square sit-in in Beijing. No breakdown of the Berlin Wall. No marches in Poland, Romania, and Czechoslovakia. And the hardliners would not have flunked Revolution 101 in the old Soviet Union last August.[23]

In mixing self-revealing, audience-directed, and content-centered emphases, Neuharth achieved multiple purposes: He established a personal bond with his audience (i.e., relational communication), gave them some messages to act on (i.e., referential communication), and added to his expert credibility by talking clearly about the world of the journalists (i.e., symbolic communication). You, too, should decide whether to emphasize yourself (i.e., personal revelations), your audience (i.e., directives to your listeners), or the subject matter (i.e., ideas and arguments about the external world) in various combinations during your talks.

Propositional Versus Narrative Style

Finally, speaking styles can be largely propositional or narrative. **Propositional style** emphasizes a series of claims, with supporting evidence for each, that culminate in a general proposition. In this style, the claims suggest what action should be taken or what policy should be adopted or rejected. **Narrative style,** however, couches claims and evidence in a more informal, often personal story that epitomizes the general claim being advanced. Thus, both argue in the sense they are claims on an audience's attention, belief, and action; however, they do so in radically different ways. In the following illustrations of propositional and narrative approaches, assume that you—the speaker—want to persuade your classmates to consult with their academic advisors on a regular basis:

Propositional Style

I. You should see your advisor regularly, because he or she can check on your graduation requirements.

A. Advisors have been trained to understand this school's requirements.

      B. Advisors also probably helped write the departmental requirements for your major, so they know them, too.

  II. You should see your advisor regularly, because that person usually can tell you something about the careers in your field.

      A. Most faculty members at this school regularly attend professional meetings and know what schools and companies are hiring in your field.

      B. Most faculty members here have been around a long time and, thus, have seen what kinds of academic backgrounds get their advisees good jobs after graduation.

 III. You should see your advisor regularly to check out your own hopes and fears with someone.

      A. Good advisors help you decide whether you want to continue with a major.

      B. If you decide to change majors, they often will help you find in another department who can work with you.

Narrative Style

   I. I thought I could handle my own advising around this school, and that attitude got me into trouble.

      A. I could read, and I thought I knew what I wanted to take.

      B. I decided to steer my own course, and here's what happened.

  II. At first, I was happy, taking any course I wanted to.

      A. I skipped the regular laboratory sciences (i.e., chemistry, biology, physics) and took "Science and Society" instead.

      B. I didn't take statistics to meet my math requirement but, instead, slipped into remedial algebra.

      C. I piled up the hours in physical education so I could have a nice grade-point average to show my parents.

 III. When I was about half done with my program, however, I realized that:

      A. I hadn't met about half the general education graduation requirements.

      B. I wanted to go into nursing.

 IV. Therefore, I had to go back to freshman- and sophomore-level courses even though I technically was a junior.

      A. I was back taking the basic science and math courses.

      B. I was still trying to complete the social science and humanities requirements.

  V. In all, I'm now in my fifth year of college—with at least one more to go.

      A. My classmates who used advisors have graduated.

      B. I suggest you follow their examples rather than mine if you want to save time and money.

Either style can be effective depending upon the audience's expectations and the speaker's resourcefulness in generating an effective argument.[24] The propositional form provides a concise, logical series of "should" statements to direct audience action. The narrative form puts your talent as a storyteller to the test. These examples suggest the use of either style as the structure for the body of an entire speech, but speeches may combine both. As mentioned,

Neuharth used a narrative style in discussing his own life experience and then moved on to a propositional form in relaying his views regarding the kinds of reforms in which journalists must engage.

Building an oral style appropriate to you, your audience, the occasion, and the subject matter takes serious thought on your part. Think through the degree of seriousness, the gender focus, the I/you-we/it emphasis, and the use of propositional or narrative forms, because shaping these carefully is the mark of a sophisticated and talented speaker.

SELECTING LANGUAGE THAT COMMUNICATES CIVILITY AND CARE FOR OTHERS

Ultimately, public speaking is a collective activity—it is the way that a society transacts its important business in face-to-face and, in some cases, in televisual ways. If we think of public speaking as the conversation of the culture, as a society having dialogues about important and even difficult matters, then we are faced with important questions regarding the degree to which speakers have an obligation to help maintain the social system and move people forward collectively.

Especially during the 1990s, American society has witnessed much concern about violations of civility—and about what some see as a hyperconcern for the treatment of others in the language we use. Those related-yet-separate concerns have been called *hate speech* and *political correctness*. Both concerns feed into a more general commitment that some think we all need to make to multiculturalism.

The Problem of Hate Speech

Hate speech is public talk that attacks or denigrates a group or class of people. It is similar to ad hominem attack, except that it is aimed at whole segments of society. Talking about women as "girls" or "chickies" is seen by some as being degrading, but other terms put them down as a group. Ethnic slurs always have been a part of the American experience, especially since the heavy immigration of the late nineteenth century. Colloquial, negative terms have been invented for the Irish, the Italians, the Puerto Ricans, the Mexicans, the African Americans, and others.

Hate speech is only possible, of course, because of the First Amendment to the U.S. Constitution's guarantee of freedom of speech. It is what is called protected speech—you are permitted to call people names publicly. The United States has guarantees on freedom of expression, but the exclusive emphasis on such individual freedoms may jeopardize collective responsibilities. The U.S. Constitution recognizes individual rights; however, it is constructed in the name of "We, the people," as its opening line names us. Public name-calling of whole segments of society can destroy the "we."

This is not to say that you should never attack someone's thinking, motives, evidence, or timing. There even are times when you should question the intentions of others publicly, but that can—and we think should—be done with rhetorical tools other than hate speech. There even are rights better left unexercised in the name of the collective good.[25]

The Question of Political Correctness

Equally difficult to deal with publicly, however, is a complementary question; the matter of political correctness. **Political correctness** is the term developed within the last 10 years for social rules about how you must refer to classes or groups of people in society. "Political correctness," of course, is a term of derision, uttered by people who believe there should not be rules about what to call groups of people: Why is it correct to say "people of color" but not "colored people" in the United States? Isn't a phrase such as "environmentally challenged" an awkward way of referring to people with disabilities?

The great difficulty associated with the idea of political correctness is that it arises out of socially positive motives—treating others with dignity—but that can itself become oppressive (i.e., a series of linguistic tests to be used to judge speakers). So, on some campuses, students are told to boycott "incorrect" speakers—a male who does not seem to appreciate feminists, a feminist who is thought by some to sound radical, or people who are too aggressively "straight" or "gay" in language they use. To be sure, hateful speech should be confronted, but to react in a knee-jerk fashion to someone who talks about a "disabled man" rather than a "physically challenged person" without examining what actually is being said is counterproductive. Listeners must learn to read past complex labels to assess ideas.[26]

The Commitment to Multicultural Visions of Audiences

In a sense, people who assert their right to call a person whatever they want as well those who judge others' motives simply on the basis of their language use need to move to another ground: *relationships between language and both the language-user and the world outside those users.* As we've suggested throughout this chapter and this book, how you use language publicly reflects both your view of the world and your understanding of the relationship with your listeners. When you say, "Gimme that pork chop," you've not only referred to a object in the environment but communicated your attitudes toward the others around you.

Public, oral language is both referential and relational, as we noted at the beginning of this chapter. Thus, whenever you speak publicly, you both talk about something and suggest (however indirectly or tacitly) your attitudes toward others—people you're talking about, and people you're talking to.

This is why a **multicultural vision** is essential to socially constructive public speaking. You almost always will be talking to a multicultural audience—men and women, young and old, rich and poor, disabled and not, and people with varied ethnic backgrounds. To ignore one or another cultural segment is to ignore potential believers in your positions. Further, to use language that seemingly demeans or rejects portions of your audience is to potentially injure your credibility or ethos. This is not to say you'll never be angry with groups of people or you'll always believe in everything other groups advocate. Of course not. Strong differences in opinion and action can exist between men and women, young and old, white and brown.

Multicultural visions do not mean that everyone melts into one lumpen society. When Americans say their civic slogan is "Out of many, one," they do not

Getting your point across depends on appropriate language choices. What kinds of choices might be involved in this scene?

mean "Out of many, all the same." All of us should be parts of what's called a *body politic*, a social-political group. Not all parts of your body are the same, however, just as not all parts of a civic body are the same. Yet all are legitimate parts—and should be accorded respect when you speak about them.

The oral, public use of language can work for good or ill, for collective action or divisiveness. Each time you use language publicly, you're participating in a destructive or a constructive social act.[27]

ASSESSING A SAMPLE SPEECH

William Faulkner (1897–1962) presented the following speech on December 10, 1950, as he accepted the Nobel Prize for Literature. His listeners might have expected a speech filled with the kind of pessimism so characteristic of his novels. Instead, he greeted them with a stirring challenge to improve humankind.

Notice in particular Faulkner's use of language. Although known for the tortured sentences in his novels, he expresses his ideas clearly and simply in this speech. His style suggests a written speech, yet his use of organic imagery and powerful metaphors keeps the speech alive. The atmosphere generally is serious, befitting the occasion. You might expect a Nobel Prize winner to talk about himself, but Faulkner did just the opposite. He stressed his craft—writing—and the commitment necessary to practice that craft. This material emphasis led naturally to an essentially propositional rather than narrative form. In addition, his stress upon the writers in his audience who would follow him meant that he was trying to use oral language to construct listeners with particular outlooks on the creative writing process. More than 50 years ago, William Faulkner offered a speech that is as relevant today as it was in 1950.

ON ACCEPTING THE NOBEL PRIZE FOR LITERATURE

William Faulkner

The language of the whole speech is forecast in the first paragraph: agony, sweat, profit, anguish, and travail versus spirit, glory, acclaim, pinnacle comprise his vocabulary. Metaphors of struggle and childbirth are contrasted with images of soul and achievement.

First, he suggests the presence of the fear and then, via restatement, comes back to it in the next three sentences. Second, he continues the linguistic contrasts between fear and spirit, human heart in conflict, and the agony and the sweat.

I feel that this award was not made to me as a man, but to my work—a life's work in the agony and sweat of the human spirit, not for glory and least of all for profit, but to create out of the materials of the human spirit something which did not exist before. So this award is only mine in trust. It will not be difficult to find a dedication for the money part of it commensurate with the purpose and significance of its origin. But I would like to do the same with the acclaim too, by using this moment as a pinnacle from which I might be listened to by the young men and women already dedicated to the same anguish and travail, among whom is already that one who will some day stand here where I am standing./1

Our tragedy today is a general and universal physical fear so long sustained by now that we can even bear it. There are no longer problems of the spirit. There is only the question: When will I be blown up? Because of this, the young man or woman writing today has forgotten the problems of the human heart in conflict with itself which alone can make good writing because only that is worth writing about, worth the agony and the sweat./2

He must learn them again. He must teach himself that the basest of all things is to be afraid; and, teaching himself that, forget it forever, leaving no room in his workshop for anything but the old verities and truths of the heart, the old universal truths lacking which any story is ephemeral and doomed—love and honor and pity and pride and compassion and sacrifice. Until he does so, he labors under a curse. He writes not of love but of lust, of defeats in which nobody loses anything of value, of victories without hope and, worst of all, without pity or compassion. His griefs grieve on no universal bones, leaving no scars. He writes not of the heart but of the glands./3

Until he relearns these things, he will write as though he stood among and watched the end of man. I decline to accept the end of man. It is easy enough to say that man is immortal simply because he

A flood of imagery washes over the listeners in his conclusion: images are auditory ("the last ding-dong of doom," "his puny inexhaustible voice," and "the poet's voice"); visual ("the last worthless rock hanging tideless in the last red and dying evening"); tactile ("the pillars" that provide support for people to "endure and prevail"); and organic ("lifting his heart").

will endure: that when the last ding-dong of doom has clanged and faded from the last worthless rock hanging tideless in the last red and dying evening, that even then there will still be one more sound: that of his puny inexhaustible voice, still talking. I refuse to accept this. I believe that man will not merely endure: he will prevail. He is immortal, not because he alone among creatures has an inexhaustible voice, but because he has a soul, a spirit capable of compassion and sacrifice and endurance. The poet's, the writer's, duty is to write about these things. It is his privilege to help man endure by lifting his heart, by reminding him of the courage and honor and hope and pride and compassion and pity and sacrifice which have been the glory of his past. The poet's voice need not merely be the record of man, it can be one of the props, the pillars to help him endure and prevail./4

William Faulkner, *"On Accepting the Nobel Prize for Literature."*
The Faulkner Reader (*New York: Random House, 1954*).

CHAPTER SUMMARY

Language is a referential, relational, and symbolic medium of communication, which means that speakers must be sensitive to how they encode their messages for the listeners who decode them. Central to effective speaking is the challenge of capturing an oral style, because public speaking is face-to-face, social, ephemeral, and enthymematic communication. One key to an oral style of language use is the need to use language competently, and part of competent oral language use is effective word choice: *accurate, simple, coherent, properly intense,* and *appropriate* language choices. Other aspects of competent language use include attention to:

- *Definitions* (dictionary, negative, etymological, exemplar, contextual, and analogical).
- *Restatements* (rephrasing, reiteration, and repetition).
- *Imagery* (visual, auditory, gustatory, olfactory, tactile, kinesthetic, and organic).
- *Metaphors.*

Oral language use also should be ethical, and speakers should think about their use of ad hominem attack, linguistic erasure, and critiquing domination (i.e., conspiratorial appeals). In selecting language that creates an oral style appropriate to you, the occasion, the subject matter, and the audience, you must make good decisions regarding serious versus humorous atmosphere; speaker-, audience-, or content-centered emphases; gendered versus gender-neutral language; and propositional versus narrative style. Speakers also should think about the larger picture—how their speeches contribute to civility and care for others. This means that speakers should raise questions about hate speech and political correctness and aim at promoting multicultural visions of their audiences.

Language choices—and the resulting ways that the oral styles of speakers are created—comprise the speaker's most crucial channel of communication.

KEY TERMS

ad hominem attack (p. 236)

analogical definition (p. 231)

atmosphere (p. 239)

clichés (p. 235)

coherence (p. 227)

competent language use (p. 226)

connectives (p. 228)

contextual definition (p. 231)

critiquing domination (p. 238)

decoding (p. 224)

dictionary definition (p. 230)

doublespeak (p. 240)

encoding (p. 224)

enthymeme (p. 225)

erasure (p. 236)

etymological definition (p. 230)

exemplar definition (p. 230)

final summaries (p. 228)

gender-linked words (p. 241)

gender-neutral words (p. 241)

hate speech (p. 245)

imagery (p. 231)

linguistic erasure (p. 237)

metaphor (p. 235)

multicultural vision (p. 246)

narrative style (p.243)

negative definition (p. 230)

oral style (p. 224)

political correctness (p. 246)

preliminary summaries (p. 228)

propositional style (p. 243)

public speech (p. 226)

referential (p. 223)

relational (p. 223)

signposts (p. 227)

stipulative definition (p. 230)

symbolic (p. 223)

tone (p. 239)

ASSESSMENT ACTIVITIES

1. Choose one of the items listed and describe it using seven types of imagery to create a portrait you could use in a speech:

   - Eating freshly picked berries on the shores of Lake Michigan.
   - A complicated machine of some kind.
   - One of the creatures from *Antz* (or any other popular movie).
   - The oldest (or newest) building on campus.

   Highlight each image that you use, and label it for your instructor.

2. Read one of the sample speeches in this textbook, and identify what methods the speaker uses to make the language effective. Were the essentials of effective word choice observed? Did the speaker create what seems to you an appropriate style, as defined here? Were rhetorical strategies of definition, restatement, imagery, and metaphor used well? Grade the speaker's competence (e.g., minimal, average, superior) as an oral stylist, and justify your grade.

REFERENCES

1. Quoted in John R. Pelsma, *Essentials of Speech* (New York: Crowell, Collier, and Macmillan, 1934), 193.

2. John Waite Bowers, "Language and Argument," *Perspectives on Argumentation,* ed. G. R. Miller and T. R. Nilsen (Glenview, IL: Scott, Foresman, 1966), 168–172.

3. Bruce Talbot, "Statement," Hearings before Senate Committee on Commerce, Science, and Transportation, *Tobacco Product Education and Health Promotion Act of 1991, S. 1088,* 14 November 1991, 102 Congress (Washington, D.C.: U.S. Government Printing Office, 1991), 77.

4. Jonathan Mann, "Global AIDS: Revolution, Paradigm, and Solidarity," *Representative American Speeches, 1990–1991,* ed. Owen Peterson (New York: H. W. Wilson Co., 1991), 88.

5. Newton N. Minow, "How Vast the Wasteland Now?" *Representative American Speeches, 1991–1992,* ed. Owen Peterson (New York: H. W. Wilson Co., 1992), 169.

6. A selection from Tom Wolfe, *The Kandy-Kolored Tangerine-Flake Streamline Baby* (Thomas K. Wolfe, Jr., 1965).

7. Elspeth Huxley, *The Flame Trees of Thika: Memories of an African Childhood* (London: Chatto & Windus, 1959), 4.

8. From Douglas MacArthur, "Duty, Honor, and Country," *The Dolphin Book of Speeches,* ed. George W. Hibbit (George W. Hibbit, 1965).

9. From Charles Schaillol, "The Strangler," *Winning Orations.* Reprinted by permission of Larry Schnoor, Executive Secretary, Interstate Oratorical Association, Mankato State University, Mankato, MN.

10. Michael Osborn, *Orientations to Rhetorical Style* (Chicago: Science Research Associates, 1976), 10.

11. Quoted on the cover of James Rogers, *The Dictionary of Clichés* (New York: Ballantine Books, 1985). On clichés, see Joe Glaser, *Understanding Style: Practical Ways to Improve Your Writing* (New York: Oxford University Press, 1999), ch. 5.

12. From Martin Luther King, Jr., "Love, Law and Civil Disobedience" (Martin Luther King, Jr., 1963). Reprinted by permission of Joan Daves.

13. Technically, the phrase *ad personam* means "to the person" in an individual sense, whereas *ad hominem* is an attack on the life circumstances of someone. So, if one argues "You're a liar and a cheat and, hence, cannot be trusted to be telling the truth on this question," that's an ad personam argument, but if one argues "You must be pro-life on the abortion question because you're a Catholic," that's an ad hominem argument. It does not really depend upon precise knowledge of the person's actual beliefs but, instead, on a circumstance—the person's baptism as a Roman Catholic. Ad hominem arguments often are class- or group-based rather than individual-based. Keep in mind, however, that this distinction is a technical one; people commonly use "ad personam" and "ad hominem" interchangeably.

14. John Locke, *An Essay Concerning Human Understanding,* abr. and ed. J. W. Youlton, Everyman Library (1695; rpt. London: J. M. Dent, 1993).

15. For arguments about the centrality of character arguments to (especially American) politics, see Bruce E. Gronbeck, "Character, Celebrity, and Sexual Innuendo in the Mass-Mediated Presidency," *Media Scandals; Morality and Desire in the Popular Culture Marketplace,* ed. James Lull and Stephen Hinerman (London: Polity Press, 1997), 122–142.

16. Philip Wander, "The Third Persona: An Ideological Turn in Rhetorical Theory," *Communication Studies* 35 (1984): 197–216.

17. For details and beautiful illustrations, see Herman J. Viola and Carolyn Margolis, eds., *Seeds of Change: A Quincentennial Celebration* (Washington, D.C.: Smithsonian Institution Press, 1991).

18. King Alfred's University College in the United Kingdom maintains a website for the Centre for Conspiracy Culture, which deals with the examples of the breadth of conspiratorial thinking in our time. See http://www.wkac.ac.uk/research/ccc/index.html.

19. For the originary discussion of the critique of domination (and the critique of freedom), see Michel Foucault, *Power/Knowledge: Selected Interviews and Other Writings,* ed. Colin Gordon, trans. Colin Gordon, Leo Marshall, John Mepham, and Kate Soper (New York: Pantheon Books, 1980). It is turned into a theory of "critical rhetoric" in Raymie E. McKerrow, "Critical Rhetoric: Theory and Praxis," *Communication Monographs* 59 (1989): 91–111.

20. Kent Ono, "Power Rangers: An Ideological Critique of Neocolonialism," *Critical Approaches to Television,* ed. Leah E. Vande Berg, Lawrence A. Wenner, and Bruce E. Gronbeck (Boston: Houghton Mifflin, 1998), 274.

21. Alan Alda, "A Reel Doctor's Advice to Some Real Doctors," in *The Art of Public Speaking,* Stephen E. Lucas (New York: Random House, 1983), 364.

22. For reviews of these and other issues relative to gendered communication, see P. J. Kalbfleisch and M. J. Cody, eds., *Gender, Power, and Communication in Human Relationships* (Hillsdale, NJ: Lawrence Erlbaum Associates, 1995).

23. Allen H. Neurath, "Acceptance Address," DeWitt Carter Reddick Award: *Address by the 1992 Recipient* [pamphlet] (Austin, TX: College of Communication, University of Texas at Austin, 1992).

24. See Bruce E. Gronbeck, "Characterological Argument in Bush's and Clinton's Convention Films," *Argument and the Postmodern Challenge: Proceedings of the Eighth SCA/AFA Conference on Argumentation*, ed. Raymie E. McKerrow (Annandale, VA: National Communication Association, 1993), 392–397.

25. Your library probably has a shelf of works on hate speech. Here are some recent works worth your time: Laurence R. Marcus, *Fighting Words: The Politics of Hateful Speech* (Westport, CT: Praeger, 1996); Judith P. Butler, *Excitable Speech: A Politics of the Performative* (New York: Routledge, 1997); Richard Abel, *Speaking Respect, Respecting Speech* (Chicago: University of Chicago Press, 1998); and Timothy Shiell, *Campus Hate Speech on Trial* (Lawrence, KS: University Press of Kansas, 1998).

26. To examine the debate over political correctness, see such works as Philip E. Devine, *Human Diversity and the Culture Wars: A Philosophical Perspective on Contemporary Culture Conflict* (Westport, CT: Praeger, 1996); Richard Feldstein, *Political Correctness: A Response From the Cultural Left* (Minneapolis: University of Minnesota Press, 1997); Cary Nelson, *Manifesto of a Tenured Radical* (New York: New York University Press, 1997); and Alan Charles Kors and Harvey A. Silvergate, *The Shadow University: The Betrayal of Liberty on America's Campus* (New York: Free Press, 1998).

27. The idea of multiculturalism has been vigorously debated in American society. For some of the positions taken, see positive statements such as Heinz Ickstadt, *Crossing Borders: Inner- and Intercultural Exchanges in a Multicultural Society* (New York: Peter Lang, 1997); Susan Stanford Friedman, *Mappings: Feminism and the Cultural Geographies of Encounter* (Princeton: Princeton University Press, 1998); and Mark P. Orbe, *Constructing Co-Cultural Theory: An Explication of Culture, Power, and Communication* (Thousand Oaks, CA: Sage, 1998). For arguments directed at the problems associated with multiculturalism, see Arthur M. Schlesinger, Jr., *The Disuniting of America* (Knoxville, TN: Whittle Direct Books, 1991); Yehudi O. Webster, *Against the Multicultural Agenda: A Critical Thinking Alternative* (Westport, CT: Praeger, 1997); and John J. Miller, *The Unmaking of America: How Multiculturalism Has Undermined the Assimilation Ethic* (New York: Free Press, 1998).

Chapter 11

Using Visual Aids in Speeches

Sue had everything ready to show slides as part of her speech—she had spent a long time working in PowerPoint to make sure points slid in as she desired, the graphics she'd added were appropriate, and even the material downloaded from the Web fit her needs. She also had practiced timing the speech, so she knew how long to show each slide before moving on. The classroom had a pull-down screen, so she didn't need to bring one. The windows had shades, so she could darken the room to enhance the visual effect. She had reserved a laptop from the Department as well as the LCD projector. The day of the speech, she brought the equipment in (and she even remembered to bring an extension cord in case it was needed), set it up, and began her speech. As she hit the first slide, she realized something was wrong—all her codes for bringing subpoints up on the slide one at a time had disappeared. Instead, the whole slide came up at once, which lessened the visual effect she had planned. After her speech, she discovered that the version of Power-Point she had used and the one on the Department's computer were not identical, and that difference in versions was sufficient to affect her slides.

Sue's experience is like that of other speakers; even with attention to preparation, one missed detail may ruin the use of visuals or lessen their impact. We fully expect that you will repeat Sue's experience—perhaps not with different versions of software, but in some other way. From a practical perspective, using visuals requires a great deal more thought and attention to detail than might at first meet the eye.

Given that, you might wonder—why use visuals at all? One answer is to consider the general impact of visuals in contemporary society. This has been called the **ocularcentric** (i.e., *ocular* = eye; *centric* = centered) **century**.[1] That is, ours has become a time when sight threatens to be the dominant sense. Television, film, transparencies, VCRs and videotape, videodiscs, CD-ROMs and related digital technologies, overhead and opaque projectors, billboards, poster art, banners trailing from airplanes, sidewalk tables with samples from a store's "today only" sale—our world is filled with visual communications. No time or place before yours has been so visually oriented. Entire companies—from famous media studios to small-town graphics shops in basements—exist because of our willingness to pay for pieces of visual rhetoric that entice the eye and affect the mind.

The public speaker, of course, always has been in the visual communication business. A speaker's physical presence before an audience is a powerful visual statement. Body language, facial expression, eye contact, and gestures—all these combine to make the visual channel of public speaking a carrier of significant messages. The use of *visual aids* makes the world of sight an essential part of oral communication transactions as well. From the objects a second grader brings to school for "show and tell" to the flipcharts sales trainers use, speakers multiply and deepen their communication messages when they use visual channels well.

Research on visual media, learning, and attitude change has revealed helpful information about the impact of visual aids on audiences.[2] Much advice, however, still flows directly from veteran speakers to those who are new at public presentations. In this chapter, we mix advice from social-scientific research with wisdom from experienced speakers. First, we deal with the general functions of visual aids, and then, we examine various types and look at some advice on how to use them to greatest effect.

THE FUNCTIONS OF VISUAL AIDS

Visual materials provide punch for any presentation in two ways: they help listeners comprehend and remember your material, and they improve the persuasive impact of your messages.

Comprehension and Recall

While the old saying that "A picture is worth a thousand words" may be something of an exaggeration, its truths are reflected in research. Visual research has demonstrated that bar graphs, especially, make statistical information more accessible; that simple drawings enhance recall; and that charts and such human interest visuals as photographs help listeners process and retain data.[3] Pictures have significant effects on children's recall and comprehension during storytelling.[4] Your own experience probably bears this out. Recall the high-school teachers who worked with models, maps, slides (transparencies) or overheads, and video. Most likely, you remember their presentations better than those in other classes where visual materials were rare or nonexistent.

Persuasiveness

In addition to improving comprehension and recall, visuals can heighten the persuasive power of your ideas because they engage listeners actively. Johnnie Cochran's oft-repeated line in the O. J. Simpson trial, "If it doesn't fit, you must acquit" depended on the jury's having watched O. J. try on the glove found after Nicole Brown's murder. Without that single visual element, Cochran's refrain would not have been possible.

Undeniably, credibility and persuasiveness are enhanced by good visuals.[5] Visual materials satisfy the "show-me" attitude prevalent in a vision-oriented or ocularcentric age and provide a crucial means of meeting listener expectations.[6]

TYPES OF VISUAL AIDS

To give you the broadest possible look at visual aids, we divide them into two large classes: **physical objects,** and **representations of objects and relationships.** Then, we examine more particular types and give you some tips on how to use them in your talks.

Chalkboard drawings are quick sketches that illustrate your ideas.

Physical Objects

The objects that you bring to a presentation, including your own body, can be categorized under two headings: *animate* (living) objects, and *inanimate* (non-living) objects.

Animate Objects.   Live animals or plants can, under some circumstances, be used to enhance your speeches. If your speech explores the care and feeding of gerbils, you can reinforce your ideas by bringing to the speech one or two gerbils in a properly equipped cage. Likewise, describing the differences between two varieties of plants may be easier if you demonstrate the differences with real plants. You might be stretching your luck, however, by bringing a real horse into the classroom to show how one is saddled or an untrained puppy to show how one is paper trained.

You want to use the actual object to focus audience attention on your speech, not to distract the audience with the object. A registered Persian cat may seem to be a perfect visual aid for a speech about what judges look for in cat shows—until a person in the first row has an allergic reaction to your pet.

You also can use your own body as a visual aid: Demonstrating warm-up exercises, ballet steps, or tennis strokes adds concreteness and vitality to such presentations. In any case, make sure those in the back rows can see the animal, plant, or demonstration. Demonstrate a yoga position from a sturdy tabletop rather than from the floor. Slow the tempo of a tennis stroke so the audience can see any intricate action and subtle movements. One advantage of properly controlled visual action is that you can control the audience's attention to your demonstration. Discretion and common sense about what's possible and in good taste will help make animate visuals work for you rather than against you.

Inanimate Objects.   Demonstrations often are enhanced by showing the actual object under discussion: A speech about stringing a tennis racket is enhanced by a demonstration of the process with an actual racket. A speech about the best way to repair rust holes in an automobile fender is clarified by samples of the work in various stages (bring in pieces, not the whole fender!). Demonstrations of cooking or house remodeling are enlivened with samples prepared before the presentation, because the presenter usually does not have time to complete the actual work during the presentation. Take a tip from TV cooking shows—they work with several copies of a dish to illustrate different stages; you can do the same if your purpose is to illustrate a sequence of events in remodeling or making something.

Whether an object is animate or inanimate, you want to keep the audience's attention focused on the message of your speech. Thus, when you are through with your gerbils in the cage, move the cage out of direct sight if possible to avoid having the audience watch the gerbils rather than listen to you. Endeavor to control the audience's focus on what you want them to hear and understand, and use visuals in a manner that maximizes their attention on you.

Representations of Objects and Relationships

When you cannot use actual objects or your own physical movement to clarify your message, you can resort to using representations—or images—that help convey an understanding of what you are discussing. These representations may be relatively concrete—such as photographs, slides, transparencies, film or videotape segments—or more abstract—such as drawings, graphs, charts, and models. They may involve a simple chalkboard or a flipchart or even equipment such as overhead transparencies, slide projectors, VCRs with television monitors, or computer-generated and controlled slides. There are advantages and disadvantages to each, however.

Photographs.   With photographs, you can illustrate flood damage to ravaged homes or depict the beauty of a wooded area threatened by a new shopping mall. One problem with photographs, however, is that audiences may not be able to see details from a distance. You can compensate by enlarging photos so that people can see them more easily. Avoid passing small photos through the audience, however, because such activity is noisy and disruptive. The purpose of a visual aid is to draw the attention of all members of the audience simultaneously.

Slides.   Slides allow you to depict color, shape, texture, and relationships. If you're giving an informative speech on Salvador Dali, you'll want to have two

---

ETHICAL MOMENTS

CAN PICTURES LIE?

Can pictures lie? Aren't they each worth a thousand words because seeing is believing, because showing is better than telling? Not really, especially in the ocularcentric age. Consider:

- Hopes for finding U.S. soldiers missing in action (MIAs) in Vietnam often depended upon photos that seemed to show American soldiers standing with signs having current dates on them. Those pictures were faked.
- Thanks to electronic scanners, you now can easily add to or subtract from pictures and print the altered photos so cleanly that the forgery is almost impossible to detect.
- During the 1992 presidential campaign, political action committees (PACs) ran ads that showed Bill Clinton holding hands in victory on the Democratic Convention stage with Ted Kennedy. What the PAC had done was put a picture of Kennedy's head on Vice-President Al Gore's body.

Pictures can be altered to "say" something that isn't true. They also can add imaginings to words to intensify them or even focus them on a particular idea that someone doesn't want to say aloud; the 1992 PAC ad seemed to be saying that "Bill Clinton is much more liberal than you think."

The visual channel can be very helpful to both speaker and audience when used in morally defensible ways. It can be destructive of the truth, however, when it is not.

or three slides that illustrate his work. If you're giving a speech on horror writer Stephen King, using a picture of the famous author or of the iron gates at the front of his home in Bangor, Maine, would be a logical way to focus attention on your topic. Using slides requires familiarity with projection equipment. Recall Sue's experience—attention to small, seemingly inconsequential details will make a major difference in how smoothly the presentation goes. For example, if you're using a slide projector instead of an LCD projector and Power-Point—that is you have actual slides to illustrate with, what happens if the bulb goes out in the middle of your presentation? Did you bring a spare, and do you know how to change the bulb? Will you need an extension cord? Do you know how to remove a jammed slide? If you operate on the assumption that whatever can go wrong will, you'll be prepared for most problematic circumstances.

HOW TO

MAKE THE MOST OF COLOR SELECTION FOR SLIDES AND OTHER VISUALS

- *Know your audience*—A conservative audience may be turned off by a yellow background; blue backgrounds are more conservative.
- *Keep your topic and purpose in mind*—If you want to sell an idea to your audience, choose colors that excite (e.g., reds and oranges). If you are discussing downsizing or an upsetting topic, use colors that calm (e.g., greens and blues).
- *Pick the background color first*—Don't choose colors that clash, and be sure to have a high degree of contrast between the text and the background.
- *Use the same color theme throughout your presentation.*
- *Do not use more than three or four colors.*
- *Do not choose a rainbow grouping of colors.*
- *Use bright colors to highlight important data.*

Further Resources

Classroom Presentations: Communicating with Color. [No date].

Technology for Teachers. [On line]. Available: http://199.78.128.9/tft/pedagogy/present/color.htm. [1997, April 18].

Hoffman, B. (1995). "Exploring Color," *Encyclopedia of Educational Technology.* [On line]. Available: http://edweb.sdsu.edu//EET/Color/Color.html. [1997, April 18].

Mandel, S. (1993). *Effective Presentation Skills* (Menlo Park, CA: Crisp Publications).

Source: Adapted from "Color Selection," available online at http://webbase.emporia.edu/slim/]]li812/project/812971/t2color.htm.

Transparencies.   If you do not have access to a slide projector or to Power-Point and an LCD projector and screen, you can still dress up the visual portion of your presentation using **transparencies** and an overhead projector. Most copy machines will allow you to reproduce directly from a print version of a document (and in color if the machine has that capability), and many printers will allow you to print transparencies directly from your file (and in color if your printer has color capability). Transparencies allow for more information on the printed page than slides. You also can download information from the World Wide Web, put it directly into your file, and then print the graphic or other visual as part of your transparency; you are not limited to just words in using an overhead projector. Because you cannot click new items to appear on the slide, as you can in PowerPoint, you'll need to cover part of the transparency to focus audience attention on the feature you wish to discuss. As you move to the next item, you also need to uncover that item. This is perhaps more cumbersome and inefficient than using PowerPoint, but it can work just as well in terms of directing audience attention to the points you want to make. Transparencies of graphs also work well using an overhead projector— and may be easier to build depending on your skill at creating slides. You also can cover the entire transparency or simply turn the machine off when you have finished with the key visuals and then turn it on again later if you need to return to specific transparencies. You even can mark the transparency quickly with respect to emphasizing a specific term or statistic or direct audience attention to one element in a table or drawing.

Document Camera.   Some classrooms and other meeting room facilities will have a **document camera** that you can use. In this instance, your original print document can be brought in (e.g., a magazine advertisement) and placed on the camera; the image then is transferred to the screen via an LCD projector. If you have more than one ad to illustrate, you simply need to remove one and place the other on the camera bed. You also can zoom in to focus attention on specific elements of the ad, or you can use a felt-tip marker to circle specific objects or attributes you want to highlight. As with any use of visuals, however, you'll want to do this fairly quickly, so as not to consume valuable time.

Videotapes and Films.   These types of visual aids also can be useful in illustrating your points. Two or three videotaped political ads can help illustrate methods for packaging a candidate. Again, familiarity with the operation of a VCR and its TV monitor or of a film projector ensures a smooth presentation. Too often, speakers assume the equipment will be provided—and a skilled technician will be available—only to find that no one knows how to run the machine properly. Such delays increase your nervousness and detract from your presentation. Slide and film projectors will require time to set up; you also may need to wheel in a monitor/VCR cart, hook it in, and get it running. Some classrooms are cable-ready, hence allowing you to show a "live" excerpt should the timing work out.

Models.   You can use models—reduced or enlarged scale replicas of real objects—to convey plans or illustrate problems. Architects construct models of new projects to show clients. Developers of shopping malls, condominiums, and business offices use models when persuading zoning boards to grant needed rights-of-way or variances. You can use models of genes to accompany your explanation of gene splicing. As with other inanimate physical objects, models need to be manageable and visible to the audience. If a model comes apart so that different pieces can be examined, practice removing and replacing these parts beforehand.

Drawings.   Whether drawn in advance or as you speak, it will be useful in some instances to construct rough line drawings or provide the audience with more formally drawn pictures to represent ideas. How "finished" these are will depend on the formality of the situation. Flipchart drawings may be sufficient to explain cell division to a small group, but when presenting the same information to a large audience, more refined visual support materials are needed. The care with which you prepare these visuals will convey to your audience an attitude of indifference or concern.

Chalkboard Drawings.   To convey an understanding of a process step by step, chalkboard drawings are especially valuable. By drawing each stage as you discuss it, you can control the audience's attention to your major points. Coaches often use this approach when showing players how to execute a particular play or defend against an opponent's play. Take care, however, not to rely on the board so much that you spend most of your speech with your back to your audience. Make sure the audience can see what you are drawing; standing in front of the drawing, with your back to the audience while talking, does little to communicate your ideas. Stand to the side, and draw away from your body, stopping to turn back to the audience at intervals so they are kept in contact with you and the development of your idea.

Regardless of the medium used to illustrate your drawing—whether on chalkboard or with a document camera (i.e., take a blank sheet, place it on the camera bed, and draw)—keep the following points in mind: First, make your drawings large enough so that the audience can see them. Second, if you continue talking to the audience as you draw, be brief; your audience's attention will wander if you talk to the board or the light source or with your head down (concentrating on drawing on the document camera's bed) for more than a half-minute. Third, as noted, consider the visual field while you draw—where should you stand to avoid blocking the audience's view of your visuals? Fourth, when you're through talking about the illustration, erase it, cover it, or turn off the projector.

Graphs.   Graphs show relationships among the various parts of a whole or variables across time. There are several types of graphs:

1. **Bar graphs** show the relationships between two or more sets of figures. If you were illustrating the difference between lawyers' and doctors' incomes or between male lawyers' and female lawyers' incomes, you would probably use a bar graph.

Representations convey information in various ways. For instance, a photograph of an in-line skate (top) *gives an audience a realistic but complicated view of the object, whereas an abstract representation, such as a diagram* (bottom), *strips away unnecessary details to illustrate the parts of the object more clearly. An action shot provides a feeling of a three-dimensional image of the object.*

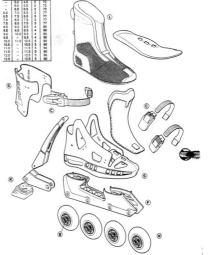

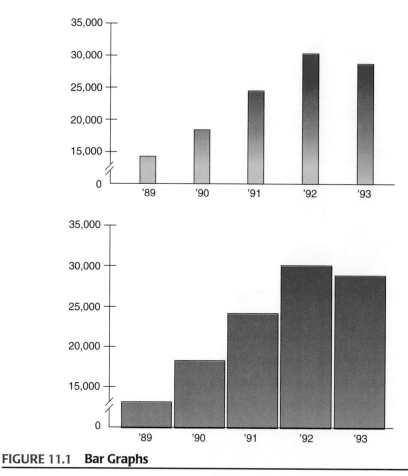

FIGURE 11.1   Bar Graphs

Bar graphs visually illustrate relationships. Changing the spacing and size of bars can affect the visual message.

2. **Line graphs** show relationships between two or more variables, usually over time. If you are trying to explain a complex economic correlation between supply and demand, you would use a line graph.
3. **Pie graphs** show percentages by dividing a circle into the segments being represented. A charitable organization could use a pie graph to show how much of its income goes to administration, research, and fund-raising campaigns. Town governments use pie graphs to show citizens what proportion of their tax dollars go to municipal services, administration, education, recreation, and law enforcement.
4. **Pictographs** represent size and number with symbols. A representation of U.S. and Russian exports of grain might use a miniature drawing of a wheat shock or ear of corn to represent 100,000 bushels; this representation would allow a viewer to see at a glance the disparity between the exports of these two countries.

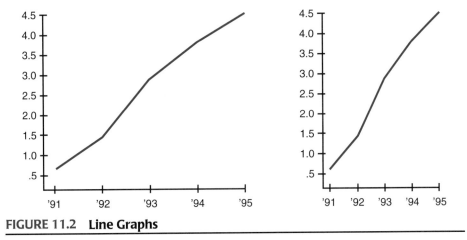

FIGURE 11.2   Line Graphs

Line graphs can reveal relationships, but they also can deceive the unwary. These two graphs show the same data, but the use of different spacing makes the increase in hotel-room prices seem much steeper in the second version than in the first. Always look at the scales and their units when trying to interpret line graphs.
Source: *Smith Travel Research, as reported in* USA Today, *October 27, 1995, B1.*

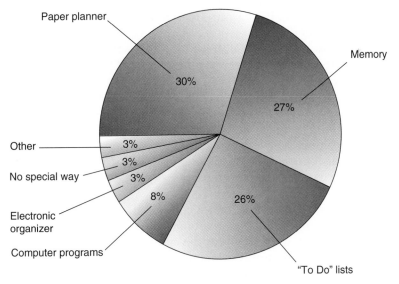

FIGURE 11.3   Pie Graph

A pie graph shows percentages of a whole; this graph shows the percentage of persons using various forms of organizational reminders. (Note the total still relying on "paper" re-sources in today's computer age!)
Source: *Opinion Research Corp. for Fuji Computer Products, as reported in* USA Today, *October 27, 1995, B1.*

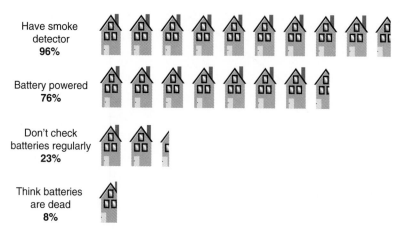

FIGURE 11.4   Pictographs

The speaker can use artistic skill to depict the number of homes with smoke detectors, those powered by battery, those not checked regularly (90% of the fires causing death were in homes with nonworking detectors), and those who think the batteries are dead. Source: *Angus Reid Group for American Sensors, as reported in* USA Today, *October 27, 1995, A1.*

Your choice of bar, line, pie, or pictorial graphs will depend on the subject and the nature of the relationship you wish to convey. A pie graph, for example, cannot easily illustrate discrepancies between two groups, nor can it show effects of change over time. If your purpose is to illustrate trends, line graphs will show increases or decreases over time, whereas bar graphs will work better to illustrate comparisons between different variables. Pie charts are excellent if your purpose is to illustrate the proportions "owned" by different variables.[7]

Regardless of the type of graph you choose, you must be very careful not to distort your information when preparing it. A bar graph can create a misleading impression of the difference between two items if one bar is short and wide but the other is long and narrow. Line graphs can portray very different effects of change if the units of measurement are not the same for each time period. You can avoid misrepresenting information by using consistent measurements and a computer to generate your graphs.

Charts and Tables.   **Charts** and **tables** condense large blocks of information into a single representation. If you want to discuss what products are imported and exported by Japan, you can break down imports and exports on a table. If you want to show the channels of communication or lines of authority in a large company, your presentation will be much easier to follow if your listeners have an organizational chart for reference.

There are two special types of charts: **flipcharts** unveil ideas one at a time on separate sheets; and **flowcharts** show the chronological stages of a process on a single sheet. Both flipcharts and flowcharts may include drawings or photos. If you present successive ideas with a flipchart, you'll focus audience attention on specific parts of your speech. If you present successive ideas with a complete chart, however, the audience may stray from your order of explanation to read the entire chart. You can use a flowchart to indicate what actions might be taken across time—for example the sequential stages of a fund-raising campaign.

If the information is not too complex or lengthy, tables and charts may be used to indicate changes over time and to rank or list items and their costs, frequency of use, or relative importance. Tables and charts should be designed so they can be seen and convey data simply and clearly. Too much information will force the audience to concentrate more on the visual support than on the oral explanation. For example, a dense chart showing all the major and minor offices of a company may overwhelm listeners as they try to follow your explanation. Thus, if the organization is too complex, you may want to develop a series of charts, with each one focusing on a smaller unit of information.

Representing Textual Material.   You are not limited to these representational forms of displaying information. You also can use any of the mentioned equipment to convey textual material, such as an outline of your talk, a list of the key items to be covered, a quotation from an authoritative source. All these can be displayed on a chalkboard or through slides, overhead transparencies, and so on. Corporate trainers, for example, often use slides created through a computer program such as PowerPoint and displayed electronically from a ceiling-mounted projector to outline their presentation and convey key information. If you are giving a seminar on how to navigate the World Wide Web, you might use visuals that duplicate what is seen on a computer screen. Saying "click the mouse here" is much easier if your audience can see where the cursor is on the screen at the front of the seminar room.

FIGURE 11.5 PowerPoint Slides

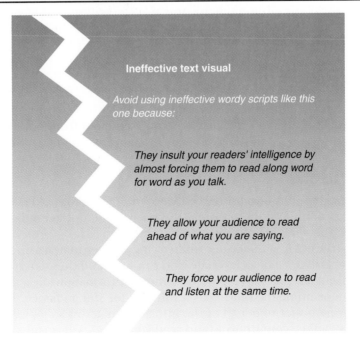

There are three things to consider when working primarily with text materials. First, keep enough "white space" on the page or slide so the audience does not get lost among the verbiage. Second, make sure the type size is large enough for the audience to see; even though you can magnify type to some extent by adjusting the distance between projector and screen, some may yet remain too small to read. Third, for slides with a presentation program like PowerPoint, the background color needs to be counter to the text color—what you see on your computer screen as you develop your slide may be easy to read, but consider the effect when you put it on a larger screen. Will the text be readable, or will the background color and text color blend to make the words hard to see?

Using Handouts.   Information also can be put on handouts and worked with while you are speaking. Charts, graphs, outlines, rough drawings—all these can be photocopied and given to each audience member. Giving one to each member is better than passing only a few copies around, which will distract listeners as they get involved in reading and passing things to each other. Often, giving each member a copy is the strategy of choice, such as if you want each person to have the material in their possession at the close of your talk. The primary difficulty you have to work against is the audience's tendency to read ahead of where you are. If you have more than one handout, you can control this by sequencing the handouts—and by having someone handle the actual distribution while you talk. You also can control the audience's access to information, at least to some extent, by using an overhead transparency. Use a separate sheet to uncover the items as you go. This won't stop all members from reading ahead, but it will focus attention on where you are at any given moment. You also can wait until the conclusion of your speech and then distribute material that you want the audience to take away with them.

ACQUIRING VISUAL AIDS

Where do you get your visual aids? Making your own, searching the Web for specific examples that you can use, or acquiring them from others are three logical resources.

Making Your Own

If you are making your own poster board to bring to class, you'll need to make sure the classroom is set up to display the board. Not all classrooms have cork strips above the chalkboard that can be used to tack up a poster. So, rather than awkwardly holding the poster while trying to refer to items on it, consider enlisting the assistance of a classmate who can hold and then put it away when you are finished. As already noted, too much information on a poster, with small letters or numbers, will make it difficult for the audience. It may take more than one poster to get all of the information across so that those sitting 15 feet away can see your drawing and read your text.

Downloading Visual Aids from the Web

Searching the Web for a suitable image or outline of the key issues you wish to discuss—and downloading that information into a slide or a file that can be printed as a transparency—has become much easier. Images, in particular, are easy to capture and move into a slide. If you are using an IBM-compatible PC with a mouse, move the cursor over the image, click on the right side, and select from the menu the "Save As" option; you will be directed next to a dialog box that asks you to select a place to file the image. You can rename it and save in any one of your file directories for easy access.[8] You then can select the file and open it in a Web site and onto your slide. For example, at the web site http://www.celebsite.com/people/stephenking/index.html, a picture of Stephen King was clicked on and saved as a JPEG file; then, with a text on screen, the file can be clicked to open onto the page. Once there, left-clicking with the mouse moves you to edit mode, and with the left button down, you can move the slide, positioning it on the page where you want it. You can move it over printed text, and when done, the text will rearrange itself around the image.

The same process will work within your slide: You can alter the size of the image and position it where you wish to have it. If your presentation will be broadcast to other sites, you'll need to place the image so that room remains for a technician to put a small picture of you speaking in one corner of the slide. Otherwise, the audience at a different site will only see the slide, or your "corner box" will cut off part of your text/image that you are attempting to illustrate.

Getting Visual Aids from Research/Others

You also can rely on your research skills (see the advice on gathering information in Chapter 6) as well as ask friends for assistance in locating appropriate images. If you wish to illustrate a specific interpersonal interaction, such as the importance of appearing credible and believable in conflict situations, think in terms of recent movies you have seen. A 30-second video excerpt from a well-known movie, for example, may be the best way to illustrate what you're talking about regarding the role of credibility in negotiating conflict. When using equipment, try and get to the classroom early enough to give the equipment (in this case, a VCR) a trial run, and make certain the tape is at the right spot to introduce the idea.

With these brief suggestions for acquiring visuals in mind, you also need to consider some of the more important ways to maximize their utility. The next section focuses on three considerations: audience and occasion, communicative potential, and using computer-generated aids.

STRATEGIES FOR SELECTING AND USING VISUAL AIDS

To decide which visual aids will work best for you, take into account:

1. The characteristics of the audience and occasion.
2. The communicative potential of various visuals.
3. The potential of computer-generated visual materials to help with your communication tasks.

Consider the Audience and Occasion

Before you select specific visual aids, common sense will tell you to think about your listeners: Do you need to bring a map of the United States to an audience of college students when discussing the westward movement of population of this country? If you're going to discuss a football team's offensive and defensive formations, should you diagram them for your audience? Can you expect an audience to understand the administrative structure of the university without providing an organizational chart?

How readily an audience can comprehend *aurally* (by ear) what you have to say is another, more difficult question to answer. It may be quite difficult, for example, to decide what your classmates know about the organization of groups such as the National Red Cross or what Rotary Club members know about the administrative structure of your college. Probably the best thing to do is speak with several of your listeners ahead of time. This and other forms of audience research can help you decide how to use the visual channel.

As part of your preparation process, take into account the speaking occasion. Certain occasions demand specific types of visual support materials. The corporate executive who presents a report on projected future profits to a board of directors without a printed handout or diagram probably will put his or her credibility in jeopardy. The military adviser who calls for governmental expenditures on new weapons without pictures or drawings of the proposed systems and printed technical data on their performance is not likely to be a convincing advocate. An athletic coach without a chalkboard at half-time on which to diagram plays probably will confuse some of the players. In short, if you speak in situations where speakers traditionally use certain visual aids, meet those expectations in your own work. If an occasion does not appear to require certain visual supports, analyze the occasion and your topic further to determine different visual possibilities. Use your imagination. Be innovative. Don't overlook opportunities to make your speech more meaningful, exciting, and interesting for your listeners.

Consider the Communicative Potential of Various Visual Aids

Remember that each type of visual aid is best at communicating a particular kind of information. Each type also must blend with your spoken presentation as well as with your audience. In general, pictorial or photographic visuals can make an audience *feel* the way you do. For example, you can use slides, movies, sketches, or photographs of your travels in Thailand to accompany a speech on social conditions in equatorial Asia. Direct representations can be filled with feeling and show an audience what you experienced in another place or situation.

Visuals containing descriptive or written materials, however, are especially useful in helping an audience to *think* the way you do. Models, diagrams, charts, and graphs about the population and economy of Thailand or the increase in AIDS cases in that country could help you persuade your listeners to conclude that the United States should increase its aid to this nation.

? HOW TO

SELECT THE RIGHT VISUAL AID

Consider the following when choosing which type of visual aids to use in a particular presentation:

1. *The purpose of the presentation.* If specific points are highlighted, a transparency or word slides might be appropriate. If the procedure is of utmost importance, a model or physical demonstration might be needed. Travel presentations often use slides or video.

2. *The nature of the audience.* What the audience knows about the subject will determine the most appropriate types of visual aids. For a presentation on diseases of vegetables to a group of homeowners with limited knowledge about gardening, it would be appropriate to have real plant specimens and slides. For commercial vegetable farmers with good knowledge of such diseases, however, perhaps you would need only slides to illustrate your point.

3. *The physical setting.* The shape, size, lighting, and equipment available in the particular environment are major considerations. Will the seating arrangement allow everyone to see the visual aids being used? If total darkness is required, is it possible? Are there enough electrical outlets for the equipment? Is an overhead projector available? A slide projector? The physical setting should be explored well before the presentation date. Time allowed for the presentation also is critical. If a short time frame is allowed, then fewer visual aids—and ones that require little explanation—should be used.

4. *The presenter's skill in using visual aids.* Only use visual aids with which you feel comfortable. Don't try using a slide projector for the first time during an important presentation without practice. Any visual aid should fit naturally into the presentation. It should not draw excessive attention to itself or be the main focus of the presentation.

Source: Adapted from information available online at http://hammock.ifas.ufl .edu/txt/fairs/11513.

Evaluate Computer-Generated Visual Materials

When considering visual aids, you can tap into the expanding world of computer graphics. You may not be able to produce results similar to those on the latest televised football game, but you still can use readily available **computer-generated visual materials.** Here are some suggestions:

- *Use computer graphics to create an atmosphere.* It's easy to make computer banners with block lettering and pictures, so hang a banner in the front of the

HOW TO

USE VISUAL AIDS EFFECTIVELY

Here are some tips and reminders to assist you in preparing and using visual aids in your presentation:

Good visuals reinforce the spoken message. They do not convey the entire message.

Have a presentation plan. Begin with an introduction, and end with a summary or set of conclusions. Identify several major points you want to cover; supporting points reinforce the main points but can be sacrificed if you're running out of time.

Words and graphics on visual aids should be kept simple.

- Complex ideas belong in a handout or paper.
- Tables generally are not effective. Schematic drawings often are too detailed, but you can modify and simplify the drawing to illustrate only the point you are making, leaving out unnecessary details.
- Organizational charts cannot be read. Simplify the chart to show only the segments you are discussing.
- Equations, by themselves, are not an effective visual aid. You

can make an equation more visually appealing, however, by adding pictorial elements.
- Bar, pie, and line charts that are too busy can confuse the audience.

Design visuals to maximize their effectiveness.

- The type size of text or characters should be 18 to 24 points.
- Use bullets and dash lines, but avoid too many subtopics.
- Use a ragged right margin.
- Bold text is preferable to underlined text.
- Avoid overcrowding.

Use—but don't abuse—available technology to produce visuals.

- Use your spill check (spell), and then proof-read.
- TEXT IN ALL CAPITALS IS HARD TO READ.
- Use color carefully: Black backgrounds cause problems. Dark blue works best, but red and blue appear to "jump" when used together.

Source: Adapted from http://omar.llnl .gov/EFCOG/tips.html.

room to set a mood or establish a theme. For example, one student urging her classmates to get involved in a United Way fund-raising drive created a banner with the campaign slogan, "Thanks to you, it works, for all of us." Initially, the banner captured attention; during her speech, the banner reinforced the theme.

- *Enlarge small computer-generated diagrams.* Most computer diagrams are too small to be seen easily by an audience. You can use a photo duplicating machine, however, that enlarges images (sometimes to 140 to 200 percent of the original size) to make a more visible diagram. Depending on the facilities available, you may be able to transfer your visual image to a large screen through use of a projector wired to your computer; this also will enlarge the diagram so that it can be seen.

- *Consider enhancing the computer-generated image in other ways.* Use markers to color in pie graphs or darken the lines of a line graph. Use press-on letters to make headings for your graphs. Convert computer-generated images into slide transparencies for projection during your speech. Mixing media in such ways can give your presentations a professional look. If you have access to the right technology, you also can create three-dimensional images of buildings, machines, or the human body.

- *Know the limitations of computer technology.* Remember that you're the lead actor and that your visuals are props. Choose visuals that fit your purpose, physical setting, and audience needs. Computers are most effective when processing numerical data and converting them into bar, line, and pie graphs.

CHAPTER SUMMARY

We asked a question in the introduction to this chapter: Why use visuals at all? At this point, the reasons should be abundantly clear. We live in an ocularcentric century. Visuals aid listener comprehension and add persuasive impact to a speech. We cannot, in a single chapter, make you proficient at all the possibilities available, but you should be able to consider your topic and occasion and make informed judgments about whether to use visuals—and about which forms would be most appropriate in your situation. You also should be able to categorize potential visual aids as physical objects and concrete or abstract representations. You also should know a bit more about using animate (i.e., living) and inanimate (i.e., non-living) objects and about using representations such as pictures, slides, transparencies, document cameras, video tapes, chalkboard drawings, graphs, charts, tables, handouts, and computer-generated materials. Just as important, you should be able to select which visual aids—and in what forms—to use in particular speeches after considering the following:

- The audience and occasion.
- The communicative potential of various visual aids.
- The best use of computer-generated materials.
- How to coordinate verbal and visual channels for maximum effect.

KEY TERMS

bar graphs (p. 260)

charts (p. 264)

computer-generated visual materials (p. 269)

document camera (p. 259)

flipcharts (p. 264)

flowcharts (p. 264)

line graphs (p. 262)

ocularcentric century (p. 253)

physical objects (p. 255)

pictographs (p. 262)

pie graphs (p. 262)

representations of objects and relationships (p. 255)

tables (p. 264)

transparencies (p. 259)

ASSESSMENT ACTIVITIES

1. Think of several courses you have taken in high school or college. How did the instructors use visual aids in presenting the subject matter of these courses? Were such materials effectively used? Was there a relationship between the subject matter and the type of visual aid used? Give special consideration to proper and improper uses of the chalkboard by instructors. When was the chalkboard use helpful, and when did it detract from the topic? Are there special problems with using visuals when audience members are taking notes while listening? Prepare a brief, written analysis of these or other questions that occur to you, including several illustrations from the classes, in answering this general question: What, in your view, constitutes appropriate and inappropriate use of visual materials?

2. Visual aids capture appropriate moods, clarify potentially complex subjects, and sometimes even carry the thrust of a persuasive message. Examine magazine advertisements and "how-to" articles in periodicals, look at store windows and special displays in museums and libraries, and observe slide-projection lectures in some of your other classes. Then, using the types of the visual materials considered in this chapter, classify those that you have encountered; assess the purposes these materials serve—clarification, persuasion, attention focusing, mood setting, and others; evaluate the effectiveness of each of the materials you have examined; and finally, prepare a report, paper, or journal entry on the results of your experiences and observations.

3. Prepare a short speech explaining or demonstrating a complex process. Use two different types of visual aids, and ask the class to evaluate which aid was more effective. The following processes might be used or might stimulate your thoughts of others to use:
   a. The procedure for gene splicing.
   b. Tapping maple trees for the production of maple syrup.
   c. Navigating the World Wide Web.
   d. The pattern of jet stream movements.
   e. The genetic inheritance of color traits in flowers.

REFERENCES

1. Jacques Ellul, *The Humiliation of the Word,* trans. Joyce Main Hanks (Grand Rapids, MI: William B. Eerdmans, 1985). See also Martin Jay, "The Rise of Hermeneutics and the Crisis of Ocularcentrism," *The Rhetoric of Interpretation and the Interpretation of Rhetoric,* ed. Paul Hernadi (Durham, NC: Duke University Press, 1989), 55–74.

2. Further information on the value of visual perception can be found in Larry Raymond, *Reinventing Communication: A Guide to Using Visual Language for Planning, Problem Solving, and Reengineering* (Milwaukee, WI: ASQC Quality Press, 1994); and Chris Jenks, *Visual Culture* (New York: Routledge, 1995).

3. William J. Seiler, "The Effects of Visual Materials on Attitudes, Credibility, and Retention," *Communication Monographs* 38 (1971): 331–34.

4. For more specific conclusions regarding the effects of various kinds of visual materials, see James Benjamin and Raymie E. McKerrow, *Business and Professional Communication* (New York: HarperCollins, 1994), 175–179.

5. Joel R. Levin and Alan M. Lesgold, "On Pictures in Prose," *Educational Communi-*

cation and Technology Journal 26 (1978): 233–244.

6. For more information on visual communication, see Paul Messaris, *Visual "Literacy": Image, Mind, and Reality* (Boulder, CO: Westview Press, 1994).

7. This is adapted from information available on line at http://www.cs.engr.uky.edu/~lewis/visuals/notes3.html.

8. See John A. Courtright and Elizabeth Perse, *Communicating Online: A Guide to the Internet* (Mountain View, CA: Mayfield Publishing, 1998).

Chapter 12

Using Your Voice and Body to Communicate

The great Greek orator Demosthenes initially had such a weak and indistinct voice that he reputedly practiced speaking by shouting into the coastal winds of the Aegean Sea and loading his mouth with pebbles to practice articulating around them. Abraham Lincoln suffered from severe stage fright. Eleanor Roosevelt appeared awkward and clumsy, speaking with a high-pitched, hoarse voice; only after years of practice could she command an audience with her delivery. John Kennedy's strong regional dialect and his repetitive, wood-chopping gestures were parodied throughout the 1960 presidential campaign and became the objects of intense speech-training sessions. Robert Dole had such trouble with speech dynamism that his staff resorted to campaign ads made of quick cuts from line to line to make him appear more animated in the 1996 presidential campaign.

ORALITY AND HUMAN COMMUNICATION

That people with the stature of Greek orators, U.S. presidents, internationally famous humanitarians, and candidates for high office took time to improve their speech delivery skills should not be surprising. These cultural heroes realized that public service comes from thinking great thoughts, yes, but also from forging strong interpersonal bonds that allow those great thoughts to become shared values and actions. Even in the age of electronic interconnectivity, it is still person-to-person contact that forms the basis of social formations. We share ideas, values, and courses of action, most fundamentally, through speech.

In Chapter 10, we started to explain the idea of orality and the importance of cultivating an oral style of speechmaking. Let's go further now. What are the characteristics of **speech delivery**—the use of voice and body to communicate with others in your presence—that enhance the importance and power of public speaking? Communication theorist and critic Walter Ong has devoted his life to answering that question in broad terms, trying to understand the ways in which oral (preliterate) cultures worked.[1] The characteristics defining oral connections between people, to Ong, include the following:

1. *Aggregative.* The best human speech gathers together ideas—commonly shared notions—and relates the subject matter to them. Maxims, folk sayings, and even clichés often are accumulated or aggregated in speeches. Even though you probably were not around when then-President Kennedy gave his Inaugural address, you undoubtedly are familiar with the refrain: "Ask not what your country can do for you . . ." (The ease with which you finish this memorable phrase is proof of its staying power as a political cliché.) The rhetorical potency of this phrase comes from its symbolism of a people willing to act on behalf of and for their country. An almost perfect political slogan, it taps into what is known as *American optimism* or *exceptionalism:* the idea that the United States believes it can always grow and overcome any problem because it is a flexible democracy with problem-solving skills provided by people assembled from all other countries.[2] The best speeches aggregate maxims, pieces of wisdom, and even clichés, tying them to the subject matter. If you gather together *only* clichés, of course, the speech is empty. The maxims and pieces of wisdom are there to bond your ideas and yourself to other members of the community, not to take the place of new ideas.

2. *Agonistic/Invitational.* There is an ineluctable tension within human speech between the forces of a combative style and those fostering a cooperative, caring spirit. On the one hand, speakers know they are struggling with ideas and with listeners, looking to speak ideas in forceful and commanding ways and to engage listeners not only intellectually but also emotionally. During his 1996 presidential campaign, Pat Buchanan was not only agonistic but also antagonistic, attacking his opponents while wrestling to convert his listeners to his antiabortion, antigovernment, anti–foreign aid messages. At the other end of the scale is Crystal Cathedral preacher Robert Schuller, a smooth, witty, and accommodating speaker. He, too, pleads with audiences and reaches out with sympathy, love, and the power of positive thinking to burrow into their psyches. Both Buchanan and Schuller know that *agonism*—struggle with others—is something that makes speeches work and that represents a form of public talk that gets things done.

    At the other extreme is a form of "invitational rhetoric,"[3] that "constitutes an invitation to the audience to enter the rhetor's world and to see it as the rhetor does. In presenting a particular perspective, the invitational rhetor does not judge or denigrate others' perspectives but is open to and tries to appreciate and validate those perspectives, even if they differ dramatically from the rhetor's own."[4] This style also strives for the same end—to "get things done"—but it seeks to do so by creating an atmosphere that is conducive to the speaker and audience coming to an understanding together, arriving at a vision of the future that is mutually held and acted on. Seeking cooperation ("Your ideas may be as valued and viable as mine, but I invite you to consider my rationale.") rather than confrontation ("It's my way or the highway.") is a resource that may be more useful in rhetorical settings.

3. *Situational.* The best speech always is grounded in the concreteness of the here-and-now, in the specific situation. Philosophical essays and poetry can try to be timeless, but speeches should always be timely, made for now. The Greek idea of ***kairos***—appropriateness for time and place—was a concept important to classical rhetoricians. That sense of timely specificity develops because speakers usually are called on or expected to speak when something is in need of repair or celebration and that something itself is concrete (e.g., you need help understanding a city council resolution, feel anger and sorrow at a friend's death, want someone to express the joy you feel when winning a game). Concreteness is important because of the sheer physicalness of person-to-person speech: words seem to flow on material sound waves from a speaker's mouth to the listeners' ears, the bodies of the speakers and listeners are present, and touch occurs when handshakes follow a talk. The very ideas discussed seem to flow from the total human body—mouth, yes, but also arms and legs, head and torso, the clothing and jewelry that adorn that body, and the technologies that amplify sound and vision. The material situatedness of public speech gives it a sense of command and presence that simply is not possible with written language, radio or television broadcasts, or Internet chat rooms.

To think about the kinds of interhuman connections that are established through vocal and bodily presence may seem too theoretical and idealistic for your tastes. If you're going to understand why control of voice and body as channels of oral communication is so important, however, you must think about such matters. Sure, you've been talking all of your life and probably have gotten along all right. But when you grab onto a lectern to address a waiting audience, hoping to achieve your general and specific purposes, you must stop to think how best to aggregate ideas, tone them powerfully, and situate yourself and your thoughts concretely enough among today's concerns to meet the audience's expectations and needs. If you do all of that well, you'll have the satisfaction of knowing you've spoken in as competent and socially successful a way as you can.

We now turn to the details, to more specific aspects of using voice and body as instruments fostering human relationships.

PUBLIC SPEAKING AS A SOCIAL PERFORMANCE

Just as you perform culture (see Chapter 4), you also perform as a public speaker. Your every action and expression is a performance of self. Whether you speak in an agonistic or combative style or in an invitational, cooperative style, what you say and how you say it intertwine in forming the audience's impression of who you are as a person. Your physical body speaks as well: "Bodies *speak*, without necessarily talking, because they come coded with and as signs. They speak social codes."[5] Consider the constraints placed on street performers—without the trappings of the theatre, they must communicate through their physical presence that they have the competence to recreate, on the street, the images and events that would normally be "staged" in a theatre.[6] The lectern functions as your "theatre" with respect to granting a sense of authority for the presentation. When you must perform without the benefit of a lectern, your body is more fully present to the audience, and like the street performer, much more is demanded of it in establishing your legitimacy as a speaker.

There is a clear, gendered aspect to what might be called a rhetoric of the body—the manner in which the body expresses itself is socially conditioned by the roles that men and women play in the public sphere. As one scholar has noted, "for men at least, the higher the role in society, the less importance the body has."[7] What this means is that for men, looks become less important than ideas or status as one climbs the social ladder; for women, appearance remains a critical component of their success. (As an illustration, consider the feeling expressed by many Hollywood actresses that once they reach the age of 40, their careers might as well be over, because Hollywood moves on to the new generation of young women). Thus, performing the body depends, in part, on the social expectations created by a society prone to differentiate on the basis of gender.

Conceiving of the body as performer is not simply a Western view of the role of discourse in society. The account of a leader of the Merina peoples of Madagascar is instructive: "The speaker began very slowly, hesitantly, and very quietly, head down, and only gradually would he appear to gain more confidence, although at no time did any excess of expression creep into his manner of delivery."[8] In the Akan society of Ghana, the norms for performance in formal situations "include the non-exclusive use of the left hand in gesticulating, baring of the shoulders, removal of footwear while addressing the chief or his proxy, and finally avoiding proxemic confrontation with the chief."[9]

In every society, adherence to the cultural norms for performing the body become part of the necessary tasks; in moving into such different cultural norms, you must be aware of what expectations are placed on your performance of self. Integrating the bodily presence with the manner of delivery is essential if you're to be considered a legitmate resource for the audience's decisions and actions. What you are seeking is **synchronicity**—a sense of oneness between your physical performance and the specific audience's expectations of that performance. In this way, you advance on a common ground with the audience; promoting the legitimacy of your ideas becomes much easier if the audience is not distracted or turned off by the manner in which your voice or body performs. Delivering your classroom speech while seated on a table or desk in the front of the room, dangling your legs (and because of nervous energy, keeping them in constant motion) probably is not the best means of expressing ideas. The audience expects a much more formal address. If, however, you are demonstrating how to do something, moving from the podium and engaging the audience's attention in a relaxed and casual manner will put them at ease—they will gain from this a sense that you are comfortable with the artifacts or objects you use in the demonstration and that they have nothing to worry about as you move forward in the speech.

How you use your voice, in addition to your body, also becomes a part of your overall performance. The next section focuses on practical advice in using the voice, and the final section of this chapter focuses on similar advice for using the body as a communicative medium.

USING YOUR VOICE TO COMMUNICATE

The human voice is the physical instrument that shapes the meanings of words and ideas. Since preliterate times, when all cultures were oral, the voice has been the primary connector between people, creating a sense of identification and community. You must learn to control your vocal sound stream to make it central to your communication habits.

You communicate your enthusiasm to your listeners through your voice. By learning about the characteristics of vocal quality, you can make your ideas more interesting. Listen to a stock market reporter rattle off the daily industrial averages. Every word might be intelligible, but the reporter's vocal expression may be so repetitive and monotonous that the ideas seem unexciting. Then, listen to Gary Thorne doing a play-by-play of a baseball or hockey game or to Billy Packer covering a basketball game. The excitement of their broadcasts depends largely on their use of voice.

Our society prizes one essential vocal quality above all others: a sense of **conversationality.**[10] The conversational speaker creates a sense of two-way, interpersonal relationship—even when behind a lectern. The best hosts of afternoon talk shows or evening newscasts speak as if they're engaging each listener in a personal conversation. Speakers who have developed a conversational quality—Geraldo Rivera, Oprah Winfrey, Barbara Walters, Kathie Lee Gifford, and Regis Philbin, for example—have recognized that they are talking *with,* not *at,* an audience.

Perceptions of the Speaking Voice

The perception that successful speakers want to create for their audiences is that their voice, as they use it to shape their ideas and emotionally color their messages, is sincere. A flexible speaking voice has *intelligibility, variety,* and *understandable stress patterns.*

Intelligibility.   **Intelligibility** refers to the ease with which a listener can understand what you're saying, and it depends upon loudness, rate, enunciation, and pronunciation. Most of the time, inadequate articulation, a rapid speaking rate, or soft volume is acceptable, both because you know the people you're talking with and because you're probably only 3 to 5 feet from them. In public speaking, however, you may be addressing people you do not know, and

Projecting your voice may require an amplifier, as is the case here.

often from 25 feet or more away. When speaking in public, you have to work on making yourself intelligible. Try the following techniques:

1. *Adjust your volume.* Probably the most important single factor in intelligibility is how loudly you speak. **Volume** is related to the distance between you and your listeners and also to the amount of noise that is present. You must realize that your own voice sounds louder to you than it does to your listeners. Obviously, you need to project your voice by increasing your volume if you're speaking in an auditorium filled with several hundred people. You shouldn't forget, however, that a corresponding reduction in volume also is required when your listeners are only a few feet away. The amount of surrounding noise with which you must compete also has an effect on your volume, as illustrated in Figure 12.1.

2. *Control your rate.* **Rate** is the number of words spoken per minute. In animated conversation, you may jabber along at 200 to 250 words per minute. This rate is typical of people raised in the American North, Midwest, or West. As words tumble out of your mouth in informal conversations, they're usually intelligible because they don't have to travel far. In large auditoriums or outdoors, however, rapid delivery can impede intelligibility. Echoes sometimes distort or destroy sounds in

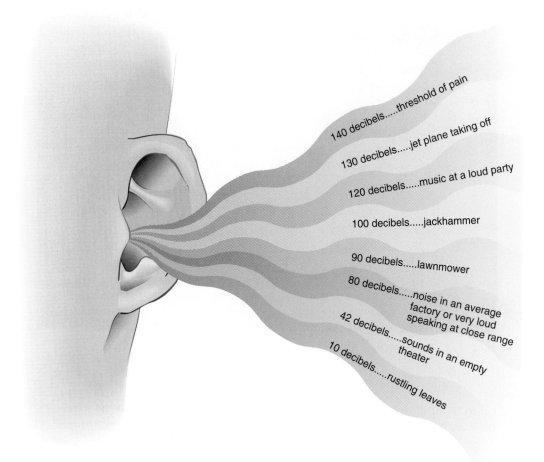

140 decibels.....threshold of pain

130 decibels.....jet plane taking off

120 decibels.....music at a loud party

100 decibels.....jackhammer

90 decibels.....lawnmower

80 decibels.....noise in an average factory or very loud speaking at close range

42 decibels.....sounds in an empty theater

10 decibels.....rustling leaves

FIGURE 12.1   Loudness Levels

As you can see, noise varies considerably. How could you adjust your volume if you were speaking to a "quiet" audience? What if you were competing with a lawnmower outside the building?

rooms, ventilation fans interfere with sound. In the outdoors, words seem to vanish into the open air.

When addressing larger audiences, cut your rate by a third or more. Obviously, you don't go around timing your speaking rate, but you can remind yourself of potential rate problems as you prepare to speak. Get feedback from your instructors and classmates regarding your speaking rate.

3. *Enunciate clearly.* **Enunciation** refers to the crispness and precision with which you form words. Good enunciation is the clear, distinct utterance of syllables and words. Most of us are "lip lazy" in normal conver-

sation, however. We slur sounds, drop syllables, and skip over the beginnings and endings of words. This laziness may not inhibit communication between friends, but it can seriously undermine a speaker's intelligibility.

When speaking publicly, force yourself to say *going* instead of *go-in*, *just* instead of *jist*, and *government* instead of *guvment*. You will need to open your mouth wider and force your lips and tongue to form the consonants firmly. If you're having trouble enunciating clearly, ask your instructor for some exercises to improve your performance. (See the box "How to Improve Your Voice" in this chapter.)

4. *Meet standards of pronunciation.* To be intelligible, you must form sounds carefully and meet audience expectations regarding acceptable pronunciation. Even if your words are not garbled, any peculiarity of pronunciation is sure to be noticed by some listeners, and your different pronunciation may distract those listeners and undermine your credibility as a speaker.

A **dialect** is language use—including vocabulary, grammar, and pronunciation—unique to a particular group or region. Your pronunciation and grammatical or syntactical arrangement of words determine your dialect. You may have a foreign accent, a white southern or black northern dialect, a New England twang, or a Hispanic trill. A clash of dialects can result in confusion and frustration for both speaker and listener. Audiences can make negative judgments about the speaker's credibility—about the speaker's education, reliability, responsibility, and capacity for leadership—based solely on dialect.[11] Paralinguists call these judgments *vocal stereotypes.*[12] Wary of vocal stereotypes, many news anchors have adopted a midwestern American dialect, a manner of speaking that is widely accepted across the country. Many speakers also become "bilingual," using their own dialects when facing local audiences but switching to midwestern American when addressing more varied audiences. When you speak, you'll have to decide whether you should use the grammar, vocabulary, and vocal patterns of middle America. The language of your audience is the primary factor to consider.

Variety. As you move from conversations with friends to the enlarged context of public speaking, you may discover that listeners accuse you of monotony in your pitch or rate. When speaking in a large public setting, you should compensate for the greater distance that sounds need to travel by varying certain characteristics of your voice. **Variety** is produced by changes in rate, pitch, stress, and pauses. For example:

1. *Vary your rate.* Earlier, we discussed normal rates of speech. Alter your speaking rate to match your ideas. Slow down to emphasize your own thoughtfulness, or quicken the pace when your ideas are emotionally charged. Observe how Larry King varies his speaking rate from caller to caller or how an evangelist changes pace regularly. A varied rate keeps an audience's attention riveted to the speech.

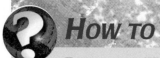

HOW TO

IMPROVE YOUR VOICE

The instructor's manual that accompanies this textbook has several exercises for voice improvement; your instructor can get it from Addison Wesley Longman. If you or others are concerned about the way you use your voice, those exercises can be most useful. Here's a sample of what you can do:

- *Breath control.* Say the entire alphabet, using only one breath. As you practice, try saying it more and more slowly so as to improve your control of exhalation.
- *Control of pitch.* Sing "low, low, low, low," dropping one note of the musical scale each time you sing the word, until you reach the lowest tone you can produce. Then, sing your way back up the scale. Now, sing "high, high, high, high," going up the scale to the highest note you can reach. Sing your way back down. Go up and down, trying to sense the notes you're most comfortable with—your so-called *optimum pitch.* Give most of your speeches around your optimum pitch.
- *Articulatory control.* Pronounce each of the following word groups, making sure that each word can be distinguished from the others. Have someone check your accuracy: jest, gist, just; thin, think, thing; roost, roosts, ghost, ghosts; began, begun, begin; wish, which, witch; affect, effect; twin, twain, twine. Or, try the following tongue twisters:

The sixth sheik's sixth sheep's sick.
Three gray geese in the green grass grazing; gray were the geese and green was the grazing.
Barry, the baby bunny's born by the blue box bearing rubber baby buggy bumpers.

---

2. *Change your pitch.* **Pitch** is the frequency of sound waves in a particular sound. Three aspects of pitch—level, range, and variation—are relevant to effective vocal communication. Your everyday or **optimum pitch level**—whether habitually soprano, alto, tenor, baritone, or bass in range—is adequate for most of your daily communication needs.

The key to successful control of pitch depends on understanding the importance of **pitch variation.** As a general rule, use higher pitches to communicate excitement and lower pitches to create a sense of control or solemnity. Adjust the pitch to fit the emotion being expressed.

Stress.   A third aspect of vocal behavior is **stress,** which is how sounds, syllables, and words are accented. Without vocal stress, you would sound like a computer. Vocal stress is achieved in two ways: through vocal emphasis, and through the judicious use of pauses.

Use Vocal Emphasis.   **Emphasis** is the way that you accent or attack words. You create emphasis principally through increased volume, changes in pitch, or variations in rate. Emphasis also can affect the meaning of your sentences. Notice how the meaning of "Now is the time for action" varies with changes in word emphasis:

1. "NOW is the time for action." (Action needs to take place now, not later.)
2. "Now is the TIME for action." (This is an appropriate time for action.)
3. "Now is the time for ACTION." (We need to act, period.)

A lack of vocal stress not only gives the impression that you are bored, it also causes misunderstandings of your meaning. Changes in rate can be used to add emphasis as well. For example, relatively simple changes can emphasize where you are in an outline: "My s-e-c-o-n-d point is . . ." Several changes in rate also can indicate the relationship among ideas: "We are a country faced with . . . [moderate rate] financial deficits, racial tensions, an energy crunch, a crisis of morality, environmental depletion, government waste . . . [fast rate], and - a - stif - ling - na - tion - al - debt [slow rate]." The ideas pick up speed through the accelerating list of problems but then come to an emphatic halt with the speaker's main concern; the national debt. Such variations in rate emphasize for an audience what is—and what is not—especially important to the speech.

Use Helpful Pauses.   **Pauses** are the intervals of silence between or within words, phrases, or sentences. When placed immediately before a key idea or the climax of a story, they can create suspense: "And the winner is [pause]!" When placed after a major point, they can add emphasis; "And who on this campus earns more than the president of the university? The football coach [pause]." Inserted at the proper moment, a dramatic pause can express feelings more forcefully than words. Clearly, silence can be a highly effective communicative tool if used intelligently and sparingly—and if not embarrassingly prolonged.

Sometimes speakers fill silences in their discourse with sounds: *um, ah, er, well-ah, you-know,* and other meaningless fillers. Undoubtedly, you've heard speakers say, "Today, ah, er, I would like, you know, to speak to you, um, about a pressing, well-uh, like, a pressing problem facing this, uh, campus." Such vocal intrusions convey feelings of hesitancy and lack of confidence. Make a concerted effort to remove these intrusions from your speech. In addition, avoid too many pauses and those that seem artificial, because they can make you appear manipulative or overrehearsed.

On the other hand, do not be afraid of silences. Pauses allow you to stress important ideas, such as the punch line in a story or argument. Pauses also intensify the involvement of listeners in emotional situations, such as when Barbara Walters or Matt Lauer pauses for reflection during an interview.

Controlling the Emotional Quality

A listener's judgment of a speaker's personality and emotional commitment often centers on that speaker's vocal quality—the fullness or thinness of the tones and whether the sound is harsh, husky, mellow, nasal, breathy, or resonant. Depending on your vocal quality, an audience may judge you as being angry, happy, confident, fearful, sincere, or sad.

Fundamental to a listener's reaction to vocal quality are **emotional characterizers,** which are cues about a speaker's emotional state. These include laughing, crying, whispering, inhaling, or exhaling.[13] Emotional characterizers combine with your words to communicate subtle shades of meaning. Consider a few of the many ways you can say, "I can't believe I ate the whole thing." You might say it as though you were reporting a fact, as if you cannot believe you ate it all, or as though eating the entire thing were an impossible achievement. You also might say it as though you were expressing doubts about whether you actually did eat the whole thing. As you say the sentence to express those different meanings, you might laugh or inhale sharply, altering your emotional characterizers. Such changes are important cues to the audience regarding how to understand what you're saying.

The vocal qualities you can control become prime determiners of your vocal style: Intelligibility is a base characteristic, for without it you have no chance whatsoever of reaching anyone with your message; variety and stress help listeners pick out the especially important parts. Emotional characterizers add the human dimensions, providing invaluable cues as to how your message should not only understood but also responded to—how we are to feel about your subject matter. These sorts of paralinguistic or vocal connections knit a speaker and the audience together.

Practicing Vocal Control

Do not assume that you'll be able to master in a day all the vocal skills we've described. To attain them, you have to train your mind, convincing yourself to express certain kinds of feelings publicly before you can, for example, fully modulate multiple vocal qualities. You also have to work on your vocal instrument—to practice aloud. Practice may not make perfect, but it certainly won't hurt. Speak in front of as many different kinds of audiences as you can, working in intelligibility, variety, and stress; this helps you engrain constructive changes in your speaking style and into everyday conversation. Then, you should be ready to seek the sense of conversationality so highly valued in this society in the enlarged context of public speaking itself.

USING YOUR BODY TO COMMUNICATE

Just as your voice communicates and shapes ideas through the oral-aural channel, so your physical behavior before an audience helps control listeners' understandings of and reactions to what you're saying. The visual channel is so important that even our word *idea* is derived from the Greek word "to see."[14]

Both the oral and visual channels can be used to create a common under-standing of your ideas and how you want others to feel about them. Questions of physical behavior usually are talked about as **nonverbal communication.**

Assessing Different Dimensions of Nonverbal Communication

Some use the phrase **nonverbal communication** to refer to all nonlinguistic as-pects of interpersonal interaction, but here, we focus on physical behavior in communication settings. In recent years, research has reemphasized the im-portant role of physical behavior in effective oral communication.[15] Basically, three generalizations about nonverbal communication should guide your speechmaking:

1. *Speakers reveal and reflect their emotional states through their nonverbal behav-iors.* Your listeners read your feelings toward yourself, your topic, and your audience from your facial expressions. Consider the contrast be-tween a speaker who walks briskly to the front of the room, head held high, and one who shuffles, head bowed and arms limp. Communica-tions scholar Dale G. Leathers summarized a good deal of research on nonverbal communication processes: "Feelings and emotions are more accurately exchanged by nonverbal than verbal means. . . . The non-verbal portion of communication conveys meanings and intentions that are relatively free from deception, distortion, and confusion."[16]

2. *The speaker's nonverbal cues enrich or elaborate the message that comes through words.* A solemn face reinforces the dignity of a wedding. The words "We must do either *this* or *that*" can be illustrated with appropriate arm-and-hand gestures. Taking a few steps to one side tells an audi-ence you're moving from one argument to another, and a smile en-hances your comment on how happy you are to be there. The degree of formality expressed through nonverbal channels also depends on the cultural context. In some cultures (Denmark, Italy), the expecta-tion is for greater informality in public settings; in others (France, Ger-many), being highly formal is the requisite behavior.[17]

3. *Nonverbal messages form a reciprocal interaction between speaker and listener.* Listeners frown, smile, shift nervously in their seats, and engage in many types of nonverbal behavior. The physical presence of listeners and the natural tendency of human beings to mirror each other when close together mean that nonverbal behavior is a mechanism of social bonding. For this chapter, though, we concentrate on the speaker's control of physical behavior in four areas: *proxemics, movement and stance, facial expressions,* and *gestures.*

Proxemics. **Proxemics** is the use of space by human beings. Two components of proxemics—physical arrangement and distance—are especially relevant to public speakers:

1. *Physical arrangements*—the layout of the room in which you're speak-ing, including the presence or absence of a lectern, the seating plan,

the location of chalkboards and similar aids, and any physical barriers between you and your audience.

2. *Distance*—The extent or degree of separation between you and your audience.[18]

Both of these components bear on the message you communicate publicly. Typical speaking situations involve a speaker facing a seated audience. Objects in the physical space—the lectern, a table, several flags—tend to set the speaker apart from the listeners. This setting apart is both physical and psychological. Literally as well as figuratively, objects can stand in the way of open communication. To create a more informal atmosphere, reduce the physical barriers in the setting: You might stand beside or in front of the lectern instead of behind it. In very informal settings, you might even sit on the front edge of a table while talking. So, what influences your use of physical space?

1. *The formality of the occasion.* The more solemn or formal the occasion, the more barriers will be used; on highly formal occasions, speakers may even use an elevated platform or stage.
2. *The nature of the material.* Extensive quoted material or statistical evidence may require you to use a lectern; the use of visual aids often demands equipment such as an easel, VCR, or overhead projector.
3. *Your personal preference.* You may feel more at ease speaking from behind rather than in front of the lectern.

The distance component of proxemics adds a second set of considerations. In most situations, you'll be talking at what anthropologist Edward T. Hall has termed a "public distance"—12 feet or more from your listeners"[19] (see Figure 12.2). To communicate with people at that distance, you obviously cannot rely on your normal speaking voice or subtle changes in posture or movement. Instead, you must compensate for the distance by using larger gestures, broader shifts of your body, and increased vocal energy. In contrast, you should lower your vocal volume and restrict the breadth of your gestures when addressing only a few individuals at a closer distance.

Movement and Posture.   The ways you move and stand provide a second set of bodily cues for your audience. **Movement** includes physical shifts from place to place, and **posture** refers to the relative relaxation or rigidity and vertical position of the body. Movement and posture can communicate ideas about yourself to an audience. The speaker who stands stiffly and erectly may, without uttering a word, be saying, "This is a formal occasion" or "I'm tense, even afraid, of this audience." The speaker who leans forward, physically reaching out to the audience, often is saying, "I'm interested in you. I want you to understand and accept my ideas." The speaker who sits casually on the front edge of a table and assumes a relaxed posture may suggest informality and readiness to engage in a dialogue with listeners. Note, however, that sitting on a table, crossing your legs, and showing the soles of your shoes to the audience, while

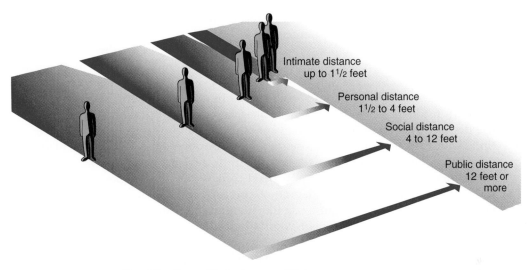

Intimate distance
up to 1 1/2 feet

Personal distance
1 1/2 to 4 feet

Social distance
4 to 12 feet

Public distance
12 feet or
more

FIGURE 12.2 Classification of Interhuman Distance

Source: *Edward T. Hall,* The Hidden Dimension *(New York: Doubleday, 1969).*

"normal" in most U. S. settings, is viewed as anything but in other cultures, where such actions are perceived as impolite—or even insulting.

Movement and postural adjustments regulate communication. As a public speaker, you can, for instance, move from one end of a table to the other to indicate a change in topic. You also can accomplish the same purpose by changing your posture. At other times, you can move toward your audience when making an especially important point. In each case, you're using your body to reinforce transitions in your subject or emphasize a matter of special concern.

Keep in mind that your posture and movements can work against you as well. Aimless and continuous pacing is distracting. Nervous bouncing or swaying makes listeners seasick. An excessively erect stance increases tension in listeners. Your movements should be purposeful and meant to enhance the meaning of your words. Stance and movement can help your communicative effort and produce the impressions of self-assurance and control that you want to exhibit.

Facial Expressions.   When you speak, your facial expressions function in several ways. First, they communicate much about yourself and your feelings. Researchers Paul Ekman, Wallace V. Friesen, and Phoebe Ellsworth call these **affect displays**—facial signals of emotion that an audience perceives when scanning your face to see how you feel about yourself and about them.[20]

Second, facial changes provide listeners with cues that help them interpret the contents of your message. Are you being ironic or satirical? Are you sure of your conclusions? Is this a harsh or a pleasant message? Researchers tell us that a high percentage of the information conveyed in a typical message is communicated nonverbally, and psychologist Albert Mehrabian has devised a formula to account for the emotional impact of the different components of a speaker's message. Words, he says, contribute 7 percent, vocal elements 38 percent, and facial expression 55 percent.[21]

Third, the "display" elements of your face—your eyes, especially—establish a visual bond between you and your listeners. Our culture values eye contact. The speaker who looks people squarely in the eye is likely to be perceived as earnest, sincere, forthright, and self-assured. In other words, regular eye contact with listeners helps establish a speaker's credibility. Speakers who look at the floor, read from notes, or deliver speeches to the back wall sever the visual bond with their audiences and lose credibility. Conversely, some cultures place a higher value on indirect eye contact, wherein the speaker avoids making direct contact with the audience. You need to consider the people you will be talking to and ascertain their degree of comfort with direct eye contact. You cannot assume that just because you like it and understand its meaning the audience likewise will accommodate your behavior.

Of course, you cannot control your face completely, which probably is why listeners search it so carefully for clues to your feelings. You can, however, make sure that your facial messages do not belie your verbal ones: When you're uttering angry words, your face should be communicating anger; when you're pleading with your listeners, your eyes should be engaging them intently. In short, let your face mirror your feelings. That's one of the reasons it's there!

Gestures.   **Gestures** are purposeful movements of the head, shoulders, arms, hands, and other areas of the body that support and illustrate the ideas you're expressing. Fidgeting with your clothing and notecards or playing with your hair are not purposeful gestures. They distract from the ideas you're communicating. The effective public speaker commonly uses three kinds of gestures:

1. *Conventional gestures* are physical movements with specific meanings assigned by custom or convention. These gestures *condense* ideas: they are shorthand expressions or symbols of things or ideas that would require many words to describe fully. A speaker can use the raised-hand "stop" gesture to interrupt listeners who are drawing premature conclusions or the "V for victory" sign when congratulating them for jobs well done.
2. *Descriptive gestures* are physical movements that describe the idea to be communicated. Speakers often depict the size, shape, or location of an object by movements of their hands and arms—they draw pictures for listeners. You might indicate the size of a box by drawing it in the air with a finger or raise an arm to indicate someone's height.
3. *Indicators* are movements of the hands, arms, or other parts of the body that express feelings. Speakers throw up their arms when disgusted, pound the lectern when angry, shrug their shoulders when puzzled, or point a threatening finger when issuing a warning. Such gestures communicate emotions to listeners and encourage similar responses in them. Facial expressions and other body cues usually reinforce such gestures.[22]

You can improve your gestures through practice. As you practice, you'll obtain better results by keeping in mind four factors that influence the effectiveness of gestures: relaxation, vigor and definiteness, proper timing, and appropriateness.

First, if your muscles are tense, your movements will be stiff and your gestures awkward. You should make a conscious effort to relax your muscles before you start to speak. You might warm up by taking a few steps, shrugging your shoulders, flexing your muscles, or breathing deeply.

Second, useful gestures are natural and animated. They reflect your emotional state and help you to physiologically describe ideas in ways that others would. Exaggerated arm movements, repetitive chopping, and random twitches of your hands call attention to your body itself, not to the ideas being formed with its aid. The best gestures reflect important mental and emotional states.

Third, timing is crucial to effective gestures. The stroke of a gesture (the shake of a fist or movement of a finger) should fall on or slightly before the point the gesture is emphasizing. Just try making a gesture after the world or phrase it was intended to reinforce has been spoken; if you do that regularly, people will think of you as either a drunk or a comedian. Timing gestures effectively demands that you be in a state of readiness, usually with arms by your sides and often with your hands resting on the lectern or held in a relaxed fashion in front of your bellybutton so they're ready to move into action. Practice making gestures until they're habitual, and then use them when you want to visualize your ideas and feelings.

Fourth, appropriateness is a serious matter when facing diverse cultural groups. Pointing at an audience or using the "A-OK" gesture may work well with most Caucasian audience members, but for non-Caucasians, these gestures are seen as insulting.[23] Knowing in advance what will insult your audience or reveal your insensitivity to their cultural norms allows you to concentrate on those gestures that are appropriate to the context.

Adapting Nonverbal Behavior to Your Presentations

You'll never completely control your physical behavior, but you can gain skill in orchestrating your gestures and other movements. You can make some conscious decisions about how to use your body together with the other channels of communication to communicate effectively. Here are some suggestions:

1. *Plan a proxemic relationship with your audience that reflects your own needs and attitudes toward your subject and your listeners.* If you're comfortable behind a lectern, use it; however, remember that it's a potential barrier between you and your listeners. If you want your whole body to be visible to the audience you feel the need to have your notes at eye level, stand beside the lectern and arrange your notecards on it. If you want to relax your body, sit behind a table or desk, but compensate for the resulting loss of action by increasing your volume. If you feel relaxed and want to be open to your audience, stand in front of a table or desk. Learn to be yourself while speaking publicly.

   Consider your listeners' needs as well. The farther you are from them, the more important it is for them to have a clear view of you, the harder you must work to project your words, and the broader your physical movements must be. The speaker who crouches behind a lectern in an auditorium of 300 people soon loses contact. Think of

A person's body also may be a communicative vehicle; artists depend as much on the rhythm of the body as on the voice to communicate personality and emotional flavoring in a message.

large lecture classes you've attended or outdoor political rallies you've witnessed. Recall the delivery patterns that worked effectively in such situations, and put them to work for you.

2. *Adapt the physical setting to your communicative needs.* If you're going to use visual aids such as a chalkboard, flipchart, or working model, remove the tables, chairs, and other objects that might obstruct your audience's view. Increase intimacy by arranging chairs in a small circle, or stress formality by using a lectern.

3. *Adapt the size of your gestures and amount of your movement to the size of the audience.* Remember what Hall noted about public distance in communication, and realize that subtle changes of facial expression or small hand movements cannot be seen clearly in large rooms or auditoriums. Although many auditoriums have a raised platform and a slanted floor to enhance visibility, you should adjust to the distance between yourself and your audience by making your movements and gestures larger.

4. *Continuously scan your audience from side to side and front to back, looking specific individuals in the eye.* Your head should not be in constant motion; *continuously* does not imply rhythmic, nonstop bobbing. Rather, take all your listeners into your field of vision periodically, and establish firm visual bonds with individuals occasionally. Such bonds enhance your credibility and keep your auditors' attention riveted on you.

Some speakers identify three audience members—one to the left, one in the middle, and one to the right—and make sure they regularly move from one to the other of them. For those who do not have trouble moving from side to side, another technique is to do the same thing from front to back, especially if the audience is not too big. Making sure that you're achieving even momentary eye contact with specific listeners in different parts of the audience creates the sense of visual bonding that you want.

5. *Use your body to communicate your feelings about what you're saying.* When you're angry, don't be afraid to gesture vigorously. When you're expressing tenderness, let that message come across your relaxed face. In other words, when you communicate publicly, use the same emotional indicators as you do when you talk to individuals on a one-to-one basis.

6. *Use your body to regulate the pace of your presentation and to control transitions.* Shift your weight as your speech moves from one idea to another. Move more when you're speaking more rapidly, and reduce bodily action and gestures accordingly when you're slowing down to emphasize particular ideas.

7. *Use your full repertoire of gestures while talking publicly.* You probably do this in everyday conversation without even thinking about it, so recreate that behavior when addressing an audience. Physical readiness is the key. Keep your hands and arms free and loose so you can call them into action easily, quickly, and naturally. Let your hands rest comfortably at your sides, relaxed but ready. Then, as you unfold the ideas of your speech, use descriptive gestures to indicate sizes, shapes, or relationships, making sure the movements are large enough to be seen in the back row. Use conventional gestures to give visual dimension to your spoken ideas. Keep in mind there is no right number of gestures to use, but as you practice, think of the kinds of bodily and gestural actions that complement your message and purpose.

Using your voice and body as the actual instruments of communication—as the vehicles that inject mere ideas with the presence and emotions of actual human beings—will significantly enhance your chances for gaining audience support for those ideas. With practice, the vocal adjustments that now sound strange to your ears and the physical movements that still feel a bit awkward will become second nature to you. You may not move with the grace of a ballerina, but everyone can learn to visualize and vocalize important dimensions of meaning in public speaking situations.

You live in a society that prizes great sound and great pictures—digitized audio and video experiences. Keep telling yourself that even more powerful than digitized reproduction is the compelling presence of a living, breathing human being. That's you behind the lectern. Unleash your vocal-visual potential for energized public talk.

CHAPTER SUMMARY

Speakers must learn to maximize the advantage of their face-to-face presence in oral communication, in part by understanding that oral communication processes are at their best when talk is *aggregative, agonistic/invitational,* and *situational*—that is, when they are completely adapted to the particular time and place in which it is occurring. Your body is a site of performance—it performs the self as you speak. Seeking *synchronicity* with your audience, wherein the message the body communicates is one that meets the expectations of the audience, will assist in legitimizing your performance as a speaker. Regarding practical advice on controlling the voice, remember that a flexible speaking voice has *intelligibility, variety,* and understandable *stress* patterns. *Volume, rate, enunciation,* and *pronunciation* affect intelligibility, as do *dialects.* Changes in *rate, pitch, stress,* and *pause* patterns create variety in your presentations. *Emotional characterizers* communicate subtle shades of meaning to listeners. Regarding nonverbal (i.e., physical or bodily) communication, three generalizations are significant:

- Speakers reveal and reflect their emotional states through their nonverbal behaviors.
- Nonverbal cues enrich or elaborate the speaker's message.
- Nonverbal messages form bonds between speaker and listener.

Speakers knowledgeable about *proxemics* can use space to create physical and psychological distance or intimacy. A speaker's *movement* and *posture* can regulate thought and feeling states. *Facial displays* communicate feelings, provide important cues to meaning, establish a visual bond with listeners, and enforce speaker credibility. If relaxed, definite, and well-timed, *gestures* enhance listener response to ideas. Speakers commonly use *conventional gestures, descriptive gestures,* and *indicators.* Practice is the name of the game—practice making your voice and body effective instruments of oral communication in a society that prizes good sound and good pictures.

KEY TERMS

affect displays (p. 287)

conversationality (p. 278)

dialect (p. 281)

emotional characterizers (p. 284)

emphasis (p. 283)

enunciation (p. 280)

gestures (p. 288)

intelligibility (p. 278)

kairos (p. 276)

movement (p. 286)

nonverbal communication (p. 285)

optimum pitch level (p. 282)

pauses (p. 283)

pitch (p. 282)

pitch variation (p. 282)

posture (p. 286)

proxemics (p. 284)

rate (p. 284)

speech delivery (p. 274)

stress (p. 283)

synchronicity (p. 277)

variety (p. 281)

volume (p. 279)

ASSESSMENT ACTIVITIES

1. Divide the class into teams, and play charades. (For rules, see David Jauner, "Charades as a Teaching Device," *Communication Education* 20 [1971]: 302.) A game of charades not only will loosen you up psychologically but will help sen-

sitize everyone to the variety of small but perceptible cues you read when interpreting messages. Talk about those cues at the end of the game.

2. Select a poem, and read it aloud. As you read, change your volume, rate, pitch, and emphasis, and use pauses. Practice reading the poem in several ways to heighten different emotions or emphasize alternative interpretations. Record three or four readings, and play them back for evaluation. Write a paragraph on each reading—describing the sound of your voice and emotional texture—and turn them in along with the tape.

REFERENCES

1. See, especially, Chapter 3 on the psychodynamics of sound in Walter J. Ong, *Orality and Literacy: The Technologizing of the Word* (London: Methuen, 1982).

2. Harold M. Zullow, "American Exceptionalism and the Quadrennial Peak in Optimism," *Presidential Campaigns and American Self Images,* eds. Arthur H. Miller and Bruce E. Gronbeck (Boulder, CO: Westview Press, 1994), 214–230.

3. Sonja K. Foss, and Cindy L. Griffin, "Beyond Persuasion: A Proposal for an Invitational Rhetoric," *Communication Monographs* 62 (1995):2–18.

4. Ibid., 5.

5. Elizabeth Grosz, "Bodies and Knowledge: Feminism and the Crisis of Reason," *Feminist Epistemologies,* eds. Linda Alcoff and Elizabeth Potter (New York: Routledge, 1993), 199.

6. David Graver, "The Actor's Bodies," *Text and Performance Quarterly* 17 (July 1997): 221–235.

7. Catherine Fouquet, "The Unavoidable Detour: Must a History of Women Begin with the History of their Bodies?" *Writing Women's History,* trans. Felicia Pheasant, ed. Michelle Perrot (Oxford: Blackwell, 1992 [Originally published in 1984]), 55.

8. Maurice Bloch, "Introduction," *Political Language and Oratory in Traditional Society,* ed. Maurice Bloch (New York: Academic Press, 1975) 7.

9. Kwesi Yankah, "Oratory in Akan Society," *Discourse and Society* 2 (1991):58.

10. Thomas Frentz, "Rhetorical Conversation, Time, and Moral Action," *Quarterly Journal of Speech* 71 (1985):1–18.

11. Mark Knapp, *Essentials of Nonverbal Communication* (New York: Holt, Rinehart and Winston, 1980).

12. Klaus R. Scherer, H. London, and Garret Wolf, "The Voice of Competence: Paralinguistic Cues and Audience Evaluation," *Journal of Research in Personality* 7 (1973):31–44; Jitendra Thakerer and Howard Giles, "They Are—So They Spoke: Noncontent Speech Stereotypes," *Language and Communication* 1 (1981):255–261; and Peter A. Andersen, Myron W. Lustig, and Janis F. Andersen, "Regional Patterns of Communication in the United States: A Theoretical Perspective," *Communication Monographs* 54 (1987):128–144.

13. Bruce L. Brown, William J. Strong, and Alvin C. Rencher, "Perceptions of Personality from Speech: Effects of Manipulations of Acoustical Parameters," *Journal of the Acoustical Society of America* 54 (1973):29–35.

14. Chris Jenks, "The Centrality of the Eye in Western Culture," *Visual Culture,* ed. Chris Jenks (New York: Routledge, 1995), 1.

15. Much of the foundational research is summarized in Mark L. Knapp, *Nonverbal Communication in Human Interaction,* 2nd ed. (New York: Holt, Rinehart and Winston, 1978).

16. Dale G. Leathers, *Nonverbal Communication Systems* (Boston: Allyn and Bacon, 1975), 4–5.

17. For a succinct review of how one might act, see Elizabeth Urech, *Speaking Globally: Effective Presentations Across International and Cultural Boundaries* (Dover, NH: Kegan Page Limited, 1998).

18. For a fuller discussion, see Leathers, 52–59 (n. 16).

19. Edward T. Hall, *The Hidden Dimension* (New York: Doubleday, 1969). The important matter here is not the exact distance, of course, but the idea that speakers must vary multiple aspects of their physical and vocal behavior as distances between them and their audiences grow.

20. Paul Ekman, Wallace V. Friesen, and Phoebe Ellsworth, *Emotion in the Human Face,* 2nd ed. (Cambridge, England: Cambridge University Press, 1982).

21. Cited in Robert Rivlin and Karen Gravelle, *Deciphering the Senses: The Expanding World of Human Perception* (New York: Simon and Schuster, 1984), 98. Of course, such numbers are only formulaic estimates and are important only as rough proportions of each other. Even if Mehrabian is off by a considerable margin, his basic point—that voice and face are the primary vehicles for emotionally bonding speakers and their audiences—is indisputable.

22. For a more complete system of classifying gestures, see Paul Ekman and Wallace V. Friesen, "Hand Movements," *Journal of Communication* 22 (1972):360.

23. For a succinct review of gestures that are perceived as obscene, see Elizabeth Urech, *Speaking Globally: Effective Presentations Across International and Cultural Boundaries* (Dover, NH: Kogan Page Limited, 1998).

Part Four

TYPES

All the ends of speaking are reducible to four; every speech being intended to enlighten the understanding, to please the imagination, to move the passion, or to influence the will. Any one discourse admits only one of these ends as the principal.

George Campbell
The Philosophy
of Rhetoric (1776)

Chapter 13

Speeches to Inform

A student, Ben, came in one day to ask his instructor how he could make an informative speech about the Vietnam War and its impacts on American life relevant to his listeners. "All that interests my classmates are bar hopping, sports, movies, dances, and television," he said. "Well, that's the key, Ben," said the instructor. "Bar hopping?" "No, the mass media! Think of all the television programs and films that have focused on Vietnam. For movies, we've had Coming Home, Apocalypse Now, The Deer Hunter, Full Metal Jacket, Platoon, Born on the Fourth of July, Heaven and Earth, The Killing Fields, *and all the Rambo movies. On television, we've had docudramas such as HBO's 'Vietnam War Stories'; on PBS, 'Vietnam: The Documentary'; on prime-time television such series as* Magnum P.I., Hill Street Blues, Tour of Duty, *and* China Beach. *And there's more! Use these movies and TV programs as ways to reach your audience."*

Reaching your audience, as we've been saying throughout this book, is the bottom line. You can talk until the sun sets and then keep talking well into the night, but if you don't reach your audience, you can forget it. Your listeners are aswarm in facts and information. You've got to find ways to grab them by the scruff of their psychological necks and the seat of their psychological pants, get them to sit up and take note, and then package facts and ideas in ways they can understand and remember. That's what informative speaking is all about

In this chapter, we first talk about information and the processes whereby "facts" become usable human "knowledge." From this, we examine the basic motives that you might tap into for "grabbing them by their psyches" and willing them to listen to what you have to say. Then, we discuss the essential features of informative speeches, after which we can examine four types of speeches and ways of building them to maximize your chances for success.

FACTS, KNOWLEDGE, AND THE INFORMATION AGE

Our society seems to worship facts. A staggering amount of information is available to us, particularly because of technologies such as electronic media, photostatic printing, miniaturized circuitry, fax machines, and digitized data storage and retrieval systems. Jumping onto America Online or your school's access to the World Wide Web puts you on an information highway with more—and bigger—lanes than the Santa Monica Freeway. The entire Indiana University library is available online, as are major collections of data from around the world. Detective Joe Friday from the old *Dragnet* television series would never dare say "Just the facts, Ma'am," today, for he'd immediately drown in data.

Furthermore, as Joe Friday knew, mere facts are not enough. Until he put those facts into a coherent order that turned them into elements of a scenario—a story of a crime—he had nothing but isolated factoids. Only after that information was patterned and hooked in cause-effect chains, and only after those chains were contextualized into the lives of particular people, did the facts produce the story of the crime. Joe Friday not only had to gather the facts but humanize them—that is, use them to probe motivations, plausible human activities, and matters of opportunity and access to the means of crime. Without structuring, clarifying, and interpreting facts, the information at hand is all but useless.

Information must be turned by competent speakers into knowledge. Think of **facts** as statements about the world upon which two or more people agree; "Gronbeck's house is 44 feet long" is a fact, which could be verified by some folks taking a tape measure to it. **Information** is a collection of facts associated with some topic. Consider the information shown in Table 13.1, which is derived from the 2509 sites Shopsearch lists for those wishing to order items via the Internet.

The challenge is to turn this collection of information into human **knowledge**—information given human significance—through your own interpretation. For example, 70 and 80 percent of the stores in Table 13.1 report orders via traditional means: mail and phone. A little less than two-thirds of the sites

TABLE 13.1 Ordering Methods on the Internet

Order Method	Number of Stores	Percent
E-mail	1450	57.88
E-mail (PGP)	12	0.47
Fax	1474	58.84
Form (secure)	675	26.94
Form (unsecure)	826	32.97
Mail	1760	70.25
Phone	2023	80.75

Source: *http://www.shopsearch.com/stats.htm*

report orders coming via fax and email. What does this mean? The Internet is growing as a source for orders via e-mail, but the many orders using more traditional means suggest people still are accustomed to older—and perhaps slower—ways of doing things. On the other hand, the growth of e-mail and fax orders also suggests that e-commerce is a growing phenomenon. Your interpretation connects the "facts" with human activity, thereby transforming mere facts into useful knowledge of buying habits.

This is what informative speaking is about: turning facts into information and then information into knowledge. To make the most of your interpretation of facts and their presentation to audiences, you also need to think in terms of the motives people have for listening to your ideas.

MOTIVATIONAL APPEALS: ENGAGING LISTENERS WHERE THEY ARE

For our purposes, human behavior will be divided into two categories: activity that results from biological needs, drives, or stimuli; and activity that results from social motives, desires, and deliberate intent.[1] External stimuli such as a stuffy room also can affect your physiological state, and attending classes between noon and 1 P.M. affects students' concentration because they're used to eating then. Satisfying a **biological need,** then, is a matter of giving in to or meeting a physiological urge. **Social motives,** however, are individual goals, desires, or behaviors that result from acting in accordance with your understanding of what others expect or value. Appeals can tap both biological and social motives. "What's a baseball game without a hot dog?" has the potential to appeal to hunger—you rushed to get to the game and haven't eaten yet—and to tradition—eating a hot dog just goes with the game. As this example attests, most biological and social motives are relatively enduring and intimately linked to the cultural environment of your own community. A word to the wise: Never underestimate the power of speech in tapping human desires and, thus, in altering beliefs, attitudes, and values.

Classifying Motives

To enable you to tap into those desires, we first introduce two classification systems that can help you group or cluster together individual motives. Then, we define "motivational appeal" and illustrate ways of expressing individual motives within speeches.

Maslow's Hierarchy of Needs.   A now-classic approach to the study of motives was proposed by Abraham Maslow. **Maslow's hierarchy of needs** has had a major impact on consumer-oriented studies of marketing and sales and on the field of communication studies. According to Maslow, the following categories of needs and desires drive people to think, act, and respond:

- *Physiological:* The needs for food, drink, air, sleep, and sex—the basic bodily "tissue" requirements.

- *Safety:* The needs for security, stability, protection from harm or injury, structure, orderliness, predictability, and freedom from fear and chaos.
- *Love and belongingness:* The needs for devotion and warm affection with lovers, spouses, children, parents, and close friends; for feeling a part of social groups; and for acceptance and approval.
- *Esteem:* The needs for self-esteem based on achievements, mastery, competence, confidence, freedom, and independence, and for recognition by others expressed in reputation, prestige, recognition, and status.
- *Self-actualization:* The need for self-fulfillment, for realizing individual potential and actualizing capabilities, and for being true to the essential self and satisfying an aesthetic sensibility.[2]

These needs and desires interrelate biological and social motives. In Maslow's theory, lower-level needs usually must be satisfied, either in whole or in part, before higher-order desires become operative. Maslow labels this interrelationship as the **hierarchy of prepotency,** which is best exemplified by considering the plight of the homeless: They have little time and energy to worry much about esteem or self-actualization, so appeals to such needs would fall on deaf ears in the soup kitchens of U.S. cities. To Maslow, needs or motivational appeals must be aimed at that level in the hierarchy where individuals' lives are centered. For the homeless, which needs are most salient at any given moment? Food and shelter would appear to be more significant needs than self-actualization. Using Maslow's strategy focuses your message on the most critical level of the hierarchy—where your audience will receive the greatest impact of the appeal being made.

McClelland's Motive Types. Generally, there are three primary motives under which more specific drives can be subsumed: affiliation, achievement, and power or social influence. **Affiliation motives** focus on the desire to belong to a group, to be well liked and accepted. **Achievement motives** relate to both the intrinsic and extrinsic desire for success, adventure, creativity, and personal enjoyment. **Power motives** involve activities in which influence over others is the primary ob-

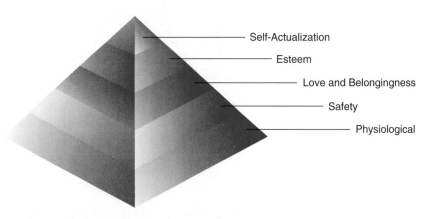

Self-Actualization
Esteem
Love and Belongingness
Safety
Physiological

FIGURE 13.1 Maslow's Heirarchy of Needs

TABLE 13.2 Comparing Maslow and McClelland

Motive Appeal	Maslow	McClelland
Prestige	Esteem	Achievement
Loyalty	Belongingness	Affiliation
Authority	Self-actualization	Power

jective.[3] These broad clusters are critical in considering your overall purpose in speaking. For example, consider the distinction between *affiliation* and *power:* will you appeal to your listeners' sense of belongingness or their sense of dominance? It's important as well to think of the relationships between *power* and *achievement* motives: Do you approach audience members with a focus on their desires to control others or their hopes for personal development and self-satisfaction? **McClelland's motive types** help you target your exploration of the specific appeal that might be most useful in addressing your audience. These motive clusters also fit well with Maslow's hierarchical approach, as Table 13.2 illustrates.

Motive Clusters

Thus far, we've treated motives as general concepts. Translating any of these into specific appeals is the focus of this section. We now are ready to move from Maslow's hierarchy and McClelland's clusters to employing specific appeals in speeches. By understanding the general thrust of each **motive cluster** and its specific appeals, you'll be in a good position to choose among the appeals we've identified when preparing your speeches and to come up with others we don't deal with. In selecting specific appeals, be guided by one principle: *Motivational appeals work only when they are relevant to audience members and have features that listeners can visualize or relate to attributes on which they want to act.* Because the motive terms virtually are self-explanatory, we list here the motive and a phrase that would be typical in its use. As you read, see how many more phrases you can create that express the motive term. For ease of reference, we employ affiliation, achievement, and power as the key clusters or groupings under which the motive terms fall.

The Affiliation Cluster. Affiliation motives are dominated by a desire for acceptance or approval. They're more focused on the social or interpersonal bonds attributed to people than with personal success or power over others.[4]

- *Companionship.* "Birds of a feather flock together."
- *Conformity.* "To get along, you need to go along."
- *Deference/dependence.* "Nine out of ten doctors recommend . . ."
- *Sympathy/generosity.* "For only one dollar a day, you could be the parent this child has never known."
- *Loyalty.* "For the past 10 years, those who have worked for the company the longest, who have lived through the bad times as well as the good times, have been the foundation on which our success is based; as new employees, I hope you will follow their example; if you do, we will surely prosper well into the future."

- *Tradition.* "It is through our sacred rituals and ceremonies that we are known as a people."
- *Reverence/worship.* "As God gives us the light to see the right, so will we act."
- *Sexual attraction.* "Nothing gets between me and my Calvins."

The Achievement Cluster.   Achievement motives are focused on individual urges, desires, and goals—a concern for self and for excellence, prestige, and success. The fourth and fifth levels of Maslow's hierarchy generally fit here; once your basic physiological and social needs are satisfied, you become centered on personal accomplishment. These motivational appeals are aimed at individual members of the audience.

- *Acquisition/saving.* "Earn good money now in our new Checking-Plus accounts!"
- *Success/display.* "Successful executives carry the Connerton electronic organizer."
- *Pride.* "Lose weight through our diet plan and feel great about your body."
- *Prestige.* "L'Oréal—Because you're worth it!"
- *Adventure/change.* "Come to Marlboro Country!"
- *Perseverance.* "If at first you don't succeed, try, try again.'"
- *Creativity.* "Dare to be different: Design your own major!"
- *Curiosity.* "Curiosity killed the cat; satisfaction brought him back."
- *Personal enjoyment.* "Let the good times roll!"

The Power Cluster.   All appeals in the power cluster focus on influence or control over others or the environment. All motives in this group feature appeals to one's place in the social hierarchy—a dominant place. People with power motives seek to manipulate or control others, but not all uses of power are negative. With power comes social responsibility—the demand that power be used in socially approved ways to benefit the group, community, and society. Appeals to power also depend heavily on appeals to affiliation, because power is most constructively used when people see it as being in their best interest to grant power to another. Appeals to power are not equivalent to forcing people to do things. Ethically, you'll need to reconcile appeals to power with those to the affiliation needs of your audience to maximize your chance of success.

- *Aggression.* "We must fight for our rights—if we are to be heard, we dare not allow others to silence us."
- *Authority/dominance.* "Under our organization's by-laws, we have the right to pursue issues in the manner we have undertaken."
- *Defense.* "Only a mean-spirited and vindictive person would draw conclusions prior to having heard all of the available information; we need to give the accused the chance to clear her name."
- *Fear.* "Friends don't let friends drive drunk."
- *Autonomy/independence.* "Just do it."

In specific terms, a **motivational appeal** is an attempt to code or translate a biological or social motive into language. Consider using the social motive *pres-*

Advertisers adapt motivational appeals to target audiences; this advertisement appears in Inc.*—a business-oriented magazine. How might this ad be revised for a sports-oriented magazine?* (Source: Inc. *magazine, January 1999, p. 35.*)

tige: "If you're elected president of this organization, people will look up to you" is an attempt to work an appeal to prestige into the language of a speech. You have two choices when attempting to encode motives into the language of speech: the **visualization process** (verbal depiction)[5] to project a scene or setting in which people are enjoying the advantages of accepting your ideas, or the **attribution process** (verbal association)[6] in claiming that someone is acting on the basis of specific motives.

Suppose you wanted your classmates to join in a demonstration against a proposed tuition hike when the Board of Regents is in town next month. Most students would, of course, like to see the school hold the line on tuition, but many would be reluctant to protest publicly. Your best bet to engage them might well be to visualize various motives:

Just think of what we can accomplish. If we all *[affiliation]* gather in front of the Administration Building, we can show the regents that this is a serious matter. We can show the regents that we're as much a part of the decision-making process as they are *[authority]* and that our voice *[independence]* deserves to be heard as much as theirs. When we present our petition to the President of the Board, even after he's tried to ignore us *[perseverance],* he'll see that we're serious and will have to admit we've got a right to be heard *[success/display].* There's no need to be afraid *[fear]* when you're among friends *[companionship]* in a cause that's right *[pride].* On that day, we'll demonstrate our solidarity *[loyalty]* and force the Board *[aggression]* to listen to our side of the story!

You also can relate motivational concepts directly to other concepts through what is technically called "a process of attribution." Instead of seeking to visualize the appeal in the audience's mind, you assert an association between an object and a specific motive appeal. You do this everyday when claiming someone acted on the basis of specific motives, such as honesty or conformity. In addition, through redefinition and relabeling, you can change the audience's attributes that they associate with a specific event or person: "While the political candidate for Governor has been labeled in the press as uncaring and unconcerned about our situation, I can tell you from firsthand experience that she is indeed committed to our cause." This process of attribution attempts to shift from a negative motive attributed to a person to one that is positive.

This discussion of individual motivational appeals is not designed to present the human psyche as if it were orderly and consistent. Rather, we're trying to give you a basic understanding of human motivation and various kinds of appeals you can use to enhance your rhetorical effectiveness. Even in all their confusing aspects, humans usually act in a motivated way. Hence, we turn next to questions concerning the use of these appeals in speech development.

Using Motivational Appeals in Speech Preparation

The material we've discussed thus far raises an extremely important question: How do you decide which motivational appeals to use in your speech? Precise choices depend on the specific group of listeners you face, the occasion, and even your own preferences and motives for speaking, but three general factors should guide your thinking about motivational appeals: the type of speech you are to give, the demographic characteristics of your audience, and your personal predilections.

Throughout the discussion of motivational appeals, we've suggested that thinking about the type of speech you're delivering helps you select appeals. For example, appeals to individuality often appear in persuasive and actuative speeches, the goals of which are to free people from previous modes of thinking.

MOTIVATIONAL APPEALS: DEVELOPING AN INTEGRATED SET

General purpose: Persuade/actuate.

Specific purpose: Having classmates pursue a flexible Bachelor of General Studies (BGS) degree.

Claim: For many students, the BGS is the best available college degree.

1. *[appeal to creativity]* Without a major and with few requirements, the BGS allows you to build a program suited to your individual desires.
2. *[appeal to adventure]* Break away from the crowd, and do something unique in structuring your life here.
3. *[appeal to curiosity]* Explore subjects as deeply as you wish.
4. *[appeal to success]* Get a feeling of achievement from designing and completing your own program.

In contrast, speeches can tap into collective motives—tradition, companionship, defense, deference, conformity, and loyalty. Exploring the demographic characteristics of your audience members—their age, educational level, and so on—also helps you sort through possible motivational appeals. As noted, for example, people with less need to be concerned about survival or safety needs are more likely to respond to appeals to creativity, independence, personal enjoyment, and generosity. As Maslow's hierarchy of prepotency suggests, a speech on urban renewal presented to inner-city tenement dwellers should feature discussions of food, shelter, and safety rather than achievement and self-actualization. Appeals to ethnic traditions and a sense of belonging work well with homogeneous audiences gathered to celebrate such occasions as Hispanic Heritage Week (*Cinco de Mayo*) or Norwegian Independence Day (*Syttende Mai*). Consider, too, McClelland's analysis of motive types, particularly the relationship between affiliation and power motives.

Illustrating the Integration of Motivational Appeals

General purpose: Persuasive/actuative.

Specific purpose: Convince the nonprofessional employees at your school that they need a labor union.

On joining the union for reasons of affiliation:

1. *[conformity]* All your friends are joining.
2. *[dependence]* The union has leaders with the strength to stand up for your rights.
3. *[sympathy]* Unions better understand the way you live and what you need than university professors do.

On joining the union for reasons of power:

1. *[aggression]* If you don't fight for your rights, who will?
2. *[dominance]* With the union, you can take charge of your workplace and run it properly.
3. *[fear]* Without a union, you can be dismissed from your job at any time and for any reason.

General purpose: Persuasive/actuative.

Specific purpose: Convince listeners to take a summer trip to Europe.

1. *[acquisition and savings]* The tour is being offered for a low price of $2000 for 3 weeks.
2. *[independence]* There'll be a minimum of supervision and regimentation.
3. *[companionship]* You'll be traveling with friends and fellow students.

These two examples give you a clear sense of how to integrate affiliation and power and add achievement to the mix in planning a speech. Never will it be the case, of course, that the audience is all achievement-oriented, affiliation-oriented, or power-oriented; life is not that simple. Assessing tendencies, however, will help you select the appeals you want to feature.

Always look to your personal predilections—your own beliefs, attitudes, and values—when framing motivational appeals. Ask yourself questions like these: Am I willing to ask people to act out of fear, or am I committed instead to higher motives such as sympathy and generosity? Do I actually believe in the importance of loyalty and reverence as they relate to this situation? Use the appeals that you think are important—and that you can defend to yourself and others. Appeals mean little without a context for their activation, and informing audiences is one such context.

ESSENTIAL FEATURES OF INFORMATIVE SPEECHES

Your goal as an informative speaker is to make it easy for your listeners to acquire and retain new information. There are five things you can do to help ensure that listeners understand and remember what you say: You should strive for (1) clarity, (2) the association of new ideas with familiar ones, (3) the effective packaging or clustering of ideas, (4) motivational appeals, and (5) relevant visualizations. Ultimately, you should communicate the sense that what you're saying is directly relevant to the lives of your listeners.

Clarity

Informative speeches achieve maximum clarity when listeners can follow and understand what you're saying. Clarity is largely the result of two factors: effective organization, and word choice.

Effective Organization. Effective organization is a matter of grouping or clustering your ideas clearly and connecting then into a coherent whole.

Limit your points. Confine your speech to three or four principal ideas, grouping whatever facts or ideas you wish to consider under these main headings. Even if you know a tremendous amount about your subject matter, remember that you cannot make everyone an expert with a single speech.

Use transitions to show relationships among ideas. Word your transitions carefully. Make sure to indicate the relationship of the upcoming point to the rest of your ideas. You might say, "Second, you must prepare the chair for caning by cleaning out the groove and cane holes"; "The Stamp Act Crisis was followed by an even more important event—the Townshend Duties"; or "To test these hypotheses, we set up the following experiment." Such transitions allow listeners to follow you from point to point.

Keep your speech moving forward. Rather than jumping back and forth between ideas, charging ahead, and then backtracking, develop a positive, forward direction. Move from basic ideas to more complex ones, from background data to current research, or from historical incidents to current events.

Word Choice. The second factor in achieving clarity is being understood. You can develop understanding through careful selection of your words. For a fuller discussion on use of language, see Chapter 10; for now, think about the following ways to achieve clarity:

Keep your vocabulary precise, accurate—not too technical. In telling someone how to finish off a basement room, you might be tempted to say, "Next, take one of these long sticks, cut it off in this funny-looking gizmo with a saw in it, and try to make the corners match." An accurate vocabulary, however, will help your listeners remember what supplies and tools to get when they approach the same project: "This is a ceiling molding; it goes around the room between the wall and the ceiling to cover the seams between the paneling and the ceiling tiles. You make the corners of the molding match by using a mitre box, which has grooves that allow you to cut 45-degree angles. Here's how you do it."

Simplify when possible. If your speech on the operation of a two-cycle internal combustion engine sounds like it came from the documentation for computer software, then it's too technical. An audience bogged down in unnecessary detail and complex vocabulary can become confused and bored, so include only as much technical vocabulary as needed.

Use reiteration to clarify complex ideas. Rephrasing helps solidify ideas for those who did not get them the first time. You might say, for example, "Unlike a terrestrial telescope, a celestial telescope is used for looking at moons, planets, and stars; that is, its mirrors and lens are ground and arranged in such a way that it focuses on objects thousands of miles—not hundreds of feet—away from the observer." In this case, the idea is rephrased; the words are not simply repeated.

Associating New Ideas with Familiar Ones

Audiences grasp new facts and ideas more readily when they can associate them with what they already know. In a speech to inform, try to connect the new with the old (see Figure 13.2). To do this, you need to know enough about your audience to choose relevant experiences, images, analogies, and metaphors to use in your speech.

Sometimes the associations you should make are obvious. A college dean talking to an audience of manufacturers on the problems of higher education

How To

Use Psychological Principles for Clarity

Clustering items of information often is useful for speakers because it makes information much easier for listeners to grasp and retain. Psychologists throughout this century have been interested in discovering why things appear the way they do to us. Four principles of perception and cognition are still current in the literature:

1. *Proximity* suggests that elements close together seem to organize into units of perception; you see pairs made up of a ball and a block, not sets of blocks and sets of balls.

2. *Similarity* suggests that like objects usually are grouped to-

gether; you see three columns rather than three rows of items.

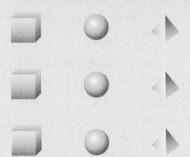

3. *Closure* is the tendency to complete suggested shapes; you see the figure of a tiger even though the lines are not joined.

FIGURE 13.2   Association of New Ideas with Familiar Ones

Snail Shell
(Single Unit)

House
(Single Unit)

Honeycomb

Condominum

4. *Symmetry* suggests that balanced objects are more pleasing to perceive than unbalanced ones.

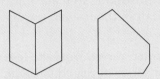

These four principles suggest ways to cluster ideas in your speeches: (1) Put your most important ideas close together so they can play off each other; (2) construct your main points in similar ways grammatically to make the structure stand out; (3) offer enough typical examples to allow for closure; and (4) balance your treatments of the main ideas to give a sense of symmetry—for example, use parallel sentences.

These principles can help you organize your speeches to take advantage of your listeners' natural perceptions.

For Further Reading

John R. Anderson, *Cognitive Psychology and Its Implications* (New York: W. H. Freeman, 1980), 53–56.

Ronald H. Forgus and Lawrence E. Melamed, *Perception: A Cognitive-Stage Approach*, 2nd ed. (New York: McGraw-Hill, 1976), 177–182.

Michael Kobovy and James R. Pomerantz, eds., *Perceptual Organization* (Hillsdale, NJ: Lawrence Erlbaum Associates, 1980).

presented his ideas under the headings of raw material, casting, machining, polishing, and assembling. He translated his central ideas into an analogy that his audience, given their vocations, would understand. If you cannot think of any obvious associations, you may have to rely on common experiences or images. For instance, you might explain the operation of the pupil in a human eye by comparing it to the operation of a camera lens aperture, and you could explain a cryogenic storage tank by comparing it to a thermos bottle.

Relevant Visualizations

Perhaps the bottom line in presenting information to others is the matter of relevance: Unless you make the information relevant to the needs, interests, anxieties, areas of known ignorance, or material conditions of people in your audience, they'll ignore you. You cannot be clear unless you know what they already know, and you cannot associate new ideas with familiar ones if you don't know what's familiar to them. Clustering ideas works only if the scheme you choose piques their interests, and motivational appeals are nothing without knowledge regarding the motivational triggers of others—you've got to know what sets them off.

In the example that opened this chapter, Ben was searching for a way to make the Vietnam War relevant to a group of people born after it was over. The instructor's talk about movies and television shows was an attempt to make the war relevant to those people by calling up known **visualizations** of the war. Think back to the discussion of language in Chapter 10—to metaphor, imagery, and ostensive definitions. To visualize information is to depict its place in someone's life. For Ben's audience, the Vietnam War lived only in the mass media, where it could be seen by them. In seeking to make information relevant to audiences, you're going to have to draw them some word pictures, such as these drawn by Jesse Jackson:

> The very issues that seem racial in content when viewed from the lens of a place like Chicago turn out not to be racial at all when viewed from the lens of Appalachia.
>
> If I were to give the same speech in Harlem as I'm giving you tonight, America would miss the point.
>
> That's why Robert F. Kennedy held a white baby from Appalachia in his arms when he was trying to rouse the conscience of a nation.
>
> That's why LBJ came to Athens when he launched his war on poverty.[7]

Jesse Jackson uses specific illustrations that are strong in affiliative appeals to connect his ideas to his listeners. Verbal depiction or visualization is a classic yet contemporary strategy for making information and viewpoints relevant to listeners' lives.[8]

TYPES OF INFORMATIVE SPEECHES

Now that we've looked at some of the essential features of competently executed informative speeches, we should examine some of the types of informative speeches you'll be asked to make during your lifetime. There are many different types of speech forms into which information is put, and the choice depends upon the situation and level of knowledge possessed by listeners. Four of those forms—*definitional speeches, instructional and demonstration speeches, oral briefings,* and *explanatory speeches*—occur so frequently, however, that they merit our attention. They represent four different yet common ways in which people package or integrate information to meet the needs of others.

Definitional Speeches

"Dad, what's a 'latchkey kid'?" "Professor Delroy, what are the differences between copper wire phone connections, ISDN phone connections, and coaxial cable connections so far as modem operations are concerned?" "Now, Jayne, I know this is a dumb question, but what's a 'dual-agency realtor,' and what's in it for me?" You've been asking questions like this all of your life; a dictionary definition just does not help. A **definitional speech** seeks to present concepts or processes in ways that make them relevant to listeners. Once Sarina knows what a latchkey kid is, she'll understand what she's been called and will want to know whether that's good or bad. Once you know about different modem-computer connections, you'll be able to assess how much it's worth to you to pay for faster data transmission. Once you understand that Jayne's able to serve both you and a seller better if she's a dual-agency realtor, you'll know how to approach an offer you want to put in on a house.

Definitional speeches demand that you present ideas clearly and coherently. This means that the ways in which you structure them are very important.

Introduction.   Because definitional speeches treat either unfamiliar or familiar concepts in a new light, their introductions must create curiosity and establish a need in the listeners. Creating curiosity is a special challenge in speeches on unfamiliar concepts; we're all tempted to say, "Well, if I've made it this far in life without knowing anything about black holes or carcinogens or trap blocking, why should I bother with learning more about these ideas now?" You

Informative speeches take many forms. A definitional speech presents concepts or processes in ways that make them relevant to listeners. An instructional speech explains a complex process verbally, and a demonstration speech adds a nonverbal illustration of such a process. A speaker giving an oral briefing assembles, arranges, and interprets information in response to a group's request. In an explanatory speech, a speaker clarifies the connections among concepts, processes or events.

need to make people wonder about the unknown. Use new information to attract attention and arouse curiosity.

Definitional speeches also must be attentive to the needs or wants of the audience. In other words, their introductions should include explicit statements that indicate how the information can affect the listeners, such as "Understanding the dynamics of trap blocking will help you better appreciate line play in football and thereby increase your enjoyment of the game every Saturday afternoon in our stadium."

Body. Most definitional speeches use a topical pattern, because such speeches usually describe various aspects of an object or idea. It seems natural, for example, to use a topical pattern for a speech on computer programming careers, organizing the body of the speech around topics such as "duties of a computer programmer," "skills needed by a computer programmer," and "training you will need to become a computer programmer."

There are occasions, however, when other patterns may serve your specific purpose even better than topical patterns. You might use an effect-cause pattern, for example, when preparing an informative speech on the laws of supply and demand. You also could enumerate a series of effects with which people are already familiar—changing prices at the gas pumps—and then discuss the laws of supply and demand that account for such changes.

Conclusion. Conclusions for definitional speeches have two characteristics: They usually include a summary of the main points, and they often stress the ways in which people can apply the ideas presented. For example, a speaker discussing diabetes could conclude by offering listeners the titles of books containing more information, the phone number of the American Diabetes Association, the address of a local clinic, or the meeting time and place of a diabetics' support group.

A speech defining diabetes could be outlined in a topical pattern as in the following sample outline. Notice several features of this speech:

1. The speaker attempts early in the speech to engage listeners' curiosity and review listeners' personal needs to draw the audience into the topic. The use of a personal example is particularly good for this kind of speech.
2. The speaker offers statistics on diabetes early so that the audience knows the disease is widespread and serious.
3. Three topics are previewed and then developed in the body of the speech to engage three aspects of listeners' thinking.
4. After offering a summary of the central idea, the speaker returns to the personal example, adding closure to the speech.

SAMPLE OUTLINE FOR A DEFINITIONAL SPEECH

WHAT IS DIABETES?

Introduction

The speaker uses a vividly devel-

I. I never knew my grandmother. She was a talented artist. She raised six kids without all the modern conveniences like mi-

oped personal example and explains the scope of the problem.

A motivation for listening is provided.

Supporting testimony shows the severity of the disease.

Listeners are warned that ignorance of the disease makes the problem worse.

The scope of the problem is expanded.

The three main ideas of the speech are previewed.

crowave ovens and electric clothes dryers, and my dad still talks about the time she foiled a would-be burglar by locking him in a broom closet until the police came. My grandmother had diabetes. It finally took her life. Now my sister has it. So do 13 million other Americans.

II. Diabetes threatens millions of lives, and it's one of nature's stealthiest diseases.

III. It's important to understand this disease, because more than likely, you or someone you know will eventually have to deal with it.

A. Diabetes is the third-leading cause of death behind heart disease and cancer, according to the American Diabetes Association.

B. More than one-third of those suffering from the disease don't even know they have it. That simple knowledge could make the difference between a happy, productive life and an early death.

C. Furthermore, diabetes is implicated in many other medical problems: It contributes to coronary heart disease; it accounts for 40 percent of all amputations and most new cases of blindness.

D. In the next few minutes, let's look at three things you should know about "the silent killer," diabetes—what it is, how it affects people, and how it can be controlled.

Body

The first main point is stated.

Diabetes is defined in medical terms.

The symptoms of diabetes are explained.

The second main point is provided.

Type I diabetes is operationally defined.

Supporting statistics show the scope of this type.

I. What diabetes is.

A. Diabetes is a chronic disease of the endocrine system that affects your body's ability to deliver glucose to its cells.

B. The symptoms of diabetes, according to Dr. Charles Kilo, are weight loss despite eating and drinking, constant hunger and thirst, frequent urination, and fatigue.

II. How diabetes affects people.

A. Type I diabetes occurs when your body cannot produce insulin, a substance that delivers glucose to your cells.

1. Only 5 to 10 percent of all diabetics have type I.

2. This type, also known as juvenile diabetes, usually shows up during the first 20 years of life.

3. Type I diabetes can be passed on genetically but also is thought to be triggered by environmental agents, such as viruses.

4. Type I diabetics must take insulin injections to treat the disease.

Type II diabetes is operationally defined. Notice how this section of the speech parallels the preceding section in development.

The third main point is provided.

B. Type II diabetes occurs when your body produces insulin but fails to use it effectively.

1. Of all diabetics, 90 to 95 percent have type II.

2. This type usually shows up after a person turns 40.

3. It often affects people who are overweight; more women are affected than men.

4. Insulin injections sometimes are used to treat the disease.

III. How to control diabetes.

A. Type I diabetes cannot be cured, but it can be controlled.

The treatments for Type I are explained.

1. Patients must take insulin injections, usually several times a day.
2. Patients need to monitor their blood sugar levels by pricking a finger and testing a drop of blood.
3. According to *Science News,* several new treatments are available:
    a. One new device uses near-infrared beams to determine blood sugar level.
    b. Insulin can be taken through the nose or in pill form.
    c. Pancreatic transplants have been performed with limited success.

The treatments for Type II are explained.

B. Type II diabetes can be controlled through lifestyle modifications.
    1. Usually these diabetics are required to lose weight by exercising, according to Dr. JoAnn Manson.
    2. Changes in diet also are required.
    3. Some people take oral hypoglycemic medications that stimulate the release of insulin and foster insulin activity.
    4. If these modifications fail, type II diabetics must take insulin injections.

Conclusion

The three main ideas are reiterated.

The speech reaches closure by referring to the introductory personal example.

Listeners are warned that diabetes could affect them.

I. Diabetes is a serious disease in which the body no longer can produce or use insulin effectively.
II. The two types of diabetes occur at different stages in life and require different measures for control of the disease.
III. My grandmother lived with her diabetes for years but eventually lost her life to it. My sister has the advantages of new treatments and future research in her fight with diabetes.
IV. As we age, many of us will be among the 600,000 new cases of diabetes each year. Through awareness, we can cope effectively with this silent killer.[9]

Instructional and Demonstration Speeches

"THIS IS NOT YOUR REAL LIFE; IF IT WERE YOU WOULD HAVE BEEN GIVEN BETTER INSTRUCTIONS." That sign testifies to the importance of instructions in daily life. You're bombarded by instructions in the classroom, at work, when purchasing or assembling a new product. Sometimes the instructions are complicated enough that you have to be shown: how a food processor works, what you need to do in a lab to isolate oxygen, how to install a water filtration system on your cold-water pipes. An **instructional speech** offers a verbal explanation of a complex process, but a **demonstration speech** goes further by providing a visual dimension, illustrating the actual product or process for the audience. To help with clarity and concreteness, both types of speeches can use visual aids—pictures, graphs, charts, overheads, and the rest.

Introduction.   In some speaking situations, such as presentations in speech communication classrooms, listener attendance may not be voluntary. On these occasions, you'll have to pay attention to motivational matters. If your audience has invited you to speak or is attending your talk voluntarily, however, you can assume listener interest. When giving instructions or offering a demonstration, you'll usually need to spend only a little time generating curiosity or motivating people to listen. After all, if you're instructing listeners in a new office procedure or giving a workshop on how to build an ice boat, they already have the prerequisite interest and motivation; otherwise, they wouldn't have come. When your audience is already motivated to listen, you can concentrate your introduction on two other tasks:

1. *Preview your speech.* If you're going to take your listeners through the steps involved in making a good tombstone rubbing, give them an overall picture of the process before you start detailing each operation.
2. *Encourage listeners to follow along.* Even though some of the steps may be difficult, urge everyone to listen. A process such as tombstone rubbing, for example, looks easier than it is: Many people are tempted to quit listening and give up somewhere along the way. If, however, you forewarn them and promise special help with the difficult techniques, they'll be more likely to bear with you.

Body.   As we suggested earlier, most speeches of demonstration and instruction follow a natural chronological or spatial pattern. Consequently, you'll usually have little trouble organizing the body of a speech of demonstration or instruction. Your problems are more likely to be technical and may include:

1. *The problem of rate.* If the glue on a project needs to set before you can go on to the next step, what do you do? You cannot just stand there and wait for it to dry. Instead, you could have a second object—already dried and ready for the next step. You also need to preplan some material for filling the time—perhaps additional background or a brief discussion of what problems can arise at this stage. Preplan your remarks carefully for those junctures so you can maintain your audience's attention.
2. *The problem of scale.* How can you show various embroidery stitches to an audience of 25? When dealing with minute operations, you often must increase the scale of operation. In this example, you could use a large piece of poster board or even a 3- by 4-foot piece of cloth stretched over a wooden frame. By using an oversized needle, yarn instead of thread, and stitches measured in inches instead of millimeters, you could easily make your techniques visible to all audience members. At the other extreme, in a speech on how to make a homemade solar heat collector, you should work with a scaled-down model.
3. *The coordination of verbal and visual methods.* Both instructions and demonstrations usually demand that speakers "show" while "telling." To keep yourself from becoming flustered or confused, be sure to practice doing while talking—demonstrating your material while ex-

Practice coordinating verbal and visual materials.

plaining aloud what you're doing. Decide where you'll stand when showing a slide so the audience can see both you and the image. Practice talking about your aerobic exercise positions while you're actually doing them; work a dough press in practice sessions as you tell your mythical audience how to form professional-looking cookies. If you do not, you'll inevitably get into trouble before your real audience. For other tips, see the advice offered in Chapter 11.

Conclusion.   Conclusions for demonstration speeches usually have three parts:

1. *Summary.* Most audiences need this review, which reminds them to question any procedures or ideas they don't understand.
2. *Encouragement.* People trying new processes or procedures usually get in trouble the first few times and need reassurance such trouble is predictable and can be overcome.
3. *Offer to help.* What sounded so simple in your talk may be much more complicated in execution. If possible, make yourself available for assistance: "As you fill out your registration form, just raise your hand if you're unsure of anything and I'll be happy to help you." Or, point to other sources of further information and assistance: "Here's the address of the Governor's Office." Such statements not only offer help but assure your listeners they won't be labeled as dim-witted if they ask for it.

Thinking through requirements of instructional and demonstration speeches might result in a speaking outline like the following one.

SAMPLE OUTLINE FOR A DEMONSTRATION SPEECH

HOW TO MAKE SHANGHAI "WONTONS"

Introduction

Listeners' interest is aroused by using questions.

I. Have you ever eaten small Chinese dumplings or "Wontons"?
II. Have you ever made Wontons? Well, you can learn, as I did from my Shanghainese mother. The steps are very simple and easy to follow, as I will illustrate.

Body

Chronological ordering used in referencing what is needed first.

I. First, you must have the proper materials.
   A. Utensils: chopsticks, dish, cup.
   B. Ingredients of Wonton filling.
      [use transparency to list ingredients]
   C. Ready-made Wonton wrappers.
II. Demonstration: folding Wonton wrappers.

The steps are shown to the audience.

   A. This is a "step-by-step procedure" that is easy to watch and to do for yourself.
      [hold up empty wrapper to show steps, then put filling in a new wrapper and repeat same steps]

Using a volunteer helps support the idea that this is an easy process.

The "So what?" question is answered in this section.

   B. With a volunteer from class, we will now show you how easy it is to do as I have done in wrapping a Wonton.
   C. Serving Wontons.
      1. Wontons can be served in chicken soup.
         [show picture of soup with dumplings]
      2. Wontons can be deep-fried and served with a hot pepper sauce.
         [show picture of deep-fried wontons]

Conclusion

The conclusion summarizes the main points.

I. With the proper utensils, the right ingredients, and ready-made wrappers, you, too, can enjoy this tasty food from my home
II. Even if you don't make them yourself, you know what they are and can try them the next time you go out to a Chinese restaurant.[10]

Oral Briefings

An **oral briefing** is a speech that assembles, arranges, and interprets information gathered in response to a request from a particular group. Briefings may be *general,* as in an overview of the general education requirements being discussed by a university committee, or *technical,* as in a class report on the award-winning concrete boat that was created by a university engineering team. Briefings are either *factual,* as in reviewing the specification for the concrete boat race and how the winning boat compared, or *advisory,* as in going beyond the factual information to provide specific recommendations for how such boats might be built by a new team.

Briefings also demand that you consider your role as an expert—as the source of predigested information for a group of people who, in turn, will act on what you have to say. That role carries the obligation to prepare with special care and the necessity to present ideas with clarity and balance. The following guidelines will help ensure your concentration on the tasks at hand:

1. *The information you present must be researched with great care.* The audience will expect you to have concrete data on which the generalizations are based, especially if those generalizations are controversial or seem extraordinary.

2. *When making recommendations rather than merely reporting information, be sure to include a complete rationale for your advice.* Suppose, for example, that as a wheelchair-bound person, you have been called on to brief your student government on the status of access for the disabled on your campus and to recommend how the assembly can help make the campus more accessible. First, you can use your own experience in listing the problems. Second, you need to gather additional information about the current status of access, especially in relation to the requirements specified in the 1991 American Disabilities Act. Information gleaned from these sources begins to build the rationale for the speech, because you want audiences to be clear about what the current status of handicapped access is on the campus.

3. *Make full use of visual aids when briefing audiences.* If your speech is short and to the point yet contains information that may be complex and new to the audience, use visual aids.

4. *Stay within the boundaries of the charge you are given.* Whether your briefing assignment is general or technical, factual or advisory, *you* are the primary source of information at that moment. Thus, being sensitive to the audience's expectations and needs is essential. What is expected of you in this situation? Were you asked to gather information only, or were you charged with offering recommendations? Does the audience assume that you'll emphasize information from the past, current trends, or future prospects? Are cost implications expected in assessing a proposal?

Oral briefings require more attention to structural considerations than other informational speeches. The following summary overviews each phase of the speech.

Introduction.   The audience is more interested in content than in being motivated to listen—they know why you are speaking. A brief reminder or recapping of the charge given sets the context. Describing the procedures used assures the audience you did your job, and forecasting the ideas or issues to be covered in the presentation prepares the audience to listen. What you want the listeners to do, believe, or know as a result of the information needs to be highlighted early in the presentation. In essence, orient listeners through a review of the past (their expectations and your preparation), the present (your goal in this presentation), and the future (their responsibilities following the presentation).

Body.   Adhere to this structural principle: *Use the pattern best suited to the topic and audience expectations.* For example, a chronological pattern will best answer the topic and expectations in a speech on the history of a group's existence or a specific problem. A cause-effect pattern would best answer an expectation for an awareness of why a problem or a group exists.

SAMPLE OUTLINE FOR AN ORAL BRIEFING

REPORT FROM THE ATHLETIC ADVISORY COMMITTEE

The reporter's "charge" is reviewed.

I. Our committee was asked to evaluate the current charge to the advisory committee and suggest changes to the President.
   A. First, you need to know that the committee is composed of faculty, staff, and students.

Orientation is completed.

   B. Second, you need to know that our Committee is Advisory to the President—we do not make policy, but we do recommend actions to make the life of student-athletes better.

The deliberative process is summarized.

II. We conducted an orderly and systematic review.
   A. First, we examined the relevance of each specific task in the current charge.
   B. Then, we interviewed two key Committee Members—the Athletic Director and Senior Women's Athletic official—to assess their views of the current charge.
   C. Next, we evaluated recent actions undertaken by the group to get a better sense of what we have been considering and its relation to the charge.
   D. With this as a baseline, we then brainstormed additional new activities with which the group could become more involved.

III. We also went outside the Committee for further information.

The recommended course of action is justified.

   A. We interviewed the President to get the opinions of "central administration."
   B. We interviewed officers in the faculty senate.
   C. We interviewed student government officers.

IV. Using this information as a basis, we then drew up a list of duties for discussion.
   A. We ranked each item as to its relative importance.
   B. We indicated our commitment to each item.
   C. Reviewing the results of A and B, we ascertained which items received unanimous, solid support from the Committee.
   D. The final list was approved.

V. The final revised document was presented to the President for approval.

Conclusion.   Direct reference to the introductory comments is a common tactic in concluding, as is thanking those who participated and made a difference in the outcome. You also may offer a motion to accept a report if the circumstances call for this parliamentary step. Inviting audience questions is another move that can be made at the close of the presentation. In essence, conclusions of oral briefings should be quick, firm, efficient, and specific regarding what you want the audience to know.

Explanatory Speeches

An **explanatory speech** has much in common with the definitional speech; both share the function of clarifying a concept, process, or event. Normally, though, an explanatory speech is less concerned with the word or vocabulary involved than with connecting one concept to a series of others. For example, a speech of definition on political corruption would concentrate on the term, telling what sorts of acts committed by politicians are included by it. An explanatory speech on corruption, however, such as on the scandal surrounding the awarding of Olympic sites, would go further into the subject and indicate the social-political conditions likely to produce corruption or the methods for eliminating it. The clarification involved in an explanatory speech is considerably broader and more complex than that of a definitional speech.

The key to most explanatory speeches is how the speaker constructs a viewpoint or rationale. Suppose, for example, that you want to explain the origins of U.S. involvement in Vietnam during the 1950s. You could offer several explanations from varied viewpoints, depending upon which story of that country and the war you wanted to tell, with a focus on the French stronghold in what was then called Indochina. Or, you could focus on allied support, including $3 billion from the United States, and its impact on Euro-American foreign policy. You might tell the cultural story of Indochina, its split between Western capitalism and Catholicism in the south and Eastern (Chinese) communism and Buddhism in the north, thereby leading to a clash of lifestyles supported by superpowers with vested social interests. The political story of Vietnam also might be told: the Cold War, the American involvement with the French and with SEATO—the South East Asia Treaty Organization, which committed the United States to defend East Asian countries against Communist aggression.[11]

Both of these approaches are "correct," and both give you a significant explanation about the importance of Vietnam to western (including U.S.) interests as they were perceived at the time. If you tried to tell them all at once, however, you'd confuse your listeners. Your best strategy in most explanatory speeches, therefore, is to identify the viewpoint you will take—"Let me tell you the story of American involvement in Vietnam from an economic [cultural/military/political] point of view. If we look at it in that way, we'll see that . . . ." Such a statement signals your viewpoint, recognizes you're not trying to offer every possible explanation, and tells your listeners what to listen for. Identifying a viewpoint helps you—and your listeners—keep the story straight.

Unlike definitional speeches, explanatory speeches can become complex and difficult to organize. We now discuss this aspect.

Introduction.   For this type of speech, motive appeals are far more important in getting audiences interested in your topic; the need to connect your topic to audience members' everyday lives is paramount. In addition, forecasting the main points will help orient the audience to your topic's development. When dealing with complex material, indicate a willingness to elaborate or note that you'll go into more detail as needed later in the presentation.

Body.   Causal or topical patterns fit most explanatory speeches. Explaining why something exists or operates as it does calls for either cause-effect or its reverse. Topical patterns allow you to order items without worrying which comes first or second.

ETHICAL MOMENTS

YOUR ETHICAL BOUNDARIES

What are your ethical limits? What are the appeals *you* would not make? Consider the following examples:

1. *[Honesty in relation to appropriateness of authority appeal]* Afraid that your listeners will not take your concerns about inadequate protections against theft seriously, you embellish statistical data obtained from campus security. Some incidents happened, but you make them appear more frequent and more serious than the statistics suggest.
2. *[Appropriateness of fear appeal]* Would you show third graders pictures of mouth sores and completely decayed teeth as a way of getting them to brush and floss better?
3. *[Appropriateness of fear appeal]* Would you bring pictures of fe-

tuses to class to show the audience what happens to the unborn during an abortion?

4. *[Honesty/openness in relation to success appeal]* Would you tell your classmates they can earn up to $5,000 a month selling encyclopedias, even though commissions average only $300 dollars a month?

Your reputation, credibility, or *ethos* is created largely by what you say and what others think about what you say. Know the limits of the audience, and more importantly, know your own limits. In that way, you won't be surprised when listeners question the motive appeals you have employed. In the process, anything you do to promote the common good and the basic humanity of others will earn you many points in life.

Conclusion. In this type of speech, most conclusions develop additional implications or calls for particular actions. Knowing what causes a disease, for example, may lead the audience to wonder how to avoid the cause or treat the effects.

Suppose your major is archaeology, and you decide to discuss recent controversial claims regarding how the first "humans" acted in their environment. Consider the following outline to see how some of this advice can be put to work.

SAMPLE OUTLINE FOR AN EXPLANATORY SPEECH

DID EARLY HUMANS "APE THE APES"?

Introduction

Raise your listeners' curiosity.

I. When did we first become more "human" than "animal-like" in our behavior?

Tie new knowledge to their desire.

II. That question cannot really be answered, but the search for an answer highlights important characteristics of human beings' development.

Body

Use both spatial and chronological patterns; and develop an understanding of the issues. Then, work with a narrative to show the sequential development of ideas.

I. The research of Louis and Mary Leakey and, more recently, their son, Richard, in Tanzania, Kenya, and Ethiopia resulted in an interpretation of "man as hunter" and "woman as gatherer."
   A. The major archaeological "finds" at Olduvai Gorge in Kenya, Koobi Fora in Kenya, and Hadar in Ethiopia are marked on the wall map to my left.
   B. The initial find was at Olduvai; Louis Leakey discovered what he termed "encampments" of men and women, with scattered bones and stone implements.
      1. He named these early humans *Homo habilis* or "handy man." They also are termed *hominids* to separate them from later humans.
      2. Leakey argued that the males were the hunters and women the gatherers.
   C. Louis and Mary's son, Richard, discovered even earlier remains in northern Kenya, at Koobi Fora. He followed the same interpretation in arguing the remains were sites of male hunters and female gatherers.

Transition

   The interpretation of the Leakeys initially was applauded but, more recently, has been challenged by others.

Interpret the facts to make knowledge claims.

II. The challenge to this interpretation asks, in effect, "How did the Leakeys know what hominids were doing millions of years ago—the evidence from the sites is insufficient to support their interpretation."
   A. Using precise geological measures, Richard Potts of the Smithsonian Institution assessed the Olduvai sites and concluded they were not encampments where men hunted and women gathered.

        1. The sites give evidence of activity by both carnivores and hominids.

        2. The sites were "caches" where implements were stored rather than actual living sites.

    B. Several arguments support Potts' conclusions.

        1. The sites were concentrated in selected areas and represent deposits over time.

        2. Bones that show evidence of being transported from an original place are marked by stone cuts.

        3. Bones also show evidence of carnivore marks superimposed on those made by stone cuts.

        4. Uncut and unformed stones were found with cut stones, indicating a "cache" where hominids might return.

Transition   C. A second conclusion based on this finding is that men and women were not definitely split in their duties and that, in fact, these early humans or hominids may have been more like their ape ancestors than later hunters.

Enlarge the interpretations to make them relevant to today's issues.   III. In challenging Richard Leakey's interpretation, there are experts who believe *Homo habilis* were scavengers, not hunters.

    A. The evidence suggests the hominids chased carnivores, such as lions, away from a kill with stones and then proceeded to take what they wanted from the carcass.

    B. The evidence also suggests the "caches" were sites to which they returned with their meat to rest and eat; when night fell, they resorted to sleeping in trees rather than on the open ground.

Conclusion

Finish with an undisputable knowledge claim.   I. These new interpretations suggest early hominids were more like apes than later humans.

    A. They did not have spears or fire; hence, stalking and killing game was not as likely as scavenging.

    B. With this in mind, we can better appreciate the difference that fire and more advanced weapons made in their lifestyle.

  II. The newer interpretations suggest how difficult it is to be certain about the lifestyle of our ancestors.

    A. As you read or hear new conclusions about our ancestors, keep an open mind.

    B. Newer findings may reveal even these conclusions to be premature.[12]

ASSESSING A SAMPLE SPEECH

The following speech, "The Geisha," was delivered by Joyce Chapman when she was a first-year student at Loop College, Chicago. It illustrates most of the virtues of a competent informative speech: It provides enough detail and explanations to be clear to a Western audience; it works from images of geishas familiar to at least some audience members, adding new ideas or correcting old ones within the frames of reference listeners might have; its topical organization pattern is simple and easy to follow; and it gives the audience reasons for listening.

THE GEISHA

Joyce Chapman

A personal reference establishes an immediate tie between Ms. Chapman and her topic.

As you may have already noticed from my facial features, I have Oriental blood in me and, as such, I am greatly interested in my Japanese heritage. One aspect of my heritage that fascinates me the most is the beautiful and adoring Geisha./1

Ms. Chapman works hard to bring the listeners—with their stereotyped views of Geishas—into the speech through comments many might have made and references to familiar films.

I recently asked some of my friends what they thought a Geisha was, and the comments I received were quite astonishing. For example, one friend said, "She is a woman who walks around in a hut." A second friend was certain that a Geisha was "A woman who massages men for money and it involves her in other physical activities." Finally, I received this response, "She gives baths to men and walks on their backs." Well, needless to say, I was rather surprised and offended by their comments. I soon discovered that the majority of my friends perceived the Geisha with similar attitudes. One of them argued, "It's not my fault, because that is the way I've seen them on TV." In many ways my friend was correct. His misconception of the Geisha was not his fault, for she is often portrayed by American film producers and directors as: a prostitute, as in the movie, *The Barbarian and the Geisha;* a streetwalker, as seen in the TV series, *Kung Fu;* or as a showgirl with a gimmick, as performed in the play, *Flower Drum Song.*/2

The central idea is stated clearly.

A Geisha is neither a prostitute, streetwalker, or showgirl with a gimmick. She is a lovely Japanese woman who is a professional entertainer and hostess. She is cultivated with exquisite manners, truly a bird of a very different plumage./3

A transition moves the listeners easily from the introduction to the body of the speech via a forecast.

I would like to provide you with some insight into the Geisha, and, in the process perhaps, correct any misconception you may have. I will do this by discussing her history, training, and development./4

The first section of the body of the speech is devoted to an orienting history, which cleverly wipes away most of the negative stereotypes of the Geisha.

The Geisha has been in existence since 600 A.D., during the archaic time of the Yakamoto period. At that time the Japanese ruling class was very powerful and economically rich. The impoverished majority, however, had to struggle to survive. Starving fathers and their families had to sell their young daughters to the teahouses in order to get a few yen. The families hoped that the girls would have a better life in the teahouse than they would have had in their own miserable homes./5

During ancient times only high society could utilize the Geisha's talents because she was regarded as a status symbol, exclusively for the elite. As the Geisha became more popular, the common people developed their own imitations. These imitations were often crude and base, lacking sophistication and taste. When American GIs came home from World War II, they related descriptive accounts of their wild escapades with the Japanese Geisha. In essence, the GIs were only soliciting with common prostitutes. These bizarre stories helped create the wrong image of the Geisha./6

A nice transition moves Chapman to her second point on the rigors of Geisha training. She discusses the training in language technical enough to make listeners feel that they're learning interesting information but not so detailed as to be suffocating.

Today, it is extremely difficult to become a Geisha. A Japanese woman couldn't wake up one morning and decide, "I think I'll become a Geisha today." It's not that simple. It takes sixteen years to qualify./7

At the age of six a young girl would enter the Geisha training school and become a Jo-chu, which means house keeper. The Jo-chu does not have any specific type of clothing, hairstyle, or make-up. Her duties basically consist of keeping the teahouse immaculately clean (for cleanliness is like a religion to the Japanese). She would also be responsible for making certain that the more advanced women would have everything available at their fingertips. It is not until the girl is sixteen and enters the Maiko stage that she concentrates less on domestic duties and channels more of her energies on creative and artistic endeavors./8

The Maiko girl, for example, is taught the classical Japanese dance, Kabuki. At first, the dance consists of tiny, timid steps to the left, to the right, backward and forward. As the years progress, she is taught the more difficult steps requiring syncopated movements to a fan./9

The Maiko is also introduced to the highly regarded art of floral arrangement. The Japanese take full advantage of the simplicity and gracefulness that can be achieved with a few flowers in a vase, or with a single flowering twig. There are three main styles: Seika, Moribana, and Nagerie. It takes at least three years to master this beautiful art./10

During the same three years, the Maiko is taught the ceremonious art of serving tea. The roots of these rituals go back to the thirteen century, when Zen Buddhist monks in China drank tea during their devotions. These rituals were raised to a fine art by the Japanese tea masters, who set the standards for patterns of behavior throughout Japanese society. The tea ceremony is so intricate that it often takes four hours to perform and requires the use of over seventeen different utensils. The tea ceremony is far more than the social occasion it appears to be. To the Japanese, it serves as an island of serenity where one can refresh the senses and nourish the soul./11

One of the most important arts taught to the Geisha is that of conversation. She must master an elegant circuitous vocabulary flavored in Karyuki, the world of flowers and willows, of which she will be a part. Consequently, she must be capable of stimulating her client's mind as well as his esthetic pleasures./12

The third point of the speech—how a Geisha develops her skills in her actual work—is clearly introduced and then developed with specific instances and explanations.

Having completed her sixteen years of thorough training, at the age of twenty-two, she becomes a full-fledged Geisha. She can now serve her clients with duty, loyalty, and most important, a sense of dignity./13

The Geisha would be dressed in the ceremonial kimono, made of brocade and silk thread. It would be fastened with an obi, which is a sash around the waist and hung down the back. The length of the obi would indicate the girl's degree of development. For instance, in the Maiko stage the obi is longer and is shortened when she becomes a Geisha. Unlike the Maiko, who wears a gay, bright, and cheerful kimono, the Geisha is dressed in more subdued colors. Her make-up is the traditional white base, which gives her the look of white porcelain. The hair is shortened and adorned with beautiful, delicate ornaments./14

As a full-fledged Geisha, she would probably acquire a rich patron who would assume her sizable debt to the Okiya, or training residence. This patron would help pay for her wardrobe, for each kimono can cost up to $12,000. The patron would generally provide her with financial security./15

The Geisha serves as a combination entertainer and companion. She may dance, sing, recite poetry, play musical instruments, or draw pictures for her guest. She might converse with them or listen sympathetically to their troubles. Amorous advances, however, are against the rules./16

So, as you can see the Geisha is a far cry from the back-rubbing, street-walking, slick entertainer that was described by my friends. She is a beautiful, cultivated, sensitive, and refined woman.[13]/17

> The conclusion is short and quick. Little more is needed in a speech that has offered clear explanations, though some speakers might want to refer back to the initial overview of negative stereotypes to remind the listeners how wrong such views are.

CHAPTER SUMMARY

Overall, informative speeches provide more interesting and greater challenges than most people realize. *Facts* and *information* are not particularly useful to listeners until they're turned into *knowledge*—assembled and structured in ways that help human beings find those facts and that information relevant to their lives.

Audiences are not always automatically interested in every topic; hence, you need to appeal to their personal motives for listening. Motives can be thought of as *springs*— needs or desires tightly coiled and waiting for the right appeal or verbal depiction to set them off. Worked by a skillful speaker, these motives can convert the individuals comprising an audience into a cohesive group, ready to think and act in ways consistent with a specific purpose. These motives, phrased in language appealing to biological needs or social motives, include three categories:

- *Affiliation motives:* The desire for acceptance and approval by others.
- *Achievement motives:* Individual urges, desires, and goals.
- *Power motives:* The desire to influence or control others or the environment.

The competent speaker will be able to draw on these motives, singly or in combination, to meet the speech purpose in an ethically sound manner. In doing so, the speaker will avoid the obvious, select appeals appropriately for the subject and occasion, and organize them effectively.

In preparing informative speeches, you must be sensitive to certain matters:

- Clarity, through effective organization and word choice.
- Ways to associate new ideas with old ones so the audience can more easily understand the new ones.
- Relevant visualization, to show listeners how information is relevant to them.

The four kinds of informative speeches discussed in this chapter—definitional speeches, instructional and demonstration speeches, oral briefings, and explanatory speeches—occur often enough in your life to demand your attention. Evaluate the organizational strategies available to you in structuring these presentations so they meet the needs of the situation and your listeners.

KEY TERMS

achievement motives (p. 300)

affiliation motives (p. 300)

attribution process (p. 303

biological need (p. 299)

definitional speech (p. 311)

demonstration speech (p. 314)

explanatory speech (p. 320)

facts (p. 298)

heirarchy of prepotency (p. 300)

information (p. 298)

instructional speech (p. 314)

knowledge (p. 298)

Maslow's heirarchy of needs (p. 299)

McClelland's motive types (p. 300)

motivational appeal (p. 302)

motive cluster (p. 301)

oral briefing (p. 317)

power motives (p. 300)

social motive (p. 299)

visualization process (p. 303)

visualizations (p. 310)

ASSESSMENT ACTIVITIES

1. In a short essay, indicate and defend the type of arrangement pattern (e.g., chronological sequence, spatial sequence, and so on) that you think would be most suitable for an informative speech on five of the following topics. Do a brief outline of first-level headings to show your reader what that speech might look like.

   The status of minority studies on your campus.

   Recent developments in genetic engineering.

   The search for the origins of human life in the Olduvai Gorge.

   How the stock market works.

   Five World Wide Web sites every college student should visit.

   Buying your first condo.

   Ways parents can control television viewing by their children.

   How the U.S. presidential caucus and primary system works.

2. Plan a two- to five-minute speech in which you give instructions. You might explain how to calculate one's life insurance needs, program a VCR so a person can watch one channel and record another, or do the Heimlich maneuver. Your instructor will grade you on the three essential criteria for all informative speeches: clarity, association of new information with old data, and your use of relevant visualization.

3. What relevant motivational appeals might you use in addressing each of the following audiences? Be ready to discuss your choices in class.

   a. A group of students protesting federal reductions in financial aid programs.

   b. A meeting of pre-business majors concerned about jobs.

   c. Women at a seminar on nontraditional employment opportunities.

   d. A meeting of local elementary and secondary classroom teachers seeking smaller classes.

   e. A group gathered for an old-fashioned Fourth of July picnic.

REFERENCES

1. Katherine Blick Hoyenga and Kermit T. Hoyenga, *Motivational Explanations of Behavior: Evolutionary, Physiological, and Cognitive* *Ideas* (Monterey, CA: Brooks/Cole, 1984), Psychologists are divided over several important issues. For example, some (e.g.,

Maslow) argue that all motives are innate, whereas others (e.g., McClelland) argue that at least some are learned. Likewise, psychologists differ on the issue of conscious awareness of motives: Are we aware of the drive, and if not, how do we control it? We won't get into such controversies, but we take the position that whether innate or learned, conscious or not, motives are the *foundations for motivational appeals* and, hence, are reasons for action. It is this characteristic that makes motives important to the student of public speaking.

2. Abraham Maslow, *Motivation and Personality*, 2nd ed. (New York: Harper and Row, 1970). In the 1970 revision, Maslow identifies two additional desires—to know and understand and an aesthetic desire—as higher states. These frequently operate as part of the satisfaction of self-actualization; hence, we've included them in that category.

3. Hoyenga and Hoyenga, Donald R. Brown and Joseph Verloff, eds. *Frontiers of Motivational Psychology: Essays in Honor of John W. Atkinson* (New York: Springer-Verlag, 1986); Abigail J. Stewart, ed. *Motivation and Society; A Volume in Honor of David C. McClelland* (San Francisco: Jossey-Bass, 1982); and Janet T. Spence, ed. *Achievement and Achievement Motives* (San Francisco: W. H. Freeman, 1983).

4. Hoyenga and Hoyenga, ch. 4 (n. 1). A classic work on affiliation is Stanley Schachter, *The Psychology of Affiliation: Experimental Studies of the Sources of Gregariousness* (Stanford, CA: Stanford University Press, 1959).

5. To understand the power of verbal depiction, read Michael Osborn, "Rhetorical Depiction," *Form, Genre, and the Study of Political Discourse*, eds. Herbert W. Simons and Aram A. Aghazarian (Charleston, SC: University of South Carolina Press, 1986), 79–107.

6. For a discussion of motivation and attribution, see Hoyenga and Hoyenga (n. 1). To review attribution theory and communication studies more generally, see Alan L. Sillars, "Attribution and Communication: Are People 'Naive Scientists' or Just Naive?" *Social Cognition and Communication*, eds. Michael E. Roloff and Charles R. Berger (Beverly Hills, CA: Sage Publishing, 1982), 73–106.

7. Excerpted from a speech by Jesse Jackson, Communications Week, Ohio University, April 27, 1998.

8. For studies dealing with rhetorical depiction and visualization, see Richard A. Cherwitz, "Lyndon Johnson and the 'Crisis' of Tonkin Gulf: A President's Justification of War," *Western Journal of Speech Communication* 42 (1978): 93–104; Donovan J. Ochs, "Rhetorical Detailing in Cicero's Verrine Orations," *Communication Studies* 33 (1982): 310–318; Michael Osborn, "Rhetorical Depiction," *Form, Genre, and the Study of Political Discourse*, eds. Herbert W. Simons and Aram A. Aghazarian (Charleston, SC: University of South Carolina Press, 1986), 79–107; Paul Messaris, *Visual "Literacy": Image, Mind, and Reality* (Boulder, CO: Westview Press, 1994); and Chris Jenks, "The Centrality of the Eye in Western Culture: An Introduction," *Visual Culture*, ed. Chris Jenks (New York: Routledge, 1995), 1–25.

9. Information for this outline was taken from Phyllis Barrier, "Diabetes: It Never Lets Up," *Nation's Business* (November 1992): 77; David Bradley, "Is a Pill on the Way for Diabetes?" *New Scientist* (June 27, 1992): 406; Chales Kilo and Joseph R. Williamson, *Diabetes* (New York: Wiley, 1987); Mark Schapiro, "A Shock to the System," *Health* (July–August 1991): 75–82; Carrie Smith, "Exercise Reduces Risk of Diabetes," *The Physician and Sports Medicine* (November 1992): 19; and John Travis, "Helping Diabetics Shed Pins and Needles," *Science News* (July 6, 1991): 4.

10. Adapted from a speech by Lam Sui Wah (Brenda), Ohio University, 1996.

11. For details on these stories, see David Halberstam, *The Fifties* (New York: Villard Books, 1993).

12. Outline adapted from Brian Fagan, "Aping the Apes," *Archaeology* 45 (May/June 1992): 16–19, 67; see also Richard Potts, *Early Humanoid Activities at Olduvai Gorge* (New York: Aldine de Gruyter, 1988).

13. Joyce Chapman, "The Geisha," *Communication Strategy: A Guide to Speech Preparation*, eds. Roselyn Schiff, et al. (Glenview, IL: Scott, Foresman, 1981). Used with the permission of Addison Wesley Longman.

Chapter 14

Speeches to Persuade and Actuate

Although spring break was still months away, Katya knew her parents would need some persuading to allow her to spend a week in Aruba. The expense, among other factors, would be a hurdle to overcome. Katya thought about the arguments she might make and considered her parents' resistance to each one. Finally, she settled on an approach that she felt was certain to work.

[Years later.] The Republican presidential convention was still months away, but Katya, a strong candidate for the nomination, felt that a "flat tax" proposal might be a distinctive feature of her campaign. Would the people in Iowa and New Hampshire, among other pre-convention states voting for delegates, buy the proposal? What if other candidates came forward with similar proposals? What arguments would entice people to see the proposal as unique, inviting, and thus an aid in getting more delegates to cast their votes for her?

While these situations are vastly different, Katya's persuasive goal in each was influenced by her knowledge of the audience that would, ultimately, determine whether her idea was acceptable. The strategies that Katya might employ in each case may be different, but the general purpose is the same: to ask that other people *change their ideas or actions in a manner that accommodates the speaker's wishes.* Speakers also may seek to reinforce the ideas or values to which people already are committed.

The speaker or writer who persuades makes a very different demand on an audience than the speaker who informs. Informative communicators are satisfied when listeners understand what's been said. Persuaders, however, attempt to influence listeners' thoughts or actions. Persuaders request or demand that the audience agree with or act upon messages. Occasionally, persuaders seek to reinforce ideas or action, urging listeners to defend the present system and reject proposed changes. Whatever the specific purpose, the general purpose of all persuaders is to convince audiences of something. Broadly, persuasion encompasses a wide range of communication activities, including advertising, marketing, sales, political campaigns, and interpersonal relations. Given this book's focus on speechmaking, however, we narrow our thinking in this chapter to three types of speeches. Persuasive speaking is the process of producing oral messages that increase personal commitment; modify beliefs, attitudes, or values; or induce action.

Before we can talk about these three types of speech—which we will call speeches of reinforcement, modification, and actuation—we need to consider some general problems you will face as a persuader:

1. The need to adapt your work to listeners' psychological states.
2. The selection of motivational appeals that will work with the particular audience you face.
3. The requirement that you recognize the diverse populations in your audience and provide each part with reasons for accepting your claims.
4. The absolute need to enhance your credibility when selling ideas to audiences.

These topics were discussed earlier, but as we reintroduce them here, the focus will be on how to use audience analysis in speeches of reinforcement, modification, and actuation.

Persuasive speaking is the process of producing oral messages that increase personal commitment; modify beliefs, attitudes, or values; or induce action.

JUSTIFYING PERSUASIVE MESSAGES: PROBLEMS FACED BY PERSUADERS

Persuading others is a challenging task. No matter what advertisers assume, people do not change their long-standing beliefs, values, or behaviors on a whim; they need convincing rationales. The natural question of "Why should I believe or act as you desire?" must be met by "good reasons" for asking listeners to alter their thoughts or actions.[1] Reasons are not "good" simply because they are perceived as rational or logically reasonable. Rather, their status is always determined by (1) listeners' psychological states, (2) the motive needs or desires of listeners, (3) sources of ideas (i.e., reference groups) acceptable to listeners, and (4) their assessment of the speaker's personal credibility. We now consider each of these problems in turn.

Adapting Messages to Listeners' Psychological States

The phrase **psychological state** refers generally to the complex of beliefs, attitudes, and values that listeners bring to a speech occasion. There are hundreds of ways to talk about psychological states, but in this chapter, we limit ourselves to three.

Psychological Orientation and the VALS Program. A popular book of a decade ago was Arnold Mitchell's *The Nine American Lifestyles.*[2] He and some teammates set up the Stanford Research Institute's **Values and Lifestyles (VALS) Program** to understand motives, lifestyles, and governing values of groups of people. They set up the program because they understood, first, that people are governed by entire constellations of attitudes, beliefs, opinions, hopes, fears, needs, desires, and aspirations that are too complex to chart neatly on paper but, second, that people nonetheless have relatively consistent ways of acting at any given time of their lives. There are patterns to people's development and actions. These can be defined as **lifestyles**—the relatively systematized ways of believing and acting in the world and the fairly consistent orientations people bring to their decision making.

The VALS program is an effort to capture those lifestyles in an analytically useful way. After considerable surveying and interviewing of Americans, Mitchell's team divided participants into four comprehensive groups that, in turn, were subdivided into nine lifestyles. The categories (see Table 14.1) and the percentages of U.S. adults in each came from 1980 research, so the specific numbers may have changed by now. Even so, the system itself is solid.

The VALS program defines groups of people who habitually respond to problems and their solutions in comparatively predictable ways:

- *Survivors* are the poverty-driven people—ill, depressed, withdrawn, undereducated, and lacking self-confidence.
- *Sustainers* are closely related to survivors but are more angry, distrustful, anxious, and have the motive to advance economically, if possible.
- *Belongers* are the stereotypical middle-class Americans—traditional, conforming, family-oriented, "moral," mostly white, and often female.

TABLE 14.1   Mitchell's VALS Typology

Need-Driven Groups (11% of U.S. adults)

Survivor lifestyle (4%)
Sustainer lifestyle (7%)

Outer-Directed Groups (67% of U.S. adults)

Belonger lifestyle (35%)
Emulator lifestyle (10%)
Achiever lifestyle (22%)

Inner-Directed Groups (20% of U.S. adults)

I-Am-Me lifestyle (5%)
Experiential lifestyle (7%)
Socially Conscious lifestyle (8%)

Combined Outer- and Inner-Directed Groups (2% of U.S. adults)

Integrated lifestyle (2%)

- *Emulators* are the great strivers, those who work hard to become richer and more successful than they are; members of this group often are young, competitive, and ambitious.
- *Achievers* are the more successful models of emulators and often are professionals—comfortable, affable, and wealthy.
- *"I-Am-Me's"* lead off the inner-directed group; they are highly emotional and flighty, both aggressive and retiring, conforming and innovative, and always searching for their true selves.
- *Experientials* are adventure-seekers, willing to experience life intensely; unlike I-am-me's, they are more involved with others.
- The *Socially Conscious* are driven by their concern for others, societal issues, trends, and events.
- *Integrated* people balance the strengths of the outer- and inner-directed people.

As these examples attest, your audiences seldom are drawn purely from one group or another. Hence, the best approach is to segment the listeners and then target appeals to each segment (as discussed in Chapter 5). Even a general analysis of psychological orientation, therefore, helps you choose among the different ways you can urge change and even phrase the specific appeals that you use.

Predisposition Toward the Topic.   An audience can have five possible attitudes toward a speaker's topic and purpose: (1) favorable but not aroused to act; (2) apathetic toward the situation; (3) interested but undecided about what to do; (4) interested in the situation but hostile to the proposed attitude,

How To

USE VALS TO CRAFT A PERSUASIVE MESSAGE FOR DIVERSE AUDIENCES

A cursory examination of your classmates should reveal something like the following:

- There will be few representatives of the need-driven groups (i.e., Survivors and Sustainers).
- There will be several outer-directed students (Emulators and Achievers).
- There also will be several inner-directed students, especially from the Socially Conscious.

Based on this quick review, suppose you are suggesting that your classmates help a neighborhood association clean up some nearby vacant lots to set up a park. For your classmates, you would want to feature appeals aimed at that particular psychological orientation:

I. We should help the neighborhood association clean the lots and build the park because:
A. You would be demonstrating that even busy college students have the ambition to take on serious community projects. [Achiever]
B. You would show the community that you have the leadership skills and technical abilities to carry it out. [Achiever]
C. You would have done something of which you could be proud and which you could put on your résumé under "community service." [Socially Conscious]

If you were to shift your focus to the neighborhood association, a cursory examination may find:

- A larger percentage of "need-driven" people would be found among the community members than might be the case in your college class.
- A majority of "Belongers" (outer-directed) would be found in the association.
- Some association members would be Socially Conscious.

For this audience, a different set of reasons would be appropriate:

I. You should be involved in the neighborhood clean up and park construction because:
A. The lots are now breeding grounds for rats and other vermin that make your life miserable. [Socially Conscious]
B. Drug dealers might be driven out of the neighborhood if those lots are cleaned up. [Inner Directed and Socially Conscious]
C. The presence of a park would increase your property value and even help those who are renters pressure your landlords to fix up your apartments. [Need Driven]
D. A park would give you a free place to visit and enjoy on spring days and summer nights. [Inner and Outer Directed]

belief, value, or action; or (5) hostile to any change from the present state of affairs. Furthermore, such predispositions can be relatively fixed or tentative, and they may vary from subgroup to subgroup within the audience. Given this sort of variability, consider the following suggestions as you design your speech:

- *A message that incorporates both sides of an issue—and contains arguments refuting one side—will be more effective across diverse persuasive situations.* Thus, if your goal is to stimulate more favorable thoughts about your proposal, use a **two-sided message** with refutation. A **one-sided message,** which focuses on the arguments for your position only, also can be effective—and is more effective than simply outlining both sides of an issue without adding refutative arguments.[3]
- *A message that recognizes the logical interdependence between ideas will target those people for whom beliefs are highly integrative.* There will be people in the audience for whom beliefs are interlocked—altering or affecting one belief will have a domino-like impact on other beliefs. Thus, a listener might believe that a "flat tax" rate would cause higher taxes for the middle class and, in turn, that higher taxes would limit the savings potential and disposable income of many people. In turn, this might harm the stock market and cause a reduction in spending for produced goods. For this listener, a speech favoring a flat tax must deal with all these implications.
- *You must also deal not only with the strength of attitudes but also with their saliency.* **Saliency** refers to the relevance and "current" interest level of a belief, attitude, or value for an individual. For example, topics currently on the front page often are highly salient, as are topics of regular conversation. The saliency of an issue should affect your persuasive strategies in significant ways: Issues will mean more or less to different members, so you need to decide how much detail to offer. The more often an issue is in the news, the more likely the audience will have opinions about it, affecting what arguments you should frame; the more they know, the more careful you must be in framing arguments.[4]
- *Recognize that audience members differ in their willingness to accept your ideas.* Audience members will have different ranges of acceptance or rejection depending on how your proposal relates to their own views. Think in terms of not going too far in either direction from your proposal for a flat tax: A rate of 2 percent might be rejected by a moderate audience simply because it would seem to generate too little revenue; conversely, a rate of 35 percent might seem too high. A proponent of the flat tax will have a larger **latitude of acceptance;** conversely, an opponent would have a larger **latitude of rejection.**[5]

Degrees of Change.   Given the differences in degrees of willingness to accept and act on ideas, you also need to recognize that people will change only so much as a result of your speeches. It is extremely difficult—except in rare circumstances, such as radical religious experiences—to make wholesale changes in people's beliefs, attitudes, and values. Generally, you should strive for **incre-**

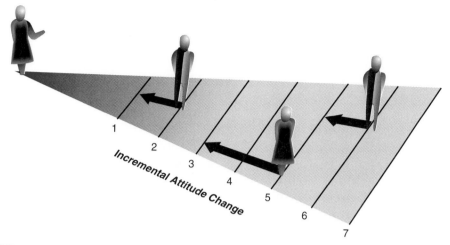

FIGURE 14.1   Incremental Approach to Attitude Change

mental change—step by step movement toward a goal. As suggested above the distance you can move a listener is determined by the initial attitude and latitude of change the person can tolerate.[6]

Obviously, you cannot interview all audience members. Indeed, few speakers (political candidates are certainly exceptions) scientifically assess the psychological states of their listeners. Good audience analysis, however, allows you to guess shrewdly and then adjust your appeals and plans of action accordingly. Talk with people. Check with civic attitude-testers such as the Chamber of Commerce. Read local newspapers and other sources of information on community problems, attitudes, and responses to those problems.

Selecting Motivational Appeals

In persuasive speaking especially, motivational appeals (see Chapter 13) are crucial to your success, because most people need strong psychological spurs to get them moving. Select motivational appeals to reach different needs or desires of different segments of your audience. A tourist agency representative urging students to take a summer trip to Europe might put together these four appeals:

1. The 3-week tour is being offered for the low price of $2,500 *[acquisition and savings]*.
2. There will be a minimum of supervision and regimentation *[independence]*.
3. You'll be traveling with other students just like you *[companionship]*.
4. We'll take you places the adult-oriented tours never get to *[curiosity and adventure]*.

In a more complete presentation, the representative also could emphasize the educational value of the trip (*self-advancement*) and side trips for special adventures such as mountain climbing. Select appeals designed to move particular portions of your audience.

ETHICAL MOMENTS

USING FEAR APPEALS

Common sense would tell you that fear appeals would be among the most potent appeals to audiences. After all, if you can make your audience feel afraid for the future if a problem is not resolved, your proposal will be just the antidote. Unfortunately, a comprehensive review of decades of research on fear appeals suggests that this common-sense notion is not that well grounded, as "existing explanations of the effects of fear arousing persuasive messages are inadequate."[7] We are not able to offer clear advice about whether the use of fear appeals to gain acceptance of a message outweighs any harms caused by frightening people—perhaps needlessly. The inability to offer such advice raises an ethical question about the use—and potential misuse—of fear appeals. Consider the following scenarios:

1. You give a speech on the increase of date rape on college campuses. To convince your audience that date rape is wrong and extremely common, you create scenarios that appeal to the fears of your listeners. Your scenarios are so vivid that several of your listeners—who are rape survivors—are visibly overcome with emotion. One of the listeners is so upset that she leaves the classroom during your speech; everyone in the audience sees her leave.

2. You feel very strongly that the college president is wrong to continue investing college money in countries where torture and imprisonment without trial are legal. You present a very persuasive speech about your feelings. In your speech, you appeal to your audience's fears by suggesting that the college president actually is propagating torture and corrupting the values of U.S. citizens to the point that, someday, torture and imprisonment without trial might be legal in the United States. Your listeners become so incensed as a result of your speech that they march to the president's house and set his car on fire.

3. You're preparing to give a speech on hate crimes in the United States. You want to make sure you have your audience's attention before you begin, so you decide to present the details of a series of grisly murders committed in your town by a psychopath—even though these murders were not motivated by hate but by mental illness (and so are not examples of hate crimes).

One final piece of advice: Avoid conspicuous appeals. Avoid saying, "I want you to *imitate* Li, a successful honors student," or "If you give to the 'Save the Children' fund, we'll print your name in newspapers so that your *reputation* will improve." Self-centered motivations—greed, imitation, personal pride, fear—should be made subtly as well.

Drawing Upon Diverse External Reference Groups

Reference groups are collections of people and organizations that affect individuals' beliefs, attitudes, and values. They are collectivities "from which an individual derives attitudes and standards of acceptable and appropriate behavior and to which the individual refers for information, direction, and support for a given lifestyle."[8] You may or may not hold actual membership in such groups; you might belong to the Young Republicans Club and not to the Sierra Club (i.e., an environmental lobby) yet be influenced strongly by both. You voluntarily join some reference groups; you might believe in the legal rights of everyone and so join the American Civil Liberties Union. You are a part of other reference groups involuntarily—for example, you are born male or female and a member of an ethnic group. Reference groups can be classified as *membership and nonmembership groups, voluntary and involuntary groups,* and *positive and negative groups.*

With this background, now consider some of the ways you can use reference groups in your persuasive and actuative speeches:

- *Make reference groups you want to use* salient *to your listeners.* You need to bring some group to a conscious level and make sure the group seems relevant to the topic at hand. For example, most students these days are heavy World Wide Web users, so appeal to their Internet experiences when talking about ways to build new circles of friends.
- *Cite the opinions of voluntary, positively viewed groups whose values coincide with positions you're taking.* This is a kind of testimony—and useful, as we saw in Chapter 6, as orienting and probative supporting materials. Before invoking the National Rifle Association in a speech opposing gun control legislation, you will need to sense whether that group is viewed positively or negatively by your audience
- *Cite voluntary, negative groups that the audience does not belong to when they oppose the position you're advocating.* Such groups are "devil-groups," or groups people vilify and actively act against. Such references play into an "us versus them" orientation, and whether you like it or not, some listeners are as willing to act against something as for something else. Drawing on the position of a Right to Life group in a speech delivered to a Pro-Choice gathering would be an example of this strategy.
- *The more significant a person's role in any group, the more the group's norms and beliefs influence that person's thoughts and behavior.* The more committed you are to a group's goals, the more likely the values of that group will influence your attitude and behavior. Groups have a normative influence with respect to setting standards—the more active you are in the group, the more impact it will have on you.[9]

- *Talk about reference groups to create a sense of security and belongingness.* Aligning your views specifically with those of positive membership groups important to listeners not only helps you create acceptance but long-lasting acceptance. If you talk to students who are active members of student clubs and organizations, noting those reference groups and their position on issues is helpful in gaining support for your ideas.

Finally, as noted throughout this book, you're usually facing diverse audiences, which means you must work many reference groups into most speeches to reach various segments of your audience. *You must aim for broad-based support of your position.*

Enhancing Personal Credibility

The issue of authority brings us to the fourth essential dimension affecting the persuasive process: credibility, or *ethos*. In Chapter 1, we outlined several factors that can determine listeners' perceptions of your credibility—their sense of your expertise, trustworthiness, competency, sincerity or honesty, friendliness and concern for others, and personal dynamism. You should work to maximize the potential impact of all these factors whenever speaking, regardless of purpose, but they are especially important when you seek to change someone's mind or behavior. The following guidelines can assist you in making decisions about the use of credibility as an effective tool in persuasion.

First, when speaking to people who are relatively unmotivated and do not have enough background information to critically assess what they hear, *the higher your credibility, the better your chances of being a successful persuader.* Conversely, if your credibility is low, even strong arguments will not overcome your initial handicap.[10] This guideline should give you a clear sense of why your own credibility is an important component in your chances for success.

Second, *you can increase the likelihood of being judged as credible when seeking to persuade an audience by taking steps to enhance your image of competence and sincerity.* People who do not take the time to weigh your reasons and evidence are unlikely to change their beliefs and values if they think you've done a poor job of researching the issues or are insincere—they are less likely to judge you as trustworthy. So, you can increase the audience's perception of your competence by (1) carefully setting forth all of the competing positions, ideas, and proposals relevant to a topic *before* you come to your own judgment; (2) reviewing various criteria for judgment to show that your recommendations or positions flow from accepted and generally held criteria; and (3) showing that the recommendations you offer actually will solve the problems you identified in the need step of your speech.

You can increase the audience's sense of your sincerity by (1) showing yourself to be open to correction and criticism should any listener wish to question you (i.e., a calmly delivered, relevant response does more to defuse hecklers than responding in kind); (2) exuding personal warmth in your relations with the audience; (3) maintaining direct eye contact with listeners; and (4) recognizing anyone who has helped you understand and work on the issue or problem.

Third, *heighten audience members' sense of your expertise, friendliness, and dynamism, especially when seeking to move them to action.* People are unlikely to change their routines on your recommendation unless they feel you know what you're talking about, you have their best interests in mind, and you're excited about your own proposal. Expertise can be demonstrated by (1) documenting your sources of information; (2) using a variety of sources as cross-checks on each other; (3) presenting your information and need analyses in well-organized ways; (4) using clear, simple visual aids when they are appropriate or necessary; (5) providing adequate background information on controversial issues; (6) competently separating causes from effects, short-term from long-term effects, hard facts from wishes or dreams, and one proposal from others; and (7) delivering your speeches in a calm and forthright manner.

A sense of friendliness and concern for others can be created by treating yourself and others as human beings, regardless of how controversial the topic is and how intensely you disagree with others, and by depersonalizing issues, or talking in terms of the "real-world" problems rather than in terms of personalities and ideologies. An audience's sense of your dynamism can be enhanced by speaking vividly, drawing clear images of the events you describe; using sharp, fresh metaphors and active rather than passive verbs; and expressing your ideas with a short, hard-hitting oral style rather than a long, cumbersome written style and with varied conversational-vocal patterns, and animated body, direct eye contact rather than reliance on your notes, and a firm, upright stance.[11]

A public speaker's principal communicative virtue is the presence of a living, active human being behind the lectern—a person who embodies a message and whose own values are expressed in and through the message. People command more attention and interest than written words, and unlike films and videotapes, people can feel, react to audience members, and create a sense of urgency and directness. Hence, personal credibility is an extremely valuable asset for the persuader and actuator.

TYPES OF PERSUASIVE AND ACTUATIVE SPEECHES

There are many ways to classify persuasive and actuative speeches, but here, we examine them in terms of the demands each type makes upon an audience's psychological state and level of activity. We examine speeches of reinforcement, modification, and actuation.

Speeches of Reinforcement

Americans are joiners. To get our political, economic, social, and personal work done, we constantly organize ourselves into groups and associations. Action-oriented groups gather and package the latest information, keep on top of issues that are important to the group members, and propose solutions to specific problems. Service groups organize charities, perform volunteer work, and provide support for other activities in communities. An inevitable fact of group life is that as time goes by, members' interest in activities declines, membership drops, and the cause for which the group was formed gets lost in the myriad other causes competing for the attention and support of people in the community. Periodically, people need to be reminded why they joined a group, what its services are, and how the group helps them meet their personal goals.

In public speaking, **reinforcement** is a process of calling up the original beliefs and values that caused people to join a group in the first place and of reinvigorating audience members so they once more contribute their time, energy, and finances to the tasks needing to be done. In a practical sense, reinforcement speeches are *epideictic:* they seek to increase adherence to—or rejection of—a particular set of values. As Perelman and Olbrechts-Tyteca observe:

> Epideictic discourse sets out to increase the intensity of adherence to certain values, which might not be contested when considered on their own but may nevertheless not prevail against other values that might come into conflict with them. . . . In epideictic oratory, *the speaker turns educator.*[12] (Emphasis added.)

Reinforcement speeches are called for when people behave as though they are unconcerned about the problem and are unwilling to actively seek remedies. The key to reinforcement speaking is motivation. People may say, "Sure, I support the Republican platform," or "Yeah, I agree with SADD's efforts to control drug and alcohol use in the schools," but they may not be motivated to act on the basis of their convictions. They need to have their original commitment resurrected.

Speeches of Modification

Unlike speeches of reinforcement, speeches of **modification** seek specific psychological changes in one's belief state, attitudes toward an object, or basic values. Speeches of this type have been the central feature in the art of rhetoric since the time of the early Greeks. Whether your present or future role is that of a student, businessperson, lawyer, minister, sales clerk, doctor, or parent, the task of changing the views of others is a constant demand of your daily life. Using the categories of beliefs, attitudes, and values described in Chapter 5, we can examine three subtypes of speeches aimed at modifying the views of listeners.

Changing Beliefs.   The psychological basis for most speeches aimed at changing someone's beliefs about the world is differentiation. That is, one can get you to change your beliefs about anything from eating seaweed to the U.S. response to conflict in the former Soviet republics by persuading you to perceive those matters in different ways. Persuaders who want you to differentiate between your old way of looking at something and a newer way of seeing it may use one (or more) of three basic strategies:

1. *Descriptive accounts.* A focus on specific characteristics of a product, event, or issue is one means of providing "good reasons" for accepting a proposal. Someone might persuade you to consider tofu as an acceptable food by assuring you that its vitamin and mineral content is superior to that of foods in your normal diet. To the extent this remains a one-sided strategy, descriptive accounts are not always the strongest move you can make. A stronger approach is to build on this strategy by considering the negatives—questions that the audience might naturally have regarding why tofu should be added to their diet—and offering reasons that make the negatives appear less influential or significant.

2. *Narrative.* A persuader may use narrative forms—for example, by telling a story about the United States preparedness level going into the Korean Conflict and ending with the moral that the country can never let down its guard. Two features of storytelling are essential if the narrative is to have persuasive force. First, listeners must perceive the story to be probable; it must make coherent sense to them. Second, the story must possess what Fisher terms "narrative fidelity"—it must appear consistent with other stories listeners have heard.[13] When both features are present, a story can function as a powerful image to move an audience.

3. *Appeals to uniqueness.* Someone attempting to get you to change your beliefs about a politician may convince you that candidate is "not like all the others," pointing to unique aspects of that person's background, experience, public service, honesty, and commitment to action.

These three strategies are effective to the extent listeners perceive the message to be important, novel, and plausible. The message must be one that is not already well internalized by the audience members (i.e., they aren't already convinced), and the rationale for change must appear credible to them. Finally, the change itself must be seen as feasible or practical.[14]

Changing Attitudes.   Attitude change probably is the most heavily researched psychological change of this century.[15] Given the previous discussion of attitude as predisposition, you're already aware this form of change involves modifying one's evaluation of an object from "good" to "bad"—or at least to "neutral."

Because attitudes are attached to beliefs (e.g., "Opportunities for women are increasing in this country [belief] and that is good [attitude]."), sometimes persuaders attempt to change an attitude by attacking a belief. If a speaker can show that the "glass ceiling" remains the norm for women's advancement, he or she then can link that assertion to a negative attitude (e.g., "The continued presence of the glass ceiling is harmful to women."). Because attitudes are organized into clusters around a value, they sometimes can be changed by getting people to think in different valuative terms.

Attitudes can be changed not only by attacking underlying beliefs or overarching values but also by direct assault. Parents attempt to instill any number of attitudes in their children by repeatedly offering short "lectures" (e.g., "Spinach is good for you," "Don't give in to peer pressure—be an individual."). Repetition often has the desired effect, because children accept the attitude as their own and live by its creed.

Changing Values.   Perhaps the most difficult challenge for any persuader is to change people's value orientations. As noted in earlier chapters, values are fundamental anchors, basic ways of organizing our view of the world and our actions in it. They are difficult—but not impossible—to change. Three techniques often are used:

1. *Valuative shifts.* Like differentiation, this technique asks an audience member to look at an issue or proposal from a different valuative vantage point. The person asking you to buy insurance, for example, tells you to look at it not simply as financial protection (a pragmatic value) but as family protection and a source of peace of mind (sociological and psychological values). Such appeals can persuade people to shift their valuative orientation and see an issue or proposal in a new way.

2. *Appeals to consistency.* When members of the Nature Conservancy hear appeals beginning with "We favor . . . ," they are being asked to approve a certain measure to remain consistent with others in their reference group. This will have an effect if approval of the reference group is a positive social value for them; if they are thinking of leaving the group, the "we" appeal will have less impact. When someone projects a value orientation from the present to the future ("If you like horror films, you'll positively love Stephen King movies."), he or she is appealing to a logical consistency between horror films as a genre and the films made from King novels as a specific example of the genre.

3. *Transcendence.* This sophisticated method for getting you to change your values approaches the issue from the perspective of a "higher" value. Notice the speeches by Representatives Richard Gephardt and J. C. Watts at the end of this chapter: Both asked listeners to view the impeachment of President Clinton in 1999 from higher values—social harmony built around "respect and fairness and decency" to Gephardt and basic issues of "right and wrong" to Watts.

Thus, speeches of modification may seek a change in beliefs, attitudes, or values. Speeches designed to bring about these kinds of changes in listeners demand a higher level of communicative competence than most other types of speeches. Again, preparation time spent thinking about the motivational springs within one's listeners is key.

Speeches of Actuation

Moving uncommitted or apathetic people to action is a chore many prefer to avoid. For example, you may have heard such expressions from friends and acquaintances as "I don't like to ask people to contribute money to a cause, even if it's worthy," "Don't ask me to solicit signatures for that petition—I feel like I'm intruding on others' privacy," or "I'm just not persuasive enough to get people to volunteer to work at the Big Brothers/Big Sisters auction—ask Maria." If all of us felt this way, little would be accomplished. In some cases, simply making a living requires that we move others to action. Even if you take one of these positions, you've undoubtedly asked others to act on your behalf in other ways ("I need a ride to Fargo this weekend; would you take me up there?"). Though such requests are interpersonal encounters, they share the same features as a more elaborate speech of **actuation**—the listener may well respond with "What's in it for me?" Getting people to see and accept the benefits that will accrue from acting as you desire is the primary purpose: *An actuative speech seeks, as its final outcome, a set of specifiable actions from its audience.* These actions may be as diverse as giving personal time to an activity (visiting a local nursing home), contributing money to a cause or product (donating to the United Way), or changing a habit (stopping smoking).

There are two types of audiences for whom actuative speeches generally are appropriate: those who believe in the idea or action but are lethargic about doing anything, and those who doubt the value of the action and are uninformed or uninvolved. The second situation is our concern here.

As in the case of speeches of reinforcement and modification, *the key to effective actuation is motivation.* No matter how wonderful the new products, exciting the political candidate, or worthy the cause, unless a listener is personally convinced that the product, candidate, or cause will make a significant change in his or her life, your speech will fail to have its intended effect.

STRUCTURING PERSUASIVE AND ACTUATIVE SPEECHES

The overall structure of a persuasive or an actuative speech incorporates the features of the motivated sequence—attention, need, satisfaction, visualization, and action—relevant to the specific type of speech. Within each step, as appropriate to the topic and occasion, other patterns of organization can be used to bring a sense of coherence and cohesiveness to each step.

The Motivated Sequence and Reinforcement Speeches

The visualization and action steps are crucial elements in most reinforcement speeches, because listeners already are convinced of the problem and are predisposed to accept particular solutions. The most important goal in a reinforcement speech is to get listeners to renew their previous commitments and charge once more into the public arena to accomplish a common objective.

COMMUNICATION RESEARCH DATELINE

RESISTANCE TO COUNTERPERSUASION

In this chapter, we've concentrated on the issue of persuading—increasing or otherwise changing people's acceptance of certain beliefs, attitudes, and values. We have not, however, focused on the ways in which you can increase your listeners' *resistance* to ideas that run counter to your own. Besides persuading them to accept your beliefs or attitudes, you also may need to protect them against *counterpersuasion*—attempts by others to influence your audience away from your position.

As in taking a vaccine to ward off a disease, you may *inoculate* your audience against your opponents' arguments. Studies by Michael Pfau and others of political advertising have found voters who received previous messages that an opponent would attack the candidate and voters who also received additional refutative arguments against the purported attack were far more resistant to the opponent's message. This offers practical support for the view that forewarning an audience may be helpful. As Benoit's analysis of the research on inoculation has suggested, it does not appear to matter whether the type of forewarning—letting audience members know in advance they'll be exposed to a counterpersuasive attempt—is general, as in "an attack on me is imminent from my opponent" or more

precise with respect to the topic and position to be taken by the attacker. Nor does it appear to matter whether the attack really is imminent or comes later.

Another strategy that increases resistance involves the amount of knowledge that people bring to a situation. For example, Hirt and Sherman found that individuals with greater knowledge are more resistant to refutational arguments. Thus, you can increase potential resistance to messages that are contrary to your own by adding to the audience's knowledge about the issues involved.

For Further Reading

William L. Benoit. "Forewarning and Persuasion," *Forewarning and Persuasion: Advances through Meta-Analysis,* eds. Mike Allen and Roy W. Preiss (Dubuque, IA: Brown and Benchmark, 1994), 159–184.

Hirt, E. R., and S. J. Sherman. "The Role of Prior Knowledge in Explaining Hypothetical Events," *Journal of Experimental Social Psychology* 21 (1985): 591–643.

Pfau, Michael. "The Potential of Inoculation in Promoting Resistance to the Effectiveness of Comparative Advertising Messages," *Communication Quarterly* 40 (1992): 26–44.

Pfau, Michael, and Michael Burgoon. "Inoculation in Political Communication," *Communication Monographs* 15 (1988): 91–111.

Beliefs, attitudes, and values are based, in part, on the traditions and customs of reference groups, although people differ in their degree of direct reliance.

USING THE MOTIVATED SEQUENCE IN A REINFORCEMENT SPEECH

PUTTING "ATHLETE" BACK INTO THE STUDENT-ATHLETE

The Situation: Your team has lost the last three games, in one instance by a lopsided margin. As you go into the final league game, the chance to gain home court for the playoffs is up for grabs—lose, and you travel; win, and you play the first game at home.

Specific Purpose: To reinforce the listeners' previous commitment to the team.

Attention Step

    I. Winning means we can look at ourselves with pride.
   II. Winning means we meet the expectations of our supporters.

Need Step

    I. We've already won as students.
       A. You are proven student athletes, with the highest academic average of any team on this campus.
       B. The seniors will graduate.
   II. What we need now is to win as athletes.
       A. You play as you practice.

B. Work ethic determines results.

C. Only we, as athletes, should determine our destiny.

Satisfaction/Visualization Step (Combined, as the Solution [*Win the Game*] is Accepted)

I. Given our last three losses, we could ask, "Why not quit now?"

    A. It insults your commitment to excellence.

    B. It lets your fans down.

    C. Anyone who quits now lets the others down.

II. Renew commitment to hard work, fun, and a winning attitude.

    A. These are the ingredients that led to our past success.

    B. They will be sufficient to carry us through this week, into the game, and beyond.

III. What does winning this final game mean?

    A. Being satisfied with your own participation as a player and team member.

    B. Recognition for you and the university.

    C. Home court advantage—and that is worth 10 points with our fans!!

Action Step

I. Now is the time to do what must be done.

    A. Practice hard.

    B. Play this last league game as if it were your last.

II. Win or lose, be satisfied with your individual effort.

    A. Individual and team integrity and discipline count.

    B. Remember, "Winning is everything" only when done for the right reasons.

The Motivated Sequence and Speeches of Modification

Regardless of the nature or scope of the psychological modification you ask of your listeners, you can use the motivated sequence. When asking people to accept your judgments about a person, practice, institution, or theory, you can seek to do these things:

- Capture the *attention* and interest of the audience.
- Clarify that a judgment concerning the worth of the person, practice, or institution is *needed* by showing why such a judgment is important to your listeners personally and why it is important to their community, state, nation, or world.
- *Satisfy* the need by setting the criteria upon which an intelligent judgment may be based and by advancing the judgment you believe to be correct and showing how it meets the criteria.
- Picture the advantages that will accrue from agreeing with the judgment you advance or the evils that will result from failing to endorse it [*visualization step*].
- If appropriate, appeal for acceptance of the proposed judgment [*action step*].

Using the Motivated Sequence in a Modification Speech

STRENGTH THROUGH CULTURAL DIVERSITY

The Situation: Henri Mann Morton presented a keynote speech at the Northwest's Colville and Okanogan National Forest conference on cultural diversity on March 23, 1989. As a Native American woman, she was in an excellent position to comment on the issues related to gaining workforce parity for all peoples. During the speech, she differentiates the Native American experience from that of others in the hope of modifying her audience's beliefs about the values and interests of Native Americans.

Specific Purpose: To modify audience beliefs about the values and interests of Native Americans.

Attention Step

I. "Thanks for honoring me with your gracious invitation to speak."
II. "We must never forget that American Indians were the first people to live in this beautiful country."

Need Step

I. The beliefs of the Native American are unique.
   A. They believe in "the dualities of life . . . sky-earth; sun/moon; love-hate; wisdom-ignorance."
   B. The most important duality is man-woman as together they are "part of the great sacred circle of life."
II. Tribal views also are unique—with different tribes holding different beliefs about women sacred.
   A. The Hopi believe in the Spider Grandmother who made the four races of people.
   B. The Iroquois give status to the Clan Mother.
   C. The Cherokee give status to the Beloved Woman.
   D. Each tribe grants respect to Indian women.
III. As a woman, I am part of that which has preceded me.
   A. "My grandmothers have been here for all time."
   B. "The land you strive to protect is my grandmother—my mother."
IV. Once the majority, we are now the "minority of minorities."
   A. We number less than 1 percent of the population.
   B. Due to our small number, policymakers are generally uninformed about our culture.
   C. "I would characterize American society as . . . 'culturally disrespectful.'"
V. Historically, American Indians have had three "agencies of oppression."
   A. Church: Christianize the pagans.
   B. Government: Assimilate them.
   C. Education: Civilize the "savages."

Satisfaction Step

   I. Policymakers should acknowledge five basic truths.
     A. "Indians have been here for thousands of years."
     B. This is their homeland.
     C. Their own distinct cultures have evolved. . . .
     D. We were not forced into abandoning our cultures.
     E. Assimilation and acculturation occur on individual's terms."
  II. The American Indian culture can contribute without changing.
     A. To the Iroquois, for example, "peace was the law."
       1. The same word is used for both *peace* and *law.*
       2. "Peace was a way of life."
     B. The allegory of the Great White Pine represents the unity of peace with law and land.
       1. For the Iroquois, the Tree symbolizes law.
       2. The Tree's branches symbolize shelter within the law.
       3. The Tree's roots symbolize the law's ability to stretch out and embrace all peoples.

Visualization Step

   I. With recognition of the Indian's true nature and contribution can come change.
     A. Change is a cause for celebration.
     B. "With clarity of vision we can celebrate the natural diversity of our universe and our world."
  II. The Indian values—patience, honest, acceptance, respect—can serve as the foundation for good interpersonal relationships in a culturally diverse world.

Action Step

   I. I applaud your commitment to a culturally diverse workforce.
  II. My tribute to you is to share with you a Cheyenne philosophical belief: "A nation is not conquered until the hearts of its women are on the ground. Then it is done, no matter how brave its warriors nor how strong its weapons."
     A. This is the power of women as equals.
     B. This is why the most powerful pairing is men and women working together.[16]

The Motivated Sequence and Actuative Speeches

Demands for action can be issued and defended very efficiently by using the motivated sequence. In fact, the desire to structure speeches that move people to action (e.g., to buy a product or engage in another specified behavior) was the impetus behind Alan Monroe's development of this organizational scheme. Read the outline here to get a clear sense of how the motivated sequence can be used in developing an actuative speech.

USING THE MOTIVATED SEQUENCE IN AN ACTUATIVE SPEECH

ENVIRONMENTAL RACISM

The Situation: You are presenting a speech to your classmates to convince them environmental racism is not only harmful but should be eliminated.

Specific Purpose: To persuade the class to believe that environmental racism should be eliminated.

Attention Step

I. "Every day I wake up and go dump my trash in the Oretega's backyard."
  A. I really don't, but the expression is an apt summary of what our government does every day—dumping garbage near the homes of the poor and dispossessed.
  B. This activity has become known as *environmental racism.*

Need Step

  I. Lower-income people and minorities suffer disproportionately higher exposure to hazardous waste.
 II. Waste facilities are not the only cause of the problem.
  A. Prisons are placed closer to lower income/minority populations.
  B. Freeways cut through these neighborhoods.
  C. Polluting industries are located nearer these areas.
III. The problem is not a small one.
  A. A study found that three out of five African-American and Hispanic families live in communities with uncontrolled hazardous waste.
  B. In Houston, Texas, for example, all five landfills and three-quarters of the incinerators are in African-American neighborhoods.
  C. In East Los Angeles, for another example, five prisons and seven freeways cut through the area, home to predominantly Hispanic and African-American families.

Satisfaction/Visualization Steps

  I. The solution is not an easy one to realize, because these areas generally are powerless to stop further encroachment.
 II. Mainstream environmental organizations need to join forces with those organizations already in the affected communities, such as Victims of a Toxic Environment United (VOTE United).
III. Only through such efforts might the United States stop trying to hide its "third world" conditions in poverty stricken, powerless communities.
 IV. Only through such efforts might ethnic and minority citizens cease to fear for their health and safety.

Action Step

  I. I am asking you to sign a petition stating support for the merging of mainstream and local environmental organizations to battle this form of racism.

II. The petition will be sent to Earthshare, a coalition of mainstream environmental organizations dedicated to fighting environmental racism.[17]

ASSESSING SAMPLE SPEECHES

The following two persuasive speeches were offered during the dramatic U.S. House of Representatives debate over Articles of Impeachment focused on President Bill Clinton, December 18–19, 1998.[18] On Saturday the 19th, both Democrats and Republicans gave time to their best speakers to offer short, persuasive speeches to justify the votes for and against impeachment that occurred in the afternoon. Among the best speakers that day were Rep. Richard Gephardt (D-Missouri) and Rep. J. C. Watts (R-Oklahoma). Both chose transcendent strategies based on value appeals, arguing that valuative commitments should guide specific actions (votes for or against impeachment).

Rep. Watts spoke before Rep. Gephardt. His strategy was dual: appeal to our care and sympathy for children *[affiliation, companionship]* and to their clear, uncomplicated sense of honesty *[conformity, loyalty, tradition]*. Especially in paragraphs 2–5, the theme of "listening" to our children and their clear sense of rightness was sketched expertly. Rep. Watts contrasted their sense with adult attitudes, which he said we could see in public opinion polls (paragraphs 6–7). Having transcended the politics of impeachment with these appeals primarily to the affiliation cluster of motivational appeals, he then asked his listeners to apply those clear moral guidelines from children to the impeachment proceedings (paragraph 8). He concluded with a negative visualization: "In this moment, our children's future is more important than our future. If our country looks the other way, our country will lose its way" (paragraph 9).

Rep. Gephardt spoke later that morning. He, too, went to affiliative motivational appeals when talking about the Founding Fathers *[tradition]* and "the altar of an unattainable morality" *[reverence]*. By paragraphs 7 and 8, he was contrasting "the death of representative democracy" *[fear]* from the power cluster with "healing" *[companionship]* from the affiliation cluster. Like Rep. Watts, therefore, Rep. Gephardt sought to transcend the political situation with social or communal appeals. He ended with negative and positive visualizations: The House now on "the brink of the abyss" in paragraph 10, contrasted with "a new politics of respect and fairness and decency" in paragraph 11. Such a new politics, he concluded, was possible only if Congress had "the wisdom and the courage and the goodness to save itself today" (paragraph 12). So, both Rep. Watts and Rep. Gephardt had warnings for their colleagues, though only Gephardt tried to turn the negative into a positive vision—and thereby, he hoped, to turn some votes for to votes against impeachment.

That there were Republican and Democratic votes both for and against impeachment—and that not all of the proposed Articles of Impeachment were passed—is testament to the power of persuasive speech.

SPEECH FOR IMPEACHMENT

Rep. J. C. Watts

Mr. Speaker, there is no joy sometimes in upholding the law. It is so unpleasant sometimes that we hire other people to do it for us. Ask the police or judges. It is tiring and thankless. But we know it must be done, because if we do not point at lawlessness, our children cannot see it. If we do not label lawlessness, our children cannot recognize it. And if we do not punish lawlessness, our children will not believe it./1

So if someone were to ask me, "J.C., why did you vote for the articles of impeachment?" I would say I did it for our children. How can we tell our children that honesty is the best policy if we do not demand honesty as a policy? How can we expect a Boy Scout to honor his oath if elected officials do not honor theirs? How can we expect a business executive to honor a promise when the chief executive abandons his or hers?/2

Whether it is a promise or a truth or a vow or an oath, a person's word is the firm footing our society stands upon, and the average kid understands that. They do not need a grand jury to enforce it. They say "cross your heart, hope to die"; "pinkie promise"; "king's X"; "blood brother." These are the childhood instincts that seek to draw a line between the honest and the dishonest, between the principled and the unprincipled./3

Ask the children. The kid who lies does not last and they do not bicker over what is and what is not a lie. They know. So do I. So do the American people./4

Time and again, we wanted the essence of truth and we got the edges of the truth. We hear, "Let's get on with the business of our country." What business is more important than teaching our children right from wrong? Some say it is all about politics and party lines. If that were true. I would have given in to popular opinion. But what is popular is not always what is right./5

Some say polls are against this. Polls measure changing feelings, not steadfast principle. Polls would have rejected the Ten Commandments. Polls would have embraced slavery and ridiculed women's rights./6

Some say we must draw this to a close. I say we must draw a line between right and wrong; not with a tiny fine line of an executive fountain pen, but with the big, thick lead of a Number 2 pencil. We must do it so every kid in America can see it./7

The point is not whether the President can prevail, but whether truth can prevail. We need to cease the cannibalizing of Members of Congress. We need to cease the attacks on the President and his family because, friends, this is not about the President of the United States. He is not the injured party. Our country is./8

In this moment, our children's future is more important than our future. If our country looks the other way, our country will lose its way./9

SPEECH AGAINST IMPEACHMENT

Rep. Richard Gephardt

Mr. Speaker, I stood on this floor yesterday and implored all of us to say that the politics of slash and burn must end. I implored all of us that we must turn away from the politics of personal destruction and return to the politics of values./1

It is with that same passion that I say to all of you today that the gentleman from Louisiana (Mr. BOB LIVINGSTON) is a worthy and good and honorable man./2

I believe his decision to retire [after sexual indiscretions were revealed] is a terrible capitulation to the negative forces that are consuming our political system and our country, and I pray with all my heart that he will reconsider this decision./3

Our Founding Fathers created a system of government of men, not of angels. No one standing in this House today can pass the puritanical test of purity that some are demanding that our elected leaders take. If we demand that mere mortals live up to this standard, we will see our seats of government lay empty and we will see the best, most able people unfairly cast out of public service./4

We need to stop destroying imperfect people at the altar of an unobtainable morality. We need to start living up to the standards which the public in its infinite wisdom understands, that imperfect people must strive towards, but too often fall short./5

We are now rapidly descending into a politics where life imitates farce, fratricide dominates our public debate, and America is held hostage to tactics of smear and fear./6

Let all of us here today say no to resignation, no to impeachment, no to hatred, no to intolerance of each other and no to vicious self-righteousness./7

We need to start healing. We need to start binding up our wounds. We need to end this downward spiral which will culminate in the death of representative democracy./8

I believe this healing can start today by changing the course we have begun. This is exactly why we need this today to be bipartisan. This is why we ask the opportunity to vote on a bipartisan censure resolution, to begin the process of healing our Nation and healing our people./9

We are on the brink of the abyss. The only way we stop this insanity is through the force of our own will. The only way we stop this spiral is for all of us to finally say "enough."/10

Let us step back from the abyss and let us begin a new politics of respect and fairness and decency, which realizes what has come before./11

May God have mercy on this Congress, and may Congress have the wisdom and the courage and the goodness to save itself today./12

CHAPTER SUMMARY

The rhetorical arts of persuasion and actuation are fundamental to any democratic society. Not only are they the heart and soul of capitalism, American mass media, and politics, but they are necessary to the operation of daily life.

Effective reinforcement, modifying, and actuative speeches are functions of the following:

- Adapting to an audience's psychological states (i.e., psychological orientations, predispositions toward the topic, and degrees of change).

- Selecting motivational appeals that will resonate with the felt needs and desires of audience members.
- Drawing upon diverse external reference groups.
- Enhancing personal credibility.

The strategies discussed under each of these topics are not exhaustive, but they suggest mental habits of audience analysis that speakers must employ each time they attempt persuasion. To increase your effectiveness, use them whenever you seek to *reinforce* an audience's commitment to shared values; *modify* listeners' *beliefs, attitudes,* and *values;* or move them to *action.* Using the motivated sequence will assist you in adapting your content and style to the audience.

KEY TERMS

actuation (p. 343)
incremental change (p. 334)
latitude of acceptance (p. 334)
latitude of rejection (p. 334)
lifestyles (p. 331)

modification (p. 340)
one-sided message (p. 334)
psychological state (p. 331)
reference groups (p. 337)

reinforcement (p. 340)
saliency (p. 334)
two-sided message (p. 334)
Values and Lifestyles (VALS) Program (p. 331)

ASSESSMENT ACTIVITIES

1. Analyze the differences between an appeal to persuade and an appeal to actuate in relation to the one or more problems faced by speakers as discussed in this chapter for each of the following situations:
   a. You want your parents to stop eating meat.
   b. You want to convince your best friend not to drop out of school.
   c. You want a stranger to donate money to the local Big Brothers/Big Sisters program.

   In what ways do your appeals differ? What variables account for the differences? Which factors are the most difficult to analyze in each of these situations and why?

2. Develop and present to the class a five-to-seven-minute speech. Follow the steps in the motivated sequence appropriate to the type of speech chosen: reinforcement, modification, or actuation. As you construct your speech, remember the strategies discussed in this chapter, both in terms of the essential features of all persuasive speeches and those specific to your speech. Adapt to the audience as you deem appropriate from your analysis of members' beliefs, attitudes, and values.

REFERENCES

1. A full theory of "good reasons" is developed in Walter R. Fisher, *Human Communication as Narrative* (Columbia, SC: University of South Carolina Press, 1987), chs. 2 and 3.

2. Arnold Mitchell, *The Nine American Lifestyles: Who We Are and Where We're Going* (New York: Macmillan, 1983).

3. For background on one-sided versus two-sided messages, see James B. Stiff, *Persuasive Communication* (New York: Guilford Press, 1994), 117–119.

4. On saliency research, see Richard E. Petty and John T. Cacioppo, *Communication and Persuasion: Central and Peripheral Routes to Attitude Change* (New York: Springer-Verlag, 1986).

5. Latitudes of acceptance and rejection are concepts that form a part of social judgment theory. See Stiff, 139–142 (n. 3); Stephen W. Littlejohn, *Theories of Human Communication*, 4th ed. (Belmont, CA: Wadsworth, 1992), 162–164; and Deirdre Johnston, *The Art and Science of Persuasion* (Dubuque, IA: Brown & Benchmark, 1994), 303–307.

6. Sarah Trenholm, *Persuasion and Social Influence* (Englewood Cliffs, NJ: Prentice-Hall, 1989), 58.

8. Frank J. Boster and Paul Mongeau, "Fear-Arousing Persuasive Messages," *Communication Yearbook 8,* ed. Robert N. Bostrom (Beverly Hills, CA: Sage, 1984), 371.

8. Philip Zimbardo, *Psychology and Life,* 13th ed. (New York: Longman, 1992), 580–581.

9. See Stiff, 52–54 (n. 3).

10. Petty and Cacioppo, 205 (n. 4).

11. A complete summary of research on credibility, which supports these conclusions, is found in Stephen Littlejohn, "A Bibliography of Studies Related to Variables of Source Credibility," *Bibliographical Annual in Speech Communication: 1971,* ed. Ned A. Shearer (New York: National Communication Association, 1972), 1–40. For some extensions of this research, see Stiff (n. 3) as well as Petty and Cacioppo (n. 4).

12. Chaim Perelman and Lucie Olbrechts-Tyteca, *The New Rhetoric: A Treatise on Argumentation,* ed. John Wilkinson and Purcell Weaver (Notre Dame, IN: University of Notre Dame Press, 1969), 51.

13. Fisher, ch. 5.

14. Donald Dean Morley and Kim B. Walker, "The Role of Importance, Novelty, and Plausibility in Producing Belief Change," *Communication Monographs* 54 (1987): 436–442. Morley develops these ideas theoretically in "Subjective Message Constructs: A Theory of Persuasion," *Communication Monographs* 54 (1987): 183–203.

15. Kay Deaux and Lawrence S. Wrightsman, *Social Psychology,* 5th ed. (Pacific Grove, CA: Brooks/Cole, 1988), 160–209. See also Gerald R. Miller, Michael Burgoon, and Judee K. Burgoon, "The Functions of Human Communication in Changing Attitudes and Gaining Compliance," in *Handbook of Rhetorical and Communication Theory,* eds. Carroll C. Arnold and John Waite Bowers (Boston: Allyn and Bacon, 1984), 400–474.

16. Adapted from a speech by Henri Mann Morton, "Strength Through Cultural Diversity," *Native American Reader,* ed. Jerry D. Blanche (Juneau, AK: Denali Press, 1990), 400–474.

17. Outline adapted from Kim Triplett, "Environmental Racism," *Winning Orations 1994.* Reprinted by permission of Larry Schnoor, Interstate Oratorical Association, Mankato State University, MN.

18. The texts for Reps. Watts' and Gephardt's speeches on 19 December 1998 are from the *Congressional Record,* Proceedings and Debates of the 105th Congress, 2nd sess. (Washington, D.C.: U.S. Government Printing Office, 1998), 144, no. 155:H11973-4, H2031-2.

Chapter 15

Argument and Critical Thinking

What action, if any, should the United States take against Iraq? Should our university institute a new technology fee? Should we rent a movie tonight? These are very different questions, yet they are alike in one major respect: Each is debatable. None of the questions automatically suggests a "right" or "true" answer with which all would agree. Answering any of these questions with a simple "yes" or "no" will invite others to ask, "Why do you believe as you do?" You will be expected to provide reasons and evidence for your position, and in turn, your response may well be challenged by your listeners. In short, this exchange involves you and your listeners in **argumentation**—the give and take involved in advancing reasons for and against a particular claim that has been advanced. This process can be discussed in terms of **argument**—the actual "product" that results from the combination of a *claim* plus supporting *reasons* and *evidence*—as well as the act of **arguing** itself.[1] As you argue, you also engage in **critical thinking**—the process of examining the relationship between your own reasons and the claim you are advocating and the reasons or evidence offered by those challenging your argument.[2]

If the questions raised are capable of being answered truthfully, without any concern for being mistaken at some later point, there is no cause for challenge. Few such questions, however, have such answers available. Hence, argument is a constant companion of those issues and ideas for which there are no certain answers. In arguing, our search is for the "best answer" we can offer given the knowledge available. We do not know for certain if taking action against Iraq will end the threat of chemical weaponry, nor do we know if a technology fee is the right way to raise money for new computer equipment. Finally, we cannot be certain that renting a movie is the optimum choice (especially if we have an exam tomorrow). Given this uncertainty, the best solution is to think critically about our choices by testing the evidence offered in support of reasons—is it reliable?—and examining the relationship between reasons and claims—do the reasons really support the claim?

As we do, two features of argumentation are worthy of comment. First, argument is a social process. Second, argument is aimed at justifying our beliefs and actions. We begin with an examination of the social process involved in arguing with others, and we then consider what is involved in justifying claims, with a focus on improving your effectiveness as an arguer.

ARGUMENT AND CULTURAL COMMITMENTS

Argument and critical thinking are bound together in public communication. Exchanging views in the social world automatically includes the critical assessment of those ideas. Engaging in argument commits you to the social conventions governing deliberation, whether in private interchanges with close friends or in public settings among friends and strangers.[3]

Commitment to Change Your Mind

You—and those who challenge you—must be willing to alter personal beliefs or actions when faced with strong counterargument.[4] Recently, the U.S. House of Representatives debated the impeachment of President Clinton. In the process of reviewing evidence, it was clear that several congressional representatives had made up their minds—no amount of counterargument, it would seem, would have moved some from their position, either as supportive of impeachment or of some form of censure. Arguing, as we define it, requires greater flexibility in positions taken. You've experienced the frustration of arguing with someone who does not accept this social convention: a stubborn friend or other opponent who believes only what he or she is saying and simply refuses to acknowledge the possibility the position being advanced is wrong.

Commitment to Knowledge

Argument fails where ignorance prevails. In addition to accepting the possibility of being wrong, both parties to an argument also must accept a commitment to learn from each other, search for new information, and test evidence to ensure that the best possible information is being used to support alternative positions. Those who are certain of their own beliefs ("Don't confuse me with facts. My mind is made up.") are closed to information counter to that which they already accept or which supports their position.

Commitment to Worthy Subjects

Ever been in a silly argument? Unfortunately, many arguments can be summarized in the following statement: "Argumentation concerns talk between the uninformed and the misinformed about the inconsequential." The value of critical thinking and the need to test ideas in private or in public are wasted on people who are just plain disagreeable and nasty. Although some have a psychological need to be contentious, more important there is a social need for argument about issues that matter, about causes that do, in fact, make a difference in how we treat and live with each other.

Commitment to Rules

Argument is a rule-governed process of arriving at a conclusion that, to the best of one's knowledge, is justifiable as a basis for belief or action. The rules may focus on the overall procedures for engaging in argument, as in using parliamentary procedures to govern who talks, when, and for how long. The rules also focus on the product itself: not any reason will support any claim—there needs to be some kind of logical, rational connection between a given reason and the claim being offered.

The reliance on reasons given for a belief or action constitutes the major difference between argumentation and mere fighting. As such, argumentation is a form of persuasion in that it seeks to change the beliefs, attitudes, values, and behaviors of others. At the same time, it also is a form of mutual truth-testing, helping participants arrive at the best possible conclusions given the information available at the time. Thus, the process is more thoroughly *rule-governed* than other forms of public presentation.

These four commitments define the social parameters of argument in the social community. Whether you are engaging in private discussion or public deliberation, the same conventions apply. The process of thinking critically about how argument proceeds depends, in addition, on understanding how one arrives at a justifiable defense—or attack—of another person's position.

ARGUMENT AS JUSTIFYING BELIEF AND ACTION

The analysis of how one justifies a position begins with the **claim** being advanced. Then, the nature of the **evidence** used in support of the claim and the major **reasoning patterns** (sometimes referred to as the *warrants* or *inferences*) used to connect evidence to claims are examined.

Types of Claims

Most argumentative speeches assert that something is or is not the case, is desirable or undesirable, or should or should not be done. The first step in constructing a successful argument is to determine clearly the nature of the claim you wish to establish.

Claims of Fact.   If you are trying to convince your listeners that "raising tuition to the levels proposed will result in fewer applications to attend this university," you are presenting a claim of fact—asserting that an audience is justified in believing this state of affairs will occur. When confronted with a **factual claim,** two questions are likely to arise among critical listeners:

1. *By what criteria or standards of judgment should the accuracy of this claim be measured?* Some standards are rather obvious. If you were asked to judge a person's height, using a yardstick or other instrument would provide the answer. Listeners look for similar kinds of yardsticks when asked to evaluate more complex claims. Before agreeing that a tuition

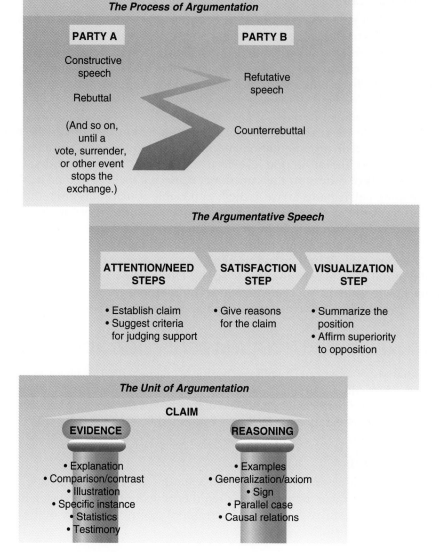

FIGURE 15.1 The Levels of Argumentation

hike will result in fewer applications, critical thinkers want to know exactly what the proposed tuition hike is as well as what constitutes "fewer"—and when does this become a significant loss to worry about?

2. *Do the facts of the situation fit the criteria as set forth?* Has the speaker identified what is meant by "fewer" such that it will be clear this is a reasonable criteria? Will 5 to 10 fewer applications constitute the truth of the claim? (In a narrow, literal sense, yes, but then what is the point of the claim if it is satisfied with one less application?) The criteria must be

seen as reasonable and making a significant difference regarding the risk associated with raising tuition. Realize that the audience may choose to disagree with your criteria as well as with your evidence. Hence, you need to be prepared to defend both.

Claims of Value.   A claim also may incorporate value judgments in asserting that your idea is worthy or that the idea of an opponent is undesirable or unjustified. In these cases, you are articulating a **value claim.** As with a factual claim, a value claim is supported by standards or criteria and by the illustration of how your value term meets those criteria. The claim that price controls cause shortages implies a value—things that cause shortages are not worthy of consideration. You must, however, do more than simply suggest a preference ("I don't like price controls."). You need to know how price controls function and what negative effects they create. This knowledge leads you to the criteria for judging the worth of price controls, which makes it easier to argue for their inadequacy because of the negative effects created.

Claims of Policy.   A **policy claim** recommends a course of action you want the audience to approve. For example, you might claim that "The federal government *should* establish a flat tax rate." The policy claim incorporates fact and value claims as its primary "proofs":

> *Policy:* The federal government should establish a flat tax rate . . . because . . .
> *Value:* A flat tax rate is an equitable tax policy because . . .
> *Fact:* A flat tax rate will simplify present IRS tax codes because . . .

Knowing your andience is critical in arguing on behalf of a client.

Fact: A flat tax rate will produce sufficient revenue because . . .

The key term in the policy claim is *should*—it identifies a proposed policy or defends a policy or action that currently is the case. For our purposes, those policy claims examined will challenge the present system, procedure, or way of doing things.

When establishing or analyzing a policy claim, four questions are relevant:

1. *Is there a need for such a policy or course of action?* If your listeners do not believe a change is called for, they aren't likely to approve your proposal. This does not mean you should avoid new ideas; rather, it suggests that the importance of establishing a need for change depends upon the audience's level of comfort with the present situation.

2. *Is the proposal practical or workable?* Can we afford the expenses it would entail? Will it meet the need as identified? Is the proposal merely being advocated for symbolic reasons, or does it actually have a chance of passage and effect change? If the policy cannot meet these basic tests, what chance does it have?

3. *Will the benefits of your proposal be greater than the disadvantages?* You may be familiar with the expression, "The cure is worse than the disease." People are reluctant to approve a proposal that promises a cure but creates conditions worse than the ones it's designed to correct. Burning a building to the ground to get rid of rats may be efficient, but it is hardly desirable. The benefits and disadvantages must be carefully weighed in concluding that a proposal is, indeed, comparatively better than the present course.

4. *Is the offered proposal superior to any other plan or policy?* Listeners are hesitant to approve a plan if they have reason to believe the current policy is more practical and beneficial. Requiring citizens to move their cars every 2 hours on downtown streets or be ticketed may seem a simple means of easing the parking crunch. Wrong! Any policy will affect some portion of the community more than others, and those whose lives are disrupted will make that known. Policy changes have consequences, and not all people will see the consequences as you do.

These claims—fact, value, policy—make different demands on you as an arguer (see Table 15.1). Your best strategy is to set forth claims, the criteria on which they are based, and the evidence used to support the claim in a straightforward, honest manner. In that way, your audience can see what standard of judgment you are using and determine how *you* see the evidence functioning in relation to the criteria and claim. In some cultures, the context in which you place the claim and evidence and how you argue the point mean more than the actual content of your message.[5]

Previewing the underlying logic of your argument at the start, unless there are solid reasons for delaying this information, enables your audience to follow your line of reasoning. Forecast your argument by saying something like the following: "I hope to convince you that there should be a salary cap on the income earned by professional athletes; if we take this action, it will result in

TABLE 15.1   Types of Claims

Claim	Description	Analysis
Fact	Assertion that something exists.	1. By what criteria is the accuracy of the claim measured? 2. Do the facts of the situation fit the criteria?
Value	Assertion that something is worthy/unworthy.	1. By what standards is something to be judged? 2. How well does the thing measure up?
Policy	Recommendation of a course of action.	1. Is there a need? 2. Is the proposal practical? 3. Are the benefits greater than the disadvantages? 4. Is the proposal better than other courses of action?

fair and equitable treatment for all athletes and will restore faith in the sport for the paying fans."

Evidence

As you discovered in Chapter 6, supporting materials clarify, amplify, and strengthen the ideas in your speech. They also provide evidence for the acceptance of a claim and its supporting points. Evidence is a crucial part of developing a clear, compelling argument, and it can be presented in any of the forms already discussed: explanation, comparison and contrast, illustration, specific instance, statistics, and testimony. As you conduct your search for information, the primary goal is to find supporting material that is both rationally and motivationally relevant to the claim being advanced.

Rationally Relevant Evidence.   The type of evidence you select should reflect the type of claim you advocate. For example, if you are defending the claim that censorship violates the First Amendment guarantee of freedom of speech, testimony from legal authorities will be useful in supporting your argument. On the other hand, examples, illustrations, and statistics work better if you are arguing that a problem exists or a change in practices is needed. If you argue that shark fishing should be more heavily regulated, you'll find that examples of poor fishing practices and statistical evidence related to overfishing and potential loss to the ecosystem will be relevant to your purpose. Always ask yourself, "Given this claim, what evidence is naturally suggested by the subject matter? What type of evidence is logically relevant?"

Motivationally Relevant Evidence.   Listeners often require more than logically relevant support. Your evidence also must create a compelling desire on their part to be involved, endorse the belief, or undertake a course of action. Why should an audience be concerned about regulating shark fishing? To motivate your listeners, you must answer the "So what?" question. To select motivationally relevant material, consider two issues:

1. *What type of evidence will this audience demand?* To orient your thinking, turn this question around and ask, "As a member of the audience, what would I expect as support for this claim to accept it?" What motivates you to accept the argument may well motivate the audience. As noted above, some evidence also seems naturally connected to certain subjects. A claim regarding relative costs of competing plans suggests things like statistical graphs or charts. If the audience is able to say "Yes . . . but . . ." after hearing your evidence, you have not motivated them to accept your claim.

2. *What evidence will generate the best response?* You should pose this question once you've determined the type of evidence required by your argument. For example, if you've decided to use expert testimony, whom should you quote? If you're using an illustration, should you use a factual example from the local group or develop your own? Will your listeners be moved more by a personal story than by a general illustration?

Forms of Reasoning (Inference)

You make connections between claims, criteria, and evidence using different forms of reasoning, or **inferences.** Forms of reasoning are the habitual ways in which a culture or society uses inferences to connect the material supporting a claim with the claim itself. In our culture, there are five primary patterns: *reasoning from example, generalization, sign, parallel case,* and *causal relations.*

Reasoning from Example.   **Reasoning from example,** which also often is called **inductive reasoning,** is the process of examining a series of known occurrences and drawing a general conclusion or of using a single instance to reason to a future instance of the same kind. The conclusion is probable rather than certain: "In every election in our community over the past few years, when a candidate leads in the polls by ten or more points with a month to go, he or she has won. Thus, my candidate will surely win next month." Maybe so—but maybe not. The inference in this case can be stated as "What is true of the particular cases is true of the whole class or, more precisely, future instances of the same class." Most reasoning from example uses multiple instances in inferring a conclusion; however, a single instance can be a powerful illustration on which to base a conclusion. You can argue for example, that one death at an intersection supports the need for a traffic light. Using relevant examples will ensure a high degree of probability and provide strong justification for the adoption of a claim.

Reasoning from Generalization or Axiom.   Applying a general truism to a specific situation is a form of **deductive reasoning.** Whereas inductive reason-

ETHICAL MOMENTS

THE USE OF EVIDENCE

The use of evidence generates several potential ethical dilemmas. Consider the following issues:

1. Should you suppress evidence that contradicts a point you are making? If your opponent is not aware of the information, should you mention it?

2. What about the use of qualifiers? Should you leave in all the "maybe's" and "possibly's" when you read or paraphrase a quotation? If you have to submit a written text or outline, you can use ellipses (i.e., the three dots that indicate something is missing from the original) where the qualifiers once were.

3. Does it make any difference if you overqualify a source? If you've discovered an article by a staff researcher at the National Endowment for the Arts on the issue of funding controversial art, will it hurt to pretend the information is from an associate director of the agency? If it increases the credibility of the information, should it be used?

4. What difference does it make if a poll is conducted by the National Right-to-Life Committee or Planned Parenthood's Pro-Choice Committee? What if each organization asks polling questions in such a way as to encourage a response favorable to their position? Can you just say that "A recent national poll found that 75 percent of our citizens favor abortion rights"? You haven't really lied in suppressing the polling agency or the actual questions asked, have you? Is this acceptable?

ing is typified by an inferential leap on the basis of the evidence, deductive reasoning produces a conclusion that is true only if the premises are true. For example, you may know that generic drugs are cheaper than brand-name drugs. On the basis of this general truism, you ask your druggist for the generic prescription whenever possible, because it will save you money. To the extent the **generalization** holds true, your experience will hold true as well.

Reasoning from Sign.   This pattern uses an observable mark, or symptom, as proof of the existence of a certain state of affairs. **Sign reasoning** occurs, for example, when you note the appearance of a rash or spots on your skin (evidence) and conclude you have the measles (claim). Signs are not causes: A rash does not cause measles, and an ambulance siren does not cause the accident or crisis it responds to. What the rash or the siren means remains open to further examination. While it may be the case that the rash is a sign of measles, it also may be a sign of an allergic reaction to medication The meaning of the siren comes closest to an "infallible sign" relationship—in that you would normally infer someone was hurt, but whether from an accident or a sudden illness you could not say. Hence, the inference that evidence is a sign of the conclusion you want to draw is not always true.

Reasoning from Parallel Case.   Another common reasoning pattern involves **parallel case**—comparing similar events or things and drawing conclusions based on that comparison. The claim that your state should adopt a motorcycle-helmet law might be supported by noting that a neighboring state, with similar characteristics, passed one and has experienced lower rates of death and head injury. In essence, you are claiming "What happened there can happen here." The political candidate's claim that what he or she has done for a community or state can be repeated in a larger arena, though not precisely parallel, draws strength from this type of argument. As the variables separating the cases grow in size and significance, however, this reasoning pattern will become less forceful.

Reasoning from Causal Relation.   **Causal reasoning** assumes that one event influences or controls other events. You can reason from a specific cause to an effect or set of effects, or vice versa. For instance, assume that alcohol abuse on a campus appears to be increasing. Is this increase the result of lax enforcement of existing rules? Do loopholes allow for greater abusive situations to develop despite the best intentions? Are students today more prone to abuse than in previous years? Pointing to one or more of these as the cause sets the stage for an analysis of potential solutions. The key is to point to connections between lax enforcement or loopholes and the resulting effect of increased alcohol abuse. The principle underlying this pattern is one of constancy: Every effect has a cause.

Testing the Adequacy of Forms of Reasoning

Central to thinking critically is testing the reasoning pattern for weaknesses, both as a user and a consumer. Each pattern has its own unique set of criteria for establishing a valid, sound argument. Within the context of each pattern, apply the questions in the box on pages 366–367 to your own arguments and those of others.

These patterns of reasoning and their tests are not the only means of evaluating the effectiveness of arguments. Arguments can be flawed in other ways as well. The following section describes common flaws or *fallacies* in reasoning.

Detecting Fallacies in Reasoning

In general, **fallacies** interrupt the normal process of connecting claims, criteria, and evidence. Here, we discuss ten of the most common, garden-variety fallacies; these are argument errors that you already have committed or have experienced as you listen to others provide reasons for their claims:

Hasty generalization (faulty inductive leap): This fallacy occurs when the conclusion is based on far too little evidence. If the answer to the question "Have enough instances been examined?" is "no," a flaw in reasoning has occurred. Urging a ban on Boeing 747 airliners because one was involved in an accident or on aerosol sprays because one blew up in a fire is insufficient support for the claim being urged.

Genetic fallacy: This argument rests on origins, historical tradition, or sacred practice: "We've always done it this way; therefore, this is the best way." That an idea or institution or practice has been around a long time may have little bearing on whether it still should be. Times change, and new values replace old ones, suggesting that new practices may be more in tune with present values.

Appeal to ignorance: The expression "You *can't* prove it *won't* work" illicitly uses double negatives. Incomplete knowledge also does not mean a claim is or is not true: "We cannot use radio beams to signal extraterrestrials, because we don't know what languages they speak." In countering such claims, use arguments from parallel cases and from examples, because they both transcend the "unknown" in providing support for a claim.

Appeal to popular opinion (bandwagon fallacy): "Jump on the bandwagon" and "Everyone is going" are appeals to group support. If others support the position, then you're pressured into supporting it as well: "There are a gzillion people who already think that Puff Daddy is one of the best." As an older advertisement put another appeal: "Eat chicken; 10,000 coyotes can't be wrong." While these may in truth have value, such claims have little probative (proof) value with respect to justifying an action. Nonetheless, this is precisely the kind of argument that has potency in changing people's minds. If audience members are receptive to popular opinion, then using that as a form of evidence will make a major difference in whether your idea is accepted. Politicians will use poll data to reflect the support that exists, even though such data in and of itself is not proof that the policy should be adopted. These claims may function as evidence of what people believe or value, but they are not, for that reason, true. The world has witnessed hundreds of widely believed but false ideas, from the idea that night air causes tuberculosis to panic over an invasion by Martians.

Appeal to authority: Citing someone who is popular but nonexpert as the basis for accepting a claim is an inappropriate use of appeal to authority. The critical question in using authoritative testimony is to ask, "Is the source an expert on this topic?" If not, why should you accept the claim?

Sequential fallacy: This phrase literally translates from the Latin (*post hoc, ergo propter hoc*) as "After this; therefore, because of this." This is a primitive kind of causal argument, because it is based on the sequence of events in time: "I slept near a draft last night and woke up with a nasty head cold" (the draft did not cause the cold, a virus did). Although the sequence may be appropriate ("The coach gave an inspirational half-time speech, and the players came out on fire."), there often are other circumstances (the players

How to

TEST ARGUMENTS

Reasoning from Example

1. *Have you looked at enough instances to warrant generalizing?* Just because you passed the last test without studying doesn't mean that not studying is the way to approach all future tests.
2. *Are the instances fairly chosen or representative?* Deciding never to shop in a store because a clerk was rude isn't exactly working on the basis of a representative, let alone sufficient, sample. You'll want to judge the store in a variety of situations. If you find that rudeness is the norm rather than the exception, your claim may be justified.
3. *Are there important exceptions to the generalization that must be accounted for?* While it is generally true, from presidential election studies, that "As Maine goes, so goes the nation," there have been enough exceptions to that rule to keep candidates who lose in a Maine primary campaigning until the general election.

Reasoning from Generalization or Axiom

1. *Is the generalization accepted?* Those who go on diets generally gain back the weight lost. People who marry young are more likely to divorce. Each of these is a generalization; you need to determine whether sufficient evidence exists to justify the claim if not already accepted as a general truism.
2. *Does the generalization apply to this particular case?* Usually, discount stores offer better deals, but on occasion, one can find better prices at sales at local neighborhood stores. While "birds of a feather flock together" applies to birds, it may not apply to a group of humans.

Reasoning from Sign

1. *Is the sign error-proof?* Many signs constitute circumstantial evidence rather than absolute certain proof. Be especially careful not to confuse sign reasoning with causal reasoning. If sign reasoning were error-proof or infallible, weather forecasters would never be wrong.
2. *Is the observation accurate?* Witnesses sometimes testify to things that later prove to be wrong. People differ in their interpretations of events. Be certain that the observation is accurate—that the sign did exist as described or explained.

Reasoning from Parallel Case

1. *Are there more similarities than differences between the two cases?* Two items may have many features in common, but there also may be significant differences that would weaken your argument. Just because two states appear similar, they may also have many more differences that would weaken the effectiveness of the parallel being drawn.
2. *Are the similarities you've pointed out the relevant and important ones?* There are two students down the hall who dress in similar clothes,

have the same major, and get similar grades; does this mean that if one is nice so is the other one? Probably not, because the similarities you've noticed are relatively unconnected to niceness. Their personal values and their relations with others would be more important criteria on which to base a parallel case.

Reasoning from Causal Relations

1. *Can you separate causes and effects?* We often have trouble with "Which came first?" kinds of issues. Do higher wages cause higher prices, or the reverse? Does a strained homelife cause a child to misbehave, or is it the other way around?

2. *Are the causes sufficient to produce the effect?* Causes not only must be *necessary* to produce an effect, they also must be *sufficient.* While air is necessary for fire to exist, it isn't all that's required, or we would be in a state of constant fire.

3. *Did intervening events or persons prevent a cause from having its normal effect?* Causes do not always produce their expected effects; they may be interrupted by other factors. An empty gun does not shoot. Droughts drive up food prices only if there is insufficient food on hand, the ground was already dry, or cheap alternatives are unavailable.

4. *Could any other cause have produced the effect?* Some effects may be produced by different causes; thus, you need to search for the most likely cause in a given situa-

Public advocates use argumentation to convince others, at times through active protest. What is the argument being promoted in this situation?

tion. Although crime often increases when communities deteriorate, increased crime rates also can be caused by many other changes. Perhaps crime only appears to have risen; in actuality, maybe people are just keeping better records.

5. *Is the cause really a correlation?* Correlations aren't necessarily causally related. Two phenomena may vary together without being related in any way. For example, since Abraham Lincoln's assassination, presidents elected in a year divisible by 20 (until President Reagan) died in office. However, the year was inconsequential in causing the death.

TABLE 15.2   Distinguishing and Testing Types of Reasoning

Form	Description	Example	Test
Example	Drawing a general conclusion from one or more examples.	I enjoy Bach, Beethoven and Ravel; I like classical music.	1. Sufficient instances? 2. Fairly selected? 3. Important exceptions?
Generalization or axiom	Applying a general truism to a specific example.	Bichons are friendly dogs; I'll buy a Bichon.	1. Generally accepted? 2. Applies to this instance?
Sign	Using a symptom or other observable event as proof of a state of affairs.	The petunias are dead. Someone forgot to water them.	1. Fallible sign? 2. Accurate observation?
Parallel case	Asserting that because two items share similar characteristics, they will share results.	Tougher enforcement of existing laws reduced drunk driving in Indiana; hence, such laws will work in Iowa.	1. More similarities than differences? 2. Similarities are relevant, important?
Causal relation	Concluding that one event influences the existence of a second, later event.	The engine won't start; the carburetor is flooded.	1. Causes and effects separable? 2. Cause sufficient to produce effect? 3. Presence of intervening events? 4. Any other cause possible, important? 5. Cause or correlation?

hate the coach but are motivated by each other) that help produce the effect. Timing alone is not sufficient to draw causal connections.

Begging the question: This is circular or tautological reasoning: "Abortion is murder, because it is taking the life of the unborn" rephrases the claim (it is murder) to form the reason (it is taking life). Nothing new has been said. In other cases, begging the question occurs in the form of a complex question: "Have you stopped cheating on tests yet?" assumes you have cheated in the past, when that may not be known. Saying "yes" admits past cheating; saying "no" admits to both past and present cheating. You cannot win either way you go. Evaluative claims are especially prone to this abuse of reasoning.

Ambiguity: A word may have more than one meaning, or a phrase may be misleading as to its intention. Using a term without clarifying its specific meaning can result in confusion and inaccurate claims: "Dog for sale: eats anything and is fond of children." Does "eats anything" include the children—sure sounds like it. Or, "Wanted: Man to take care of cow that does not smoke or drink"; when was the last time you saw a cow smoking? Or, consider President Clinton's tortured use of "sexual relations" in the statement he made that he had not had "sexual relations with that woman" in referring to Monica Lewinsky. As later events revealed, what he construed as "sexual relations" was not the ordinary meaning usually associated with that phrase.

Persuasive definition: Value terms and other abstract concepts are open to special or skewed definitions that are unique to the person or group offering them: "Liberty means the right to own military weapons"; "Real men don't wear cologne"; "A true patriot doesn't protest against this country while on foreign soil." Each of these definitions sets up a particular point of view that is capricious and arbitrary. You could say that persuasive definitions are self-serving, because they promote an argument at the expense of more inclusive definitions of the same terms. If you accept the definition, the argument is essentially over.[6] Substituting a definition from a respected, widely accepted source is a way of challenging this fallacy.

Name-calling: There are several forms of this fallacy; all involve attacking the person rather than the argument. You may attack special interests ("Of course you're defending her; she's your cousin.") or personal characteristics ("No wonder you're arguing that way; dweebs [or geeks] always think that way."). In these two cases, being related is not proof of defense, and dweebs may have ideas as good as anyone else's. Claims should be judged on their own terms, not on the basis of the people or ideas with which they may or may not be connected. On the other hand, note the powerful effect of name calling as used by political candidates—or others. To label someone is also to reject other possible labels for that person. Name-calling, or what is sometimes called *ad hominem* ("to the person") argument, may well be persuasive.

These are some of the fallacies that find their way into casual and formal argumentation. A good, basic logic book can point out additional fallacies.[7] If you know about fallacies, you'll be better able to construct sound arguments and assess the weaknesses in your opponent's arguments. In addition, thinking critically can protect you from being taken in by unscrupulous politicians, sales personnel, and advertisers. The process of protecting yourself from irrelevant appeals can benefit from the model for organizing and evaluating arguments that is presented next.

A Model for Organizing and Evaluating Arguments

As noted earlier, arguments are about contingent matters—events that could be other than they are or than what is proposed. The Toulmin model uses a visually clear pattern that isolates all the implicit and explicit elements in the argument. This patterning of relationships will aid you in analyzing and critiquing your arguments and the arguments of others:

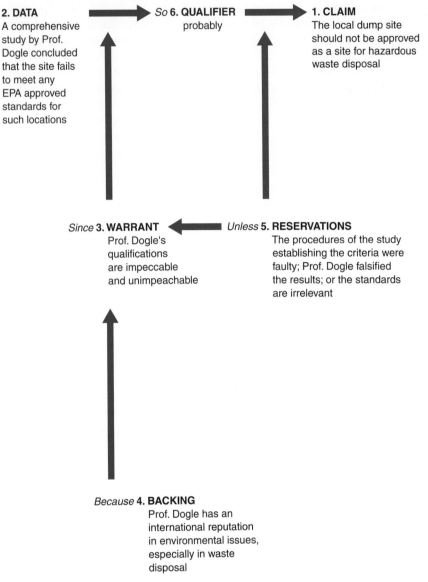

2. DATA
A comprehensive
study by Prof.
Dogle concluded
that the site fails
to meet any
EPA approved
standards for
such locations

So **6. QUALIFIER**
probably

1. CLAIM
The local dump site
should not be approved
as a site for hazardous
waste disposal

Since **3. WARRANT**
Prof. Dogle's
qualifications
are impeccable
and unimpeachable

Unless **5. RESERVATIONS**
The procedures of the study
establishing the criteria were
faulty; Prof. Dogle falsified
the results; or the standards
are irrelevant

Because **4. BACKING**
Prof. Dogle has an
international reputation
in environmental issues,
especially in waste
disposal

FIGURE 15.2 The Toulmin Model of Argument

These six elements operate as a general framework for the construction and analysis of an argument. The interrelationships among the elements can best be displayed through a visual diagram. The numbers in the diagram correspond to the elements discussed.

1. *Claim:* Put simply, what are you proposing for audience consideration: fact, value, or policy?
2. *Data:* What materials—illustrative parallels, expert opinion, statistical information, research studies, and the like—can you advance to support the claim?

3. *Warrant:* What is the relationship between the parallel case, statistical data, or expert opinion and the claim? On what kind of assumption or inferential pattern does its acceptance as support for the claim depend? Materials do not function as evidence or support for no reason; *facts do not speak for themselves.* What makes an audience believe in the strength of the reasons as support lies in the following kinds of assumptions that warrant acceptance of the link between data and claim:

a. An expert knows what he or she is talking about.

b. Past economic, social, or political practices are reliable predictors of future occurrences.

c. Inferential patterns (e.g., cause, sign) suggest that the linkage is rational.

We know, for instance, that an expert's credibility is a major determinant in gaining acceptance of the opinions being offered. In the development of the argument, this factor operates as an implicit *warrant* connecting the opinion to the claim. In matters involving economics, we know that the regularity of certain marketplace functions such as supply and demand exerts a powerful influence on events. Hence, when we claim the prices of finished products will rise because of the increases in the cost of raw materials, we are tacitly assuming the normal operation of the marketplace. Likewise, the value of using parallel cases as support for a position rests on the regularity of an inferential pattern: When two cases are parallel, similar results can be expected.

4. *Backing:* Does the audience accept the relationship between the data and the claim as given? If not, what further data would help support the warrant? When the warrant linking a reason and claim is accepted by the audience, explicit development of this facet of the argument is unnecessary. When a relationship between the reason and the claim is not automatically accepted, however, the speaker must provide additional support focused on the warrant rather than the original claim. Thus, in supporting an argument claiming that price controls would cause food shortages with authoritative testimony from a politician, you may need to establish her expertise to increase audience acceptance.

5. *Reservations:* Can significant counterarguments be raised? In most cases, arguments on the opposite side not only are readily available but even may be as strong as your own reasons. Anticipating reservations in advance will help you strengthen your own argument. In general, these can be thought of as "unless" clauses in your argument.

6. *Qualifiers:* How certain is the claim? Note that we do not ask how certain *you* are; you may be absolutely sure of something for which you cannot offer verifiable support. How much can your listeners bank on the claim you are putting forward as an acceptable basis for belief or action? Are you *sure* that price controls will have the claimed effect? Qualifiers such as *probably, presumably, virtually,* and *may* should be incorporated into the claim to reflect the strength of the argument.

HOW TO

DEVELOP ARGUMENTATIVE SPEECHES

Consider the following practical suggestions in developing an argumentative speech:

- *Organize your arguments, using the strongest first or last.* This takes advantage of a **primacy-recency effect.** Presenting strong arguments at the outset sets the agenda for how listeners will think about your claim. On the other hand, your last argument will be retained more easily; hence, you may wish to build toward it, carrying your audience with you as you provide stronger and stronger reasons for adopting the claim.

- *Use a variety of evidence.* You cannot bank on any one piece of material to move an audience toward your position; hence, a broad variety of evidence appealing to relevance and motivation will strengthen your effectiveness. For example, if you wish to argue for restrictions on shark fishing, you can cite statistical evidence of overfishing depleting the population or present a graphic video clip showing de-finned sharks being dumped back into the ocean to die (shark fin soup is an expensive delicacy in some countries). The

This model has three principal uses in organizing your arguments. First, by setting forth the arguments' components in the manner indicated, you'll be able to capture visually the relationships among the components. How, for example, are the data you present linked to the claim? What sort of warrants (assumptions, precedents, rules of inference) are you using to ensure the audience sees the connection between the data and the claim? Second, once you've written a brief description of the data and identified the warrant on which its relationship to the claim rests, you can more clearly determine whether you wish to offer the claim as definite, only probable, likely, or possible. You'll also be reminded to reflect on the audience's grasp of the warrant. Is it a generally accepted relationship; will it be in this case? Finally, thinking through the possible reservations that others will have to your argument puts you in a better position to shore up weaknesses in advance and, where necessary, build a stronger base from which to respond to issues that might undermine rather than directly refute your case.[8]

Applying the elements also sharpens your ability to question an argument. The data may be misleading or in error. The relationship between the data and claim may be highly questionable (lacking a strong warrant). There may be so many reservations that the claim must be highly qualified, and advocates may

latter is a more moving illustration of the reason for restrictions on fishing.

- *Know the potential arguments of your opponent.* The best defense is a good offense, but it stands to reason that prior knowledge of the opponent's reasons will go a long way toward strengthening your own claims. Investigating your opponent's position as thoroughly as possible gives you a competitive advantage; you'll be less likely to be surprised or caught off guard by an argument.

- *Finally, practice constructing logical arguments and detecting fallacious ones.* Ultimately, arguing well depends on your understanding of logical reasoning. The common denominator of all arguments, despite their different content, is the patterns of reasoning people use. If you have a clear grasp of the basic building blocks—including the material presented in this chapter—your skill development will proceed at a much faster pace.

be pushing claims harder than the data warrant. Using the model as a means of thinking about arguments can help you determine whether a claim goes beyond what can reasonably be supported by the evidence and available warrants.

ASSESSING A SAMPLE SPEECH

Policies are supported by particular factual assertions as well as values. The advisability of an action is based on the credibility of the facts offered in its support and on the audience's willingness to accept the value judgments being made.

In many cases, a speaker must reorient listeners' thinking, especially if they take something for granted, such as their own listening skills. Prof. Carol Koehler addressed this problem in arguing that one of the reasons for poor physician-patient relationships can be traced to an inadequate appreciation for—and skill in—listening.[9] As a professor of communication and medicine, she is in a unique position to develop an argument. The problem is set up in paragraphs 1 to 6, and the reasons that link poor listening to the problem then are evaluated (paragraph 7). She then raises a rhetorical question regarding what solution is available: providing "care over cure" (paragraph 8). In the remainder of her argument, she illustrates how her solution responds to the problem (paragraphs 9–14). In her conclusion, she uses an appropriate quotation to pull together the strands of her argument that caring is as essential as curing in the medical arena.

MENDING THE BODY BY LENDING AN EAR: THE HEALING POWER OF LISTENING

Carol Koehler, March 19, 1998

Setup of the argument

I would like to start this morning by telling you two different stories. Each story has the same two characters and happens in the same location. Both stories occur within a twenty-four hour period./1

Over the Christmas holidays my husband and I were invited to a formal black tie wedding. This was to be an elegant event so we put on our best evening clothes. Adding to that, I wore my mother's diamond jewelry and this fabulous mink coat that I inherited. Just before we left the house I telephoned my 86-year-old mother-in-law for her daily check up. When she answered, her voice sounded a little strange so my husband and I decided to stop at her apartment to make sure she was alright before we went to the wedding./2

When we arrived she seemed slightly disoriented (she was 86 years old but wonderfully healthy, sharp-witted and self-sufficient). We called her physician to ask his advice and he said to bring her to the local Emergency Room and have her checked out. We did that. This was a Saturday night so the Emergency Room was pretty active. When we arrived I, in my mink and my husband in his tux, we looked noticeably different from the general population in the waiting room. While my husband filled out forms, the doctors took my mother-in-law into a makeshift curtained room. When I noticed that the staff had removed both her glasses and her hearing aid, I realized she would experience some anxiety, so at that point I decided to stay with her to keep her from being frightened. As I went into the room, a young doctor said, "Mam, you can't go in there." Without missing a beat I said "Don't be ridiculous." With that I went and found a chair in the waiting room, brought it into the examination room and sat down. I remember thinking the staff looked a little bewildered but no one challenged me at any time. When my mother-in-law's hands felt a little cool, I asked for a heated blanket and one was brought immediately. So it went for the entire evening, we missed the wedding but finally got my mother-in-law in a permanent room about 2 A.M./3

The next morning I went to the hospital about 10 o'clock in the morning, dressed in tennis shoes, a sweat suit and no make-up. As I arrived at my mother-in-law's room, an unfamiliar doctor was just entering. I introduced myself and asked him to speak up so my mother-in-law would be aware of why he was there and what he was doing. I told him that she tends to be frightened by the unexpected and without her glasses or hearing aid, she was already frightened enough.

This thirty something male doctor proceeded to examine my mother-in-law without raising his voice so that she could hear, and without acknowledging me or my request in any way. Actually he never really looked at either one of us./4

In both those scenarios, I was listened to, not by ears alone, but by eyes, by gender, by age judgments, and by social status assessments. That started me thinking . . . /5

Transition to claim

Why did a recent article in the *Journal of the American Medical Association* indicate high dissatisfaction in traditional doctor-patient appointments? Why is it the *Wall Street Journal* claims that perception of physician concern and not physician expertise is the deciding factor in the rising number of malpractice suits? Why did *The New England Journal of Medicine* report that the care and attention quotient is causing "alternative" medical practices to grow by leaps and bounds? Given this litany of events, what does it really mean to listen? And why, in the name of science don't we produce better listeners in the medical profession?/6

Causes of the problem

The reasons are so obvious that they are sometimes overlooked. First, listening is mistakenly equated with hearing and since most of us can hear, no academic priority is given to this subject in either college or med school (this by the way flies in the face of those who measure daily time usage). Time experts say we spend 9% of our day writing, 16% reading, 30% speaking and 45% listening—just the opposite of our academic pursuits. Second, we perceive power in speech. We put a value on those who have the gift of gab. How often have you heard the compliment, "He/she can talk to anyone?" Additionally, we equate speaking with controlling both the conversation and the situation. The third and last reason we don't listen, is that we are in an era of information overload. We are bombarded with the relevant and the irrelevant and it is easy to confuse them. Often it's all just so much noise./7

How can we address this depressing situation? Dan Callahan, a physician and teacher, argues that primacy in health care needs to be given to the notion of care over cure. Caring as well as curing humanizes our doctor patient relationships./8

Transition to solution

Let's talk about what that might mean for health care. What comes to mind when someone is caring? (The audience responded with the words warm "giving," "interested," "genuine" and "sincere"). Now, what comes to mind when you think of the opposite of care? (The audience volunteered "cold," "uninterested," "egotistical," "busy," "distracted" and "selfish")./9

What might a caring doctor be like? If we take the word CARE and break it down, we find the qualities that are reflective of a therapeutic communicator, in other words, someone who listens not with ears alone./10

Breakdown of solution

C stands for concentrate. Physicians should hear with their eyes and ears. They should avoid the verbal and visual barriers that prevent real listening. It may be as simple as eye contact (some young doctors have told me they have a difficult time with looking people in the eye, and my advice is, when you are uncomfortable, focus on the patient's mouth and as the comfort level increases, move to the eyes. In the placement of office furniture, try and keep the desk from being a barrier between you and the patient. Offer an alternative chair for consultations—one to the side of your desk and one in front of the desk. Let the patient have some control and power to decide their own comfort level./11

A stands for acknowledge. Show them that you are listening by using facial expressions, giving vocal prompts and listening between the lines for intent as well as content. Listen for their vocal intonation when responding to things like prescribed medication. If you hear some hesitation in their voice, say to them, I hear you agreeing but I'm getting the sound of some reservation in your voice. Can you tell me why? And then acknowledge their response. Trust them and they will trust you./12

R stands for response. Clarify issues by asking "I'm not sure what you mean." Encourage continuing statements by saying "and then what?" or "tell me more." The recurrent headache may mask other problems. Provide periodic recaps to focus information. Learn to take cryptic notes and then return your attention to the patient. (Note taking is sometimes used as an avoidance tactic and patients sense this). Use body language by leaning toward the patient. Effective listening requires attention, patience and the ability to resist the urge to control the conversation./13

E stands for exercise emotional control. This means if your "hot buttons" are pushed by people who whine, and in walks someone who does that very thing, you are likely to fake interest in that patient. With your mind elsewhere, you will never really "hear" that person. Emotional blocks are based on previous experiences. They are sometimes activated by words, by tone of voice, by style of clothes or hair, or by ethnicity. It is not possible for us to be free of those emotional reactions, but the first step in controlling them is to recognize when you are losing control. One of the most useful techniques to combat emotional responses is to take a long deep breath when confronted with the urge to interrupt. Deep breathing redirects your response and as a bonus, it is impossible to talk when you are deep breathing. Who of us would not choose the attentive caring physician?/14

Conclusion   As it nears time for me to take that deep breath, I would just like to reiterate that listening is a learned skill and learning to listen with CARE has valuable benefits for health care professionals and patients. As a wise man named J. Isham once said, "Listening is an attitude of the heart, a genuine desire to be with another which both attracts and heals."/15

Thank you very much./16

CHAPTER SUMMARY

Argumentation is a persuasive activity in which a speaker offers reasons and support for claims in opposition to claims advanced by others. Arguing with others engages people in tasks central to critical thinking: assessing the reasons offered in support of claims. Within single argumentative speeches, particular arguments consist of the following:

- The claim to be defended.
- The evidence relevant to the claim.
- The reasoning pattern, or inference, used to connect the evidence to the claim.

Claims of fact assert that something is or is not the case. Claims of value propose that something is or is not desirable, and claims of policy attempt to establish that something should or should not be done. Evidence is chosen to support these claims because it is rationally or motivationally relevant.

There are five basic reasoning patterns: reasoning from example, reasoning from generalization or axiom, reasoning from sign, reasoning by parallel case, and reason-ing from causal relation. Each of the inferential, or reasoning, patterns can be tested by applying specific questions to evaluate the strength or soundness of the argument. Critical thinkers also should be on the alert for fallacies committed during an argumentative speech. The garden variety fallacies or flaws in the construction of arguments discussed in this chapter are hasty generalization; genetic fallacy; appeals to ignorance, popular opinion, and authority; sequential fallacy; begging the question; ambiguity; persuasive definition; and name-calling. Through the use of the Toulmin model of argument and its elements—(claim, data, warrant, backing, reservations, and qualifiers)—you can better assess the quality of your arguments as well as the arguments addressed to you. If you are seeking to develop argumentative speeches, either to initiate support for a position or refute of an opponent's position, you should consider the general strategies presented in this chapter. As you become more adept at constructing your own presentations, you'll also increase

KEY TERMS

ambiguity (p. 368)

appeal to authority (p. 365)

appeal to ignorance (p. 365)

appeal to popular opinion (p. 365)

arguing (p. 355)

argument (p. 355)

argumentation (p. 355)

backing (p. 371)

begging the question (p. 368)

causal reasoning (p. 364)

claim (p. 357)

critical thinking (p. 355)

data (p. 370)

deductive reasoning (p. 362)

evidence (p. 357)

factual claim (p. 357)

fallacies (p. 364)

generalization (p. 363)

genetic fallacy (p. 365)

hasty generalization (p. 365)

inductive reasoning (p. 362)

inferences (p. 362)

name-calling (p. 364)

parallel case (p. 369)

persuasive definition (p. 364)

policy claim (p. 359)

primacy-recency effect (p. 372)

qualifiers (p. 371)

reasoning from example (p. 362)

reasoning patterns (p. 357)

reservations (p. 371)

sequential fallacy (p. 365)

sign reasoning (p. 363)

value claim (p. 359)

warrant (p. 371)

ASSESSMENT ACTIVITIES

1. How influential are political debates in campaign years? Locate studies of presidential debates, and present your critical summary in written form or as part of a general class or small group discussion.

2. Assume you're going to give a speech favoring mandatory military service to an audience of students hostile to your proposal. Outline your arguments using the Toulmin model of argument. What factors do you consider as you construct and frame your argument? Assume that several counterarguments are offered by your fellow students; what new factors must you consider in rebuilding your case for service?

3. Prepare a ten-minute argumentative exchange on a topic involving you and one other member of the class. Dividing the available time equally, one speaker will advocate a claim, and the other will oppose it. Adopt any format you both feel comfortable with. You may choose from the following:

a. A Lincoln/Douglas format—the first person speaks four minutes; the second, five, and then the first person returns for a one-minute rejoinder.

b. An issues format—both speakers agree on, say, two key issues, and then each speaks for two-and-a-half minutes on each issue.

c. A debate format—each speaker talks twice alternately, three minutes in a constructive speech, two minutes in rebuttal.

d. A heckling format—each speaker has five minutes, but during the middle of each speech, the audience or opponent may ask questions.

REFERENCES

1. For a summary of the senses in which the term can be employed, see Joseph Wenzel, "Three Perspectives on Argument: Rhetoric, Dialectic, Logic," *Perspectives on Argument,* eds. Janice Schuetz and Robert Trapp (Prospect Heights, IL: Waveland Press, 1990): 9–26

2. Harvey Siegel, *Educating Reason: Rationality, Critical Thinking, and Education* (New York: Routledge, 1988), 1–47. The importance of critical thinking has been underscored in two recent national reports on higher education: The National Institute on Education's *Involvement in Learning: Realizing the Potential of American Higher Education* (1984); and the American Association of Colleges' report *Integrity in the College Curriculum: A Report to the Academic Community* (1985). For a summary of research on critical thinking in the college setting, see James H. McMillan, "Enhancing College Students' Critical Thinking: A Review of Studies," *Research in Higher Education* 26 (1987): 3–29.

3. For a discussion of argument as justification, see Raymie E. McKerrow, "The Centrality of Justification: Principles of Warranted Assertability," *Argumentation Theory and the Rhetoric of Assent,* eds. David Cratis Williams and Michael David Hazen (Tuscaloosa, AL: University of Alabama Press, 1990), 17–32.

4. For a discussion of cultural constraints on arguing, see Iris Varner and Linda Beamer, *Intercultural Communication: The Global Workplace* (Boston: Irwin, 1995).

5. For a clear discussion of why one should acquiesce in the face of a stronger argument, see Douglas Ehninger, "Validity as Moral Obligation," *Southern Speech Communication Journal* 33 (1968): 215–222.

6. Charles L. Stevenson, *Ethics and Language* (New Haven, CT: Yale University Press, 1944).

7. For further study of informal logic, see Irving M. Copi and Keith Burgess-Jackson, *Informal Logic,* 2nd ed. (New York: Macmillan, 1992).

8. Sarah Trenholm, *Persuasion and Social Influence* (Englewood Cliffs, NJ: Prentice-Hall, 1989), 242–243.

9. Carol Koehler, "Mending the Body by Lending an Ear: The Healing Power of Listening," *Vital Speeches* 64 (June 15, 1998): 543–544.

Chapter 16

Building Social Cohesion in a Diverse World: Speeches on Ceremonial Occasions

*I*nforming, persuading, and arguing within the public domain carries an obligation to provide as full and complete a picture of the event or issue as you can. In these speeches, your ideas about what exists—and what should be created or altered—are of paramount importance. Through audience analysis, you'll also focus on the needs and aspirations of your listeners to convey information or persuasive arguments in the most acceptable form.

Nowhere is this process of adapting your message to the audience as critical as in **special occasion** speeches. The task of creating, maintaining, or strengthening the community's sense of togetherness is critical to the special occasion format, particularly regarding speeches of tribute and those designed to create goodwill. Speeches of introduction and nomination also carry an obligation to connect in some way with community values and, thereby, strengthen the bond between the person introduced or nominated and the audience that is asked to judge that person's qualities. In these settings, the presentations aim to uplift the human spirit, acknowledge humility in the face of adversity, and praise the generosity of others.

On these and other special occasions, our consciousness of the role we should play as a representative of a select community, as in the case of entertainers, poets, or athletes, dictates the ground rules for speaking. Prior tradition—how speakers have handled their duties on previous occasions—at awards presentations, at Fourth of July commemorations, and other events specifies how we should perform. As presenters, we have a natural desire to do well, to earn the respect and admiration of the community on our return from the podium.

In this chapter, we look at several kinds of speeches you may give in the presence of—or as the representative of—such a select community. Before we discuss those speech types, however, we return to an issue dealt with in Chapter 4: *the challenge of communicating in an age of diversity.* Special-occasion speeches are absolutely crucial types of public talk. Unless we're willing to think about what holds us together—what makes us a *community*—informative, argumentative, and persuasive speaking will produce no results. In this chapter, therefore, we return to our discussion on the nature of cultural diversity and then turn our attention to speeches of introduction, tribute, nomination, and goodwill.

CEREMONY AND RITUAL IN A DIVERSE CULTURE

The word "community" comes from the Latin *communis,* meaning "common" or, more literally (with the *-ity* ending), "commonality." A community is not simply the physical presence of people—say, those who live in the same town (i.e., a local community) or who worship together (i.e., a religious community). A **community** is a group of people who think of themselves as bonded together, whether by blood, locale, class, nationality, race, occupation, gender, or other shared experiences or attributes.

The phrase "who think of themselves" is key here. Of course, you share a blood type with members of your family, but why is that important to your concept of family? There are biological differences between males and females, but why should gender be a factor in determining who gets paid more, draws combat duty in time of war, or generally is expected to raise the kids? Yes, skin comes in many different colors, but why have we made so much of that fact? To understand why, we need to recognize one fundamental truism:

> *While physiological, psychological, and social differences between people are real, the importance attached to those differences is socially constructed in arbitrary ways.*

Social Definitions of Diversity

A **social construction** is a mechanism used by group members to understand, interpret, and evaluate the world around them. There is no such thing, as Nelson Goodman notes, as "perception without conception."[1] Human beings cannot "see" their world without framing it, usually in language. Words store our experience of the world. Just uttering "pit bull" brings to mind, for most people, frightening stories of their own or other people's experiences. Words encode our common attitudes; as noted in Chapter 10, we have multiple words for the same object ("officer of the law," "cop") because our feelings about such people vary. Words express our evaluations. The difference between a "student-athlete" and a "jock" is a difference in how we value what the person does while at school. Saying that "we socially construct our world" is not to say that we create it in some brute way; the physicality of the world is real, solid—and you'll literally hurt your toe when it bumps into a desk. Rather, we are saying that *human beings orient themselves to the world via language.* We see, interpret, and evaluate the world via language.

It follows, then, that at one level or another, communication is always the attempt to get others to see, interpret, and evaluate the world as you do. The language you share within your social community builds a socially cohesive world; unfortunately, that language may not have the same impact outside your own community. Words vary from time to time, from place to place, from context to context, and even from person to person. "Democracy" means one thing in the United States and another in the Russian republic because of differing traditions, governmental institutions, and personal experiences. When a U.S. and a Russian citizen talk to each other about democratic institutions, they must be careful to indicate very concretely how each is seeing, interpreting, and evaluating the world when using that term. Within our own communities, such care is critical: Building consensus across diverse ethnic, racial, and class groupings in our larger cities is not an easy task. One thing we have learned: *In an age of diversity, there is a tendency to fragment society rather than to share beliefs, attitudes, and values as a community.* The great challenge of special-occasion speaking is to get a society to live together while valuing their individual differences. We can become "one"—we can live in harmony with others—without sacrificing our own identity through the language that we employ in building social cohesiveness, a sense of togetherness as we struggle to define our common purpose.

Public Address as Community Building

Within your own community, the groups you belong to have a special influence on your beliefs and actions. Whether you are part of a religious group, a member of the university swim team, a fraternity or sorority member, or an active member of a residence hall council, the group functions as a reference point in your life: you draw self-definition from the groups you belong to, and you use these same groups for reinforcement or for new information on problems. As noted in Chapter 4, culture is performed through language. The specific cultural frame that you choose to communicate from is heavily influenced by your **reference group;** the frame serves as a guide in defining you and your role in the community.

When seen as relevant to a problem or event, a group helps direct the choices you have and even may dictate what should be done to remain in good standing within one or more of the groups. Just as your group memberships change over time, so does the power of particular groups to affect your thought and actions.[2] Yet, traces of groups from your youth follow you through life. The question we face in this chapter goes beyond that social-psychological truth: *Your sense of group identity, of community, is created largely through public talk.* The language of reference groups is inscribed in your memory. If you were a Boy or a Girl Scout, you can still, to this day, recite the oath expressing your commitment to the group. Your civic education begins with pledging allegiance to the flag; it broadens when you participate in Memorial Day, Fourth of July, and Labor Day ceremonies (which include public addresses); and it is reviewed every time the president appears on television or candidates campaign for local, state, and national office. Your sense of community undoubtedly is built out of bits and pieces of social constructions reinforced in you since your childhood.

As Michael Walzer puts it, "The state is invisible; it must be personified before it can be seen, symbolized before it can be loved, imagined before it can

ETHICAL MOMENTS

A COUNTEREXAMPLE: CHALLENGING THE COMMUNITY'S VALUES

Special occasions also are open to the possibility of challenging an audience—such occasions may or may not represent what the community or nation needs at this moment in time.

Over the years, several notable acceptance speeches have been given by celebrities—some notable because they violated the expectations of the audience. At a recent American Music Awards for example, Garth Brooks was named Artist of the Year. His acceptance speech was decidedly nontraditional, however, because he refused to accept the award, leaving it on the lectern as he left the stage. Two decades earlier, three women were nominated for a National Book Award. As the following excerpt suggests, they, too, used the occasion to make a statement that violated audience expectations:

We, Audre Lord, Adrienne Rich, and Alice Walker, together accept this award in the name of all the women whose voices have gone and still go unheard in a patriarchal world, and in the name of those who, like us, have been tolerated as token women in this culture, often at great cost and in great pain. We believe that we can enrich ourselves more in supporting and giving to each other than by competing against each other; and that poetry—if it *is* poetry—exists in a realm beyond ranking and comparison. We symbolically join together here in refusing the terms of patriarchal competition and declaring that we will share this prize among us, to be used as best we can for women.[3]

The three women had agreed in advance that, should one of them win, this acceptance would be delivered by the award recipient on behalf of all three. What's going on here? This is, after all, a **special occasion**—a time to thank the award sponsors and those whose assistance made it possible for one person to win. It's as if, instead of a stirring call to national pride on the Fourth of July, a speaker were to soundly berate Americans for small-mindedness. What's going on is that the speakers believed their approach was the only viable one if they were to remain true to their own values.

Consider these questions:
- Do you agree with this analysis?
- Why, or why not?
- What are the ethical commitments that are placed in question in this kind of challenge to community practices?
- When a speaker violates expectations, is it ever ethical?
- When would it not be ethical to violate those, even if to remain consistent with the community would mean contravening your own values?

be conceived."[4] The same is true with most reference groups in your life. You cannot see group standards, only the behavior of individuals; you cannot feel the influence of groups outside of the words and other symbols they use to define their claim upon you.

You may not be consciously aware of the influence of particular reference groups, but their claim on your self-identity, beliefs, and actions is brought home to you on special occasions, in special rituals. David Kertzer has described **ritual** as follows:

> Ritual action has a formal quality to it. It follows highly structured, standardized sequences and is often enacted at certain places and times that are themselves endowed with special symbolic meaning. Ritual action is repetitive and, therefore, often redundant, but these very factors serve as important means of channeling emotion, guiding cognition, and organizing social groups. I have defined ritual as action wrapped in a web of symbolism.[5]

Symbolization is the key here. Some highly standardized sequences of behavior, such as brushing your teeth or getting dressed, have little or no symbolic significance; they are simply habits or routines. Rituals, however, are structured actions to which we attach particular collective significance—often about how the past relates to the present and how the present should affect the future. A political ritual, Kertzer notes, "helps us cope with two human problems: building confidence in our sense of self by providing us with a sense of continuity—I am the same person today as I was twenty years ago and as I will be ten years from now—and giving us confidence that the world in which we live today is the same world we lived in before and the same world we will have to cope with in the future."[6] As a community, we celebrate our pasts and construct our futures in the present; ritual is the mechanism of that celebration.

The notion of power comes into the picture when we consider politics as the process whereby vested interests in a society struggle for domination: Republicans fight Democrats for legislative or executive control. Parents in a local school neighborhood come together to protest the school's closing. The Hispanic voters of Texas ask presidential candidates to take stands against the "English-language only" movement. Political struggle can be harsh—even fatal, in some societies. Citizens attempt to ritualize political fighting: They invent rules of "parliamentary procedure" to ritualize partisan debate, and the transfer of power from one executive to another is ritualized in inaugural ceremonies. The power in such rituals, according to Kertzer, lies in their abilities to control the actual struggles for power and to help convince the witnesses the populace) that authority is being wielded benevolently, in their name. The rhetoric of special occasions, thus, is a two-edged discourse of power and community maintenance. This can be seen in such activities as confirmation or bat mitzvah services, "hooding" a new Doctor of Philosophy during graduation, and reciting the Pledge of Allegiance in school—these are kinds of ritual actions that Kertzer is talking about. All rituals are structured, standardized, and repetitive, with times and places set aside for ritual observances. Ritual is

ETHICAL MOMENTS

WAVING THE BLOODY SHIRT AND THE BURNING FLAG

The phrase "waving the bloody shirt" dates from the year 1868, when tax collector and school superintendent A. P. Huggins was roused from his bed, ordered to leave the state, and given 75 lashes by members of the Ku Klux Klan. Huggins reported the incident to the military authorities, and an officer took his bloodied shirt to Washington and gave it to Radical Republican Congressman Benjamin Butler of Massachusetts. Later, when giving a speech in support of a bill permitting the president to enforce Reconstruction laws with military force, Butler waved Huggins' shirt. From then on, Republican orators regularly "waved the bloody shirt," blaming the South for starting the Civil War and accusing it of disloyalty to the Union and its flag.

Similarly, in the late 1980s and early 1990s, people have burned the U.S. flag to protest nationalism and call attention to threats to freedom of speech and the Bill of Rights. In reaction, many people have "waved the burning flag," denouncing flag burning as unpatriotic and as a symbol of anti-American sentiment. "Waving the bloody shirt" and "waving the burning flag" represent particular persuasive strategies in special-occasion speaking. In such speeches, you're likely to hear patriotic recitals of the lives of martyrs who died that we might enjoy freedom, of traditional values and their symbols, and of the United States as the democratic bulwark, impervious to the assaults of all other political systems around the world.

Buried in this kind of public speaking are difficult ethical moments. Certainly, as Americans, we should know our history and who our martyrs were. We should be able to openly discuss values and the topics of patriotism and allegiance. And the United States, for better or worse, is expected to play a significant role in the international scene.

1. What if, however, our definition of patriotism begins to preclude discussion of alternative viewpoints?

2. What if references to traditional American values halt the examination of values of subgroups within our own society?

3. When does the defense of democracy become cultural imperialism—an attack on all other cultures, economies, and political systems?

Special-occasion speaking *is* a time for reflecting upon one's own culture and belief systems, but such situations can easily be used to batter someone else's culture and thoughts. What the Greeks called *epideictic* oratory—the oratory of praise and blame—is talk filled with ethical minefields. At what point does waving the bloody shirt or the burning flag stop, rather than encourage, dialogue?

imbued with symbols and with public address to provide the means of channeling, guiding, and organizing that Kertzer mentions.

Speeches on special occasions are themselves, then, ritualized—they follow a set pattern and, hence, may seem trite or even uninteresting. If many nomination speeches sound alike from campaign to campaign, that's because few of us really want surprises in our campaign processes. Surprise could lead to change, which in turn could upset our political system. In speeches for special occasions (except, as we shall see, speeches to entertain), you meet expectations by following the ritualized tradition—you invite revolutionary change when you violate those traditions. In one form or another, the goal of these speeches is always to socially construct the world in ways consonant with group traditions: to get you to see, interpret, and evaluate the world through the eyes of the group in which the public address is occurring.

In many ways, the challenge that is set before us on special occasions is the most daunting of those faced by any speaker:

> *In an age of diversity, when each of us has been socialized into any number of specific ethnic, social, political, and religious groups, each of which makes demands upon our beliefs, attitudes, and values, how can we create a sense of shared community?*

We proposed five strategies for building cohesive communities in Chapter 4: recognizing diversity while calling for unity, negotiating among diverse values, accepting multiple paths to shared goals, working through the lifestyle choices of others, and maintaining self-identity in the face of cultural difference. Through use of these strategies, you'll find developing appropriate themes and the language to express them a much easier task than it may, at first, seem. With these strategies, it is possible to share "community" when people are divided into two genders, innumerable religions, age groups ranging from the young to the elderly, multiple ethnic groups, a growing number of political parties, and even Mac versus IBM users.

In the following sections, we look at some types of special-occasion talk—speeches to introduce, pay tribute, to nominate, and to create goodwill. How do we create unity while retaining our diversity? That is the challenge as we review the special occasions you may encounter.

SPEECHES OF INTRODUCTION

The **speech of introduction** usually is given by the group's leader or the person responsible for bringing the speaker before the group. These speeches are designed to prepare that group to accept the featured speaker and his or her message into the group's community and standards. In a sense, a speech of introduction paves the way; it gains permission to speak. In the case of a nonmember of the group or community, that permission is based upon what the person brings. What knowledge or skill, above and beyond what the group itself might already possess, does the speaker offer? If the speaker is a member of the group, the introduction should serve as a reminder of his or her role and accomplishments within the community.

Presenting ideas with confidence and presenting individuals with enthusiasm is important in any forum.

Style and Content in Speeches of Introduction

Always, the speech should motivate the audience to listen to the presentation. Everything else must be subordinated to this aim. You are not being called upon to make a speech yourself or to air your own views on the subject. You're only the speaker's advance agent; your job is to sell him or her to the audience. This task carries a twofold responsibility. First, you must arouse the listeners' curiosity about the speaker and subject, thus making it easier for the speaker to get the attention of the audience. Second, you must do all that you reasonably can to generate audience respect for the speaker, thereby increasing the likelihood that listeners will respond favorably to the message that's presented.

When giving a speech of introduction, your manner of speaking should be suited to the nature of the occasion, your familiarity with the speaker, and the speaker's prestige. It is never appropriate to tell a story that embarrasses or otherwise demeans the character or integrity of the person you introduce—it makes no difference whether the person is a friend or stranger or you think it is a "safe" story that person should not find embarrassing or demeaning. If you are introducing a professor to your club or student government, this is not the time to tell a presumably funny story about a class experience—don't even chance it! Match your introduction to the seriousness of the occasion.

As you consider the occasion, gauge the amount of time you need to spend talking by how well known the speaker is to the audience—a well-known speaker does not need a long repetition of her accomplishments. For a lesser-known speaker, you may need to spend more time building her or his credibility for the audience. In general, however, observe these principles:

- *Talk about the speaker.* Who is the speaker? What's her position in business, education, sports, or government? What experiences qualify the speaker to talk on the announced subject? Build up the speaker's identity, and tell what he knows or has done. Don't praise his or her ability as a speaker, however. Let speakers demonstrate their skills.
- *Emphasize the importance of the speaker's subject.* For example, in introducing a speaker who will talk about the budget cuts facing your university, you might say, "All of us pay tuition, and we know first hand that budget cuts may mean a tuition hike for us. Knowing why the budget cuts are imperative, and what is likely to happen as a result, is in our self-interest."
- *Stress the appropriateness of the subject or the speaker.* If your town is considering a program of renewal and revitalization, a speech by a city planner is likely to be timely and well received. If an organization is marking an anniversary, one of the speakers may be its founder. As in the previous example, you could go on to note the speaker is the university's vice-president for finance and administration and, hence, is in a position to know the reasons for the current crisis.

Organizing Speeches of Introduction

The necessity for a carefully planned introduction depends upon the amount of time available and the need to elaborate on the topic's importance or the speaker's qualifications. A simple introductory statement—"Ladies and gentlemen, the President of the United States"—obviously requires little in the way of organization. For longer, more involved introductions, consider how much attention should be devoted to the background and expertise of the speaker and to the interest, importance, or urgency of the topic. A good way to start is to make an observation designed to capture the attention of the audience and then develop topics that relate the speaker and message to group interests, desires, or needs. Remember, your introduction should not be longer than the speech it introduces, so aim for brevity.

ASSESSING A SAMPLE SPEECH

The virtues of an excellent introduction—displaying tact, brevity, sincerity, and enthusiasm—are evident in the following introductory speech.

INTRODUCING A CLASSMATE

Benita Raskowski

We've all come to know Sandy Kawahiro in this class. When we introduced ourselves during the first week of the semester, you learned that Sandy was raised in Hawaii, later moving to the West Coast to live with an uncle. Sandy's first speech dealt with his experiences in California's Sonoma Valley as a minority person for the first time in his life and of the pressures those experiences put upon his values and behavior. In his second speech, Sandy offered an explanatory speech on his post-collegiate career, industrial relations./1

Today, Sandy's going to combine his personal and professional life. If you followed the state legislature's recent public hearings on discrimination on the job, or saw CBS' special report on work environments in Japan two nights ago, you know how important human relations training can be to a successful business operation. This morning, Sandy will continue some of those ideas in a speech arguing for further development of human relations programs in executive training packages. The speech is entitled "Human Relations Training on the Job: Creating Color Blindness."/2

SPEECHES OF TRIBUTE

As a speaker, you may be called upon to give a **speech of tribute** to praise a person's qualities or achievements. Such occasions range from the awarding of a trophy after a successful softball season to dedicating a new recreational facility to delivering a eulogy at a memorial service. Sometimes tributes are paid to an entire group of people—teachers, soldiers, mothers—rather than to an individual. In all these circumstances, however, the focus is upon relationships between the community and the individual or group being paid tribute. This focus is reflected in the sample speech at the end of this section; Susan Au Allen, president of the Pan Asian American Chamber of Commerce (PAACC), speaking in honor of a ten-year Excellence 2000 Awards program initiated by the PAACC, reminded her listeners of past award winners and the values they reflected. Honorees were held up for praise because they personified the community's values. Her speech is an excellent illustration of how community building takes place through ceremonial discourse. The following occasions—farewells, dedications, memorial services—call for tributes of one kind or another.

Farewells

In general, the **speech of farewell** falls into one of three subcategories. When people retire or leave one organization to join another or persons who are ad-

How To

ORGANIZE SPEECHES OF TRIBUTE

Consider the following strategies in preparing your tribute:

- *Direct the attention of the audience toward those characteristics or accomplishments that you consider most important.* There are two commonly used ways to do this: make a straightforward, sincere statement of these commendable traits or achievements or of the influence they have had upon others; and relate one or more instances that vividly illustrate your point.
- *Dramatize the impact of the persons' accomplishments by noting obstacles that were overcome.* Thus, you might describe the extent of the loss to a family when their home burned before praising the Habitat for Humanity group that came to their aid, with special mention of the college students who participated in rebuilding the home.
- *Develop the substance of the tribute itself. Relate a few incidents to show how the personal or public problems you have outlined were met and surmounted.* In doing this, be sure to demonstrate at least one of the following:

How certain admirable traits—vision, courage, and tenacity, for example—made it possible to deal successfully with these problems.

How remarkable the achievements were in the face of the obstacles encountered.

How great the influence of the achievement was on others.

---

mired leave the community where they've lived, the enterprise in which they've worked, or the office they've held, public appreciation of their fellowship and accomplishments may be expressed by associates or colleagues in speeches befitting the circumstances. Individuals who are departing may use the occasion to present farewell addresses in which they voice their gratitude for the opportunities, consideration, and warmth given them by coworkers and, perhaps, call upon those who remain to carry on the traditions and long-range goals that characterize the office or enterprise. In both situations, verbal tributes are being paid. What distinguishes them is whether the departing person is *speaking* or is being *spoken about*. More rarely, when individuals—because of disagreements, policy differences, or organizational stresses, for example—resign or sever important or long-standing associations with a business or governmental unit, they may elect to use their farewell messages to present publicly the basis of the disagreement and the factors prompting the resignation and departure from the community.

Dedications

Buildings, monuments, and parks may be constructed or set aside to honor a worthy cause or commemorate a person, group, significant movement, his-

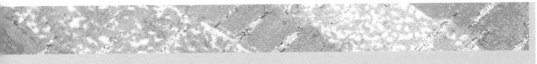

- *Synthesize the attributes of the person or group into a vivid composite picture of the accomplishment and its significance.*

There are several ways to do this. Introduce an apt quotation. Try to find a bit of poetry or a literary passage that fits the person or group to whom you're paying tribute, and introduce it here.

Draw a word picture of a world (e.g., community, business, profession) inhabited by such persons. Suggest how much better things would be if more people had similar qualities.

Mention the sense of loss that will occur after the individual or group leaves. Show vividly how much he, she, or they will be missed. Be specific: "It's going to seem mighty strange to walk into Barbara's office and not find her there ready to listen, advise, and help."

- *In closing, connect the theme of the speech with the occasion on which it is presented.* Thus, in a eulogy, suggest the best tribute the audience can pay the person being honored is to live as that person did or to carry on what he or she has begun. In a dedication speech, suggest the appropriateness of dedicating this monument, building, or plaque to such a person or group, and express hope that it will inspire others to emulate its accomplishments. At the close of a farewell speech, extend to the departing person or persons the best wishes of those you represent, and express a determination to carry on what they have begun. If you are saying farewell, call upon those who remain to carry on what you and your associates have started.

toric event, or the like. At such **dedications,** the speaker says something appropriate about the purpose to be served by whatever is being set aside and about the person or persons, event, or occasion thus commemorated.

Memorial Services

Services to pay public honor to the dead usually include a speech of tribute, or **eulogy.** Ceremonies of this kind may honor a famous person or persons, perhaps on the anniversaries of their deaths. For example, many speeches have paid tribute to John F. Kennedy and Martin Luther King, Jr. More often, however, a eulogy honors someone personally known to the audience and recently deceased. At other times, a memorial honors certain qualities for which that person stood. In such a situation, the speaker uses the memorial to renew and reinforce the audience's adherence to ideals possessed by the deceased and worthy of emulation by the community.

Style and Content in Speeches of Tribute

When delivering a speech of tribute, suit your manner of speaking to the circumstances. A farewell banquet usually blends an atmosphere of merriment with a spirit of sincere regret. Dignity and formality are, on the whole, characteristic of memorial services, unveiling of monuments, and similar dedicatory ceremonies. Regardless of the general tone of the occasion, a simple, honest expression of admiration presented in clear and unadorned language is the most appropriate form.

Frequently, a speaker attempts to itemize all the accomplishments of the honored person or group. This weakens the impact, however, because in trying to cover everything, it emphasizes nothing. Instead, focus your remarks:

- *Stress dominant traits.* If you are paying tribute to a person, select a few aspects of his or her personality that are especially likable or praiseworthy and relate incidents from the person's life or work to illustrate these distinguishing qualities.
- *Mention only outstanding achievements.* Pick only a few of the person's or group's most notable accomplishments. Let your speech say, "Here is what this person [or group] has done; see how such actions have contributed to the well-being of our business or community."
- *Give special emphasis to the influence of the person or group.* Show the effect the behavior of the person or group has had on others. Many times, the importance of people's lives can be demonstrated not so much by their particular material accomplishments as by the influence they exerted on associates.

ASSESSING A SAMPLE SPEECH

As noted, Susan Au Allen presented the following remarks at the tenth anniversary of the Excellence 2000 Awards and in Celebration of Asian Pacific American Heritage at a meeting of the U. S. Pan Asian American Chamber of Commerce in Washington, D.C.[7] In the first two paragraphs, she acknowledges her connection to the Awards program and sets forth the objective of her presentation—to examine "where we are heading in the future"—and sets the rationale for a review of the preceding decade's awards—a task well suited to a tenth-anniversary celebration. In paragraphs 3 to 13, she reviews the principal themes and values underlying the celebration of Asian Pacific American Heritage months in the preceding years. She then extends the review of the current year, 1998 and its accomplishments, before returning to her central question in paragraph 20. In the remainder of the presentation, she extols the values central to the organization, including the presentation of awards to people who are not of Asian descent; past recipients have been African American and Bosnian, because they were "the most qualified" applicants.

IN PURSUIT OF THE TIGER: TRADITIONS AND TRANSITIONS

Susan Au Allen

Setting the purpose

I am honored that you are here to celebrate this occasion with us tonight. When I started this program ten years ago. I could only dream that it would become what it is today./1

The 10th anniversary Excellence 2000 Awards program of the U.S. Pan Asian American Chamber of Commerce, brings forth a vital question—where are we heading in the future, based on the traditions and transitions we have been through? But before we can answer that question, let us look together at where we have been in the last ten years./2

Briefly illustrating past themes/values

In 1989, when we inaugurated the program, there was a serious need to celebrate achievements by the many Asian Americans in the arts, science, sports, business, education and public service. We looked back and praised 15 Asian Americans for their extraordinary achievements in these areas. They demonstrated vividly that America remains a land of opportunity for any and all who embraced its basic concept of freedom and personal accountability./3

For each of the ensuing years, in May during Asian Pacific American Heritage month, we would celebrate our heritage and chose a theme to guide our lives and businesses in the coming year./4

In 1990, our theme reflected what we all believed—that we were "Proud to be Americans."/5

In 1991, we embraced "Success through Merit"—not preferential treatment based on race, national origin or gender./6

In 1992, our theme was the "Asian American Success Story," to underscore and perpetuate the profound belief shared by our members, that we are an integral part of America and its unique history wherein neither ethnic nor racial origin decides the main characters./7

Then a year later in 1993 the debate over militant and government-mandated cultural diversity exploded across the land. In response to this dangerous trend toward division and group conflict, we embraced "A New Horizon" to remind the country that although injustices still remained, the doors of opportunity were opening wider to ever increasing numbers of Americans. We affirmed that for us, just as for others who previously had faced barriers, hardship, and prejudices in America, with opportunity when combined with hard work, skills and merit, comes success./8

That tumultuous year was followed in 1994 with a surging rise in national crime rate. Our response was "A New Palladium," a metaphor we borrowed from Washington's farewell address and he borrowed from the ancient Greeks, signifying a strong unified foundation. In our case, it is a foundation of good citizens of all creeds, colors and races, unified to form a solid foundation built on the principles of equality, justice, freedom and the pursuit of happiness. We urged the country to use these vital forces to ward off the evil spirits of greed and crime./9

In 1995, when the U.S. Congress threatened new restrictions on legal immigration, we responded with "We Immigrants. We Citizens," to remind the Congress, as President Franklin Roosevelt did, that we are all descended from immigrants and revolutionists./10

Throughout these years, as we continued to do in 1996, we involved ourselves in "Reaching, Teaching and Inspiring," to lay the foundation for more promising futures. And over these years we awarded 38 college scholarships./11

For 1997, we celebrated "An Auspicious Journey," to memorialize that Asian Americans are strangers no more to the American

Dream. We have been and are in all walks of life. From building the Trans Continental Railroad, to fighting for America during World War II, to winning Olympic Gold medals and Nobel Prizes, Asian Americans had undeniably become an essential part of the American fabric. For example, in December 1996, Time Magazine named Dr. David Ho, "Man of the Year" because of his groundbreaking AIDS research./12

In 1998, he joined our Asian American Hall of Fame, with world class architect I.M. Pei, cellist Yo-Yo Ma, Nobel Laureate Subrahmanian Chandrasekhar, Olympians Sammy Lee and Kristi Yamaguchi and 63 others, all featured in tonight's program book./13

This brings us up to date on the Excellence 2000 story./14

For 1998, we have the theme, "In Pursuit of the Tiger: Traditions and Transitions."/15

Reviewing the values embraced in 1998's theme

1998 is the Year of the Tiger in Chinese culture. Coincidentally, one of our honorees tonight is named Tiger. Also, my father will celebrate his 80th birthday this year and he was born in the Year of the Tiger—and so was his much younger son-in-law Paul, my husband, both are in the audience with my mother and one of the jewels in the family crown, our younger son Edward. Our older son, Mark, is at the University of Chicago, studying, I hope. My sister May May is also here. They are my backbone./16

I'd like my family to stand so that I can thank them publicly for their patience, support and love./17

The tiger in Chinese folklore is known for its valor, power and readiness to take risks to preserve his or her values. And I propose the spirit of the Tiger be the guiding philosophy for the Excellence 2000 program in the next ten years./18

In pursuit of the tiger, we intend to preserve the time-honored traditions that have been the Asian American legacy—family, personal responsibility, knowledge, industry, self-restraint, respect for those who came before us, care for those who come after us, compassion for those less fortunate than us, and the wisdom to pass the torch of excellence from one generation to the next./19

Importantly, these are the very same values honored by millions of people who arrived on these shores over the last 220 years. Many of us have succeeded because we have held onto these traditions, and have done well on account of our own efforts. As one Excellence 2000 scholarship recipient said to me. "I am responsible for my life. I do not ask for breaks. I make them, instead."/20

Returning to the central question and answering it

Now, the vital question is—Where are we heading in the next ten years? Now that we have achieved success in so many areas, Asian Americans are moving into politics and government. More than ever, we are participating in the political process. This is a good thing. However, we must be careful not to fall prey to reliance on the government to do the work for us./21

As a minority group with little political power, we have come a long way without government help. The formulae we used, the traditions I mentioned earlier, have worked for us, as they have worked for other ethnic groups. They are the proven means to success, and we should preserve them at all costs./22

Here at the U.S. Pan Asian American Chamber of Commerce, we embrace voluntary diversity and merit. As a result, many of our members are non-Asian./23

Our Bruce Lee Scholarship was awarded to an African American student in 1996. Why? Quite simply because she was the most qualified applicant. This year, the Bruce Lee Scholarship will be awarded to an immigrant from Bosnia. He, too, is the most qualified./24

Correctly, we support legislation that would open the doors for competition to small businesses. For example, the proposed Small Business Lawsuit Abuse Protection Act would prevent frivolous lawsuits, and arbitrarily large punitive damage awards that have ruined countless small businesses, destroyed jobs and reduced American competitiveness./25

The free market economy is the ideal environment to practice and preserve the traditions that we hold dear. All Americans involved in politics must honor this sacred truth. Such an economy promotes a limited and responsive government, one that would reduce taxes and reform regulations; and act as the arbiter of right from wrong, instead of an advocate for endless special interests./26

As we have looked back together tonight at the history of Excellence 2000 and look forward to our 1998 honorees, we see that all of the honorees—Tiger Woods, Andrea Jung, Scott Oki and Robert Nakasone—personify the traditions we value./27

Looking ahead into 2000 and beyond

Now as we stand at this important transition to the next century, it is my hope that these traditions will continue to be the guiding force for our lives, businesses and organization./28

Like the Chinese adage, "When we drink the water, we remember the source." So as we embark on new careers and new frontiers, such as politics and government, we ought to remember the source—our traditions./29

Concluding with a return to the present purpose—the current Awards program

So, it is to the vital task of preserving this miracle of the free market that the U.S. Pan Asian American Chamber of Commerce must bring the valor, power and readiness to take risks embodied in the spirit of the Tiger./30

Welcome to the 10th Anniversary Excellence 2000 Awards program and I ask you to join me in the noble challenge before us./31

In summary, by isolating character traits that others can emulate, dramatizing accomplishments so that others are inspired, illustrating the honoree's vision and courage, and synthesizing the person's significance in terms of group standards, you not only honor an individual's accomplishment but also pull the listeners together in a community. Even a highly diversified audience can be galvanized into a collective if your topics and language help individual listeners to see the world of the honoree in a particular way.

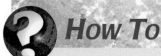

How To

PRESENT A NOMINATION

1. Because this is, fundamentally, a speech to actuate, begin with the declaration of intent: "I rise to place . . . in nomination for the office of . . ."

2. Describe the qualifications required by the job, problems to be dealt with, and personal qualities needed in the individual to be selected.

3. Relate your candidate's qualifications—training, experience, success in similar positions, and personal qualities—to those required.

4. Urge audience endorsement of your candidate, and close by repeating your formal announcement: place the person's name into nomination.

SPEECHES OF NOMINATION

The **speech to nominate** contains elements found in both speeches of introduction and speeches of tribute. Here, too, your main purpose is to review the accomplishments of an admired person. Instead of standing as an end in itself (i.e., tribute) or of creating a desire to hear the person (i.e., introduction), however, this review is made to contribute to an actuative goal—obtaining the listeners' endorsement of the person as a nominee for an elective office.

In U.S. political culture, one of the primary occasions for a speech of nomination is at the Republican and Democratic National Conventions. While it may be clear who the front-runner is for the nomination, tradition calls for each candidate still in the running to be placed in nomination before the assembled delegates. Speakers use this opportunity to extol the virtues of their candidate seriously. In the case of unlikely winners, this may be the last chance to air a candidate's position before the delegates and, in turn, a nationwide audience.

On these occasions, the manner of speaking is dignified, formal, and in keeping with the traditions of the respective conventions. In general, the content of the speech follows the pattern of a speech of tribute, but the illustrations and supporting materials are selected to highlight the nominee's qualifications for the office in question.

The steps outlined in the accompanying box assume that the candidate's interest in the position is well known and positively received by many in the audience. In the event you are introducing a relative newcomer or a person whose nomination will alienate the audience, it may be better to refrain from naming that person at the outset. First, establish the qualities needed for the position and then, in naming your candidate, indicate how this nominee's qualifications satisfy the requirements. Not all nominations, of course, need to be supported by a long speech. Frequently, and especially in small groups and clubs, the person nominated is well known to the audience, and his or her qualifications already appreciated. Under such circumstances, all that is required is the simple statement: "Given her obvious and well-known services to our club in the past, I nominate Marilyn Cannell for the office of treasurer."

SPEECHES TO CREATE GOODWILL

The fourth type of special-occasion speech we discuss is the **speech to create goodwill.** Ostensibly, the purpose of this special type of speech is to inform an audience about a product, service, operation, or procedure, but the actual purpose is to enhance the listeners' appreciation of a particular institution, practice, or profession. Thus, the goodwill speech also is a mixed, or hybrid, type. Basically, it is informative—but with a strong, underlying persuasive purpose. There are numerous situations in which goodwill speeches are appropriate. The most common include luncheon meetings of civic and service clubs such as Rotary or Kiwanis, training programs such as those sponsored by schools or companies, and special demonstrations at conventions or product shows. In each case, speakers have the opportunity to show their appreciation for being invited to speak and to increase appreciation for the company or product they represent.

Style and Content in Goodwill Speeches

Three qualities—modesty, tolerance, and good humor—characterize the manner of speaking appropriate to goodwill speeches. On most occasions, you'll find the audience well disposed to hear you speak. The company you represent or the product you wish to introduce already is viewed positively by the audience—they simply want to know more about what is going on, or they want to know how to use the product in their own work. In other cases, the audience may be downright hostile. A state official coming into a community to indicate why a proposed school cannot be built will likely have more difficulty creating goodwill. Speakers must be able to act not only as information sources on the company but also as persuaders, working to change uninformed beliefs and hostile attitudes. You must know and present the facts clearly and show a tolerant, patient attitude toward others. You also can communicate your awareness of the depth of feelings you face and recognize that alternative opinions have merit.

On these occasions, you also face the challenge of diversity, because audiences are likely to have stereotypical views that may make your task more difficult. If you are speaking to a local group about your fraternity's proposal to build a new house for members, you'll face problems if they believe all college students are lazy no-accounts whose only goal is to party. Overcoming such views is never easy. The challenge is to array information and valuable appeals in such a way as to attack those stereotypes. On most occasions, you must talk

How To

ORGANIZE GOODWILL SPEECHES

Use the following advice in organizing your speech:

- *Attention Step.* Establish a friendly feeling, and arouse the audience's curiosity about your profession or the institution you represent. You can gain the first of these objectives by a tactful compliment to the group or a reference to the occasion that has brought you together. Follow this with one or two unusual facts or illustrations concerning the enterprise you represent.
- *Need Step.* Point out certain problems facing your audience—problems with which your institution, profession, or agency is vitally concerned. For example, if you represent a radio or television station, show the relationship of good communications to the social and economic health of the community. By so doing, you'll establish common ground with your audience. Ordinarily, the need step is brief and consists largely of suggestions developed with only an occasional illustration; however, if you intend to propose that your listeners join in acting to meet a common problem, the need step will require fuller development.
- *Satisfaction Step.* Tell your audience about your institution, profession, or business, and explain what it is or what it does. Relate interesting events in its history. Explain how your organization or profession operates. Describe the services your organization renders. Tell what your firm or profession has done for the community: people employed; purchases made locally; assistance with community projects; or improvements in health, education, or public safety. Do not boast, but make sure that your listeners realize the value of your work to them.
- *Visualization Step.* Crystallize the goodwill that your presentation of information in the satisfaction step initially created. Do this by looking to the future. Rapidly survey the points you have covered, or combine them into a single story or illustration. To approach this step from the opposite direction, picture for your listeners the loss that would result if the organization or profession you represent should leave the community or cease to exist. Be careful, however, not to leave the impression there is any real danger that this will occur.
- *Action Step.* Make your offer of service to the audience. For example, invite the group to visit your office, or point out the willingness of your organization to assist in a common enterprise.

An educational program provides the public with critical information while creating goodwill in the process.

like a modest, tolerant, good-humored individual—not like a person who is angered by the attitudes you hear.

In selecting materials for a goodwill speech, keep three suggestions in mind. First, present novel and interesting facts about your subject. Make your listeners feel that you're giving them an inside look into your company or organization. Avoid talking about what they already know; instead, concentrate on new developments and on facts and services that are not generally known. Second, show a relationship between your subject and the lives of your listeners. Make them see the importance of your organization or profession to their personal safety, success, or happiness. Third, offer a definite service. This offer may take the form of an invitation to the audience to visit your office or shop, help them with their problems, or answer questions or send brochures.

As with every type of speech, the style, content and organization of the goodwill speech must be adapted to meet the demands of the subject or occasion. You should, however, never lose sight of the central purpose for which you speak: to show your audience that the work you do or the service you perform is of value to them, that it will somehow make their lives happier, more productive, interesting, or secure.

CHAPTER SUMMARY

Speeches on special occasions are grounded in the ceremonies or rituals that define and reinforce the fundamental tenets of a community. On such occasions, speakers face the special challenge of getting diversified audiences to see, interpret, and evaluate the world through the beliefs, attitudes, values, and rituals of the group observing the occasion. We define ourselves and live up to standards of behavior within reference groups, yet when those groups clash, unifying social constructions of the world must be built through language. Types of speeches on special occasions include speeches of introduction, speeches of tribute (farewells, dedications, memorial services), speeches of nomination, and speeches to create goodwill. Most of these forms are built to construct and reinforce community standards.

KEY TERMS

community (p. 381)

dedications (p. 391)

eulogy (p. 390)

reference group (p. 382)

ritual (p. 384)

social construction (p. 381)

special occasion (p. 380)

speech of farewell (p. 389)

speech of introduction (p. 386)

speech of tribute (p. 389)

speech to create goodwill (p. 397)

speech to nominate (p. 396)

ASSESSMENT ACTIVITIES

1. This chapter has argued that goodwill speeches usually are informative speeches with underlying persuasive purposes. Describe various circumstances under which you think the informative elements should predominate in this type of speech, and then describe other circumstances in which the persuasive elements should predominate. In the second case, at what point would you say the speech becomes openly persuasive in purpose? If you prefer to work with advertisements, scan magazines to find public service ads that emphasize what a company is doing to help society with its problems or promote social-cultural-aesthetic values. Then, ask yourself similar questions about these advertisements.

2. In this chapter we have discussed speeches of introduction and tribute but ignored speakers' *responses* to them. After you have been introduced, given an award, or received a tribute, what should you say? Knowing what you do about speeches of introduction and tribute, what kinds of materials might you include as attention, satisfaction, and visualization steps?

3. Your instructor will give you a list of impromptu, special-occasion speech topics, such as the following:

   a. Student X is a visitor from a neighboring school; introduce him/her to the class.

   b. You are Student X; respond to this introduction.

   c. Dedicate your speech-critique forms to the state historical archives.

   d. You are a representative for a speechwriters-for-hire firm; sell your services to other members of the class.

   You will have between five and ten minutes to prepare a speech on a topic assigned or drawn from the list. Present this speech in class, and be ready to discuss the techniques you used in putting the speech together.

REFERENCES

1. Nelson Goodman, *Ways of Worldmaking* (Indianapolis, IN: Hackett, 1978), 6.

2. For a discussion of the kinds of group activity that reinforce the power of groups over your life, see James E. Combs, *Dimensions of Political Drama* (Santa Monica, CA: Goodyear, 1980), "The Functions of Ritual," 20–22. Cf. Philip G. Zimbardo, "Constructing Social Reality," *Psychology and Life,* 13th ed. (New York: HarperCollins, 1992), 595–607.

3. Adrienne Rich, Andre Lord, and Alice Walker, "A Statement for Voice Unheard," *Inviting Transformations,* eds. Sonja K. Foss and Karen A. Foss (Prospect Heights, IL: Waveland Press, 1994), 148–149.

4. Michael Walzer, "On the Role of Symbolism in Political Thought," *Political Science Quarterly* 82 (1967): 194.

5. David I. Kertzer, *Ritual, Politics, and Power* (New Haven, CT: Yale University Press, 1988), 9.

6. Kertzer, 10 (n. 4).

7. Susan Au Allen, "In Pursuit of the Tiger: Traditions and Transitions," *Vital Speeches of the Day,* 64 (July 15, 1998): 604–607.

Chapter 17

Speaking at Conferences and Meetings

Walk into any hotel with meeting space in the United States, check the "Activites Today" listing of events, and you'll find at least one meeting with a featured speaker scheduled. Examine the various texts of speeches published in *Vital Speeches of the Day,* and note the occasion—in most instances, the speech selected for publication was presented at a conference or celebratory event. Meetings—and speeches—seem to go together in our society. The chances that you will be in attendance at such events in the near future is very good; the chance that you will be the featured speaker at such an event is perhaps less remote, but not as far from reality as you might first suspect. In fact, your college campus union schedule lists any number of meetings, so that you may speak or have already spoken in front of a student group on more than one occasion before graduating is not a "far reach." For that reason, knowing in advance what to prepare for and what to do as a speaker before a special meeting or conference will be helpful. This chapter considers some general advice for communicating at meetings and conferences; then, it discusses three distinct types of speaking obligations that might occur: after-dinner talks, keynotes, and panel discussions.

MEETINGS AND CONFERENCES AS SPECIAL OCCASIONS

The advice given in the preceding chapter about meeting the needs of the audience and occasion carries over into this chapter as well. You are well advised to pay particular attention to the "culture" of the group to whom you are being asked to speak—it may be a weekly luncheon meeting of a service organization, such as Rotary or Kiwanis, or it may be a campus meeting of the student activities board seeking advice on programming for the coming year. In each case, a safe presumption is that the group has been meeting for a time and has its own, informal rules about what to expect from invited speakers. Rotary or Kiwanis members, for example, will be looking for a speech that connects to their reason for being at the meeting, so whatever information or policy argument you present must acknowledge their role as members of a service organization. In a campus group, the culture may be much less well developed, but the group still has a serious concern about receiving information that fits within its purview as an organization. Speaking to a student activities board about the administration's antagonism toward Greeks, for example, may find a sympathetic ear, but it also may cause members to wonder, "Why talk to us—isn't this more appropriate for the student senate?" They may well be correct in their assessment of your topic choice. As with other "special occasions," the freedom to talk about anything, in the manner you desire, is constrained by the tradition of the group that has invited you to speak.

Direct eye contact in speaking before groups is essential in making the audience feel involved in the presentation.

Extending an invitation to speak does have an advantage: the audience has gathered for a distinct purpose and already has decided that you would be a credible, capable spokesperson for a particular topic. Knowing that purpose in advance—and adapting your comments so that they meet the expectations of the audience—is far easier when the audience comes with a shared sense of what they want to accomplish. In a classroom, the instructor may give you fairly free rein in choosing a subject—with the provision that it's purpose be to inform or persuade. In a meeting or conference, on the other hand, the selection of the subject often is predetermined or highly restricted. Even in meetings such as those of Optimist or Civitan service organizations, the choice of what to speak about is not wide open. Members do not wish to waste their time with frivolous subjects, nor do they wish to be put "on the spot" regarding their commitment to particular causes without advance warning. If you are coming in as a director of a local American Cancer Society chapter or a representative of the Red Cross, the expectation is that a portion of your talk will be about ways in which the service organization can assist you in meeting your goals. Hence, in these instances, audiences will not feel accosted by a "plea" when it is presented. On the other hand, if you are invited not in that capacity but because you recently took a trip to the Middle East and have been asked to speak about your experiences, adding a special plea on behalf of your organization will not be as well received. The members may remain polite, but their willingness to assist—even at a later time—will have been lessened by your poor choice of timing (recall the discussion of *kairos* in Chapter 12).

In general, even when audiences disagree with your position or argument, they may be more receptive in these settings, because they will assume you are talking to them about issues they deem important. Indicating at the outset that you, likewise, value their position and their sense of the importance of the issues will increase the chances of the audience giving you a fair hearing. If they believe you to be sincere in your respect for their position while remaining committed to your own, they may yet disagree but will be more likely to be cordial and hospitable in hearing your ideas.

The same will be true at conferences. On these occasions, special pleading on behalf of specific causes will depend largely on the purpose of your invitation to speak as well as on the goals of the conference itself. If it is meeting to determine the ways to best advance a "city parks for the new millenium" proposal, then placing before the group a special-interest plea that competes with that goal will not be in your best interest. If the conference is an academic one, the presenters generally will be expected to eschew political presentations and, instead, engage in discussions that may be critical of political events but in a manner designed to provide greater knowledge about how such events have occurred—or ways to prevent their reoccurrence. Your contribution to intellectual ideas also may well be what the audience seeks; students in various majors participate in such events through honors organizations as well as student chapters of various national organizations. Submitting a paper to an undergraduate research conference in your discipline may be a way to experience such occasions firsthand. In fleshing out more precise advice with respect to meetings and conferences, we now deal with discrete meetings first and then consider conference speaking.

AFTER-DINNER TALKS: ENTERTAINING WITH A PURPOSE

Although it is by no means the only form of speaking at specific meetings, we focus here on the speech to entertain as a specific type of after-dinner meeting presentation. To entertain an audience, especially one that meets late in the evening and is just finishing a banquet meal, presents special challenges to speakers. As you may recall, we identified "to entertain" as an independent type of speech in Chapter 2 because of the peculiar force of humor in speechmaking. Discounting slapstick (of the slipping-on-a-banana-peel genre), most humor depends primarily upon a listener's sensitivities to the routines and mores of society; this is obvious if you have ever listened to someone from a foreign country tell jokes. Much humor cannot be translated, in part because of language differences (e.g., puns do not translate well) and in even larger measure because of cultural differences. After-dinner occasions are not the only situations for an entertaining speech, but they are an apt use of this genre of speaking. Because the audience is at the end of what, for many, may be an already long day, to hit them hard with a serious, intellectually demanding talk is asking of them more than they may have to give in terms of attention and focus at that moment. At the same time, humor does not work well if used only as an end in itself. Merely being funny is not enough in these occasions—the audience may well wonder why they didn't just invite a professional comedian (at least then the jokes would be better). In place of humor for itself, the speech to entertain combines humor with a moral purpose. It seeks to ease the audience into more serious thought rather than brow-beating them over the head with abstract theoretical musings. Hence, the title of this section: to entertain with a purpose. More often than not, that purpose is to make a point about some facet of society's values or some event of mutual concern to you and your audience. This is precisely the manner in which Martha Dunagin Saunders used humor to put her audience in a more receptive frame of mind at a ceremony honoring honors students, as you will see later in her sample speech.

Style and Content of Speeches to Entertain

Like most humor in general, a **speech to entertain** usually works within the cultural frameworks of a particular group or society. Such speeches may be "merely funny," of course, as in comic monologues, but most are serious in their force or demand on audiences. After-dinner speeches, for example, usually are more than dessert. Their topics normally are relevant to the group at hand, and their anecdotes usually are offered to make a point. That point may be as simple as deflecting an audience's blasé attitude toward the speaker, as group-centered as making the people in the audience feel more like a group, or as serious as offering a critique of society. To entertain does not always have

HOW TO

ORGANIZE SPEECHES TO ENTERTAIN

The following sequence works well for speeches to entertain:

1. Relate a story or anecdote, present an illustration, or quote an appropriate passage.
2. State the essential idea or point of view implied by your opening remarks.
3. Follow with a series of additional stories, anecdotes, quips, or illustrations that amplify or illuminate your central idea. Arrange those supporting materials so they are thematically or tonally coherent.
4. Close with a restatement of the central point you've developed. As in step 1, you can use another quotation or one final story that clinches and epitomizes your speech as a whole.

to mean "be funny all of the time." You want the audience to relax and enjoy the moment, but you also want to say something worth their listening. Simply stringing unrelated anecdotes together, as in a comic monologue, is not what we have in mind in discussing this type of speaking. The difference between "to entertain" and to inform or persuade, then, is in the emphasis placed on humor as a vehicle in obtaining audience attention and interest in your views.

Speakers seeking to deflect an audience's antipathy often use humor to ingratiate themselves. For example, Henry W. Grady, editor of the *Atlanta Constitution,* expected a good deal of distrust and hostility when, after the Civil War, he journeyed to New York City in 1886 to tell the New England Society about "The New South." He opened the speech not only by thanking the Society for the invitation but also by telling stories about farmers, husbands and wives, and preachers. He praised Abraham Lincoln, a Northerner, as "the first typical American" of the new age; told another humorous story about shopkeepers and their advertising; poked fun at the great Union General Sherman—"who is considered an able man in our hearts, though some people think he is a kind of careless man about fire"; and assured his audience that a New South, one very much like the old North, was arising from those ashes.[1] Through the use of humor, Grady had his audience cheering every point he made about the New South that evening.

Group cohesiveness also can be created through humor. Politicians, especially when campaigning, spend much of their time telling humorous stories about their opponents, hitting them with stinging remarks. In part, of course, biting political humor degrades the opposition candidates and party; however, such humor also can make one's own party feel more cohesive. In the sample speech that follows, note how the speaker connects with her audience through mention of her son's assistance in providing some relevant "wisdom" for this day of honor for those being inducted into the national scholastic honorary, Phi Kappa Phi, or being honored by the University's Honors Program Medallion Ceremony. The use of humor at the outset makes this an entertaining yet productive address that is appropriate to the ceremony it intends to honor.

ASSESSING A SAMPLE SPEECH

LEAVING MORE THAN FOOTPRINTS IN THE SAND: TO SEE WHAT OUGHT TO BE

Martha Dunagin Saunders

On occasions such as this, the speaker is supposed to impart a few words of wisdom for the audience to consider as they reflect on the importance of such a day. But to be honest with you, by this time of the semester wisdom is, for me, in somewhat short supply. My son, the psychology student, suggested I might share some Deep Thoughts by Jack Handey. He e-mailed a few of his favorites:/1

"If you ever drop your keys into a river of molten lava let 'em go, because man, they're gone."/2

Or, "To me, it's a good idea to always carry two sacks of something when you walk around. That way, if anybody says, 'Hey, can you give me a hand?' you can say 'Sorry, got these sacks.'"/3

Or, "If a kid asks where rain comes from, I think a cute thing to tell him is, 'God is crying.' And if he asks why God is crying another cute thing to tell him is, 'Probably because of something you did.'"/4

And my favorite, "If you ever catch on fire, try to avoid seeing yourself in the mirror, because I bet that would really throw you into a panic."/5

But I didn't get the idea for today's speech from Jack Handey. I found it, instead, where I get a lot of my inspiration—at Pensacola Beach. If you have ever been there, you probably have seen a number of signs with the following message: Please leave only your footprints on our sand. The signs were erected by the Island Authority as a polite reminder to visitors to pick up any trash or litter before they leave. But today I want to encourage you to disregard the message on the Pensacola Beach sign and leave more than your footprints in this place, because what's important in life is usually what we leave behind./6

The idea started to gel when I, like millions of Americans, spent Easter Sunday evening watching "The Ten Commandments" on television. Some of you may have watched it too, and some of you may have first seen it, as I did, many years ago in a movie theater. I remember what a big deal the movie was to us, it was the "Titanic" of its day, sweeping the Oscars. It, too, was a v-er-y long movie, and still is. But there I was, last Easter Sunday, stretched out on my living room sofa, groggy from a chocolate hangover, watching "The Ten Commandments". . . again./7

I stayed awake for most of my favorite parts, like when Moses (played by Charlton Heston) turned all the plagues onto the pharaoh in an attempt to persuade him to free the children of Israel from slavery in Egypt. The frogs, the hail, the water turning to blood. To be sure, the special effects in that movie are downright primitive compared to today's high-tech wonders like "Jurassic Park," and "Titanic," but I still get a thrill when the waters of the Red Sea pull back so that Moses and his people make their getaway./8

But no matter how many times I see it, I always seem to notice something new. This time it happened during the scene when Moses had been thrown out of Egypt by Yul Brynner and would have died of thirst in the desert, but he passed out near a well and some kindly shepherd girls found him and gave him water./9

Now I've probably seen that scene a hundred times, but this year I found myself thinking, "Wasn't it lucky that somebody just happened to build a well there?" If somebody hadn't taken the time to dig it, Moses would have died and the story would have taken a very different turn. But lucky for Moses, somebody had prepared a place of shelter and comfort for him to use. Somebody had left more than footprints in the sand. And that is what I would like for you to consider today. The idea of leaving something behind for others to use. Something that will stand long after everyone in this room is gone./10

Today, 30 years after the opening of this university, we can walk around this beautiful campus and smell flowers we didn't plant, and sit in buildings we did not build, and benefit from wisdom we did not amass from books we did not write. And we take it all for granted./11

And not all contributions come in the form of books or buildings or programs. Sometimes a place such as this has been made better by an improved spirit of cooperation, or the settling of a conflict, or an idea for making the little things go more smoothly. For the past two years I have enjoyed the benefits of a well I did not dig as Director of the University Honors Program. Nearly every week, I come across a memo from the first director, Jack Salmon, who laid a strong academic foundation. Or I find myself relying on a procedure the second director, Dr. Mary Lowe-Evans, took the time to set up. And I can refer to orderly files and archives put together by secretaries who took pride in their work. And I have good and accurate records recorded by careful clerks who left this place before I arrived. Everyday I drink from a well I didn't dig. We all do./12

The important question of the day then, is what will we leave for others to use after we are gone from The University of West Florida? Some in this room have already made great contributions. Others are in the process, and it is our role as university leaders to do just that./13

Cervantes wrote: "There is a strange charm in the thoughts of a good legacy" and I'll admit to being charmed by the thought of leaving UWF better for my stay here. So my wish for us all today is to have the vision to see what ought to be, the courage to make it a reality, and the generosity to leave more than foot-prints in the sand./14

Congratulations Honors graduates and Phi Kappa Phi inductees./15
Thank you.[23]/16

KEYNOTE SPEECHES

The **keynote speech** is one that requires a clear sense of the mission or purpose of the conference being addressed. The audience will expect that you have asked the right questions in advance and that your presentation conveys an implicit—if not explicit—understanding of who they are and why they have gathered at this time and place. The keynotes you may well recall are those traditionally delivered during Republican and Democratic National Conventions. In each instance, the speaker serves as a symbolic representative of the party gathered to select a presidential candidate. Likewise, in each case, the speaker spends some time acknowledging the work of the party members attending— and also offers a critique of the "other party" as a means of solidifying support for the agenda of those listening.

On other occasions, the keynote speaker is brought in from "outside," as in the case of John Hope Franklin's keynote address at a recent National Communication Association Convention. In this instance, Franklin acknowledged the connection between communication faculty concerns and his own concerns as Chair of the Advisory Board to President Clinton's Initiative on Race. As a further illustration, consider the sample speech provided here: Carol Quinn's keynote at the Secretary's Day Breakfast at the Argonne National Laboratory is typical of the kinds of addresses delivered at conferences across this country. As Director of Human Resources for the same organization, she knew many, if not all, of those assembled. Her remarks began by acknowledging her

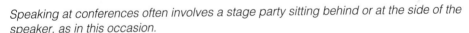

Speaking at conferences often involves a stage party sitting behind or at the side of the speaker, as in this occasion.

own connection to their current positions, talking about lower-level positions she had experienced during her younger years. Through a narrative style, she develops stories that the audience can relate to in their own lives. She then goes on to develop six themes that relate directly to their experience as secretaries and the rationale behind celebrating their role. In this fashion, she accomplishes the major task set forth for a keynote speech: honor the audience by knowing who they are—and why they are present.

ASSESSING A SAMPLE SPEECH

PLAYING TO YOUR STRENGTHS: LEADERSHIP

Carol Quinn

Good morning everyone. I am delighted to be here and am honored that you have selected me as your keynote speaker for Secretary's Day. Most of you have coffee, or juice, or perhaps tea. What I have here in this glass is Kool-Aid. But I'm not going to drink it./1

Why I have this Kool-Aid and why I'm not going to drink it are in a sense what I want to talk about this Secretary's Day./2

What I would like to share with you today are six suggestions for maximizing your career success by playing to your strengths./3

This glass of Kool-Aid represents the worst job I've ever had./4

Yes, you are looking at a former "Kool-Aid taste-tester" for General Foods. There really is—or at least "was"—such a job. When we weren't taste-testing Kool-Aid, we were expected to taste daiquiri mixes, or nibble potato chips, or smell soap, or otherwise play the role of "average consumer."/5

I came away from that with a long-standing aversion to Kool-Aid. Which is why I'm not going to drink this./6

The second-worst job I've held was waitress. It wasn't that the work itself bothered me. But it seemed as though the better I did the job, the lower the tips. The customers liked me better when I played an inept "struggling college student." This was my first and only encounter with a job where it was possible to be "too good."/7

There are other early jobs on my list—none of which seemed especially amusing at the time, but many of which cause me to laugh now. Not one of them was wasted effort, either. Because each one helped prepare me for the career I have today./8

It may not be immediately clear how this Kool-Aid helped point me toward law school and then into a career in Human Resources management. But it did./9

That and every other professional experience I've had showed my strengths, showed me what I was good at, and helped me understand what I enjoyed. Sometimes those insights were gained "in reverse" in jobs which showed me what I did not want in a career. The Kool-Aid falls in that second category./10

To know your strengths you must experience different options, alternatives, lifestyles. Experience is what you get when you don't get what you want. As Aldous Huxley once said, "Experience is not what happens to you, it is what you do with what happens to you."/11

I long have believed this is the first requirement for professional success—know your strengths./12

The second requirement is . . . play to your strengths./13

Knowing what you're good at is not enough. One must select a career path where her, or his strengths are an asset. Put another way, one must avoid professional situations where he or she is at a disadvantage due to skill or temperament or interest./14

When I was about to graduate from law school, I faced the question of whether to join a law firm. Law firms are about argument. People there argue for a living, and success is measured in part on how good you are at arguing./15

Now some of my colleagues today may be surprised—perhaps shocked—I know my husband would be amazed—to hear me say this, but I do not enjoy arguing. Even though I came from a family of five, plenty of fodder for gaining an expertise in the art of argumentation, I do not enjoy arguing./16

So, playing to my strengths, I by-passed the law firm system and joined a corporation where talent and skill at counseling, interpretation, negotiation, and management were more important than arguing./17

Oh, I must pause here and tell you a corporate story./18

It's about how a chauvinist named Earl endorsed the worth of secretaries, without ever knowing he did so./19

Earl was an enormous guy, and no one would ever claim it was "all muscle." Earl also was a supervisor who had a fist-fight with an employee half his size. The employee charged Earl with assault. The employee had a broken nose I might add. My job as a young attorney was to go to criminal court with Earl and defend him. With 6,000 employees I didn't know Earl nor did he know me. I met him on the courthouse steps./20

So, as we all must occasionally do, I "held my nose" and did what was required./21

We got lucky. Earl's "victim" didn't show up, so the state's attorney dropped the charges. I told Earl all charges had been dropped, and he was very pleased—so pleased that he later called my boss to tell him what a good job I had done. Or, more precisely, to tell him what a good job "the secretary" had done./22

Earl was so confident of the skills of secretaries that he was willing to let one represent him in criminal court. We know what diverse skills are required by a secretary in the 1990s. Still, I'm sure we would all prefer to be represented by experienced counsel in a criminal case./23

Since I technically won the case—my first and only criminal court case—I can honestly say I have a 100% success rate as a litigator./24

My story about Earl digresses somewhat from the point I am trying to make—but I love that story. I want to emphasize again the importance of selecting an occupation which maximizes your talents, and defending accused individuals in a criminal proceeding did not play to my strengths./25

As Philip Metzer wrote in Managing Programming People. "Practically every secretary is a typist but not every typist is a secretary." Likewise, every criminal lawyer is a lawyer, but not every lawyer can be or should be a criminal lawyer. And that's what my brief criminal law career taught me./26

No one knows better than human resources professionals that even with the best education in the world a person will fail to excel at a job that does not maximize their strengths./27

What the English historian John Ruskin stated in 1850 is still true: "In order that people be happy in their work, these three things are needed:

They must be fit for it;
They must not do too much of it; and
They must have a sense of success in it."
Play to your strengths./28

Well thus far I've offered two suggestions for success—know your strengths, and play to your strengths. Here's another:

Look to the future, not the past or present./29

Think about what you want to be doing professionally three or five years from now, and what will be required then. Once you've done that, you can start working now to satisfy what the requirements will be./30

When I entered the Human Resources field (well, actually it was dubbed "personnel" in those days) it wasn't necessarily an asset to be a lawyer. But I knew it would be. The increasing volume of federal and state employment law, and the equally expanding body of case law, told me that the HR field would soon become so legally complex that being a lawyer would be a real plus. And here I am./31

Back in 1986 management consultant Buck Blessing stated, "The secretary you hire this year will need a higher level of computer competency than mid-level manager did seven or eight years ago." How many of you are spending time teaching your supervisors the intricacies of E-mail or the complexities of cyberspace? I am not going to take a poll, but I would suggest quite a few./32

Learn by your past experiences, but remember you don't learn anything the second time you are kicked by the mule. In Human Resources we are often told to recruit employees for where a program is going, not where it is. Handle your own career in the same manner./33

A related part of that future orientation is that one should act, talk, and dress for the job you want, not the job you have. Those visual and verbal cues help supervisors to think of you as a candidate for that new position. Although one should never judge a man by his clothes—a man should be judged by his wife's clothes./34

Look to the future not the past or present./35

Now, a related suggestion: Never quit learning./36

People retain the capacity to learn for as long as they live. Some, though, choose to stop learning—believing perhaps that a job title, or a certificate, or a Ph.D., or an J.D. means they now know all that one needs know. That's not only nonsense, it's also short-sighted./37

The world keeps evolving, whether we want it to or not./38

In my field, the tax-related implications of Human Resources are expanding. Look at the financial options and decisions every employee deals with here at Argonne—options and decisions regarding your medical coverage, and your benefit plans, including your retirement accounts. These are issues your parents never had to address, because years ago employers made all these decisions for employees. These also are often complex decisions that are important to you and your families. So what happened because of this shift? Responsibility is now yours. And as Erica Jong so correctly stated, "Take your life in your own hands and what happens? A terrible thing: No one to blame." If I and my staff are to give you the best possible advice to help you make those decisions, then we must know the topics to help you make intelligent choices—which is why I presently am enrolled in a Master's program in tax law./39

Learning is a constant part of life./40

And while I'm emphasizing the importance of continuous learning and it's place in my ability to perform my job duties, I want to speak to you about the type of learning that is "tremendously important" to success in anyone's life./41

This is probably the most useful thing that I will tell you today so please listen up./42

To be a success you must take responsibility for your investment planning—for most of us this means retirement funds—and this means more than taking the advice of Billy Rose to never invest your money in anything that eats or needs repainting."/43

Am I saying that proper investment planning/learning is essential to the pursuit of success? Absolutely, unequivocally—YES./44

Take advantage of services offered by HR and others. Read books and use other vehicles to learn about investing. The knowledge gleaned will remove a great source of anxiety, make you feel self-confident and in control . . . and it makes for great cocktail party banter. It can also make a positive difference for you and your family in the way you live./45

Never quit learning./46

So your job is a part of life. But not all of it./47

In Human Resources, we often encounter people who have forgotten that—the workaholics who are always "on duty," always talking business, always canceling vacations because "now isn't a good time." They are not usually the employees being subjected to disciplinary action. However, the lack of work-life balance is hard on you, hard on your family, and it is not the best way to contribute to the organization. Frenetic constant work activity does not always equate to maximum effectiveness./48

Over time, the superior performers are those who have learned to balance their lives./49

So my fifth principle for ensuring success is to suggest that you seek a balance in your life. Take your vacations, remember to exercise your mind and body, and above all enjoy the company of your family and your friends. Not only is that the best course for you as individuals, it also is the best course for Argonne./50

Don't, for the sake of earning a living, forget to live./51

Have you ever heard of anyone who asked that their tombstone read, "I Should Have Worked Harder"?/52

No, what you often hear from people near the ends of their lives is that they should have spent more time with their spouses and their children—that they should have enjoyed life more./53

Each of us can do that now, rather than regret not doing it later. As with death, taxes and childbirth, there's never a convenient time for any of them. But somehow the time must be made Don't sacrifice your marriage, relationship with your children or your passions because of your work./54

Balance your life./55

My sixth and final point is: Think of yourself as a business partner, not an employee./56

I always remind myself that the job of each employee is as important to him or her as mine is to me. As Jack Welch, chairman of General Electric, wrote speaking of supervision: "It is embarrassing to reflect that for 90 years we've been dictating equipment needs and managing people who knew how to do things much better and faster than we did."/57

No matter your job title, pay grade, or rank, you have a right to an opinion and a right to be heard./58

To which I would also add "and a right to be respected."/59

The best companies and organizations to work for—and Argonne is included in this list—go beyond tolerating differences and work to build a culture of respect which views diversity for culture and opinions as the fuel for creative thought./60

Here's a story illustrating the right of each employee to speak his mind—and to seize authority and responsibility where it has been delegated. It's a story about the CEO of a large company visiting one of his plants. Deciding to eat with workers in the employee cafeteria, he asked a young man behind the counter for a second scoop of ice cream on his cone./61

"Sorry," said the worker. "One scoop to a customer."/62

The CEO was taken aback. Then he said, "I guess you don't know who I am, son. I'm the chairman of this company. I sign your paycheck."/63

The young man was unimpressed./64

"Well, I guess you don't know who I am," he said./65

"No, I don't," said the agitated executive. "Who are you anyway?"/66

"I'm the guy in charge of the ice cream."/67

Take the initiative and take charge of your career./68

A few things you can do to accomplish this are:

Understand the business—look to the Argonne Information Center Read booklets.
Lose that "it's not my job" attitude
Study your leaders—what traits made their success possible
Build shortcuts into the regular work process
Become active in professional organizations to hone you job skills

A partner has an equity stake in a business—he or she is an owner./69

Approach your career as an owner, a partner, because you most definitely have an equity share in your career. Perform outside the confines of your current position description. A General Winfield Scott once said, "Any fool can keep a rule; God gave him a brain to know when to break the rule."/70

Be a partner not an employee./71

So to recap here are six suggestions for maximizing you talents:/72

1. Know your strengths.
2. Play to your strengths.
3. Look to the future, not the past or present.
4. Never quit learning.
5. Balance your life.
6. Think of yourself as a business partner not an employee.

If I really wanted to end this speech with flair, I would now drink this glass of Kool-Aid./73

But there being no power on the planet which could force me to drink another glass of Kool-Aid, I will instead wish you health happiness, a wonderful day and . . . you know what? . . . strawberry Kool-Aid is really the best./74

Thanks for inviting me./75

PANEL DISCUSSIONS AT MEETINGS

Inviting experts to appear as participants in a **panel discussion** is a common feature of most conferences or conventions. Generally, four to six individuals are asked to present a brief "position statement" and then discuss the issues raised, both among themselves and with members of the audience. These can be "pro/con" sessions, with experts invited to speak on either side of a controversial issue, or they can be "random" sessions, with experts asked to present their personal views and with mixed agreement/disagreement between and among the panelists.

Preparing for Panel Participation

As part of a group of presenters, you have an obligation to take the possible positions of others into account as well as to prepare remarks that permit others equal time to convey their thoughts. Speaking "off the cuff" seldom is a good idea in these settings, because the audience will rather quickly conclude you have not given much thought to how your ideas will fit with those of others. Hence, it is incumbent on you to spend some time thinking about the situation and how your ideas will fit—and to prepare an outline from which you might speak extemporaneously. Adhering to the following guidelines will make it easier to make the best use of your time as part of the panel.

First, *address the theme.* This constrains your choice a bit more than in other speaking situations, because you need to address the issues that others will also be considering. Your "take" on the issues may be different from others, and you may emphasize different facets of the problem or theme. Still, you will need to satisfy the other panel members and the audience that you have indeed paid attention to the reason for being a participant.

Second, *consider whether it would be wise to divide issues in advance of the presentation.* If you know the other participants, a conference call organizing the presentation may be in order. In this way, you will avoid duplication as well as the feeling that, as the last speaker, everything you planned to say has already been noted by preceding speakers.

Third, *plan your own remarks in advance.* This may include reviewing the information you already have for significant gaps that need to be filled before you participate. Doing additional research on the issue, whether to fill gaps or bring your own knowledge up to date, may be essential if you are to come across as well versed in the issues. If the issue is controversial, you also may want to develop a more specific point of view to assemble your points in support. Rambling around, in, and under a topic does little to merit confidence that you have a commitment to the ideas. You also should anticipate the impact of your thoughts on the panel as well as the audience. If your position will be controversial, think about the kinds of objections that will be raised and consider how you might answer queries or arguments counter to your position.

Fourth, when the moment arrives that you have the floor, *speak in a direct, friendly, conversational style.* Even if your ideas are not well accepted, that you are willing to address others in a cordial and collegial manner will assist in keeping the follow-up questions in a similar tone. Your specific contribution to the panel should be presented so that it appears straightforward, precise, and succinct. Succinctness will make it easier to keep your remarks within an allotted time frame so as to not monopolize the time set aside for the panel presentation. In most conferences, events are tightly structured, with only so much time allotted for each program. As the first or second speaker, in particular, you will want to make sure the remaining participants have ample time to present their own views.

Finally, *speak in a conciliatory tone during the follow-up discussion.* By and large, the purpose of panel sessions is not to come to specific decisions about what to do but to stimulate audience thought about the options available, with each speaker giving a specific slant to the possibilities. Thus, being perceived as open to alternatives—even though you may have a favorite solution in mind— is essential if the panel is to achieve its objective. You may marshal evidence and critique other alternatives as part of the follow-up discussion, but the overriding objective is to get as many ideas on the floor for discussion as possible. Hence, remaining calm and tolerant of dissenting views is as important as saying something meaningful.

With these guidelines in mind, you are well on your way to a successful and productive panel session.

CHAPTER SUMMARY

The guidelines for speaking at meetings and conferences are, in general, no different than those for other ceremonial or special-occasion speeches. The key difference between such events and those involving classroom speeches is that you have more constraints on your freedom to select and develop a topic of your own choosing. After-dinner speaking—and particularly entertaining with a purpose—is one of the common types of speech occasions that you will en-counter. You also may be asked to present a keynote address or participate in a panel discussion at a conference, in these cases, adapting your presentation to fit the conference or panel's theme and conveying to the audience an appreciation for their reasons for coming to the meeting will be important. Following the guidelines for participation in panel discussions, in particular, will be helpful in making the best use of your time—as well as the time of the audience.

KEY TERMS

keynote speech (p. 409)   *panel discussion (p. 415)*   *speech to entertain (p. 405)*

ASSESSMENT ACTIVITIES

1. Develop a speech that entertains as it promotes a specific point of view or moral. As you collect specific jokes or stories that are humorous, consider whether anyone in the intended audience might find them more offensive? Can you adapt the story so as not to give offense? What might be the consequence of going ahead with the story as written? Is this a consequence you want to accept? Ask the audience, in particular, to evaluate your choice of entertaining stories and jokes—how accurate is your sense of what might be funny as well as nonoffensive?

2. Select a conference or convention that focuses on an issue, product, or theme that is important to you. You can use the *Chronicle for Higher Education*'s list of conferences (though that will be limited primarily to academic conferences) or student organizations you belong to as one resource, or you can check trade publications in your university library to see when and where such conferences are held. Once you have a conference in mind, develop a keynote address that fits the theme of the conference. If you have the opportunity to present the speech in class, indicate in advance the nature of the conference and its theme, and ask that the audience "role play" conference attendees in evaluating your presentation.

3. Divide the class into small groups. Each group will consider one of the following topics and develop a panel presentation centered on the topic:
   a. The ethics of lying—when is it ok to tell a lie?
   b. The ethics of plagiarism—is it ever ok to borrow from the works of others? (Note that some cultures do not have the same strictures placed on "borrowing" as does our culture.)
   c. The status of civil discourse in this society—are we in an "age of incivility," and if so, what should we do to in-

crease the occurrence of civil discourse?

d. [select a topic that is of current concern on your campus or in your community]—What are the causes of the "problem," and what solutions might be proposed?

REFERENCES

1. Henry W. Grady. "The New South," *American Public Addresses: 1740–1852,* ed. A. Craig Baird (New York: McGraw-Hill Book Co., 1956): 181–185.
2. Martha Dunagin Saunders, "Leaving more than Footprints in the Sand: To See what Ought to Be," *Vital Speeches of the Day* 62 (July 15, 1998): 607–608.
3. Carol Quinn, "Playing to Your Strengths: Leadership," *Vital Speeches of the Day* 64 (June 15, 1998): 508–510.

Credits

"Common Ground and Common Sense" by Jesse Jackson in *Vital Speeches of the Day*, August 15, 1988, 54(21):651.

From Minister Louis Farrakhan's Remarks at the Million Man March, October 17, 1995. Reprinted by permission of Louis Farrakhan.

Excerpt from website www.library.ucla.edu/libraries/ college/instruct/web/ critical.htm. Reprinted by permission of Esther Grassian, UCLA College Library.

"Sexual Assault Policy a Must" by Maria Lucia R. Anton in *Winning Orations 1994*. Reprinted by permission of Larry Schnoor, Executive Secretary, Interstate Oratorical Association, Mankato State University, Mankato, Minnesota.

"Persecution and Politicization: Roma (Gypsies) of Eastern Europe" by Carol Silverman from *Cultural Survival Quarterly*, Summer 1995:43-49. Reprinted by permission.

"Special Projects Update" from *Cultural Survival Quarterly*, Summer 1995:8-9. Reprinted by permission.

"I've Been to the Mountaintop" by Martin Luther King, Jr. Reprinted by arrangement with The Heirs to the Estate of Martin Luther King, Jr., c/o Writers House, Inc. as agent for the proprietor. Copyright 1968 by Martin Luther King, Jr., copyright renewed 1996 by The Estate of Martin Luther King, Jr.

"Love, Law and Civil Disobedience" by Martin Luther King, Jr. Reprinted by arrangement with The Heirs to the Estate of Martin Luther King, Jr., c/o Writers House, Inc. as agent for the proprietor. Copyright 1963 by Martin Luther King, Jr., copyright renewed 1991 by Coretta Scott King.

Acceptance speech by Allen H. Neurath upon receiving the DeWitt Carter Reddick Award, published by the College of Communication, 1992. Reprinted by permission of the author

"Upon Receiving the Nobel Prize for Literature" by William Faulkner from *Essays, Speeches and Public Letters by William Faulkner* edited by James B. Meriwether. Copyright © 1950 by William Faulkner. Reprinted by permission of Random House, Inc.

Excerpt from *The Nine American Lifestyles: Who We Are and Where We're Going* by Arnold Mitchell, New York: Macmillan 1983.

"Environmental Racism" by Kim Triplett from *Winning Orations*, 1994. Reprinted by permission of Interstate Oratorical Association.

"Mending the Body by Lending an Ear" by Carol Koehler, Ph.D., in *Vital Speeches of the Day*, June 15, 1998:543-544. Reprinted by permission of the author.

Excerpt from *Persuasion and Social Influence* by Sarah Trenholm. Copyright © 1989 Allyn & Bacon, pp. 242-243.

"In Pursuit of the Tiger" by Susan Au Allen from *Vital Speeches of the Day*, July 15. 1998:605-607. Reprinted by permission of the author. "The Guerrilla Girl's Pop Quiz" poster. Copyright © 1990 Guerrilla Girls. Used with permission.

"Leaving More Than Footprints in the Sand" by Martha Dunagin Saunders in *Vital Speeches of the Day*, July 15, 1998:607-608. Reprinted by permission of the author.

"Playing to Your Strengths: Leadership" by Carol Quinn in *Vital Speeches of the Day*, June 15, 1998:508-510. Reprinted by permission of Argonne National Laboratory.

"Wrapping Wanton" by Brenda Lam. Reprinted by permission of the author.

"The Geisha" by Joyce Chapman from *Communication Strategy: A Guide to Speech Preparation*, Roselyn Schiff, et al. (eds). Glenview, IL: Scott Foresman, 1981. Used with the permission of Addison Wesley Educational Publishers.

Index